St. Nicholas and Mary Mapes Dodge

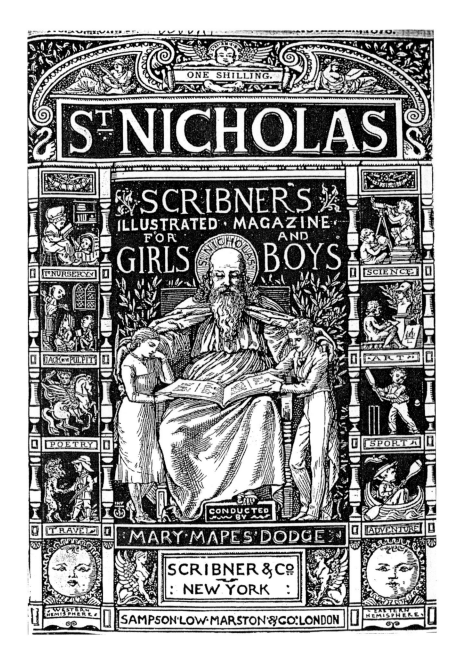

St. Nicholas and Mary Mapes Dodge

The Legacy of a Children's Magazine Editor, 1873–1905

Edited by SUSAN R. GANNON,
SUZANNE RAHN, *and*
RUTH ANNE THOMPSON

McFarland & Company, Inc., Publishers
Jefferson, North Carolina, and London

To Joe, John and Frank.

Frontispiece: The cover for the British edition of *St. Nicholas* was created in 1877 by Walter Crane.

LIBRARY OF CONGRESS CATALOGUING-IN-PUBLICATION DATA

St. Nicholas and Mary Mapes Dodge : the legacy of a children's magazine editor, 1873–1905 / edited by Susan R. Gannon, Suzanne Rahn, and Ruth Anne Thompson.
    p.   cm.
Includes bibliographical references and index.

ISBN-13: 978-0-7864-1758-2
(softcover : 50# alkaline paper) ∞

1. St. Nicholas (New York, N.Y.)   2. Dodge, Mary Mapes, 1830–1905. I. Gannon, Susan R. II. Rahn, Suzanne. III. Thompson, Ruth Anne.
PN4900.S75S7   2004
081'.083 — dc22   2004003507

British Library cataloguing data are available

On the cover: British edition of *St. Nicholas*, 1877, by Walter Crane

Manufactured in the United States of America

McFarland & Company, Inc., Publishers
Box 611, Jefferson, North Carolina 28640
www.mcfarlandpub.com

Table of Contents

Introduction: What Was *St. Nicholas* Magazine?

SUSAN GANNON

St. Nicholas,[1] edited by Mary Mapes Dodge from its inception in 1873 to her death in 1905, has often been called the best of all children's magazines. A member of the influential circle of writers and intellectual leaders associated with *Scribner's Monthly* (later the *Century*), Dodge was able to induce many famous authors to write for "*St. Nick*," among them Louisa May Alcott, Thomas Bailey Aldrich, L. Frank Baum, Frances Hodgson Burnett, Rudyard Kipling, Henry Wadsworth Longfellow, Thomas Nelson Page, Frank Stockton, Theodore Roosevelt, Mark Twain, and Kate Douglas Wiggin. Dodge's publishers paid handsomely, and *St. Nicholas*, with its beautiful layout, illustration, and design, was an excellent showcase for writers and artists. Dodge and her staff worked intensively with contributors to create what she liked to call a "pleasure ground" for children, and *St. Nicholas* under her guidance became an important influence on what has been called the golden age of American children's literature.[2] Many stories, serials, feature articles, verses and other special items were republished later as popular books, usually with their elegant *St. Nicholas* illustrations by artists like John Bennett or Reginald Birch. Among the children who read the magazine and went on to contribute to it through the St. Nicholas League were F. Scott Fitzgerald, E. B. White, Stephen Vincent Benét and Edna St. Vincent Millay.

But despite its cultural, historical, and literary importance, *St. Nicholas* has not received the scholarly attention it deserves. Aside from a handful of unpublished dissertations, a biography of Dodge authorized by her family, a brief study of Dodge's work, and two popular anthologies drawn from its contents, there are no full-length studies of the magazine or its editor. Much background material that might illuminate the way Dodge operated as a cultural gatekeeper remains buried in publishers' archives and research libraries, despite growing scholarly interest in American periodicals and their role in the development of children's literary culture. So this collection is designed to bring together pioneer work on *St. Nicholas*, essential resources for its study, and new essays setting the magazine and the Dodge legacy in fresh contexts.

I. The Making of *St. Nicholas*, 1873–1905

Many of the essays in this collection draw on previously unpublished material from publishers' archives and the correspondence of the magazine's editors. The first section, "The Making of *St. Nicholas*, 1873–1905," includes Dodge's essay "Children's Magazines," originally a letter to Roswell Smith of Scribner and Company, who liked her ideas about writing for children so well that he published her letter in *Scribner's Monthly* (without her byline) and offered its author the editorship of his new and as-yet unnamed children's magazine. William Fayal Clarke's intimate portrait of Dodge, "In Memory of Mary Mapes Dodge," is a major source of information about the founding and running of the magazine, written by a close friend and colleague. Clarke, who came to *St. Nicholas* before he was quite old enough to vote, in 1878 replaced the versatile Frank Stockton as Dodge's assistant. In 1893 he became associate editor, and as Dodge entered her seventies she began to rely heavily on him to manage the magazine. After her death in 1905 he became editor-in-chief, and carried on in the Dodge tradition until his own retirement in 1927; so he had a unique insider's knowledge of the magazine's philosophy and operation.

Susan R. Gannon's "Fair Ideals and Heavy Responsibilities: The Editing of *St. Nicholas* Magazine" draws on Dodge's literary correspondence and editorial memos to illustrate the difficulties involved in turning the theories expounded in her 1873 essay for Roswell Smith into practice. One of Dodge's key ideas was that the ideal children's magazine must be superbly illustrated. She and her art director, Alexander Drake, worked very hard to make *St. Nicholas* exemplify the highest standards in illustrative art, layout, and printing. Michael S. Joseph's "Illustrating *St. Nicholas* and the Influence of Mary Mapes Dodge" is a meticulous account of this aspect of her editorial work, also drawn largely from original archival sources.

One useful but often neglected resource for the study of children's periodicals is the commercial advertising and in-house promotional material inserted in the front or back of each monthly number. These materials, often stripped from library copies when the magazines were bound, are hard to come by, but offer a great deal of otherwise unavailable information about the marketing of the magazine, the demographics of its readership, and the interests of both publishers and readers. In "'Here's to *Our* Magazine!' Promoting *St. Nicholas*," Susan Gannon uses in-house promotional copy, ads in other contemporary magazines and retrospective essays like Clarke's "Fifty Years of *St. Nicholas*: Brief Anniversary Compilation of Chronicle and Comment," also excerpted in this section, to trace the development of the magazine and the shaping of its public image during its first three decades.

II. "Jacks and Jills": *St. Nicholas* and Its Audience

To understand *St. Nicholas* in the Dodge years only in terms of its editorial program, or its promotional agenda for the eager audience of parents, children, and caregivers that looked forward to the magazine's arrival each month, would be a mistake. Even looking at the magazine as a carefully designed occasion of a complex reading experience does not give sufficient weight to the interactive nature of the reading and writing process. The second section of this book, therefore, focuses on the magazine's unique relationship with its young community of readers and the way Dodge acted as intermediary between that community and one of its favorite authors, Louisa May Alcott.

In three related pieces, Suzanne Rahn explores the special bond between Dodge's magazine and its readers, examining the way the interactive features of the magazine worked to make it, in the words of one young reader, "the medium of feeling between all the boys and girls in the land" (*SN* 11[Feb. 1884]:340). In "*St. Nicholas* and Its Friends: The Magazine-Child Relationship," Rahn places Dodge's handling of the "Letter-Box" in the context of other such features in earlier magazines and shows how her personal column, "Jack-in-the-Pulpit," set the ground rules for a pleasant "community in which children would be first-class citizens."[3] Selections here from children's letters and other contributions illustrate the development of the different interactive features and let the young readers speak for themselves of their diversity, their mutual affection, and their devotion to their favorite magazine. In "Young Eyewitnesses to History," Rahn demonstrates that the "Letter-Box" also represents a remarkable cache of historical material — history seen through the eyes of children, who in their letters described some of the most striking events of their time. The St. Nicholas League for young contributors is justly famous, and Rahn, who has studied it closely, tells, in "In the Century's First Springtime: Albert Bigelow Paine and the St. Nicholas League," of the way the founder of the League nurtured its first generation of young writers and artists.

Among the young contributors who went on to outstanding literary careers was E. B. White. In this book we have the privilege of reprinting White's tribute to *St. Nicholas* that appeared in *The New Yorker* in 1934; and in "A Debut in the League," Rahn looks at selected appearances by the very young White and his wife-to-be, Katherine Sergeant. When his memoir "Onward and Upward with the Arts: The St. Nicholas League," describing how much it meant to him to see his work in print, appeared in the *New Yorker* in December of 1934, White sent a copy of the piece to William Fayal Clarke, then seventy-nine and long retired. Clarke replied graciously in a valuable letter describing the founding of the League. We are pleased to be able to include both White's essay and Clarke's reply here.

Just as the in-house ads for *St. Nicholas* and the other promotional material published on its behalf provide an enlightening context for its contents, so do the commercial ads it carried. Ads for books and magazines, household or institutional furnishings, boarding schools, nostrums of one sort or another, clothing and travel schemes can tell a good deal about the target audience for *St. Nicholas* at any given time or place. (The British edition's upscale ads in the eighties, for example, point to the relative aᵒuence of its subscribers.) As Dodge herself observed, young readers tend to read as they please, and give their attention only to what genuinely interests them. So it was a real challenge to ensure that they would read ads, especially ads that appeared to be directed toward adults. Still, it was in the interest of the advertisers to have their copy read with attention by the younger generation, who might become loyal customers as they grew up. Ellen Gruber Garvey provides an intriguing picture of the way the advertisers in *St. Nicholas* trained readers of the magazine to pay close attention to ad copy by involving them in competitions similar to the League contests, but commercial in their aim. Apart from exercising the wits of the readership, these contests were shrewdly designed to shape the habits of future consumers at the dawn of the advertising age. Garvey's essay, "The *St. Nicholas* Advertising Competition: Training the Magazine Reader," explains the ingenious tactics advertisers used to get young readers not only to peruse their ads attentively, but to engage them imaginatively in the ad game, "to play with it, to fantasize within its terms, using its images."[4]

Daniel Shealy, who co-edited a recent edition of Alcott's letters, offers a close reading of the editorial relationship between Alcott and the "compassionate editor who understood the pressures of juggling a professional career alongside domestic responsibilities."[5] Generous excerpts from Alcott's letters to Dodge show Dodge offering sympathetic support and good pay, but constantly angling for more crowd-pleasing stories like *Eight Cousins,* while the anxious and over-taxed Alcott tries her best to oblige with something that will serve her devoted readers "wisely as well as cheerfully."[6]

III. *St. Nicholas* and Its Worlds: Cultural Messages

The articles in the final section of this collection situate *St. Nicholas* in the cultural history of its time and place. Fred Erisman in "The Utopia of *St. Nicholas*: The Present as Prologue" reminds us that the publishers of *St. Nicholas* intended it to be "the qualitative equivalent of the adult magazine, conveying and reinforcing the values of its upper-middle-class readers."[7] So it is important to understand the view of the world presented in the magazine's pages. *St. Nicholas,* for Erisman, presented a "humane, conservative world somewhat at odds with the practical world of reality," but its suggestion that the modern world could at least be made compatible with such a picture had a utopian message for young readers who might be in a position to bring about the necessary changes.[8]

R. Gordon Kelly, in his pioneer study *Mother Was a Lady: Self and Society in Selected American Children's Periodicals, 1865–1890,* saw the social function of formulaic fiction in magazines like *St. Nicholas* as the reaffirmation of traditional standards of behavior held by the gentry elite. He read such stories as allaying parental fears about intergenerational tensions in a time of rapid social and economic change and reassuring children that even in a period when the future might be very different from the present, parents were still a reliable source of guidance. We have been able to include only a brief excerpt from Kelly's book, but his approach to understanding formulaic fiction as an embodiment of "the values, expectations, assumptions, hero types, and needs of a social group" that might resolve tensions arising out of "conflicting needs"[9] has been influential, and his view of these texts as efforts to persuade children to "act on … particular definitions of self and society" opened up significant lines of inquiry into narrative fiction for children.[10]

Historian Anne MacLeod's "Money: The Change-of-Fortune Story in *St. Nicholas Magazine*" examines the way some fiction in the magazine expressed the anxieties and aspirations of middle-class Americans in a time when unpredictable economic swings could suddenly make or break a family's financial and social status. The stories she selects for analysis respond to particular concerns of the historical moment, but the social problems on which they center are with us yet, especially those of "the working poor, the exploited immigrants, children without homes or hope, consumerism without restraint, the very rich rich and the very poor poor."[11] Another source of middle-class anxiety at the turn of the century was the threat of social unrest and disruption represented by the wretchedness of the crowded slums in America's rapidly growing cities. Greta Little, in "*St. Nicholas* and the City Beautiful, 1893–1894," sets a memorable series of articles on the great cities of the United States in the context of the "City Beautiful Movement," an approach to city planning that gained major attention as a result of the Chicago World's Fair in 1893. The announced intention of the series was to celebrate the wonders of the nation's great cities at a time when the country expected many visitors from abroad. But the detailed descriptions of each city's ideal parks, playgrounds, schools, boulevards and handsome buildings, accompanied by suggestions that these are the sort of places needed to nurture better citizens in the future, presented yet another strong utopian message to young readers.

Putting what *St. Nicholas* said to its special audience about war and militarism in the context of the larger discussion of such matters in the adult press, Marilynn Strasser Olson, in "'When Did Youth Ever Neglect to Bow Before Glory?' *St. Nicholas* and War," builds a formidable case that Dodge's editorial treatment of these subjects lacked the requisite balance and nuance presented by — for example — the *Century*, in its famous series on the Civil War, prepared for adult consumption. Like the other contributors to this section, Olson sees the selections she discusses as instrumental in the preparation of youth for an uncertain future. But Olson's unusually comprehensive and detailed study of the idealization of war and sacrificial valor in *St. Nicholas* raises serious questions about how well this carefully modulated picture of grim realities may have served its audience.

This section concludes with an account from literary historian Gillian Avery of the way British readers responded to the picture of American childhood and family life that they saw in *St. Nicholas.* In "Young England Looks at America" she cites the sentiments about American life, manners, food and dress that turned up in a wide range of contemporary British fiction, and observes the appeal of American child characters in *St. Nicholas* who were so different from British readers, so "independent, resourceful, spirited, informal with their parents, unabashed by adults and easy with strangers."[12] Throughout her meditation on Americanness in *St. Nicholas,* Avery uses her wide knowledge of British and American fiction of the time to compare plot lines, characterization and thematics. A refrain that runs through the piece is the way British children enjoyed the participatory domestic coziness of American fiction, and its "real people."[13] This warm picture of ordinary American home life, with its relative informality and opportunities for early independence, seems to have generated its own brand of utopian fantasy in the minds of properly brought-up transatlantic readers.

In its own way, each of the essays in this section deals with the possible impact on readers of the idealized world of Dodge's "pleasure ground," which could offer such a striking contrast to their personal experience of the constraints and contingencies of "real life." To give Dodge her due, her readers were from the very first encouraged to be intellectually curious, and diligent in seeking honest answers to their questions about the world. And she acknowledged that "harsh, cruel facts" had their claim, even on the inhabitants of a "pleasure ground." But she insisted that such facts should "march forward boldly, say what they have to say, and go."[14] Like its sister periodical, the *Century*, *St. Nicholas* found the vigor of contemporary realism tempting enough to publish Mark Twain and John Townsend Trowbridge. But like her colleague Richard Watson Gilder of the *Century*, who said that "since all art is selection, there was no real *real* in literature," Dodge chose to "temper realism with idealism."[15] The implications and effects of this choice have been addressed here in terms of the way readers might have been invited to think and feel on the subjects of utopian reform, "fallen fortunes," urban renewal, military glory and family life. But these studies can only suggest what might be done far more comprehensively by the kind of broadly based interdisciplinary, collaborative scholarship historical children's periodicals are beginning to get — and richly deserve.

IV. The Rest of the Story

What happened to *St. Nicholas* after 1905? It had a long life. Dodge had "conducted" it for thirty-two years, and the faithful William Fayal Clarke carried on very much in her tradition for twenty-two more. Unfortunately, Dodge's warm personal touch and ability to network on behalf of the magazine were inimitable. Many well-known writers for children continued to publish in *St. Nicholas,* but Clarke could not match her ability to persuade first-rank writers for adults to write for the magazine. He did create a number of interesting new departments and took a special interest in seeing that current events were covered in "The Watch Tower." After Albert Bigelow Paine, its first director, left the St. Nicholas League to work on Mark Twain's papers, Clarke took over the running of the

League in addition to his other chores, and did it very well, having learned a good deal from Paine's example. After Clarke's retirement in 1927, George F. Thompson (1927–1929) and Albert Gallatin Lanier (1929–1930) edited the magazine for the Century Company. But in 1930 the Century Company decided to sell *St. Nicholas,* and thereafter it passed successively to a series of publishers, none of whom could make a success of it. Later editors included May Lamberton Becker (1930–1932), Eric J. Bender (1932–1934), Chesla Sherlock (1934–1935), Vertie A. Coyne (1936–1940) and Juliet Lit Sterne (1943). Many of them spoke earnestly of wanting to revive the glories of the Dodge years, but for a variety of reasons, that seems to have been impossible.

However, in 1973, an American literary magazine for children was founded with the "avowed aim" of trying to "bridge the gap existing in children's magazine publishing since *St. Nicholas* ceased publication," and it has had considerable popular and critical success.[16] The editors at *Cricket: The Magazine for Children* and its whole family of age-oriented literary journals for the younger set are today doing quite well with the *St. Nicholas* formula, including a Cricket League for young contributors, modeled explicitly on the St. Nicholas League.

So it might be said that the legacy of Mary Mapes Dodge *does* live on in the example she set, in the classic children's stories she nurtured into being, in the accomplishments of artists and writers whose work is constantly being "re-discovered" by scholars and ordinary readers. Many American families still possess treasured bound copies of the magazine. Research libraries still have complete runs, and old copies in decent condition don't stay in the used bookstores very long. The volumes produced during the Dodge years are presently available on microfilm from University Microfilms, and it is to be hoped that in the near future some enlightened and well-endowed scholarly enterprise will make a full-text searchable database version available online.

A new generation of scholars interested in children's literary studies, cultural studies, American studies and history of the book would certainly find such a tool appealing, for the magazine is a rich mine of resource material in all their special fields. The pages of *St. Nicholas* in the Dodge years reveal much about the cultural program espoused for their children by three generations of anxious achievement-oriented parents, and show how American families dealt with the tensions and conflicts generated by a period of unprecedented and disorienting change. As a heterogeneous collection of materials representing many different voices and viewpoints, the contents of *St. Nicholas* are more diverse and more variable in quality and in message than the critical literature might suggest, often representing an interesting compromise between what its editors wanted and what they could get. Any comprehensive study of such a vast and unwieldy subject must be a large-scale effort, broadly based, interdisciplinary, representing many differing perspectives. For readers who wish to explore the subject more comprehensively, the Bibliography at the end of the volume provides suggestions for further study. But the best way to begin will always be to settle down in a comfortable chair with a volume of *St. Nick* for a few hours of fascinating — and provocative — reading.

Notes

1. Until July 1881, the magazine's full title was *St Nicholas: Scribner's Illustrated Magazine for Girls and Boys*; for the rest of Dodge's editorship, it was titled *St. Nicholas: An Illustrated Magazine for Young Folks*. For convenience it will be referred to here as *St. Nicholas* in text and cited in notes and references as *SN*. This practice will be followed throughout this volume.

2. Mary Mapes Dodge, "Children's Magazines," *Scribner's Monthly* 6 (July 1873) : 354.

3. Suzanne Rahn, "*St. Nicholas* and Its Friends: The Magazine-Child Relationship," Chapter 6 in this volume.

4. Ellen Garvey, "The *St. Nicholas* Advertising Competition: Training the Magazine Reader," Chapter 11 in this volume.

5. Daniel Shealy, "'Work Well Done': Louisa May Alcott and Mary Mapes Dodge," Chapter 12 in this volume.

6. Alcott to Dodge 17 Sept. [1879], *The Selected Letters of Louisa May Alcott*, ed. Joel Myerson and Daniel Shealy; Madeleine Stern, assoc. ed. (Athens: University of Georgia Press, 1995).

7. Fred Erisman, "The Utopia of *St. Nicholas*: The Present as Prologue," Chapter 13 in this volume.

8. *Ibid.*

9. R. Gordon Kelly, "Two Narrative Formulas," *Mother Was a Lady: Self and Society in Selected American Children's Periodicals 1865–1890* (Westport, CT: Greenwood Press, 1974). Chapter 14 in this volume.

10. *Ibid.*, xvi.

11. Anne S. McLeod, "Money: The Change-of-Fortune Story in *St. Nicholas Magazine*," Chapter 15 in this volume.

12. Gillian Avery, "Young England Looks at America," Chapter 18 in this volume.

13. *Ibid.*

14. Dodge, "Children's Magazines," 354.

15. Arthur John, *The Best Years of the* Century: *Richard Watson Gilder*, Scribner's Monthly, *and* Century Magazine, 1870–1909 (Urbana: University of Illinois Press, 1981).

16. Mary D. Manning, "*Cricket: The Magazine for Children*," *Children's Periodicals of the United States,* ed. R. Gordon Kelly (Westport, CT: Greenwood Press, 1984): 132.

Part I

THE MAKING OF *ST. NICHOLAS*, 1873–1905

1

Children's Magazines

MARY MAPES DODGE

(*Scribner's Monthly*, July 1873)

Sometimes I feel like rushing through the world with two placards—
one held aloft in my right hand, BEWARE OF CHILDREN'S MAGAZINES!
the other flourished in my left, CHILD'S MAGAZINE WANTED! A good
magazine for little ones was never so much needed, and such harm is
done by nearly all that are published. In England, especially, the so-called
juvenile periodicals are precisely what they ought not to be. In Germany,
though better, they too often distract sensitive little souls with grotes-
querie. Our magazines timidly approach the proper standard in some
respects, but fall far short in others. We edit for the approval of fathers
and mothers, and endeavor to make the child's monthly a milk-and-
water variety of the adult's periodical. But, in fact, the child's magazine
needs to be stronger, truer, bolder, more uncompromising than the other.
Its cheer must be the cheer of the birdsong, not of condescending editorial babble. If it *mean* freshness and heartiness, and life and joy, and
its words are simply, directly, and musically put together, it will trill its
own way. We must not help it overmuch. In all except skillful handling
of methods, we must be as little children if we would enter this king-
dom.

If now and then the situation have fun in it, if something tumble
unexpectedly, if the child-mind is surprised into an electric recognition
of comical incongruity, so that there is a reciprocal "ha, ha!" between the
printed page and the little reader, well and good. But, for humanity's sake,
let there be no editorial grimacing, no tedious vaulting back and forth over
the grim railing that incloses halt and lame old jokes long ago turned in
there to die.

Let there be no sermonizing either, no wearisome spinning out of facts, no rattling of the dry bones of history. A child's magazine is its pleasure-ground. Grown people go to their periodicals for relaxation, it is true; but they also go for information, for suggestion, and for today's fashion in literature. Besides, they begin, now-a-days, to feel that they are behind the age if they fail to know what the April *Jig-jig* says about so and so, or if they have not read B — 's much-talked-of poem in the last *Argosy*. Moreover, it is "the thing" to have the *Jig-jig* and the *Argosy* on one's drawing-room table. One must read the leading periodicals or one is nobody. But with children the case is different. They take up their monthly or weekly because they wish to, and if they don't like it they throw it down again. Most children of the present civilization attend school. Their little heads are strained and taxed with the day's lessons. They do not want to be bothered nor amused nor taught nor petted. They just want to have their own way over their own magazine. They want to enter the one place where they can come and go as they please, where they are not obliged to mind, or say "yes ma'am" and "yes sir," — where, in short, they can live a brand-new, free life of their own for a little while, accepting acquaintances as they choose and turning their backs without ceremony upon what does not concern them. Of course they expect to pick up odd bits and treasures, and to now and then "drop in" familiarly at an air castle, or step over to fairy-land. They feel their way, too, very much as we old folk do, toward sweet recognitions of familiar day-dreams, secret goodnesses, and all the glorified classics of the soul. We who have strayed farther from these, thrill even to meet a hint of them in poems and essays. But what delights *us* in Milton, Keats, and Tennyson, children often find for themselves in stars, daisies, and such joys and troubles as little ones know. That this comparison holds, is the best we can say of our writers. If they make us reach forth our hands to clutch the star or the good-deed candle-blaze, what more can be done?

Literary skill in its highest is but the subtle thinning of the veil that life and time have thickened. Mrs. Browning paid her utmost tribute to Chaucer when she spoke of

> "_____his infantine
> Familiar clasp of things divine."

The *Jig-jig* and *Argosy* may deal with Darwinism broadly and fairly as they. The upshot of it all will be something like

> The mouse ran up the clock.
> The clock struck one

Frontispiece for the first issue of *St. Nicholas.*

> "Hickery, dickery, dock!
> And down she ran —
> Hickery, dickery, dock!"

And whatever Parton or Arthur Helps may say in that stirring article, "Our Country Today," its substance is anticipated in —

> "Little Boy Blue!
> Come, blow your horn!
> The cow's in the meadow
> Eating the corn."

So we come to the conviction that the perfect magazine for children lies folded at the heart of the ideal best magazine for grown-ups. Yet the coming periodical which is to make the heart of baby-America glad must

ST. NICHOLAS.

Vol. I.   NOVEMBER, 1873.   No. 1.

DEAR GIRL AND BOY—No, there are more! Here they come! There they come! Near by, far off, everywhere, we can see them,—coming by dozens, hundreds, thousands, troops upon troops, and all pressing closer and closer.

Why, this is delightful. And how fresh, eager, and hearty you look! Glad to see us? Thank you. The same to you, and many happy returns. Well, well, we might have known it; we *did* know it, but we hardly thought it would be like this. Hurrah for dear St. Nicholas! He has made us friends in a moment.

And no wonder. Is he not the boys' and girls' own Saint, the especial friend of young Americans? That he is. And isn't he the acknowledged patron Saint of New York—one of America's great cities—dear to old hearts as well as young? Didn't his image stand at the prow of the first emigrant ship that ever sailed into New York Bay, and wasn't the very first church the New Yorkers built named after him? Didn't he come over with the Dutch, ever so long ago, and take up his abode here? Certainly. And, what is more, isn't he the kindest, best, and jolliest old dear that ever was known? Certainly, again.

Another thing you know: He is fair and square. He comes when he says he will. At the very outset he decided to visit our boys and girls every Christmas; and doesn't he do it? Yes; and that makes it all the harder when trouble or poverty shuts him out at that time from any of the children.

Dear old St. Nicholas, with his pet names—Santa Claus, Kriss Kringle, St. Nick, and we don't know how many others. What a host of wonderful stories are told about him—you may hear them all some day—and what loving, cheering thoughts follow in his train! He has attended so many heart-warmings in his long, long day that he glows without knowing it, and, coming as he does, at a holy time, casts a light upon the children's faces that lasts from year to year.

Never to dim this light, young friends, by word or token, to make it even brighter, when we can, in good, pleasant, helpful ways, and to clear away clouds that sometimes shut it out, is our aim and prayer.

Mary Mapes Dodge's letter to her readers in the first issue of *St. Nicholas*.

not be a chip of the old Maga block, but an outgrowth from the old-young heart of Maga itself. Therefore, look to it that it be strong, warm, beautiful, and true. Let the little magazine-readers find what they look for and be able to pick up what they find. Boulders will not go into tiny baskets. If it so happen that the little folks know some one jolly, sympathetic, hand-to-hand personage who is sure to turn up here and there in every number of the magazine or paper, very good: that is, if they happen to like him. If not, beware! It will soon join the ghosts of dead periodicals; or, if it do not, it will live on only in that slow, dragging existence which is worse than death.

A child's periodical must be pictorially illustrated, of course, and the pictures must have the greatest variety consistent with simplicity, beauty and unity. They should be heartily conceived and well executed; and they must be suggestive, attractive and epigrammatic. If it be only the picture of a cat, it must be so like a cat that it will do its own purring, and not sit a dead, stuffed thing, requiring the editor to purr for it. One of the sins of this age is editorial dribbling over inane pictures. The time to shake up a dull picture is when it is in the hands of the artist and engraver, and not when it lies, a fact accomplished, before the keen eyes of the little folk. Well enough for the editor to stand ready to answer questions that would naturally be put to the flesh-and-blood father, mother, or friend standing by. Well enough, too, for the picture to cause a whole tangle of interrogation-marks in the child's mind. It need not be elaborate, nor exhaust its theme, but what it attempts to do it must do well, and the editor must not over-help nor hinder. He must give just what the child demands, and to do this successfully is a matter of instinct, without which no man should presume to be a child's editor and go unhung.

Doubtless a great deal of instruction and good moral teaching may be inculcated in the pages of a magazine; but it must be by hints dropped incidentally here and there; by a few brisk, hearty statements of the difference between right and wrong; a sharp, clean thrust at falsehood, a sunny recognition of truth, a gracious application of politeness, an unwilling glimpse of the odious doings of the uncharitable and base. In a word, pleasant, breezy things may linger and turn themselves this way and that. Harsh, cruel facts—if they must come, and sometimes it is important that they should—must march forward boldly, say what they have to say, and go. The ideal child's magazine, we must remember, is a pleasure-ground where butterflies flit gayly [sic] hither and thither; where flowers quietly spread their bloom; where wind and sunshine play freaks of light and shadow; but where toads hop quickly out of sight and snakes dare not show themselves at all. Wells and fountains there may be in the grounds, but water must be drawn from the one in right trim, bright little buckets; and there must be no artificial coloring of the other, nor great show-cards about it, saying, "Behold! A fountain." Let its own flow and sparkle proclaim it.

2

In Memory of
Mary Mapes Dodge [Excerpts]
Died August 21, 1905
WILLIAM FAYAL CLARKE
(*St. Nicholas* Magazine, October 1905)

Long before this number of ST. NICHOLAS reaches its readers, the daily newspapers will have brought to them the sad news of the death of the beloved editor of this magazine. Mrs. Dodge had been suffering from a severe illness for several months, and it was hoped that the usual sojourn in her summer cottage in Onteora, New York, might restore her to health. But she steadily grew weaker until the end, which came peacefully on the morning of Monday, August 21st.

To all who knew and loved her it seems almost unbelievable that one who was so vital a part of the lives of those around her has vanished forever from our sight. Mrs. Dodge was always so triumphantly alive and joyous, so "in love with life and raptured with the world"; she had served so long and faithfully in her chosen field; she belonged so thoroughly to her great task, and held so high a place in both public and private esteem, that, as many a sorrowing friend has written, "We cannot imagine life without her." The recognized leader in juvenile literature for almost a third of a century, she was universally honored by the children of America and even of the world—for from shore to shore of our country and across the widest seas her name was held in reverent affection by child-readers and their parents. Two generations of girls and boys have known her work and learned to love the noble, gifted, kindly nature which that work revealed. Children's faces all over the land broke into smiles of joy at the mention of her name; parents all over the land, knowing well the debt which they and their children owed to her, said many a quiet "God bless her!" in their hearts. Upon her desk today are loving, grateful letters from children whose fathers and mothers sent her just such letters in the cramped handwriting of their own childhood twenty-five years ago. "And we love you, dear Mrs. Dodge, as much as we love ST. NICHOLAS!" was always the burden of these missives. Every copy of ST. NICHOLAS made a personal friend for Mrs. Dodge of every girl and boy who read it, and everywhere she was honored and beloved as one who had done a great work in the world.

The portrait of Mary Mapes Dodge from William Fayal Clarke's memorial. "As her pictures show," wrote Clarke, "she had a fair and noble countenance, but the first and the most lasting impression which she made was that of a singular radiance and cheer." *SN* 32 (Oct. 1905): 1068.

But it was not by any luck or good fortune that she accomplished that work; it was by patient, devoted, conscientious labor — by the exercise of noble gifts to a noble end. It was her mission to minister to the thoughts and interests and aspirations of childhood, and for this she was divinely fitted. From first to last — in her delight in simple things, in her simple faith, and in her eager impulses and quick sympathies — she was herself a child. But not in powers — for her powers were of the rarest and the greatest; not in knowledge and wisdom — for there have been few wiser or more accomplished women; not in courage — for her courage nothing could daunt. Yet these high endowments, with all the other manifold gifts of her nature, she consecrated to the service of childhood. To make child-readers happy first, and through this happiness to lead them on to higher and nobler living, — this was her aim and work. And all the joy and sweetness and enlargement which she brought into their lives, they have still and cannot lose....

After the publication in leading magazines of several essays and stories for grown-up readers, Mrs. Dodge brought out, in 1864, her first book — made up of short tales for children — under the title "Irvington Stories." So great was its popularity that the publisher begged for a second series or a sequel. But Mrs. Dodge, meantime, had begun work upon a longer narrative. She was really improvising it as a "good-night story" for her boys—"making it up as she went along," as children say. From Motley's histories and other books her mind was filled with admiration of the sturdy, heroic little nation which for centuries had held its own against the mightiest powers of Europe and a still mightier enemy—the sea. In the heat of kindled imagination she began to tell her children a story of life in Holland, weaving into it much interesting material from the history of that quaint and valiant country, which at that time she had never seen.

The subject grew more and more absorbing to her. She worked upon the manuscript from morning till night, and sought eagerly for every source of information which could make her pages more true to life or more entertaining to her readers. "She ransacked libraries, public and private, for books upon Holland; made every traveler whom she knew tell her his tale of that unique country; and submitted every chapter to the test of the criticism of two accomplished Hollanders living near her. It was the genius of patience and toil, the conscientious touching and retouching of the true artist, which wrought the seemingly spontaneous and simple task."

From the day of its issue, "Hans Brinker" found multitudes of readers, and more copies of it are still sold every year than of the average newly-written juvenile story. Besides its large circulation in America, it has passed through several editions in England; has been published in French at Paris; in German at Leipsic; in Russian at St. Petersburg; and in Italian at Rome. The French Academy awarded it one of the Monthyon prizes of fifteen hundred francs. In Holland itself a Dutch translation has found a sale of many editions. By a curious coincidence, too, when Mrs. Dodge was in Amsterdam with her son in 1873, a copy of this Dutch edition was recommended to him by a bookseller as the best and most faithful juvenile story of Dutch life that was known in Holland. It was a pleasant experience for Mrs. Dodge when the boy, having purchased a copy, proudly presented it to her, repeating the bookseller's comment, and confiding to him that she was the author of the story. Today, in our own country and in all English-speaking lands, "Hans Brinker" is a veritable classic of juvenile literature. Even if Mrs. Dodge had done nothing more than to write this book, her place would be forever secure in the affections of child-readers.

But after bringing out, in 1869, a clever little book of home pastimes entitled "A Few Friends," she accepted, in 1870, the position of associate editor of "Hearth and Home," a weekly family paper, of which the editors were Mrs. Harriet Beecher Stowe and Mr. Donald G. Mitchell. On this journal she took charge of the household and juvenile departments, and ere long Mrs. Dodge's reputation as editor equaled that which she had already attained as author. The circulation of the periodical was greatly increased, and the department itself rapidly grew into a very prominent feature of the weekly issues. It was her work in this field which first attracted the attention of Dr. J. G. Holland and Mr. Roswell Smith when, early in the seventies, as directors of the company which now publishes "The Century Magazine," they began to consider the publication of a new juvenile monthly. Their decision really hinged upon hers, for they were heartily ready to undertake the project provided they could obtain her consent to its management and become its editor.

Let it be confessed that she had other aims. Ambition tempted her. She was eager to try her hand at novel-writing. Her triumphs in juvenile literature had already exceeded her expectations; she longed for other fields to conquer. Thus her mind reasoned; but her heart — her heart turned again to thoughts of the children. Many gifted men and women were writing novels; no one was doing all that could be done — that ought to be done — for the boys and girls. Not without a pang of regret, but without further hesitation, she obeyed the call of duty. How clearly she heard, how faithfully she answered the cry of children all the world knows today.

For thus it was that St. NICHOLAS was founded; and from the choice of its title and its first issue, in November, 1873, the best years of Mrs. Dodge's life have been devoted to St. NICHOLAS.

Looking back upon it from the standpoint of to-day, what a vast performance it represents! In no wise can it be measured by the size or contents of the single magazine which the postman leaves every month at the door. It means twelve of these, each year, for more than thirty years. A complete set, in book-form, means fifty-eight large bound volumes, which would almost fill an ordinary book-case. But it means, also, such a golden treasury of stories, verses, pictures for boys and girls— such a children's library in itself— as, in the form of a single publication, can be found nowhere else in the world.

We must remember, too, that at the time when St. NICHOLAS first appeared it was such an advance upon any preceding juvenile periodical that it might justly be called an absolutely new creation. A comparison of the last issues of "The Riverside Magazine" or "Our Young Folks" with the very first number of St. NICHOLAS showed at a glance the immeasurable superiority of the new magazine. From the first, Mrs. Dodge set herself to prove the truth of her own statement —

> The child's magazine must not be a milk-and-water variety of the periodical for adults. In fact, it needs to be stronger, truer,

bolder, more uncompromising than the other; its cheer must be the cheer of the bird-song; it must mean freshness and heartiness, life and joy. Therefore look to it that it be strong, warm, beautiful, and true. Most children of the present attend school. Their heads are strained and taxed with the day's lessons. They do not want to be bothered nor amused nor taught nor petted. They just want to have their own way over their own magazine. They want to enter the one place where they may come and go as they please, where they are not obliged to mind, or say "yes, ma'am" and "yes, sir," — where, in short, they can live a brand-new, free life of their own for a little while, accepting acquaintances as they choose and turning their backs without ceremony upon what does not concern them. Of course they expect to pick up odd bits and treasures, and now and then to "drop in" familiarly at an air-castle, or step over to fairyland. A child's magazine is its playground.

Even with the opening issues, the child-readers of the country recognized that they had come into their own at last. It was the aim of both editor and publishers to produce the most beautiful and entertaining periodical for youth which it was possible to create. Mrs. Dodge was at her prime, and she made the magazine a marvel of inventiveness and youthful jollity; of absorbing stories, helpful articles, and historical sketches; of nonsense verse and genuine poetry — a rich mine, in short, of entertaining reading fitted with wonderful skill to the tastes and the wholesome development of the boys and girls. And all her conscientious labor was heartily seconded by her generous publishers. As Mrs. Dodge has said of him, Mr. Roswell Smith, the founder of the magazine, was "ambitious for the work in hand, rather than for himself. He counted no cost too great for the carrying out of a plan; and the success of ST. NICHOLAS has rested upon his energy and liberality." In her editorial work, also, she was fortunate in having capable and devoted assistants who shared her own enthusiasm for the magazine and its readers. The work was never drudgery to her nor to them. Her ardent zeal, keen wit, and tireless invention brightened with zest the dullest hour and the hardest task. Winter or summer, her spirits were unflagging, her powers always mettlesome and ready. Her mind teemed with ideas. Many a time, to fill a page or two in ST. NICHOLAS, she has written at white heat and while the presses were waiting, contributions in prose and verse that are now household favorites in the land.

An incident connected with her editorial career on "Hearth and Home" illustrates the spirit which always animated her. A happy idea came to her that would, she knew, greatly improve the number of the paper just then going to press. But — it involved a change of many pages, the rewriting of almost the entire contents of her department, and — the presses were waiting. A consultation was quickly held; the project was outlined and was promptly declared by all to be an inspiration. But could it be carried out in time? A half-hour went by in discussion; and then the decision was gently broken to Mrs. Dodge in the words: "It is impossible. We are very sorry, but it is impossible."

"Yes, I know. It *is* impossible, of course. But let's do it just the same! Why not?" was the quick, inspiring reply; and it was done — to the final enthusiastic admiration of all concerned.

What she attempted, she performed. There was no emergency, great or small, to which she was not equal; there was no Hill of Difficulty which she did not easily climb; for she believed with Emerson that "difficulties exist to be surmounted."

Perhaps it is not too much to say that with the advent of ST. NICHOLAS the Children's Age began. Assuredly, nothing to compare with it had ever been known before. In proof of this, let us quote from a recent issue of the New York "Evening Post" this cordial recognition of what the magazine did in those days:

> In that golden era the St. Nicholas published several of Trowbridge's best tales, "The Young Surveyor" and others of the "Jack Hazard" series; Noah Brooks's "Boy Emigrants," Miss Alcott's "Eight Cousins," and some of the wittiest and most whimsical of Frank R. Stockton's short sketches. Surely that is a noble muster-roll. Graybeards of forty will testify to the eagerness with which they awaited the mail that brought the St. Nicholas, to the gusto with which they plunged into the fresh instalment [sic] of Trowbridge or Miss Alcott, to the earnestness with which they begged to sit up a little later that night, and to the bright, troubled dreams in which they lived over the fascinating adventures. But in a day or two the magazine had been read from cover to cover, including the alluring advertisements of bargains in foreign stamps and jig-saws; and twenty-eight long days stretched away before the next issue.

"Aren't you going to ask me to write for ST. NICHOLAS?" asked Mr. Rudyard Kipling, when he met Mrs. Dodge for the first time.

"I am not sure that you can! Do you think you are equal to it?" was the bantering reply, to which he quickly answered:

"Oh, but I must and shall! For my sister and I used to scramble for ST. NICHOLAS every month when I was a kid."

How gloriously he redeemed his vow and earned the lasting gratitude of the ST. NICHOLAS editor and readers is indeed a cause of congratulation not only to the magazine but to the world. For a few weeks later, at Mrs. Dodge's home, he outlined the wonderful stories of little "Rikki-Tikki-

Tavi" and "Toomai of the Elephants," and her joy may be imagined, as those were the first two of the famous "Jungle Stories" which were written especially for this magazine. The incident illustrates, however, Mrs. Dodge's editorial gift of enlisting great writers in the service of children and of getting from each of them his or her best. She had always the fitting word for every occasion, and her wide and intimate acquaintance with the greatest writers of the time was made to contribute to the benefit of the eager-minded boys and girls. It was through her personal friendship with William Cullen Bryant, Henry W. Longfellow, and John G. Whittier that those distinguished poets became frequent contributors to ST. NICHOLAS. But she had also the gift of inspiring all contributors with her own zeal in behalf of her beloved army of child-readers, and it was invariably in their name, and not for her own sake, that she made her appeal, as this extract from a letter to her good friend Mr. Whittier will testify:

> Dear Mr. Whittier: I cannot help hoping that among your unwritten poems there may be some song or story for children — some Christmas thought or some personal reminiscence of a sleigh-ride or boyish coasting — in short, a legend or something from school-life, home-life, or thought-life that you may feel like giving to the children. If so, thousands upon thousands of them will be glad — and so will we editors be — and so will you be, for I know you truly enjoy making others happy.

The gentle poet responded, in due time, with a characteristic story in verse.

Even Lord Tennyson was persuaded by an irresistible letter to contribute the two exquisite child-songs which appeared in ST. NICHOLAS in 1880. There is little doubt that personal friendship — the authors' liking for Mrs. Dodge as well as for the magazine — helped to secure for ST. NICHOLAS such serials as Mrs. Frances Hodgson Burnett's "Little Lord Fauntleroy," the most popular juvenile story of its day, and Mark Twain's "Tom Sawyer Abroad"; besides notable single contributions by leading writers, including President Roosevelt, John Hay, Bret Harte, Mrs. Oliphant, Mary E. Wilkins, W. D. Howells, Edmund Clarence Stedman, Bayard Taylor, George W. Cable, John Burroughs, Frank R. Stockton, Charles Dudley Warner, and other authors of equal reputation.

Who shall measure the benefit which she thus conferred upon the boys and girls of America and upon their parents?

But, after all, this was only the lesser part of the service which she rendered. Far greater than any contribution or set of contributions to the magazine, was the patient, ceaseless, ardent attention which the editor herself bestowed upon its pages, and the conscientious, unremitting thoroughness of her work upon it from month to month and year to year.

No mention of Mrs. Dodge's editorial life would be complete without reference to the department which was her own especial joy and pride — though, all too modestly, she never even acknowledged its authorship. What reader of the early volumes of ST. NICHOLAS will ever forget the famous "Jack-in-the-Pulpit," the inimitably wise and witty little preacher whose tiny discourses of the keenest sense and most inspiriting nonsense — sometimes uttered from the "pulpit" direct, and at others through the blithe "Little School-ma'am" or good "Deacon Green"—were a feast for the minds and souls of young folks every month? It is no betrayal of a confidence, now, to reveal that Mrs. Dodge was herself "Jack-in-the-Pulpit," "Deacon Green," and the "Little School-ma'am" all in one. These were very actual and charming personages, however, to the boys and girls of that time. Like Shakespeare's characters to children of a larger growth, they were quite as "real" as many of the living, breathing folk whose voices we hear and whose hands we touch. There was never so delightful a department for young readers as "Jack-in-the-Pulpit," nor one so endeared by matchless wit and wisdom to every youthful heart....

In her personality, Mrs. Dodge was one of the most lovely and lovable of women. There was in her face a higher quality than what the world calls beauty. As her pictures show, she had a fair and noble countenance, but the first and most lasting impression which she made was that of a singular radiance and cheer.

Mr. Frank R. Stockton used to relate quietly, but with a twinkle of the eye, a story of his first meeting with Mrs. Dodge. From the fact that she was "a writer and editor for little folks," he had conceived an ideal of her as "a tall, spare, angular woman, very old-maidish in appearance, with a Maria Edgeworth type of face, spectacles at her eyes, and little round curls dangling in front of her ears." When, therefore, on entering her sanctum in the office of "Hearth and Home," he was greeted warmly, as he has often said, by "one of the most attractive and brilliant women he had ever seen," aglow with enthusiasm and wit, he was surprised almost to the point of embarrassment. It is needless to say that it was a fortunate meeting for both, and the beginning of a long association in which they were the happiest and heartiest of co-workers. Mr. Stockton soon joined the editorial staff of "Hearth and Home"; when Mrs. Dodge took charge of the new magazine, ST. NICHOLAS, he accepted at her request the position of assistant editor, which he retained for several years; and until the close of his life each of these two favorite writers for children had no better friend than the other....

Mrs. Dodge would have been the last to claim the entire credit for the success of ST. NICHOLAS. Every magazine is, of course, the work of many minds and many hands. No one more promptly or willingly acknowledged how much ST. NICHOLAS owed to the business energy and foresight of its publishers, and to the diligence and devotion of her editorial associates. No one gave heartier recognition to the generous cooperation of its contributors and artists. The editorial authority was hers, but she trusted her assistants more and more with the actual making of the magazine; and in her later years she had, of necessity, to depend upon them more and more as she gradually withdrew from active management.

In one sense, she neither will or can have any successor. But the work which she established and directed so ably will be continued, and will endure, a source of pleasure and of benefit to thousands, adapting itself to new conditions as they arise, and fulfilling — or even enlarging, let us hope — its mission and its influence.

To have sent out into the world a story that is a classic of juvenile literature, and unnumbered verses that have gone straight to the heart of childhood with joy and innocent laughter; to have created the best of magazines for children, and to have made it vital with the best thought and fancy of the time; to have written poems which touch the soul to a new love of beauty and a stronger faith in God — many a writer would be proud to have achieved any one of these successes. She achieved them all, and with seeming ease. But the reason is not far to seek; for what she did was merely the expression of what she was. All that she wrote and accomplished was as natural as the fruit upon the bough or the blossom on the stem. It was but the flowering of a royal nature — of noble gifts patiently and faithfully used for noble ends.

Her best memorial is already builded by her own life-work, for the volumes of ST. NICHOLAS and the copies of her books that are to be found in thousands of homes to-day will never lie dust-covered, but will continue to gladden the family life, and to inspire a love for goodness, truth, and beauty in the hearts of those who are to come after us. It is given to few to exercise so far-reaching an influence upon young minds, and thus upon the future of the nation. She left the world not only happier, but better than she found it. Few lives have been more worthy and high-minded, more useful and successful, more devoted and unselfish. Perhaps it was a part of her recompense that she retained to the last the charm of inexhaustible youth — the radiance of the morning-time of life. Through all her cares, responsibilities, and sorrows, as through all her laureled years of triumph and success, her heart was as the heart of a little child.

William Fayal Clarke

3

Fair Ideals and Heavy Responsibilities: The Editing of *St. Nicholas Magazine*

SUSAN R. GANNON

"It is certainly a heavy responsibility as well as a high privilege to have the ear of Young America once a month."[1]

Mary Mapes Dodge, editor (1873–1905) of *St. Nicholas Magazine*,[2] said in what might be called her literary manifesto: "Sometimes I feel like rushing through the world with two placards—one held aloft in my right hand, BEWARE OF CHILDREN'S MAGAZINES! The other flourished in my left, CHILD'S MAGAZINE WANTED!"[3] Dodge kept a keen eye on her competition at home and abroad, and thought most children's periodicals—including her own—often missed the mark. Conscientious and self-critical, she was decidedly uneasy about what she felt to be wholesale and rather undiscriminating praise heaped on her magazine when it first appeared on the literary scene (Dodge to Whitelaw Reid, 16 October 1874, WR: LC). She was inclined to lament the "trials and disappointments" of the editorial life. "Fair ideals," she once complained, "get so woefully squeezed under printing and binding presses!" (Dodge to Scudder, 4 December 1866, HS: HN).

Though more "has been written about *St. Nicholas* than about any other American children's magazine," much "is repetitious and devoted to uncritical appreciation."[4] The story of the early years of *St. Nicholas* has often been presented in terms deriving from the idealized image of the journal, its editor, and its readership fostered by the ardent publicists at Scribner and Company. It has been assumed that, under the leadership of its maternal "Conductor," and with the generous funding of its publishers, the magazine went from triumph to triumph with apparent ease, but things were never quite that simple. So this study will not only look at its founding editor's editorial philosophy, and her publishers' program for the magazine, but will examine what Dodge's correspondence, her publisher's archives, and the pages of *St. Nicholas* itself say about the daily struggle Dodge and her staff faced for over three decades, as they tried to live up to their publicity and translate their ideals into twelve solid issues a year. "Along the way" as Dodge might put it, it will pick up, from time to time, one minor but exemplary strand of the story: her professional dealings with one of the contributors most closely identified with *St. Nicholas* in those early years, John Townsend Trowbridge.

I. "Fair Ideals": The Program of *St. Nicholas*

What did Scribner and Company, Dodge's publishers, expect from their new journal? A note in *Scribner's Monthly* announcing its arrival said:

> As we have undertaken to make Scribner's Monthly as good as labor and money can make it, so no pains will be spared to make the St. Nicholas the best juvenile that lives.... It will be adorned with beautiful and costly pictures, it will be filled with contributions by the best writers, it will be edited by Mrs. Mary Mapes Dodge. What more can be said of it, except to assure fathers and mothers and children everywhere that they will want it, and must have it. Wherever "SCRIBNER" goes, "ST. NICHOLAS" ought to go. They will be harmonious companions in the family, and the helpers of each other in the work of instruction, culture, and entertainment.[5]

The new children's magazine, then, was designed to carry out the cultural program of its adult counterpart. The editors of *Scribner's Monthly* aimed to "heal the estrangement of religion and science," "to bridge the gap between culture and the common people,"[6] and to make a good deal of money. It was the hope of men like J. G. Holland and Richard Watson Gilder that "the American middle class, if sufficiently exposed to the traditional culture and traditional values" espoused by Scribner and Company, "would move to a higher plane of appreciation for literature and art, would impose morality on American public life, and would create a just, ordered, and gracious society."[7] Passing on the values of the genteel upper-middle class to a younger generation was the task they assigned *St. Nicholas.* Their two magazines would share many of the same contributors, have the same brilliant art director and innovative printer. The mix of literature, features, and art in both their pages would have a family resemblance, and the aesthetic, moral, and political values informing their editorial perspectives would be identical.

But the editors assigned to carry out Scribner and Company's ambitious scheme for reforming American culture through shaping the attitudes of its children would have their work cut out for them. No matter how carefully they might try, it would prove impossible to gain complete control of the incoherent mix of voices and the complex flow of heterogeneous detail in even the most carefully-edited issue. And there would be so many pressures and unexpected contingencies to deal with: publishers, advertisers, and printers would make demands; willful contributors would resist advice; deadlines would prove inexorable; and readers— young and old— would turn out to have agendas of their own.

How did the editor of *St. Nicholas* see her own role? Most commentators have approached this question by citing a letter publisher Roswell Smith of Scribner and Company asked Dodge to write for him on what the ideal children's magazine should be like.[8] She wanted the letter back to publish in *Hearth and Home*, the publication she was working for at the time, but Smith was so pleased with what she had said that he sent her a check for the piece, and saved it to publish in *Scribner's Monthly*—just three months before *St. Nicholas* made its debut. Critics usually focus on a few quotable phrases in Dodge's essay that epitomize editorial practices observable in her work at *St. Nicholas*. But the essay is even more interesting for the sense it gives of Dodge's apprehensiveness about the task ahead of her, and for the ambivalence it expresses toward the whole process of editing for children: you can do so much harm, Dodge says; and there are so many ways to go wrong.

Dodge, in her letter to Smith, pointed out a key difficulty in the creation of a child's magazine: it must not be an imitation of an adult one, but speak to children — tactfully and sensitively — in their own terms. Perhaps she had an inkling that Smith would offer her a job, and wanted, delicately but firmly, to express a certain independence, as well. Any child's magazine she might edit for him would not meekly follow *Scribner's Monthly*; sometimes it might lead the way. Dodge observed that American children's magazines "timidly approach the proper standard in some respects, but fall far short in others. We edit for the approval of fathers and mothers and endeavor to make the child's monthly a milk-and-water variety of the adult's periodical. But, in fact, the child's magazine needs to be stronger, truer, bolder and more uncompromising than the other" (352). In her personal correspondence "true" was a word that Dodge used to mean almost "ideal, having all the best qualities of something."[9] This call for a "stronger, truer, bolder, more uncompromising" journal for children might mean, then, one that more perfectly fulfilled its own nature. "The perfect magazine for children," she told Smith in her letter, "lies folded at the heart of the ideal best magazine for grown-ups" (353).

II. The Launching of *St. Nicholas*

For Dodge, the practical realities of editorial life at *St. Nicholas* meant attending to her publishers' orders, wooing reluctant or recalcitrant contributors, keeping artists happy and printers calm, learning how to please a demanding divided audience of parents and children, and somehow managing to meet deadlines with good-humored efficiency. Given her high standards, Dodge found herself constantly scrambling for suitable material, but no deadline meant as much as the first one. There was enormous pressure to come up with an opening issue that lived up to the grandiose expectations raised by Scribner and Company's advertising copy.

When, in 1873, Dodge agreed to edit the new magazine, she gratefully accepted Roswell Smith's offer of $5000 a year, which amounted to a handsome increase in salary for her. (Her job at *Hearth and Home* had only paid $3000.) But Dodge was tired. It had been a trying year at *Hearth and Home*, and — though she really wanted the new job — she took the risk of making two conditions: the new journal was not to come out until January of 1874, and she was to be allowed to spend the intervening time how and where she wished. Smith accepted her conditions, and in March, as soon as her labors at *Hearth and Home* were over, Dodge set to work.

Her first move was to bring the talented and energetic Frank Stockton, a colleague from *Hearth and Home*, aboard as her assistant. The two tried to line up distinguished contributors to give the new magazine the best send-off possible. But it was harder than they expected to entice the famous to a new and untried periodical. Dodge's sister Louise described her as much in need of rest at this time, as "low spirited" and worried over "the insurmountable things which seem to come up at every turn in her preparation for starting."[10] Louisa May Alcott — later to become a *St. Nicholas* stalwart — refused Dodge flatly, citing loyalty to the *Youth's Companion*. Dodge was forced to turn to her father's old friend William Cullen Bryant and to her former editor at *Hearth and Home*, Donald K. Mitchell, to add luster to her roster of contributors. Noah Brooks, Lucy Larcom, and Rebecca Harding Davis also came through for her, but between them Dodge and Stockton ended up having to write two thirds of the first issue themselves, using their own names, as well as various pseudonyms.

The whole process was not made easier by Dodge's decision to take a badly-needed working vacation that summer, networking, lining up contributors in England, and taking the cure for an ailing knee at Aix-les-Bains. It was fortunate that the reliable and hard-working Stockton was in New York, holding the fort, when Dodge sailed for England in May of 1873, because events began to take an interesting turn while she was gone. As it happened, she would have much less time to prepare her new journal for the critics than she had been promised. Despite the tensions and concerns of the emerging financial panic of 1873, Roswell Smith had boldly decided to buy out the most likely competitor of his new monthly children's magazine. In 1870, on speculation, he had bought Horace Scudder's distinguished but failing *Riverside Magazine* and merged it with *Scribner's Monthly*. Now he snapped up a healthier rival, Ticknor and Fields's *Our Young Folks*. Anxious to make the most of his investment by securing as many of *O.Y. F.*'s subscribers as possible, Smith pushed back the opening number of *St. Nicholas* to November 1873, and made it clear that he wanted very much to be able to retain the services of *O. Y. F.*'s editor, John Townsend Trowbridge, whose engaging serials about down-to-earth, adventurous boys were a mainstay of his magazine. The ability to announce Trowbridge's continuance and to promise future Trowbridge serials would be a powerful inducement for *O. Y. F.*'s readers to maintain their subscriptions. Though he was later to speak feelingly of the perfect confidence he had reposed in Dodge, Smith seems to have wanted to bring Trowbridge on as an editor as well. Dodge's feelings about this matter are not on record. She wrote graciously to Trowbridge suggesting that he would be welcome on the magazine's staff, though it is likely that she was vastly relieved when he declined the offer. Unlike the genial Stockton, who almost invariably saw things her way, Trowbridge could be difficult, and he was still upset and a little bitter about losing his own magazine.

In Dodge's correspondence at Princeton there is an undated fragment of a letter from Trowbridge on *Our Young Folks* stationery.[11] The whole tone of the note suggests how wounded he felt, and he cannot have been easy to deal with in this mood. He asks for complimentary copies of the January number of *St. Nicholas* to be sent to a list of "personal friends, who have received the 'O. Y. F.' : which they are never to see more." When a magazine ceased publication or was bought by another it was customary to print a "card" of farewell or of explanation to the subscribers. Trowbridge made it clear that he had been more or less ordered to write an appropriate one for his readers and was complying as best he could in the time allotted: "The card which you have kindly proposed to make room for, was prepared in great haste in response to the telegram from Scribner

& Co.: I only regret that I could not have had more time to consider what should be said in so brief a space at such a time."

To Dodge's "courteous intimation that assistance from … [him] would be agreeable" Trowbridge wrote, " I should be glad to make a worthy and substantial response. But since the death of 'O. Y. F.,' a variety of applications and propositions have poured in upon me, and as yet I am at a loss to know what I shall do, or what, in justice to myself, I ought to do. For the present, therefore, I can make no positive promises. But I cannot but feel a deep interest in 'St. N' & shall look eagerly to see the results of your splendid opportunity." Still, as an editor who had just lost his own magazine, he could not resist slipping in a little criticism of the first issues of *St. Nicholas*: "Perhaps it is not fair to judge the magazine by its first numbers, but these have seemed to me designed rather to tickle the fancy, than to create a strong interest in the minds of children — those intense little realists, who wish to have the most extravagant fairy tale made, for the moment at least, vivid & actual to them."

That frank comment — rare among early responses to the magazine in its acknowledgment that some improvements might be useful — recommended just the combination of fancy and realism that would become the trademark of *St. Nicholas*. Trowbridge was an experienced editor with a good track record, and though Dodge might not have enjoyed his criticism of her first efforts, she could recognize good advice when she got it. "Permit me to add," he said, "that I think it unfortunate that more of the features of 'O. Y. F.' could not have been transferred to 'St. N.' The 'Letter Box' with its … correspondents was an especial favorite with our readers. Since you invite suggestions, I have with diffidence allowed myself to say so much."

Now Dodge had had some experience of managing a letter box and other interactive audience-participation features in the past, and while she understood their advantages, she had some ethical qualms about them. She particularly worried about encouraging an unwholesome precocity or self-consciousness among young correspondents. And perhaps she thought that the kind of devices she had used to whip up circulation at *Hearth and Home* –contests, puzzles, correspondence columns— would be out of place in the decidedly more upscale *St. Nicholas*. But here again, Trowbridge's advice proved to be right on target. And Dodge was soon to find that her "Letter-Box" feature would indeed be a key factor in the success of the new magazine. Despite his prickly manner and their rather different notions of style, propriety, and what was right for a children's periodical, Dodge patiently accepted Trowbridge's advice and criticism, and did everything she could to secure him as an ally. He would, in the long term, prove a good friend both to Dodge and *St. Nicholas*, but working with him would never be easy.

Dodge's handling of Trowbridge exemplifies the tact and forbearance with which she could turn potential rivals into valuable collaborators. A key colleague at Scribner and Company was Richard Watson Gilder, editor of *Scribner's Monthly*, later the *Century*. Gilder had been a family friend and a protégé of Dodge's when he was first working as a young journalist in Newark. Everyone seemed to expect that since Gilder and Dodge had been close, they would enjoy working side by side in the Scribner offices, but something personal happened when Dodge first entered the scene — it is not clear what it was — that caused a strain between them never completely overcome on either side. Nevertheless, the records show that Dodge was able to forge an amicable professional relationship with Gilder that allowed her access to many of his contributors and made it easier to share the services of art director Alexander Drake and master printer Theodore De Vinne.

IV. Addressing Young Readers

Dodge appears to have been almost as much concerned with finding the right voice to use with her readers as with deciding what to say to them. She was keenly aware that — plan as she might — her readers themselves would decide not only *whether* they would read her magazine, but *how* they would read it. Adults may be bullied or flattered into reading what they think they should be reading, but children "do not want to be bothered nor amused nor taught nor petted. They just want to have their own way over their own magazine."[12] She would be dealing with readers who would read opportunistically and idiosyncratically, "accepting acquaintances as they choose and turning their backs without ceremony upon what does not concern them" (353).

Editorial aims are often more clearly articulated in the specific requests editors make of contributors than in the high-flown rhetoric of manifestos and publishers' blurbs. In the spring of 1873 Dodge sent an announcement to certain prospective authors outlining the requirements of the new and as yet unnamed magazine for children she would edit. It warned contributors to avoid preachy piety. The magazine was to be "entirely unsectarian in character," so "anything like formal teaching or preaching" would be quite inappropriate. (This was an important signal in a period when children's magazines were often scrutinized for their orthodoxy, and when Sunday school libraries constituted a lucrative market.) Pleasure would be its keynote: "The spirit of mirthfulness shall be invoked from the first, and all things fresh, true, and child-like, heartily commended, while every way to juvenile priggishness shall be bolted and barred as far as the management can effect."[13] The terms "fresh," "true," and "childlike," are vague — perhaps deliberately so. What Dodge meant by them is best seen in the quality of the material she and Stockton provided in the early issues, in their editorial revisions and advice to contributors, and in the image of themselves young readers found in their magazine — especially in the letters and contributions chosen for publication in the "Letter-Box" and "Jack in the Pulpit" features. In her essay on "Children's Magazines" Dodge had suggested that a warm "jolly, sympathetic hand-to-hand personage who is sure to turn up here and there in every number might be appealing to children" (353). Dodge's inventions, the kindly "Uncle Tim" and "Little Schoolm'am," had given a warm human presence to the children's pages of *Hearth and Home*. Now she proposed to speak to the readers of *St. Nicholas* authoritatively — but without condescension — by creating a new persona, a voice that could convey a good deal of useful information and advice without being preachy or priggish. Dodge's device for doing this was unusual, but it worked. Her editorial column was headed each month by an engraving of a huge wildflower — a jack-in-the-pulpit — from which there emerged a beaming "preacher," addressing a congregation of happy and attentive children. During the first twelve issues this figure was rather loosely drawn and resembled a plant more than a human being. The sketch was re-drawn more carefully for the second and succeeding years, transforming the speaker into a smiling figure with spectacles, vaguely resembling Mrs. Dodge. "Jack" was a wildflower, but also a vivid human character, and a male one, at that. Though the audience reaction to the spirited columns was positive from the first, some readers just didn't know what to make of "Jack." So Dodge replied to some puzzled readers in typical teasing fashion in her column for November of 1875:

> That reminds me: Am I a real Jack-in-the-pulpit? you have asked — a true plant, growing and preaching out in the sunshine? Well perhaps no. Perhaps yes. This much is certain: I *do* live in the sunshine; I *do* try to grow; and I do love to talk to the boys and girls of *St. Nicholas* — to open their eyes and their minds by pointing out all sorts of queer truths here, there, and yonder — and to put into their hearts grateful loving thoughts toward the Giver of all Good. So my darlings, if you're satisfied with this explanation, I am [*SN* 3 (1875) : 54].

"Jack in the Pulpit" was a miscellany of tidbits: jokes, anecdotes, discussions of natural history. Children were invited to send in their questions and observations and their letters were printed. This correspondence, when it appeared in print, was carefully selected to provide young readers with an image of themselves as lively, unspoiled, interested in learning things for themselves and sharing what they have found out. Though Dodge privately expressed exasperation with the often messy, ill-spelled letters she received, *St. Nicholas,* unlike other magazines of the time, neither preserved children's errors because they were cute, nor lectured them on spelling or grammar. Her practice of silently correcting errors and of excerpting natural, appealing letters was noted in a contemporary review and reprinted in the magazine's own advertising: "the letters printed are worth it, and those condensed are not only judiciously but kindly so" (*Springfield Republican,* quoted in "What the American Press Says of the Bound Volume," *SN* 3 [January 1875]: ad p. 4).

For many of her adult contributors it was not easy to find a voice with which to speak effectively to the young. A child's magazine, Dodge insisted, is a child's pleasure ground. Writing for *St. Nicholas* had not only to be fresh and hearty but clear, coherent, and to the point. In an age when writers were paid by the page, long-windedness was profitable, and Dodge had to work very hard to curb the habitual verbosity of many a resentful adult contributor. Helen Hunt Jackson complained constantly about required cuts, and in one letter E. C. Stedman moaned about having to disguise the scars left by the "amputations" she demanded, though, as usual, he finally conceded to them.[14] On the other hand, a number of authors learned from experience how clever she could be at cutting and arranging their material for her particular readership, and her correspondence is full of grateful comments from the likes of Frances Hodgson Burnett, Mark Twain, and Louisa May Alcott, who readily granted her the right to snip and trim their work as she saw fit.

Dodge knew the appeal of suspense to young readers: she often got frantic letters from children beseeching her to tell them what would happen next in an exciting serial. So she stressed the importance of ending episodes as interestingly as possible. But she had also suffered the wrath of young readers ba°ed by the occasional story that ended too ambiguously for their comfort. When the financially hard-pressed Mark Twain was anxious to be able to continue his novel *Tom Sawyer Abroad* in a series of sequels, he gave Dodge a first draft of the novel that assiduously avoided closure. Dodge did not want to offend Twain, who was a dear friend as well as an unparalleled star turn, but she simply could not accept that lame ending. "With a serial," she told him, "readers are more clamorous for some sort of definite ending than in the case of a book; and young folks you know, are particularly exasperating in this respect. Of course no one could ask you to finish Tom Sawyer — that would be murder! But would it not be practicable to 'satisfactorize' the present conclusion, say by a few paragraphs that would at least lure the fascinated reader into the belief that he had it all?"[15] Twain grumbled, and said it broke his heart to do it, but he finally gave in and made the required changes.

Sometimes authors writing on complex, grown-up matters for *St. Nicholas* had to be instructed on the best ways to draw young readers into their subject. When she asked poet Lucy Larcom to write a series of articles introducing children to poetry, Dodge felt she had to outline not only the content she had in mind, but the way she wanted it approached — and this though Larcom had been an editorial colleague of Trowbridge's on *Our Young Folks* and should have known how to talk to children. The tone Dodge specified was "light and gossipy, yet full of tender spirit and feeling."[16] When Larcom's first article proved turgid and unreadable, Dodge urgently advised changes in the next installment that would catch young readers' attention and lead "them into the subject with a clearer comprehension of its significance."[17] Meanwhile, Dodge tried frantically to promote the series in her "Jack in the Pulpit" column, no doubt aware that — despite all her efforts — the articles would appeal to few of her young readers.

Indeed, features on books and reading were never quite as successful as Dodge seems to have wished. She tried a variety of formats but none of them seemed to take off with readers. She read her mail from young readers carefully, and in 1881, after a decade of trying to respond to their wishes and raise their reading standards through a careful selection of fiction, poetry, serials and features, she undertook to poll them on the direction they wanted *St. Nicholas* to take. They apparently wrote to her frankly, telling her exactly what they liked best, but it was not what she wanted to hear, as they clearly preferred light fare and immediate satisfaction. She wanted to expand their horizons and help them grow as readers. So she thanked them for their counsel, but advised: "You will find that, in this hurrying, busy, nineteenth-century life of ours, your present tastes will change or new tastes develop more rapidly than you can now imagine, and *St. Nicholas*, if it is truly to be your magazine, must keep pace with, and even anticipate your growth" ("Letter-Box," *SN* 10 [Jan. 1882]: 260).

Sometimes, when she thought authors utterly clueless about how to speak to young readers, Dodge would tactfully present them with bound volumes of earlier issues, as she did when she traveled to Cambridge to visit Longfellow. Getting what she wanted from celebrated authors was often a long, trying process. Each time Longfellow gave her something to print, she thanked him effusively for giving her poetry that was not actu-

"OH, MOTHER! DAD 'S GOT MY ST. NICHOLAS!"

St. Nicholas proved successful in attracting a "secondary audience" of adult readers, as this stylish cartoon suggests. SN 46: (Aug. 1919): 884.

ally written for children but which could still be read by them with profit. And then she would add a broad hint about how wonderful it would be if he would write something especially for her readers. The first volume of the magazine had included contributions from many well-known men of letters who had had little experience writing for children. Her strenuous efforts to assist them were acknowledged by the *New York Tribune*, which expressed admiration for the tact with which Dodge had enabled such men as "Bryant, Ik Marvel [Donald K. Mitchell], Bret Harte, Charles Dudley Warner, C. P. Cranch, Clarence Cook, John Hay, and T. W. Higginson" to "find themselves no less at home in the nursery than in the arena of politics and in the higher walks of literature" (*New York Tribune* qtd. Advertising Supplement, *SN* [Jan. 1875]).

V. Addressing the Adult Audience

Of course, while *St. Nicholas* was nominally addressed to children, as her publishers had noted in their announcement of it, the new journal would have a very important secondary audience of adults whose tastes and preferences had to be considered. Working for Scribner and Company meant that Dodge was expected to adhere to the standards of propriety set by *St. Nick's* sister magazine, *Scribner's Monthly* (later to become the *Century*) "where the editors shielded readers from direct contact with the crude phenomena of life in various forms." For the adult readers of these elite magazines, "in scenes of violence, blood might be indicated but not literally spilled," "drunkenness ... was suggested, not portrayed," "characters might not sweat nor blow their noses," "profanity was outlawed, and there was a rule against slang or 'undignified' English" (John 155).

Scribner's Monthly, like most successful magazines of the period, addressed present issues and even looked to the future, but the values expressed in its pages were those with which its middle-class readership felt comfortable. Its editor, Josiah Holland, favored the temperance movement, opposed women's suffrage, was a sentimental, nationalistic patriot. He published some undeniably racist material, yet spoke up for minority rights and social reform. Though she agreed with Holland, Smith, and Scribner on some matters, Dodge was much less stuffy, less inclined toward what she called "churchiness." Dodge had a simple but fervent religious faith and an earnest desire to do good, but she was also a sophisticated New Yorker who could banter with Mark Twain, enjoy a good game of poker, and call champagne "a bottled Sermon on the Mount" because "it made everyone blessed."[18] Her dearest friends included strong-minded and independent women like Kate Field and Libbie Custer, as well as Holland's bête-noire, Walt Whitman, who was "very fond" of her (Hutton 223).

It seems clear that because she thought the Scribner and Company imprimatur guaranteed a certain standard of propriety and committed her to a specific moral and social agenda, Dodge went out of her way to exclude from the pages of her magazine much that she did not personally find objectionable. She appeared to feel that parents bought *St. Nicholas* relying on her endorsement of the contents, and perhaps the wholesome reputation of her publishers. She frequently expressed her regret to authors over cuts and changes she was obliged to make. And she often went out of her way to "puff" books which had been cut, polished, and "Scribnerized" for serial publication in *St. Nicholas*, when, subsequently, they were published in full elsewhere.

As a matter of policy, Dodge refused to publish anything she found morally offensive, overly didactic, dull, or morbid. Anything too sectarian or likely to be politically divisive was also ruled out. She tried to avoid excessively sentimental pieces of a teary sort, though now and then one slipped through. One of the trickiest problems she faced was how to handle material adults might see as setting a bad example to their children.

There are innumerable stories about alterations in illustrations that Dodge had to require for fear of offending adult sensibilities. Young ladies' skirts could not be allowed to billow too widely, lest it cause scandal; Tom Sawyer and Huck Finn could not be shown with bare feet, because that would be vulgar; and Gellett Burgess's Goops were not allowed to stick their tongues out for fear young readers would follow suit.

Mark Twain was a close personal friend of Dodge's and his children insisted he offer her his *Tom Sawyer Abroad* for their favorite periodical. Twain, with an eye toward the special needs of the *St. Nicholas* audience, told his publisher that when writing this piece, he had "tried to leave the improprieties all out," and if he didn't, "Mrs. Dodge can scissor them out."[19] Dodge claimed she would use the scissors "very sparingly and with a reverent hand,"[20] but nonetheless cut approximately 2,000 words of Twain's text. Some of these alterations were stylistic. Twain tossed off the 40,000 word story in a month, and some of his sentences needed tightening up. But many of the changes toned down his use of dialect and eliminated some, but by no means all, of the "improprieties," including crudely racist references.

Like Twain, John T. Trowbridge specialized in rather unbuttoned realism and thereby presented Dodge with some tricky editorial problems. When he was editor of *Our Young Folks*, Trowbridge wrote his lively and entertaining serial yarns by the episode, printing them as he went along. The first installment of *Fast Friends*, featuring the further adventures of his popular Jack Hazard, was already in type when Roswell Smith bought the magazine out from under him. But Smith persuaded Trowbridge to let *St. Nicholas* have the serial (already promised to *Our Young Folks'* subscribers) and to print the first installment in its own January '74 issue. Smith and Dodge knew that printing the story immediately would be the best way to assure the continuance of former *O.Y. F.* subscribers. But as the novel developed, Trowbridge's characters moved in an ever-more-raffish ambiance. Jack Hazard and his friend George met people who not only talked in an un-genteel fashion, but chewed tobacco, indulged in petty crime, got drunk, and gambled. The boys stayed in a shabby boarding house, went to a saloon and a gaming house, consulted a pawnbroker, and even went backstage at a dubious stage-show — all situations guaranteed to give the editors at *St. Nick* heartburn.[21]

The illustrations presented Trowbridge's regular fellows— one of whom at least was old enough to shave — as innocent-looking, sweet-faced youngsters. When a drunk scene occurred in one episode, Dodge absolutely refused to have it illustrated. In March of 1874 Trowbridge wrote to her, reluctantly agreeing to her "course in rejecting the tipsy scene as subject

The young heroes of J. T. Trowbridge's serial *Fast Friends*, unable to pay their rent, are forced to visit a pawnbroker. Such sordid scenes of urban life caused difficulties for Mary Mapes Dodge as editor of *St. Nicholas*. SN2 (Aug. 1874): 570.

for a picture." He maintained stiªy that he "had thought that in Mr. White's hands it might be made … funny, & not at all revolting: everything depends upon how such things are managed." Defending a gaming house scene that apparently raised eyebrows at *St. Nicholas*, Trowbridge told Dodge that she could tell Mr. Smith that he would use it in "the book, as I should have used it in 'Our Young Folks,' without hesitation; my only objection being the juvenile characterless appearance of our young heroes. It seems almost impossible that the artist could have read the story, & got so false an impression of them from it."[22]

Trowbridge noted with satisfaction that his novel was—by Dodge's own admission—being found "interesting" by the young *St. Nicholas* readers, and he stressed his innocent intentions in writing it for them. He claimed that he had not tried "to make it in any sense sensational, but true to life; & in introducing the gaming and drunken scenes" he claimed to have been as careful as he could be "not to excite a morbid curiosity, or to shock even the most delicate minded, while at the same time the vices are made to appear unattractive."[23] It is clear that while Trowbridge's story sailed close to the wind in some ways, *St. Nicholas's* young readers simply loved it and wanted more. Despite their worries about parental objections, the editors knew they had to secure Trowbridge's services for the long haul. He confided in his autobiography that he had "confidently expected to finish ... [Jack Hazard's] career in Fast Friends [sic]." But he added: "That story had been running hardly half a year when I was invited to New York for a conference with Mr. Roswell Smith and Mrs. Dodge, regarding a serial for the ensuing year (1875).... For a couple of days Mr. Smith, whose guest I was, gave a large part of his leisure to making my visit pleasant; and I came home with a commission to write a fifth Jack Hazard story, The Young Surveyor [sic]."[24]

Trowbridge's later novel *His One Fault*, a "choice of life" story, is set in a wholesome rural locale quite unlike the sleazy world of *Fast Friends*. But even so it presented problems. In a revealing memo preserved in the Century Company files, Dodge's assistant, William Fayal Clarke, reminds Trowbridge of Mrs. Dodge's "hearty appreciation & admiration of the story as a whole" and makes it clear that "the few modifications" he must suggest "are asked for the *magazine version*, on *account of* the peculiar limitations & requirements of 'St. Nicholas'." Trowbridge was required to modify some of the incidents in his story. A wheezing asthma attack had to be shortened, he was asked to "tone down" a rather brutal beating, omitting the teasing suggestion that the beating might be fatal to the protagonist, and to de-emphasize one character's cruelty to his wife. Clarke seems very apologetic, and stresses that Dodge herself had no problem with the material as written: "Mrs. Dodge appreciates the truth to nature and dramatic value of these, as now described — if written for a book, or for older readers — but for 'St. Nicholas' the changes suggested must be an improvement."[25]

Trowbridge prided himself on a good ear for dialect, and his characters, like Twain's, speak in a colorful, pungent fashion. But as Clarke had to tell Trowbridge in his memo, "St. Nicholas [sic] is seriously crippled in the use of dialect by the demands of parents & teachers for strictly grammatical language in the magazine." Recognizing that realism had its claims, Dodge and her staff struck a compromise with Trowbridge and just toned down the use of dialect and slang. In an effort to "avoid extremes and try to be both natural & grammatical as far as possible, "Clarke asked for permission" to make such slight alterations in text as seem to us necessary to avoid too much criticism of the kind we have mentioned." The memo is regretful, and Clarke went out of his way to show Trowbridge a simple way of marking changes in his manuscript so that the original readings could readily be restored when the manuscript was being typeset for publication in book form."[26]

The changes suggested by the editors at *St. Nicholas* made it possible for them to publish *His One Fault*, but while the story remained entertaining, it lost a little of its edge and its fresh appeal in the process. A comparison of the serialized version and the story as published later by Trowbridge makes it clear how much color and vitality were lost when his slyly critical view of various parental figures was modified and the regional speech of the characters was sanitized for genteel readers.

Editorial comments, advertising inserts, testimonials, correspondence, and features directed toward parents give ample evidence that adults were an important audience for the magazine. They were represented in the correspondence columns and their interest in the magazine, their read-aloud activities, and their enthusiasm for its fiction are attested to in the accounts of family reading sessions to be found in the "Letter-Box." Part of Dodge's editorial task was to provide sufficient material in the magazine that would appeal genuinely to the interests and needs of her dual audience of adults and children. The formula fiction which filled the pages of *St. Nicholas* is highly repetitive in its plots, characters, and issues. Plucky waifs find good homes, heroic child patriots save the day, young entrepreneurs make unlikely successes. The rapt attention given to these stories by young and old seems, on the surface, hard to account for. But parents and children recognized the basic dilemmas dramatized in these stories and were clearly fascinated by watching familiar conflicts play out in a fictional context. Children were shown how dependent youngsters might negotiate for greater autonomy, while parents could observe the way the adults rather like themselves might respond to the dependency of the young and their desire for self-realization.

Like other reform-minded people of her circle, Dodge looked to individual charitable effort to provide for the needs of the marginal, dependent, and powerless. *St. Nicholas* did address the specifics of many reform projects in the public sphere in editorials and articles on such subjects as boys' clubs, children's hospitals, orphan homes, and "fresh air schemes." It is evident from her letters, her fiction, and her verse that she thought she had a special mission to use the magazine to awaken the individual sympathies of adult readers toward children and their needs. So it is possible to see some of the more sentimental fiction, poetry, and art she published as part of a pedagogical project aimed at enlisting adults in the reform efforts of the genteel establishment. While it may be difficult to assess the precise ethical and rhetorical effects of the sentimental enterprise upon adult readers of the magazine, it seems easy enough to note at least one effect upon its editor: suspending her ordinary critical standards in aid of what she seemed to see as a good end, Dodge printed many verses and stories that seem to exist only to describe children as innocently touching an adult's sensibilities because of their weakness, tininess, or inability to speak correctly. In such pieces, children's normal limitations become something to be doted on for the feelings of protectiveness and superiority they evoke in adults. *St. Nicholas* even printed some appalling baby-talk poems, a few of the worst contributed by Dodge herself.

VI. Ethical Issues

Dodge was extremely concerned about getting the record straight. The pages of the magazine are full of apologies for misattributions of credit and minor errors of fact. She agonized over misprints, telling a poet whose work had been marred by an error that she fully understood the occasional impulse to murder a printer. But the issue that really troubled her was plagiarism. She took the matter very seriously, and it was a perennial problem with young contributors' columns. Sometimes as she read a manuscript she would detect something wrong, and out would go a polite but firm note to the author, or the author's parents, asking for assurance that the piece in question was original. When Dodge was taken in by a fraud of one sort or another she took it much to heart. Ordinary child plagiarism might be expected, but when she had run *Hearth and Home*, the letters of a saintly little invalid named Minnie had attracted much reader interest, and the "little sufferer" had become a character in a sort of continuing soap opera. Dodge herself was evidently touched by the child's ability to smile through her tears. But when at last it became evident that Minnie was a fraud, Dodge saved and labeled a final letter carefully, as though to warn herself against this sort of imposture in future.

On April 21, 1880, an item appeared in the "Literary Notes" column of the New York *Tribune* suggesting that even the sharp-eyed editor of *St. Nicholas* occasionally failed to spot a case of plagiarism. The piece went on to note the report that a story in the April number was taken almost word for word from a book published two decades earlier. [27] Dodge responded in a pained note of explanation to editor Whitelaw Reid, assuring him she thought it a good thing that papers like his would publicize frauds like this, even though in this case, it had to be at her own expense.[28]

Dodge felt strongly about the property rights of authors. Along with many other American writers, Dodge expressed her concern for the need of an international copyright law in an open letter to the *Century*. Dodge made herself very clear about her ethical position, saying: "In the present stage of civilization, a great republic — unless it is willing to be a moral anomaly — must allow and secure International Copyright. It is high time that on this question our law-makers should cease to interpret 'the rights of man' as meaning only the rights of Americans."[29] The whole *Century* crowd seems to have signed on to a similar party line, led by editor Richard

Gilder and the very committed Edward Eggleston. Trowbridge himself contributed a ringing denunciation of what he termed "the easy plunder of authors' rights," in which he argued "that the facility with which a thing may be stolen is no valid excuse for the theft, and that simple justice to the author requires that literary property should be protected like any other property."[30] Dodge's reaction to Trowbridge's letter is not on record, but might have been interesting, considering something that had happened eight years before.

The *St. Nicholas* files at the Century Company Archive (NYPL) record a touchy affair involving misappropriation of literary property, the culprit in the case being John Townsend Trowbridge himself. In 1878 Trowbridge had sent Dodge a twenty-three stanza poem called "King Cheese," recounting the story of how the Swiss sent a great cheese to the Paris Exhibition of 1867. When, presumably, the poem was advertised, an angry Mrs. Maud Christiani got in touch with Dodge's staff—in her absence—and complained that she had previously submitted a similar item to Trowbridge as editor of *Our Young Folks*. She was able to provide a copy of her own piece, and though the immediate reaction of the editorial staff had not been sympathetic to her claim, it is clear that on her return, Dodge investigated and was appalled to find that the claim was justified. Dodge wrote to Mrs. Christiani, telling her that since she had called "three times" at Mrs. Christiani's residence "without the good fortune" of finding her at home, the lady was invited to come to see Dodge at *her* home, where she would be "all the afternoon and evening." Dodge said that she would at that time "be very glad to assure" Christiani in person of her "sincere regret that the managers of St. Nicholas" during her absence had "given ... offense." Dodge knew that it was essential to make some accommodation with the injured author. She assured her that Scribner and Company was willing "notwithstanding the contingent delay and expense, to set aside the first form of the large edition of 'St. N.' for August *already printed*, throwing out Mr. Trowbridge's version of [her] story, and substituting something else in place of it." This would have been quite a concession. But Dodge hints at some possible scheme of amendment that might be in Mrs. Christiani's interest: "Certainly I, for one, would not consent to that version being printed in St. Nicholas without your assent. But this point, and others of more importance to yourself, (as it seems to me), can be talked over today, if you will see me at my rooms as proposed."[31]

Dodge and Mrs. Christiani seem to have made a deal. Trowbridge's piece appeared in the August *St. Nicholas*, but after a decent interval, Dodge, citing a transparently unlikely reader demand for more information about the famous Swiss cheese, printed Mrs. Christiani's version of the story in the "Letter-Box" for February, 1879. It is hard to imagine why Trowbridge would attempt such a fraud, especially since his own earlier letterbooks from *Our Young Folks* now held at Harvard's Houghton Library are full of stern remonstrances to young plagiarists. But the incident apparently did not exhaust Dodge's patience sufficiently to do any lasting harm to her working relationship with Trowbridge, who went on to contribute a total of eleven serials to the magazine, as well as assorted shorter pieces, though no more poems.

VII. Shaping the "Editorial Mosaic" over Time

Dodge once wrote to a fellow editor, "to my mind ... the best editorial work is not so much connected with the material at hand, important as that often is, but in the foresight and insight that gives new life to the very heart of one's magazine"[32] Her most challenging task in editing *St. Nicholas* was the long-range planning required to shape the journal's identity over time, with an eye to the future effects of every decision. The miscellaneous periodical is an open-ended form, full of gaps and discontinuities. It is the editor's job to give readers the variety and novelty they desire in a format that seems comfortably familiar and provides structure and coherence to the reading experience over the years. Dodge's personal taste and her priorities shaped the roster of contributors to *St. Nicholas* and determined the standards by which pieces were selected, edited, and rewritten. Her commitment to the social and cultural agenda of her publishers and to her own vision of the reader-oriented magazine as pleasure-ground provided a strong unifying element to the magazine. Yet these same commitments guaranteed a focus on the future and a stress on constant change and improvement.

To please her readers and keep them interested, Dodge learned to pay close attention to her mail, reproducing popular features and developing artful schemes for linking one issue, one volume, to the next. She took pains to cultivate the loyalty of a group of authors who became identified with the magazine. Their stories, poems, and articles got top prices and were illustrated by the best talent to be had. The quality of the illustrations offered a particularly potent appeal to writers, since they knew that if the Century Company didn't want to publish the final product in book form, Dodge could be counted on to give her full support to her contributors' efforts to publish elsewhere, suggesting alternative venues, patiently writing letters of recommendation, and — best of all — arranging to let other publishers have the first-rate illustrations done for *St. Nicholas* at a good break in price.

Dodge's letters to authors were extremely artful. She knew just how to flatter, tease, and cajole, till she got what she wanted from them. Part of her long-term strategy for shaping her magazine's content involved making valuable contributors into personal friends, who might visit with her at her summer home in Onteora, attend her receptions and "at homes" in New York, and correspond not only about business but personal matters as well. She networked for them, did them courtesies, gave them good advice, and fussed over them, their families, and their precious manuscripts. When Louisa May Alcott's inspiration failed, she sent off a set of illustrations that inspired her "Spinning Wheel Stories." And when the poor woman got writer's cramp, Dodge offered to arrange to have her fair copies made by a professional to spare the aching hand. Always helpful, ready to sympathize and advise, and generous to a fault, Dodge, over the years, turned an initially reluctant contributor into one of "*St. Nick's*" staunchest friends.

Dodge's editorial relationship with Kipling involved much mutual respect and affection, but it also illustrates the challenges and stresses of the editorial game as Dodge played it. The story is documented in letters and memos most of which are held in various collections at Princeton, and has been well told by Dodge's biographer, Catherine Morris Wright.[33] In 1892, Kipling and his bride arrived in New York on their honeymoon. Two days later, he was honored at a men-only luncheon at the University Club. Many important social events in the New York literary world were held in venues that did not admit women, but Dodge had loyal agents who were quick off the mark. Frank Stockton left the party and went straight to her apartment to report. And Will Carey of the *Century* staff dashed off a note telling her that Kipling had confided he'd be proud to be invited by Mrs. Dodge to write for *St. Nicholas*. Dodge wasted no time, and initiated a correspondence with Kipling immediately.

To her delight, Kipling told her how he and his sister had tussled over "*St. Nick*" as children, and explained that much as he would like to address the child audience, he knew they were very discriminating readers with strong likes and dislikes. He worried about being able to strike the right note with them, and was only able to face the difficulties of the task by reflecting that after all, he had been a reader of her magazine since he was a child. All of this was promising, but Kipling's first offerings to Dodge turned out to be a weak verse story written by a friend, and a less than impressive tale about a princess shut up in a pickle jar, burdened with the off-putting title "The Potted Princess." Their subsequent correspondence and her personal memos on the subject show how skillfully Dodge could bargain down the price for the verse without alienating either Kipling or the friend who had written it and reserve comment on a story by Kipling that was not a favorite. As a later memo to herself indicates, however, Dodge was pleased that each new story Kipling sent was stronger than the last, and more unmistakably in his own special vein. The young writer seemed to be full of ideas for stories drawing on his Indian experiences. Their letters show him presenting tentative scenarios and Dodge eagerly encouraging him to fill out their details. It was under the gentle pressure of her insatiable curiosity that he was encouraged to develop such strong and memorable series as the *Jungle Book* tales of Mowgli and the *Just So Stories*. (One letter from Dodge urges him to go ahead and tell her more about a boy named Kim, whose adventures would be developed into a novel for older readers a few years later.)

Michael Joseph has amply documented Dodge's painstaking efforts to deal with the demands of authors like Kipling with strong views on the way their pieces should be illustrated.[34] When Kipling proposed that Dodge hire his friend Oliver Herford to do some illustrations, she was gracious, but firmly suggested the polished *St. Nicholas* stalwart, Reginald Birch. Kipling was wryly critical of the Birch illustrations, but accepted the editor's decision. Dodge and the kindly Fayal Clarke graciously found other work for Herford, who learned over time that he could always place a little drawing or set of verses with them when he was pressed for cash.

Kipling, who had been an editor, appreciated the importance of getting stories in on time, so that Dodge might fit them in to the larger plan of the year's work, with special attention to the all-important November, December, and January issues. And he was shrewd enough to state boldly his own preferences on such matters as the price he wanted per word for each piece; rights to subsequent publication; typing assistance; the Century Company's policies on reading of proofs; the kind of revisions needed when turning a serial into a book. His correspondence with Dodge shows that he, like Mark Twain and Frances Hodgson Burnett, could be a formidable business adversary on those occasions when he and his editor did not see eye to eye. Dodge and her stable of authors needed each other: she did her best to please and pay them well, and her cordial business letters rarely betray the strains of constant negotiation so visible in the draft letters and personal memos preserved in her files. These documents show the apparently confident editor puzzling over what to do, weighing alternatives, working out strategies for getting her way, and looking for fallback positions in case she must compromise. Dodge was very good at the game, and more often than not, carried the day, but it was time-consuming and stressful work.

As the guiding spirit of the magazine, Dodge had to be very attentive to the patterning of issues, volumes, even of whole runs of the magazine. For her, the editor's vision shaped what she termed the "editorial mosaic" of a magazine.[35] Each issue had to represent a balance of instruction and entertainment, had to include a variety of genres and subjects, and there had to be something for everyone in the audience. A Trowbridge serial that might appeal to boys and older readers would have to be balanced by something for girls or little children. When extensive reports from the Agassiz Association, a fast-growing reader interest group focusing on natural history, threatened to dominate whole issues, Dodge had to make a hard decision: it was clearly time to spin off a separate periodical for budding scientists.

Among the devices Dodge had contrived to provide continuity to the magazine were participatory activities for readers— like the Agassiz Association — and a variety of departments appealing to different interests. Despite her initial reservations about publishing children's work, the "Letter-Box" feature, her interactive column "Jack in the Pulpit," and the St. Nicholas League for young contributors all engaged readers in the development of their own magazine over time, offering them a carefully constructed image of themselves as members of a group of like-minded young people and thus providing a consistent position from which to read, yet one that could accommodate growth and change.

A particularly delicate matter for the editor of a magazine intended to be improving was deciding how the didactic impulse would be managed. Dodge stressed that the best sort of children's magazine would instruct its readers "indirectly." There was to be "no sermonizing," no wearisome spinning out of facts, no rattling of the dry bones of history" ("Children's Magazines" 353). She was by no means opposed to teaching moral lessons. She just thought that "a great deal of instruction and good moral teaching may be inculcated in the pages of a magazine ... by hints dropped incidentally here and there; by a few brisk, hearty statements of the difference between right and wrong; a sharp, clean thrust at falsehood, a sunny recognition of truth, a gracious application of politeness, an unwilling glimpse of the odious doings of the uncharitable and base" (354).

What *St. Nicholas's* editor and her contributors saw as right, wrong, false, true, uncharitable, or base was translated into a recognizable — though loose and inconsistent — didactic program, one that was probably all the more effective for its indirection. In its conscious idealism, the editorial agenda of *St. Nicholas* resembled that of its sister magazine, the *Century*. Both magazines celebrated hard work, self-discipline, cultural uplift, religious principle and love of country, though any assessment of their ethical stance must note a lamentable tendency to confuse the attitudes of genteel upper-middle-class New York with eternal verities. So despite the reformist idealism of its program, *St. Nicholas* during the Dodge years did include stories, verses, and illustrations presenting painful racial and ethnic stereotypes, and the editor's taste for dialect humor (as in the stories of her close friend, Ruth McEnery Stuart) must have offended some readers. As Marilynn Olson notes elsewhere in this volume, *St. Nicholas* also glorified warfare and military action.[36] And there was much unthinking class and gender bias. The poor were presented most sympathetically when they shared genteel values, or at least aspired to them. Those whose hardships might have made their common humanity harder to perceive from a middle-class point of view were sometimes presented as objects of fear or condescension. Though English manners and traditions were rather admired, and the folkways of other Northern Europeans were treated with interest and respect, *St. Nicholas* at this period too often presented "foreigners" as quaint, peculiar, or sadly backward. Shaped as it was by the cultural suppositions of genteel New York, the best of children's magazines, even in its "golden age," had its blind spots and limitations.

Dodge's mentor, Horace Scudder, editor of the pioneering *Riverside*, had complained to Dodge about the way an issue would sometimes get away from him and head off in a direction he had not intended. His magazine was a brilliant editorial experiment that foundered after only four years, in part because Scudder never managed to create a compelling editorial persona, or persuade his publishers to endow him with sufficient resources to carry out his program. Dodge, on the other hand, seemed born to the business. Roger Burlingame, whose father knew her well, was one of the first generation of young readers to be enthralled by *St. Nicholas*. In his view, "to say that Mrs. Dodge 'conducted' this brilliant performance was an understatement; she dictated it, she was its absolute queen, and she endowed it with a personality which endeared it to three generations of hard-to-please growing Americans."[37] Burlingame, writing a history of the House of Scribner in 1946, saw Dodge as a ground-breaking journalist who had created "the first of the truly personal magazines; it was warm, tangible flesh, blood and heart—companionable, responsive, amusing, amused and loyal."[38] His description of the satisfactions of reading the magazine as a little boy shows how its first readers felt about "*St. Nick*":

> You sat in its lap, it buttoned your shoes, it said what you, inarticulate, wanted to say; it took you where you wanted to go and it never preached or scolded. It strained your eyes in the gaslight until the sandman shut them, it spent the night under your pillow, regaled you in hungry hours of early daylight. *St. Nicholas*

was "for boys and girls" and nothing before or since has ever been so wholly theirs [199].

Though in life, as in her writing, Dodge had an engaging manner and a way of making all she did look easy, constant micro-managing of her magazine took its toll on her. Her personal working style made the busy editorial offices of *St. Nicholas* a gracious and home-like place that visitors remembered not only for the art on the walls, the bowls of flowers, the soft carpets, but for the warm atmosphere and the congeniality of the staff. Her home life, on the other hand, was constantly invaded by her work. Dodge seemed perpetually busy. Though she did not come into the office every day, messengers regularly delivered "budgets" of work to her midtown apartment, where she maintained a home office. She relied on Frank Stockton and later Fayal Clarke to handle many of the office details, but she was a very "hands-on" editor who initialed and commented firmly on much of the material passed on to them for further action. Because she was involved in every aspect of the business, she worked a heavy schedule: reading and editing manuscripts, preparing novels for serialization, visiting the studios of likely new artists, soliciting new work, networking with the *Century* crowd, and carrying on a very extensive and burdensome personal and business correspondence, mostly in longhand.

Dodge's health was not robust, so her tendency to overwork worried her friends and associates. From time to time, her doctors felt it necessary to order her to rest, or to prescribe long trips away from New York — once to California, once as far as the pyramids of Egypt. When, in her later years, it became imperative that she find some refuge far enough from the office to offer some respite from her labors, Dodge would build a summer home in the Catskills. But even there, she found only a partial escape, for she settled in Onteora Park, a club-like community of artists and writers mostly from the *Century* circle, many of whom wrote for *St. Nicholas*. Her editorial associate, William Fayal Clarke, was a frequent houseguest, fetching manuscripts from the office in New York, and conveying her orders and decisions to the staff in the city. Her summer neighbors at Onteora included Twain as well as *Century* colleagues like Laurence Hutton and Richard Watson Gilder. There is no question that Dodge enjoyed her work, and she met its challenges with wit, zest, and energy. Yet, given the stresses and strains of the editorial life, it is perhaps not surprising that she remarked in the nineties to Horace Scudder, then editor of the *Atlantic Monthly*, that she'd often "noticed that the more 'new life' there is in a magazine the less there is left in its editor!"[39]

VIII. Conclusion

No doubt J. T. Trowbridge would have agreed with Dodge. When, back in 1874, Trowbridge got that telegram from Scribner and Company asking him to write a "card" of farewell for the readers of *Our Young Folks* to be published in *St. Nicholas* right after the first installment of his *Fast Friends*, he took the occasion to look back over the nine years of his editorship and to acknowledge that he and his fellow editors had had some hard times. Though theirs had been "the pioneer of the better class of juvenile periodicals, there were many things about it which we would gladly have made different could we have gone back, with our acquired experience, and projected its form and character anew." It was his generous hope, though, that from the grave of his own periodical, "'violets'" would "'spring,'" to "blossom amid the leaves of a more beautiful and more beloved successor." And he expressed a wish that *St. Nicholas* "crown its present promise with fulfillment" (*St. Nicholas* 1 [Jan. 1874]: 160).

Translating her "fair ideals" into twelve lively issues a year would never be easy for the "Conductor" of *St. Nicholas*; inevitable "trials and disappointments" would come with the "heavy responsibility" and "high privilege" of having "the ear of Young America once a month." Dodge knew that high editorial standards could sometimes make an editor's working life miserable, but they were also a magazine's "stronghold"[40] and the "best guarantee" that "success is sure to come."[41] Though she felt she had not achieved all she might have done, Dodge came to believe that the quality of the magazine through the years demonstrated the soundness of her editorial principles. In 1902, Dodge and her staff were in a position to look back at the first three decades of *St. Nicholas*, and the following note to readers was printed in the first editorial "Books and Reading" column of the year:

> With this number ST. NICHOLAS begins its thirtieth volume. During its whole life—for a magazine lives, just as a creature lives—it has been conducted by one editor, and so has an identity such as few periodicals can claim. It has changed as the times have changed; it has grown in ways that can hardly be understood except by a comparison with its early numbers. We advise our readers to put an early volume side by side with one that is just closed, and compare them carefully.
>
> See the difference in the style of stories, the style of illustration, note the names of the writers and the artists. And the readers of the new volume are the sons and daughters of those who were the little boys in the distant seventies. To such readers as ST. NICHOLAS has, it is not necessary to preach a little sermon upon this text. It will be enough if they will give an hour or two

to an understanding of all that the magazine has been to a whole
generation of Americans and of English-speaking people throughout the world.

The twenty-nine volumes of ST. NICHOLAS have well stood
the test of time, and they offer the soundest warrant for the
principles upon which the magazine has been conducted [*SN*
30 (Nov. 1902): 90].

Unlike the mass of "indiscriminate" praise usually heaped upon the
magazine, this assessment is modest, sober, shrewdly professional. It
stresses the essentials of editorship as Dodge saw them: the "foresight and
insight" that allowed her — despite all the stresses and difficulties — so carefully to balance the claims of tradition and innovation that she kept her
magazine alive and growing, crowning, as her old ally Trowbridge might
have put it, its early "promise" with long years of "fulfillment."

Notes

1. Mary Mapes Dodge to Horace Scudder, 4 Dec. 1866, Horace Scudder Papers.
Permission has been given to quote from the following sources: Century Company
Archives, New York Public Library, cited as C: NYPL; Donald and Robert Dodge Collection of Mary Mapes Dodge, Princeton University Library, cited as DRD: P; Horace
Scudder Papers, The Huntington Library, cited as HS: HN; Mary Mapes Dodge Collection, Princeton University Library, cited as MMD: P; Unpublished material from
the Whitelaw Reid Papers, Library of Congress, has also been consulted.

2. Dodge's official title was "Conductor" of the magazine. Her first associate editor was Frank R. Stockton, who was also a frequent contributor.

3. "Children's Magazines," *Scribner's Monthly* 6 (July 1873): 352 (reprinted in this
collection, 13–17).

4. R. Gordon Kelly, preface to *Children's Periodicals of the United States* (Westport,
Conn.: Greenwood Press, 1984), xiv.

5. Unsigned comment, *Scribner's Monthly* 6 (July 1873): 115, quoted in Fred Erisman, "*St. Nicholas*" in Kelly, *Children's Periodicals*, 378.

6. Samuel B. Chew, *Fruit Among the Leaves: An Anniversary Anthology* (New York:
Appleton-Century Crofts, 1950), 77.

7. Arthur John, preface to *The Best Years of the* Century: *Richard Watson Gilder,*
Scribner's Monthly, *and the* Century Magazine, *1870–1909* (Urbana: University of Illinois Press, 1981), ix.

8. "Children's Magazines," *Scribner's Monthly* 6 (July 1873): 352–54.

9. She used the word that way, for example, in a condolence letter to Mark Twain
and his wife, calling their daughter Susy "the rarest truest girl I ever knew" (qtd., Olivia
Clemens to Mary Mapes Dodge, 25 October 1896 in Catherine Morris Wright, *Lady
of the Silver Skates: The Life and Letters of Mary Mapes Dodge* (Jamestown, R.I.: Clingstone Press, 1979), 96.

10. Marie Louise Mapes to Catherine Tylee Mapes Bunnell, Spring 1873, qtd. in
Wright, *Lady of the Silver Skates*, 73.

11. DRD:P.

12. "Children's Magazines," 353.

13. "Announcement to Prospective Contributors," HS: HN. This item, of great

interest for the guidelines it presents, was preserved among Horace Scudder's papers because there is a note from Mary Mapes Dodge to Scudder, 15 May 1873 on its reverse side.

14. Edmund C. Stedman to Dodge, 31 January 1893, qtd. in Susan R. Gannon and Ruth Anne Thompson, *Mary Mapes Dodge* (New York: Twayne, 1992), 39.

15. Dodge to Samuel Clemens, 19 November 1892, in Wright, *Lady of the Silver Skates,* 182–183.

16. Dodge to Larcom, TS, 27 March 1876, (DRD: P).

17. Dodge to Larcom, TS, 17 June 1876, (DRD: P).

18. Laurence Hutton, *Talks in a Library with Laurence Hutton,* recorded by Isabel Moore (New York: G. P. Putnam's Sons, 1905), 422.

19. Mark Twain to Fred J. Hall, 10 August 1892, *Letters to His Publishers, 1867–1894,* ed. Hamlin Hill (Berkeley and Los Angeles: University of California Press, 1967), 324.

20. Dodge to Mark Twain, 19 November 1892, in Wright, *Lady of the Silver Skates,* 183.

21. In his autobiography Trowbridge termed *Fast Friends* a minor work, but noted that some of the material came straight from his own experience. John Townsend Trowbridge, *My Own Story with Recollections of Noted Persons* (Boston and New York: Houghton Mi°in and Company, 1903).

22. Trowbridge to Dodge, 31 March 1874 (DRD: P).

23. *Ibid.*

24. Trowbridge, *My Own Story,* 325.

25. William Fayal Clarke, "Memoranda Concerning His One Fault" (C: NYPL).

26. *Ibid.*

27. Enclosure, Dodge to Whitelaw Reid, 21 April 1880 (WR: LC).

28. Dodge to Reid, 21 April 1880 (WR: LC).

29. Dodge, "Open Letters," "International Copyright: Plain Speech from American Authors," *Century* 31 (Feb. 1886): 630.

30. John Townsend Trowbridge, *ibid.,* 633.

31. Dodge to Mrs. Maud Christiani, 9 July 1878 (C: NYPL).

32. Dodge to Richard Watson Gilder, April 1880, qtd. Wright, *Lady of the Silver Skates,* 116.

33. Catherine Morris Wright, "How *St. Nicholas* Got Rudyard Kipling: And What Happened Then," *Princeton University Library Chronicle* 35 (Spring 1974): 259–89.

34. See Michael Joseph, "Illustrating *St. Nicholas* and the Influence of Mary Mapes Dodge," in this collection.

35. Dodge to Horace Scudder, 13 January 1868 (HS: HN).

36. See Marilynn Olson, "'When Did Youth Ever Neglect to Bow before Glory?': *St. Nicholas* and War" in this collection.

37. Roger Burlingame, *Of Making Many Books: A Hundred Years of Reading, Writing, and Publishing* (New York: Charles Scribner's Sons, 1946), 199.

38. *Ibid.*

39. Dodge to Scudder, 9 September 1891 (HS: HN).

40. Dodge to Scudder, 9 May 1867 (HS: HN).

41. Dodge to Scudder, 4 December 1866 (HS: HN).

4

Illustrating *St. Nicholas* and the Influence of Mary Mapes Dodge

Michael S. Joseph

In her powerful essay on children's periodicals, written for Roswell Smith's *Scribner's Monthly*, Mary Mapes Dodge argued the case for illustration with humor and passion:

> A child's periodical must be pictorially illustrated, of course, and the pictures must have the greatest variety consistent with simplicity, beauty, and unity. They should be heartily conceived and well executed; and they must be suggestive, attractive, and epigrammic. If it be only the picture of a cat, it must be so like a cat that it will do its own purring, and not sit, a dead, stuffed thing, requiring the editor to purr for it. One of the sins of this age is editorial dribbling over inane pictures. The time to shake up a dull picture is when it is in the hands of the artist and engravers, and not when it lies, a fact accomplished, before the keen eyes of the little folk.[1]

If *Scribner's* wide renown as "a magazine of art" encouraged Mrs. Dodge to express herself freely, her words revealed an intimate understanding of the expressive potential of the medium she was praising. The daughter of a painter, James Mapes, whose home served as a meeting place for other artists and writers, Mary Mapes Dodge learned to sketch and sculpt while still a child, and formed friendships with girls whose talents in the visual arts destined them for prominence.

James Jay Mapes, whom friends called "The Professor," was a man of many versatile talents (Mapes 26). Although his major contributions were in agricultural science, Mapes experimented with pigments and taught the chemistry and natural philosophy of colors in the National Academy of Design between 1835 and 1838. A member of the St. Nicholas Society and the Sketch Club, he anticipated the illustrious career of his famous daughter as well by briefly editing, from 1840 to 1842, the *American Repertory of Arts, Sciences & Manufactories,* and, in the 1850s, *The Working Farmer.* Mapes also achieved distinction as a skilled painter whose compositions appeared on exhibition. In a letter to Mrs. Dodge, written late in his life, the painter and print-maker John Sartain spoke of having recently resumed work on a portrait of her father, and hoped that, after so many years, he would soon finish it. In defense of taking a brush to the painting of a man more than twenty years in the grave, Sartain wrote, "I would like it for two reasons. First that I flatter myself that the work is a success, and secondly that the public may see the resurrection of an old painter."[2]

While such celebrated men of letters as Washington Irving and Horace Greeley were counted among Mapes' friends and colored the rich flow of life within the Mapes' household, visual artists, such as Sartain, Samuel F. B. Morse and Asher Durand, were also Mapes' companions. Mrs. Dodge and her sisters not only grew up among easels and artists, but practiced art as well. Sophie, by report the most artistically talented of the sisters, grew proficient as a painter under Sartain's tutelage, and Mrs. Dodge "sketched and modeled with a sure hand" (Mapes 25). Spencer Mapes, in his unpublished biography of his great-aunt, notes that she "spent much time sketching and sculpturing, unable to decide which of these two mediums she preferred (Mapes 25). Mrs. Dodge's youthful art studies brought her into the company of other talented young artists, including Emily Sartain, who would rise to become art editor of *Our Continent* and the principal of the Philadelphia School of Design for Women, and Mary A. Hallock, who would become a favored illustrator-author for *St. Nicholas* and one of the ablest designers on wood in America (Hamilton 129).

The professor devoted a part of his daughters' instruction to hand printing, a skill he had acquired as a boy (Mapes 19). As a young girl, Lizzie learned to set type and operate a hand press—one basis, perhaps, for the abundant advertisements for tabletop hand presses she published in the early numbers of *St. Nicholas*—and when her sons, James and Harry, were old enough to grasp a composing stick, Mrs. Dodge followed her father's example by teaching the black art to them. "The boys had a little press and their mother helped them set up many a form at the printer's case" (Mapes 97). As young men, both were able to earn money by job printing.

As author, editor and as a recruiter of authors, Mrs. Dodge's influence upon the literary excellence of *St. Nicholas* has been carefully assessed, beginning with William Fayal Clarke's "In Memory of Mary Mapes Dodge."[3] However, discussion of the art of *St. Nicholas* has often turned to indexing the contributions of its dazzling array of illustrators, or to recording the visual vocabularies shifting over the course of the magazine's long run.[4] Surveys such as these fall shy of elucidating the method by which particular decisions were made regarding the illustration and physical appearance of *St. Nicholas*, and how these decisions related to Mrs. Dodge. Her correspondence, and the mechanics of graphic reproduction at Scribner and Company and, after 1881, the Century Company, suggest the history of the course of illustrating *St. Nicholas*.

Producing the art in *St. Nicholas* engaged all of the magazine's editors. Mrs. Dodge monitored every key point of the process, recruited and commissioned artists, reviewed their compositions, reviewed layouts and oversaw the printing of the engraved wood blocks. The process of reproducing illustrations also came under the jurisdiction of the chief editor. As Spencer Mapes notes: "With the utmost care [Mrs. Dodge] edited and censored every bit of art work submitted and then conferred with Drake, Fraser and DeVinne to make sure there would be no hitch in the reproduction" (Mapes 216).

Alexander Wilson Drake, for almost forty years art superintendent for both *St. Nicholas* and *Scribner's Monthly* (later, the *Century Magazine*), assumed responsibility for presenting the engraved wood blocks for printing. An art instructor at the Cooper Institute before coming to work for Smith in 1870, the mild-mannered, debonair and indefatigable Drake had been educated in art and wood engraving. The accurate reproduction of pictures deeply interested him, and he and the distinguished printer Theodore Low DeVinne together spent much time and effort experimenting with different kinds of ink and paper and costly refinements of printing techniques to secure the best illustrations.

Drake sought to improve upon the conventional method of creating an image on the surface of the block. At the time of *St. Nicholas's* birth, little had changed in the hundred years that had elapsed since Thomas Bewick reinvented wood engraving in Newcastle. Artists were required to render their design in reverse upon the block's prepared surface, sometimes using pen and sometimes India ink washes. Scribner (and, later, Century) retained no staff of illustrators, preferring to commission each picture independently, and so, if an illustrator traveled or moved out of town, the precious boxwood blocks would have to be entrusted to the mail.[5] When illustrations were to be made from existing works of art, draftsmen were called upon to copy the original on the block, translating tones into line, radically simplifying and frequently reducing the scale — and, unfortunately, the quality.

Obviously this system was not only ungainly but costly and highly impractical for the requirements of a major illustrated monthly. Drake worked to adapt one of several extant methods for transferring an image to the block through the use of photography. By laying a very thin, photosensitive emulsion on the block's surface, the desired image could be reproduced upon it with a camera. Thus, it was no longer necessary to have illustrators compose or copy their designs on the block surface, and engravers were able to keep the original illustrations (or a likeness of the original illustration) beside them as a guide while they cut their way through a photographic copy. This not only facilitated the incision of truer images, but also

Among the finest engravings in *St. Nicholas* were those of animals, exotic plants and birds, such as this falcon in "A Bird That Is Fond of Sport." *SN* 14(Apr. 1887): 457.

inspired the more imaginative engravers to experiment with unusual effects (e.g., the textures of oil paintings and sculptures) and to venture beyond their traditional role as copyists or interpreters. They could portray landscapes and city views *ad vivam,* without the intervention of a paintbrush or lithographer's crayon. In the skilled and sensitive hands of artists such as Elbridge Kingsley and Timothy Cole, American wood engraving attained unprecedented heights of expressiveness and technical virtuosity. In 1879 Scribner's found it profitable to issue a *Portfolio of Proof Impressions Selected from* Scribner's Monthly *and* St. Nicholas, a successful undertaking repeated by the Century Company in 1881.

Neither Scribner nor Century managed a department of engravers, but they commissioned work from independent sources on a per item basis. Among the many *St. Nicholas* engravers was Elbridge Kingsley, one of an elite minority of engravers who could also boast a reputation as an accomplished artist, and who "shook the pillars of tradition by appearing with an engraving direct from Nature" (Kingsley 43). In old age, Kingsley could recall "Cole, Juengling, Smithwick, Wolf, Evans, Kelly, King, Davis, and Marsh;"[6] almost a half-century later, he spoke feelingly of "how we climbed the stair to Mr. Drake's office, did our own memoranda, took out our blocks and brought them back with fear and trembling lest they have to be done over..." (Kingsley 42).

The many talented engravers whose work appeared in *St. Nicholas* include dozens of names forgotten or unknown to Kingsley. Donald Nichols, overlooked in Kingsley's recollection, executed an immense number of extremely delicate engravings for *St. Nicholas* including the frontispiece to its crucial first number. William J. Linton[7] and Andrew Anthony,[8] two revered engravers and relentless critics of the so-called New School of Engraving, also did business with *St. Nicholas*. Writing to Mrs. Dodge sometime between 1874 and 1876, Mary Hallock Foote, who had been a former student of Linton's, sent an illustration and asked "as a great favor that Mr. Linton or Mr. Anthony engrave ... [the] block" for it.[9]

Foote's request hints at the manner in which artists and engravers were brought together at *St. Nicholas*. Kingsley, in his unpublished autobiography, *Life and Works of Elbridge Kingsley, Painter-Engraver: Consisting of Paintings in Oil and Water Colors ...* (v. 1), draws the picture more clearly:

> As I remember the routine at Mr. Drake's office while on Broadway, it was something like this: We waited our turn in a little anti [sic] room, going in one at a time to do business. If an artist had taken a fancy to an engraving by Kingsley, maybe I would find my name on a small block with the copy waiting. Then I would take a piece of brown paper, outline my block upon it, mark on it the title, dates of starting and finishing; put this record in Mr. Drake's desk and then away to make room for the next artist or engraver. With the finished work I generally hunted up the artist, and perhaps proved several times before the finish. If complete Mr. Drake signed the order for my pay [Kingsley 88].

Despite the narrow four months lead-time with which the magazine had to work, Drake would commission engravings only following the completion of preliminary layouts. Over the course of Mrs. Dodge's long stewardship, layout was handled by many. Until he departed the magazine in 1877, Frank Stockton, also a practiced wood-engraver, did layouts, with the cooperation of Alexander Drake, as did his replacement, William Fayal Clarke. After he joined the Century in the early 1880's, William Lewis Fraser, the art manager, handled layouts as well and, later, after he became

Mr. Drake's assistant, so, too, did Frank Crowninshield. When layouts were ready, they would be critically reviewed by Mrs. Dodge who would give Drake his final directions (Mapes 183).

In the concluding stage of the process, the blocks of rare boxwood, deftly scored with the fine, dense, mesh of nicks and narrow grooves that would translate into inked illustrations within the pages of *St. Nicholas*, were secured on the flatbed press by the *St. Nicholas* printer, Theodore Low DeVinne. To ensure the best possible fidelity of printed image, DeVinne worked ceaselessly at creating the ideal make-ready for every impression. By sticking bits of paper of varying thickness underneath sections of the woodblock, a discerning printer could achieve an extraordinary variety of tonal qualities in the wood engravings he printed. DeVinne, "the great champion" of this process of "overlay pictorial relief printing" (Tatham 119), sometimes allowed his presses to stand idle for days while he coaxed the most nearly perfect image from the *St. Nicholas* wood blocks.

The responsibility for gathering art into the offices of *St. Nicholas* fell to all. As Mrs. Dodge's assistant, Clarke regularly corresponded with contributors to discuss work in progress, their missed deadlines, lost drawings and additional assignments. Not surprisingly, the versatile James Montgomery Flagg, only twelve years old when he sold his first drawing to *St. Nicholas,* remembered the assistant editor as "a charming but seemingly slightly harassed gent."[10] Alexander Drake, in addition to working with DeVinne and the engravers, actively recruited illustrators such as Harrison Weir, Frank Beard, E. B. Bensell and Livingston Hopkins, thus expanding the group he had cultivated for *Scribner's Monthly*. Drake's Art Department offered artists a place to drop in and fraternize, in mood not unlike the art department managed at Harper and Brothers by Drake's opposite number, Charles Parsons.

Mrs. Dodge, who looked closely at all phases of the illustration process, the minutiae of the print shop not excepted, also recruited new illustrators aggressively as a function of her office, and continually refreshed relationships with the artists that had become old friends, such as Mary Hallock Foote. Her documentary, exquisitely drafted, observations of young adulthood and the American West graced the pages of *St. Nicholas* for many years. Mrs. Dodge's intimacy with this multi-talented artist, sealed in their childhood, endured even after marriage swept her off into the hinterlands of California, and beyond. In June of 1889, writing from British Columbia, she told Mrs. Dodge she would soon be entrusting to her an entire "sketchbook of Victoria" and instructed her to "take what you will for *St. Nicholas*."[11]

Just as *St. Nicholas* authors could be counted upon to bring other authors into the fold, or, at least, to assist Mrs. Dodge in canvassing fresh material,[12] so *St. Nicholas* illustrators introduced Mrs. Dodge to other illustrators. Walter Crane wrote in 1887 expressly to recommend the work of Heywood Sumner, who had collected and illustrated a sheaf of old country songs.[13] Mrs. Dodge discovered Daniel Beard, who would provide art for one of *St. Nicholas's* finest serializations, Mark Twain's *Tom Sawyer Abroad,* while paying a visit to the studio of his older brother, Frank, a *St. Nicholas* mainstay (Mapes 219).

Mrs. Dodge's entrée to New York's intimate salons where artists and writers assembled to discuss their work enabled her to make the acquaintance of many other potential contributors (Mapes 273). Artists' receptions were a frequent occurrence at the Tenth Street Studios, where the more prominent artists could be found, as well as at the countless more modest studios. Mrs. Dodge would drop in on these and made the effort to keep current with the activities of New York's artistic circles.

As the reputation of *St. Nicholas* spread, Mrs. Dodge found admired illustrators could be approached successfully through the mails. Clarke wrote to the renowned English illustrator Kate Greenaway who replied:

> In the Winter months I might be able to send some small sketches now and then, if I might be quite free as to subject; but I could not undertake to contribute anything at stated times or regular intervals.
> I am sorry I have no published drawings but all those made have been for some purpose for which they have been used.
> I am very pleased that Mrs. Dodge should hold my work in such esteem....[14]

At the close of her letter Greenaway expresses a wish to have her drawings returned after "photographs had been taken." A standard practice of modern publishing, the notion of returning art was extraordinary at the time. For many years, *St. Nicholas* officers would simply divide up the year's collection of artworks among themselves (Tatham 122). Gelett Burgess, whose comical Goops drawings appeared in *St. Nicholas* in the 1890's, credited Oliver Herford for having taught him "early on to demand the return of all my drawings from magazine editors."[15] Mrs. Dodge also initiated, through Roswell Smith, a correspondence with Walter Crane and secured from him in June of 1877 a new design for a *St. Nicholas* cover, unveiled in that year's Christmas issue. In that November issue, Mrs. Dodge had written two paragraphs praising the English artist, "most widely known in America by his designs of colored picture-books for children."[16]

Of course, once the reputation of *St. Nicholas* became established, Mrs. Dodge found illustrators approached her. Spencer Mapes noted that "most of them came to Mrs. Dodge's home or office with their drawings," and her "relationships with artists were mostly by personal contact" (Mapes 314). Burgess reminisced, "One always thought of her, somehow, as an ultimate friend to whom one could confide anything," and recalled being treated warmly by Mrs. Dodge even while he was still "more or less a stranger!"[17]

Edith Holman Hunt (nee Marion Edith Waugh), the wife of the Pre-Raphaelite Brotherhood artist, wrote in the autumn of 1888 to broach the possibility of sending a story modeled on recent archaeological excavations, and mentioned two pieces of artwork, one watercolor (which she bade Mrs. Dodge instruct the engraver to handle carefully), and a pencil sketch. With these, she put her services as an illustrator at Mrs. Dodge's disposal. Choosing first to acknowledge the offer rather than to accept it, Mrs. Dodge then instructed the hopeful amateur in the customary procedures for republishing magazine illustrations in book form, adding very graciously:

> [A]lthough it has been the rule of the Century Co. in cases of republication, to sell to book publishers, at half price, the illustrations used in the magazine, we should, of course [be] willing to supply you a set of electrotypes[18] of any illustrations furnished by yourself and reproduced in *St. Nicholas*.[19]

The publishers of *St. Nicholas* would have welcomed the opportunity to merchandise their electrotypes (which Hunt had asked for specifically in her letter), since it would provide them with a means of offsetting part of the expense of illustration which at the time was significant. By the late 1880's, the cost of engraving a block to cover a full page had reached $500 (Pyle 30). Then again, Mrs. Dodge may have doubted that the chances of the story being republished between boards were strong.

During the same period, hoping to capture a story from William Dean Howells, Mrs. Dodge found herself sought after by the author's young daughter instead, who courted her with pictures and poetry:

> I have some fear that you may think [still another rhyme that I have just finished] a little too awful but if you will only consider it carefully you will see that it isn't as bad as it seems.
> I send some illustrations with it and if these are too many, you can use those, which you please.[20]

Mrs. Dodge evidently admired the writing more than the illustrations, but diplomacy prompted her to accept both, as the Howells' paterfamilias had himself written to her on the subject of "Pilla's" work.[21]

Mrs. Dodge played the "nice" editor/"mean" editor trick with her mild-mannered Art Superintendent, Alexander Drake, on more than one occasion. It seemed a particularly serviceable ploy when she thought authors sought to usurp editorial prerogatives. When Rudyard Kipling agreed to publish in *St. Nicholas*, he proposed his father might render satisfactory illustrations. Mrs. Dodge wrote back, assuring him that the celebrated artist of *Little Lord Fauntleroy*—"Mr. Birch, our best illustrator"—would do the pictures.[22] It was a convention of magazine illustration that the literary compositions of both the most and the least marketable authors would be interpreted by only the most popular illustrators, and Mrs. Dodge was obviously paying Kipling the compliment of including him among the former.

Perhaps because time was short, Kipling did not receive illustrated proofs, although it was Mrs. Dodge's usual practice to post them to her authors. When "Collar-Wallah and the Poison-Stick" and "The Potted Princess" appeared two months later, Kipling expressed his dissatisfaction with Birch's drawings. His letter of 29 January 1893 complained:

> Birch does not know too much about monkies [sic]. He's gone and drawn a man coming back from a dinner in a pith hat — the sort of thing you go and stalk tigers in! His old buffalo is an Italian beast and the yoke is a patent I don't know. He's a ripsnorter in the Fauntleroy act but menageries isn't [sic] his stronghold. All the same, people who haven't been in India won't know.[23]

If Mrs. Dodge had been proud to secure children's stories from Kipling, she now had cause to be irked by his attitude, both towards Birch, who was a current favorite, and to her commitment to the magazine's educational component. The off-putting tone of the author's comments may be explained in the following exchange of letters. Kipling had written on 11 January 1893:

> Oliver who is called Herford has just strolled in from the other side of the Atlantic. He broke the Umbria's screw shaft en route (probably tried to draw the poor thing) but don't you think that he'd be the man to illustrate "Toomai of the Elephants?" He knows beasts intimately and he knows me and I know him and perhaps by the grace of heaven we could get him to work on it. He's not exactly a hog (in a manner of speaking) on swift enterprises but if his Daemon interests him in "Toomai" and the weather is fine and he feels happy in his inside he might do lovely drawings. Do you think it could be arranged?[24]

The Princeton Library's manuscript copy of Mrs. Dodge's reply bears numerous revisions, evidence of the agitated state of her thinking. Certainly, she did not wish to encourage authors to decide who would illuminate their writing. Moreover, the implication that Herford and Kipling had already discussed the possibility of collaborating might have galled her. Yet Kipling, already widely admired, was only twenty-seven years old and still a rising star. Herford, too, having made a name for himself through his numerous whimsical contributions to *St. Nicholas,* as well as to *Life,* New York's latest satirical weekly, was also ascendant. It would be better for *St. Nicholas* if she could make them happy. As of 23 January 1893, the body of her reply read:

> As to the illustrating of "Toomai" we shall bear your sugges-
> tion in mind, but in all matters of picture making I ought really
> to consult the managers of our Art Department, and I have had
> no opportunity yet to talk this over with them. Mr. Clarke tells
> me that Mr. Herford will probably be in town for some time,
> and so if it be settled that he is to illustrate "Toomai" we have
> him within reach. But whoever is to illustrate that epic of the
> jungle must have a realizing sense of the responsibilities laid
> upon him, and by prayer and fasting, if necessary, prepare him-
> self for the biggest thing he ever did in his life.[25]

Evidently, Mrs. Dodge chose, at first, to grant Kipling's request, adopting a playful if slightly patronizing tone. But, this obviously did not satisfy her. The margins of the letter contain meaningful alterations and addi-tions. The authoritative "We always consult Mr. Drake, the Manager of the Art Department" is penciled in to replace the weaker and more plas-tic "I ought really to consult the managers of the Art Department." In the left margin, she has added a full paragraph, more likely aimed at the artist's edification, whose tone can accurately be termed threatening:

> It is sometimes well for us to have our artist — even one whose
> work is well known — to draw but one picture before putting
> the whole matter of illustration in his hands. I appreciate Mr.
> Herford's work and so do we all at the Century, but sometimes
> our best artists have disappointed us and we are cautious before
> placing the matters of illustration in their hands.[26]

We do not know upon which form she settled to show Kipling (and, presumably, over his shoulder, Herford), or that she sent either. An undated letter suggests that perhaps Mrs. Dodge ultimately preferred to treat the challenge neither diplomatically nor combatively but, sensibly, editorially:

> ... the illustrating of Toomai should be worthily — that is to say
> *superbly*— done. One of our best draughtsmen (and no other
> need apply) should have a clear six weeks allowance for the
> work....[27]

It may have been that Mrs. Dodge's semi-refrain "one of our best

Although Reginald Birch was considered "our best illustrator" by Mary Mapes Dodge, Rudyard Kipling was dissatisfied with his work on "The Potted Princess" and "Collar-Wallah and the Poison Stick." *SN* 20(Jan. 1893): 164.

draughtsmen" answered Kipling's retaliatory broadside against Birch, to whom Mrs. Dodge had referred earlier in their correspondence, as "our best illustrator." However, the matter was settled; W. H. Drake,[28] whose specialty was animals, received the task of illustrating "Toomai," — as well as its successors, "Mowgli's Brothers," "Rikki Tikki Tavi" and "Tiger, Tiger." Mrs. Dodge did favor Kipling's request four years later. In an undated letter (probably written during the summer of 1897), Kipling told Mrs. Dodge about a new set of stories he'd just finished "of that brand of nonsense much more difficult to write than any sense,"[29] that would be called "the 'Just-So Stories.'" He suggested once again, "Herford might be the one to illustrate them very nicely." And, beginning in December 1897 and continuing through February 1898, Oliver Herford's illustrations appeared alongside Kipling's "Just So Stories."

Mrs. Dodge received many requests similar to Kipling's, and her usual tendency was to assist authors in realizing the visual image of their work, where possible, by accommodating them. In 1876, the popular novelist, Thomas Bailey Aldrich, whose "The Story of a Bad Boy" had first appeared in *St. Nicholas's* predecessor and early rival, *Our Young Folks*, wrote concerning one of his submissions: "When I put it in book-form, I intend — if I can find my artist — to have the text *sprinkled* with small silhouettes, somewhat in the fashion of the English edition of *The Bab Ballads*."[30] Mrs. Dodge seized upon Aldrich's suggestion and decorated his humorous ballad, "The Cat and the Countess," with the vivacious silhouette embellishments of Livingston Hopkins, another illustrator whose work straddles the fields of satire and children's literature. Documenting her attention to the matter, Mrs. Dodge penciled in the margin of Aldrich's letter: "the whole story illustrated with fine original silhouettes by L. Y. Hopkins."

After his own children's periodical, *Our Young Folks*, ceased publication, John Townsend Trowbridge agreed to place one of his popular "Jack Hazard" stories with the new children's monthly. In his rather detailed letter, dated the very month *St. Nicholas* first appeared, we are afforded a glimpse of the rigorous demands that monographic series made upon the illustrator as well as the difficulty of their graceful accommodation within the scheme of a magazine:

> In regard to the illustrations for "Fast Friends" I do not know that I need add anything to Mr. Ticknor's communication to you on the subject. I supposed that you had learned from him that I prefer to have them all made by the hand that executed the first, in such a shape as would enable us to use them afterwards in a vol. of the "Jack Hazard" series. For this purpose the ordinary "text-blocks" should not exceed 3/4 inches in width. The full-page cuts (for the book) may be of the size of the largest one in the Jan. installment. There will probably be 4 or 6 of this size, if you will kindly allow so many. When drawn — as in time … they may be — with the figures perpendicular to the longitude of the block, this will exactly fit the *St. Nicholas* page filling the space in width occupied by the 2 columns. As in the previous stories of the series, I had intended to have two cuts to each number, after the first. In the 2nd number, which I suppose Mr. Ticknor has sent to you, I shall be pleased to have Mr. White [the artist, G.G. White] take his choices of subjects.[31]

Horace E. Scudder, an old friend and advisor to Dodge, had also been the editor of a prestigious children's periodical. The *Riverside Magazine* had been absorbed by Scribner and Company in advance of their formation of *St. Nicholas*.[32] One of Scudder's major editorial accomplishments had been acquiring eleven original stories from Hans Christian Andersen

One of Henry Sandham's illustrations for *The Land of Fire* by Captain Thomas Mayne Reid. *SN*11 (Mar. 1884): 376.

written expressly for the *Riverside,* and an additional six tales never before translated into English (Schiller 33). In the summer of 1876 he wrote to Mrs. Dodge:

> I have received from Copenhagen the final volumes of Andersen's stories, 3 vols. very abundantly illustrated by Frolich.[33] I found one long story — "Godfather's Picture Book" which has never appeared in English dress. I should recommend it very strongly to you, as it is a series of picturesque incidents from Danish and especially from Copenhagen history. It has 34 very effective little vignettes by Frolich. Would you like me to send you the book to see if you want to use the story in *St. Nicholas?* I suppose you could get electrotypes from the Danish publisher and I would translate the story....[34]

In Scudder's recommendation, the educational value and originality of the material deserve the attention *St. Nicholas,* but of no less importance is its supply of "very effective" illustrations. The importance of illustration seems, coincidentally, to form the subtext of Scudder's letter as well, in which he described the history ("picturesque") and the language ("English dress") in visual metaphors.

If illustrations attracted *St. Nicholas* subscribers, they also drew the attention, and occasionally the indignation, of the magazine's authors, as well. Their ample correspondence on the specifics of illustration possesses overlapping and idiomatic, as well as idiopathic, concerns. Where Kipling rued, after the fact, the artist's heedless infidelities, Thomas Mayne Reid expressed anxiety in advance about the potential harm to which the narrative drama of his tale might be exposed by the artist's overbearing fidelity, and dictated:

> If the Portsmouth scenes should be illustrated no hint [should] be given either by *inscript* on the picture, or otherwise, that the three curious specimens of humanity are natives of Tierra del Fuego. An acknowledge[ment] of that fact in the reader ... would detract from the interest of my tale by a too early revelation of the plot....[35]

Reid, whose story *The Land of Fire* would appear in 1884, illustrated by the historical and maritime specialist, Henry Sandham, also supplied Mrs. Dodge with the admonition that "if the artist can procure a copy of the *Straits of Magellan* by King and Fitzroy"[36] he would locate pictures to give an idea of the Fuegian people's appearance and costumes.

References of this kind were routine, particularly from authors of non-fiction. Evidence suggests Mrs. Dodge may even have solicited them. In 1897, she negotiated with her old friend, Frank Stockton, for his pirate histories. Stockton, who would have been thoroughly familiar with Mrs. Dodge's working method, pointed out that "a great many striking pictures can be made"[37] and, like Reid, averred that "authentic portraits of some of the buccaneers"[38] could be found "at the Astor Library, in ... *The Buccaniers of America*, by John Esquemeling."[39]

A consideration of the illustration history of Louisa May Alcott's work for *St. Nicholas* demonstrates the author's concern that her stories be well illustrated and Dodge's unremitting efforts to appease her. In 1873 *St. Nicholas* published *Eight Cousins* [40] with illustrations by Addie Ledyard, an artist whose warm, broad curves conveyed a wonderfully idealized sense of languorous well being eminently suited to the picture books of that era. Alcott, however, expressed the view that *Eight Cousins* was poorly served by Ledyard and, consequently, eager to please her celebrated author, Mrs. Dodge commissioned Mary Foote for Alcott's next serialization, *Under the Lilacs.* While at work on *Under the Lilacs,* which would be published in 1878,[41] Alcott wrote:

> I will send you the first few chapters during the week for Mrs. Foote, & with them the schedule you suggest so that my infants

may not be drawn with whiskers & my big boys & girls in
pinafores as in "Eight Cousins."[42]

Alcott's letter continues by expressing solicitude for the artist's new-
born child, although anxieties concerning her illustration soon crowd in:
"I hope the new baby won't be set aside too soon for my illustrations, but
I do feel a natural wish to have one story prettily adorned with good pictures, as hitherto artists have much a°icted me."[43] Alcott then turns to the
influence motherhood was likely to exert upon Foote's art, concluding
merrily: "I shall expect the small tots to be unusually good since the artist
has a live model to study from. Please present my congratulations to the
happy mamma & Mr. Foote Jr."[44] She was to be disappointed. Alcott's
opinion of her illustrator's failing found terse expression in a letter penned
to Mrs. Dodge that September: "I have selected the parts I should prefer
for illustrations. Mrs. F. does not choose lively ones & half the fun is spoiled
by a spiritless picture."[45]

Like many other authors, Alcott was anxious to see that certain scenes
were chosen for illustration. Trowbridge had recommended subjects for
illustrations (and had them rejected), and Mayne Reid had indexed the
illustratable scenes in his manuscript out of a stalwart sense of obliga-
tion.[46]

For *Jack and Jill*, Alcott's next serialization,[47] Mrs. Dodge commissioned the German-born Frederick Dielman, the future Director of the
Art School of Cooper Union, to create the illustrations. Unfortunately, no
correspondence conveying the author's anxiety or regard for Mr. Dielman's efforts survives. However, Alcott's letters frequently provide light
chat about her views on the capacities of illustrators, having found in Mrs.
Dodge a perceptive and sympathetic colleague.[48]

> I like Mr. Ennis's drawings better than Miss E. B. Greene ... her
> children were altogether charming, their little fat legs captivate
> me entirely. But I love E. B. G. and don't mind her infants' drop-
> sical heads very much.[49]

From the earliest days of her editorial career, Dodge had turned to
pictures already in hand for inspiration when writing stories. From time
to time, illustrations would be sent to authors to inspire their writing.
Alcott termed this method of composition "writing up to pictures," and
admitted that she found illustrations "very suggestive, especially ... when
invention is at a low water mark."[50]

It was easier for an editor to secure an artist's spontaneous sketch
than an agreement to illustrate text within an inflexible timetable. Many
of *St. Nicholas's* best-known artists, such as Kate Greenaway, whose first

submission appeared in 1879 beside one of Mrs. Dodge's compositions, would have been otherwise unobtainable.

Mrs. Dodge found Celia Thaxter adept at poetizing pictures and elicited many contributions from her over the course of a long association. Thaxter's correspondence with Mrs. Dodge[51] resonates with the poet's genuine pleasure in making rhymes to match *St. Nicholas* illustrations. In one of her final letters, Thaxter exclaims: "I think it's a heavenly little picture — I wish I were Tennyson to do it justice!"[52]

Mrs. Dodge's tactful, playful way of teasing poetry from her contributors, and her intuitive openness to the ambiguities in the relationship of text and illustration are demonstrated in a letter to the poet and one-time editor of *Our Young Folks*, Lucy Larcom, who, at the time of the writing of this letter, was one of Mrs. Dodge's old friends.

> Do you feel like giving our little folks some verses to which the enclosed pictures will be complementary? I hope so. We would *very much* like to have them for our Xmas issue. You will see that the print represents the Parable of the Sower, but your poem need not necessarily follow it. I should think a mere allusion would suffice....
>
> If you would rather not allude *by word* to the Parable, we can simply put the text directly under the picture.[53]

The editorial practice of allowing a loose semiotic fit between text and illustration prevailed in American publishing as early as the 1850's, when the publishers of gift books often deemed it more judicious to let the picture ornament or decorate rather than reconceptualize a text (Tatham 87). Mrs. Dodge's idea of complementarity follows this practice closely. It may also illuminate her understanding of pictorial "unity," one of the three graces she invoked at the birth of *St. Nicholas*. Henry Wadsworth Longfellow, generally wary of the power of illustration to subvert poetry (Tatham 89), humorously ridiculed one danger of overly close correspondence in his objection to the illustration tentatively paired with his poem, "The Three Kings":

> I am afraid we must let the poem go without illustration. There is as good authority for horses as there is for camels, that is, none at all. But as the Wise Men came from the East and not from the South, they probably came on horseback.
>
> I have looked to see if the verses could be changed but find it impossible. Horses might be turned into camels; still the caskets on the saddle-horns remain. Could not some artist turn the camels into horses?
>
> After all, I come back to the conclusion that we had better have no illustration whatever.[54]

Mrs. Dodge took Longfellow's point and "The Three Kings" appeared beside a wood engraving of Ittenbach's *The Holy Family* instead. Mrs. Dodge herself possessed a fastidious eye and a sense of humor, as is demonstrated by Rodman Gilder's version of an often repeated anecdote:

> A newly painted poster by Maxfield Parrish had just arrived at the Century Co. office ... and several *St. Nicholas* and *Century* editors were examining the painting. It showed ... nude figures seated (with the inevitable Parrish bent knee) in, as I recall, bright green grass. One man exclaimed "Lovely! A girl just budding into womanhood!" Another "I should say it is a boy just budding into manhood. Here's Miss Dodge; she will settle the question. Miss Dodge came down the corridor, was asked to decide & after a careful examination, said "It is a boy budding into womanhood."[55]

It is unlikely, though, that such a design, as successful as it may have been on the cover of *Scribner's Monthly*, would have appeared in *St. Nicholas*.[56] However "heartily conceived" cartoons might get, Mrs. Dodge would never permit her own sophistication to condone relaxed moral standards. As we have noted, Mrs. Dodge "edited and censored every bit of art work submitted" (Mapes 216). Her readiness to wield the red pen on behalf of the first of her avowed principles, "simplicity," which is to say, innocence (a touch of prudishness, perhaps) is amply attested.

> One ... sketch of a cow was sent back so the udders could be removed. A design for a kite was refused because it was in the image of a woman and, although just the feet showed beneath the skirt, it was objected that the kite could be seen from below [Mapes 256].

Mrs. Dodge chided Dan Beard for including vulgarity in his rough sketches for *Tom Sawyer Abroad* by displaying the boys' bare feet. (In the published text, Tom and Huck are both politely shod.) Another artist had his drawing of a boy swimmer returned several times because of excessive nudity until, in good natured exasperation, he submitted the drawing once again with the boy completely covered (up to his eyes) by swaddling clothes (Mapes 257).

Depicting intoxication was also not acceptable in *St. Nicholas*. Upon being so advised, the savvy, detail-conscious John Townsend Trowbridge replied: "I entirely approve of your course in rejecting the tipsy scene as a subject for a picture. Mr. White and MMD better left altogether with choice of subjects for illustrations."[57]

Mrs. Dodge demonstrated equal implacability on purely aesthetic matters, making sure, precisely as she had asserted to Roswell Smith, that

St. Nicholas contained only illustrations that met a certain standard of beauty. That standard was hers, and she was a vigilant guardian. Even Charles Scribner, the publisher of *St. Nicholas*, was not beyond the reach of that unbribable eye.

> The other day some Japanese drawings came to me, from you, I think, at Mr. Smith's request. I have handed them to Mr. Clarke to return to you with the message that they are not available for *St. Nicholas* though they certainly are remarkably fine in finish. They seem to me to have not enough dash and life in them to be satisfactory as Japanese productions....[58]

Mrs. Dodge's influence upon the art and iconographic program of *St. Nicholas* continued far beyond the days of her editorship, as evidenced by the activities of the St. Nicholas League. For Mrs. Dodge, and for Clarke, the overriding significance of the League was its promise as "an amazing encourager, inspirer and developer of latent artistic abilities in children the world over" (Mapes 334).

While, over the years, *St. Nicholas's* "Letter-Box," its frequent picture contests and monthly rebus puzzles, had consistently registered high reader response to the magazine's artwork, Leaguers now looked at art with intensified purpose and self-interest. In their quest for the badges that *St. Nicholas* awarded to the lucky young artists whose illustrations it published, and the personal recognition that prizes conferred, children now looked *and* analyzed: they learned their lines by heart. While its writers exerted a considerable attraction, *St. Nicholas* illustrators attained the rarified level of celebrities: "Artists, in particular, were closely aped by the boys and girls who were familiar with the work and style of each *St. Nicholas* artist," Spencer Mapes noted (334).

Leaguers began to write in declaring their favorites, which produced the idea of a popularity contest. Fanny Y. Cory (the Montana artist and illustrator of L. Frank Baum and Margaret Sidney) outpolled the rather impressive competition as the Leagues' favorite *St. Nicholas* illustrator. She was followed, in turn, by Reginald Birch, Charles Dana Gibson, Howard Chandler Christy, Howard Pyle and Charles M. Relyea.[59]

The high degree of visual literacy and excitement among the readers of *St. Nicholas* reflects the program of the journal's editor. While the League had been an invention of Albert Paine and flourished under his inspired direction, this was an invention for which Mrs. Dodge had created the theme. The League crystallized one of her guiding editorial principles, to "draw her readers into a close-knit group by encouraging their participation in the magazine."[60] Indeed, readers of *St. Nicholas* must have perceived the League as an outgrowth of the principles embodied in the early

"Bird-defenders" and the Agassiz Association. The St. Nicholas League clearly focused the third of Mrs. Dodge's editorial objectives as well: "To inspire [children] with an appreciation of pictorial art."

The League's importance as a force for heightening youthful interest in illustration and fostering visual literacy inspired the venerable father of the Brandywine School to write a letter of support in 1901. Howard Pyle had come to New York City two decades earlier at the invitation of Roswell Smith and found needed encouragement to develop his raw artistic talent from Mrs. Dodge. Pyle first published in *St. Nicholas* in February 1877 and remained a frequent contributor until October 1903 — a period of years that roughly shadows Mrs. Dodge's editorship. He wrote in praise of the *St. Nicholas* League as a stimulus of young talent:

> Who knows but that some great future artist who is destined, after awhile, to reach high pinnacled altitudes is here essaying his first unfledged effort at flight; who knows but that some future man of might may some time look back to the very page of the Magazine which I hold open in my hand and may see in it his first young work that are the thoughts that make the pages of the League so interesting to me....
>
> I wish you every success in your endeavors to stimulate such young efforts in so beautiful a field of life-work....

Put into their proper context, Pyle's excited impressions of the St. Nicholas League stand as a vivid testament to Mrs. Dodge's dynamic influence as the presiding genius of the nineteenth century's most successful and artistically accomplished illustrated children's periodical.

Notes

1. Mary Mapes Dodge, "Children's Magazines," *Scribner's Monthly* 6 (July 1873): 353.

2. John Sartain, letter to MMD, Nov. 1893, Donald and Robert M. Dodge Collection of Mary Mapes Dodge, Princeton University Libraries. Hereafter referred to as Dodge Collection.

3. William Fayal Clarke, "In Memory of Mary Mapes Dodge," *SN* 32 (Oct. 1905): 1068–70.

4. See, for example, Jennie L. Keith, "Selected Illustrators of Children's Literature in *St. Nicholas* Magazine, 1873–1900" (Master's thesis, Kent State University, 1974); Mary Alice Hunt, "Trends in Illustrations for Children as Seen in Selected Juvenile Periodicals, 1875–1900" (Ph.D. dissertation, Indiana University, 1973); Mary June Roggenbuck, "*St. Nicholas* Magazine: A Study of the Impact and Historical Influence of the Editorship of Mary Mapes Dodge" (Ph.D. dissertation, University of Michigan, 1976).

5. Mary A. Hallock Foote, writing from Milton, N.Y., to Frank Stockton attests this practice: "Thank you for sending two blocks — they are quite right as to size. The larger drawing can be as easily reduced to one size as another — its shape being like that of

its composition." Mary Hallock Foote, letter to Frank Stockton, 1 Oct. [1874 or 1875], *St. Nicholas* Correspondence, de Grummond Collection, University of Southern Mississippi. Hereafter referred to as de Grummond.

6. The engravers were Timothy Cole, Frederick Juengling, John G. Smithwick, Henry Wolf, W. Evans, John Edward Kelly, Frances S. King, John P. Davis and Henry Marsh.

7. William James Linton, engraver and historian, was probably the most celebrated wood engraver of his time. An Englishman by birth, Linton came to America in 1866 and taught wood engraving at the Cooper Institute in New York. Among his published works are *Some Practical Hints of Wood-Engraving for the Instruction of Reviews and the Public* (Boston: Lee and Shepard, 1879) and *The History of Wood-Engraving in America* (Boston: Estes and Lauriat, 1882).

8. Andrew Varick Stout Anthony (1835–1906) rose to prominence in the 1850's-1860's as a director of illustrated books for the literary publisher, Ticknor and Fields (Tatham 94, 322, 323).

9. Mary Hallock Foote, letter to MMD, 29 Oct. [1874 or 1875], de Grummond.

10. James Montgomery Flagg, letter to Spencer Mapes, 3 Dec. 1935, Dodge Collection.

11. Mary Hallock Foote, letter to MMD, 28 June 1889, Dodge Collection.

12. Bayard Taylor introduced Laura C. Redden, who took Howard Elynder for a pen name; Celia Thaxter worked effectively on Mrs. Dodge's behalf to obtain material from the aged John Greenleaf Whittier; Charles Godfrey Leland recommended Miss Elizabeth Robins, the wife of the artist Joseph Pennell; Edmund Gosse elicited a contribution from the aged Capt. Mayne Reid.

13. Walter Crane, letter to MMD, 11 Jan. 1887, Dodge Collection.

14. Kate Greenaway, letter to William Clark, 15 Apr. 1880, Dodge Collection.

15. Gelett Burgess, letter to Spencer Mapes, 29 Mar. 1937, Dodge Collection.

16. *SN* 5 (Nov. 1877): 69.

17. Gelett Burgess, letter to Spencer Mapes, 29 Mar. 1937, Dodge Collection.

18. Electrotypes were copper facsimiles of engraved woodblocks, cast from the original finished block. Invented in 1839, electrotypes were used as substitutes for blocks in the printing process. Their greater durability over wood ensured larger press runs, and, if they became nicked or worn, they could be easily replaced.

19. MMD, letter to Edith Holman Hunt, 1 Oct. 1888, Dodge Collection.

20. Mildred Howells, letter to Mary Mapes Dodge, 11 Apr. [1889?], Dodge Collection.

21. William Dean Howells, letter to MMD, 5 Jan. 1890, *SN* Correspondence of Mary Mapes Dodge, Princeton University Libraries (hereafter referred to as PUL).

22. MMD, letter to Rudyard Kipling, 19 Oct. 1892, Dodge Collection..

23. Rudyard Kipling, letter to MMD, 11 Jan. 1893, qtd. in Catharine Morris Wright, "How *St. Nicholas* Got Rudyard Kipling and What Happened Then," *Princeton University Library Chronicle* Spring (1974): 283.

24. Rudyard Kipling, letter to MMD, 11 Jan. 1893, Dodge Collection.

25. MMD, letter to Rudyard Kipling, 23 Jan. 1893, Dodge Collection.

26. MMD, letter to Rudyard Kipling.

27. MMD, letter to Rudyard Kipling [Jan. 1893], *St. Nicholas* Correspondence of Mary Mapes Dodge, PUL.

28. William Henry Drake (1856–1926).

29. Rudyard Kipling, letter to MMD, [Summer 1897?], Private collection of Betsy Beinecke Shirley.

30. T. B. Aldrich, letter to MMD, 14 Feb. 1876, Archive of Charles Scribner's Sons, PUL.

31. John Townsend Trowbridge, letter to MMD, 29 Nov. 1873, *St. Nicholas* Correspondence of Mary Mapes Dodge, PUL.

32. The Huntington Library alone contains 65 of their letters, stretching from 1866 to 1893.

33. Lorenz Frolich, 1820–1908.

34. Horace E. Scudder, letter to MMD, 5 July 1876, Dodge Collection.

35. Mayne Reid, letter to MMD, 7 June 1883, *St. Nicholas* Correspondence of Mary Mapes Dodge, PUL.

36. Mayne Reid to MMD: The book Reid intended would have been *Voyages of The Adventure and Beagle*, by Darwin, King & Fitzroy.

37. Frank Stockton, letter to MMD, 5 June 1897, *St. Nicholas* Correspondence of Mary Mapes Dodge, PUL.

38. Frank Stockton to MMD.

39. Frank Stockton to MMD.

40. Louisa May Alcott, *Eight Cousins*, SN 2 (Jan. 1875–Oct. 1875).

41. Louisa May Alcott, *Under the Lilacs*, SN 5 (Dec. 1877–Oct. 1878).

42. Louisa May Alcott, letter to MMD, 3 June [1878?], Dodge Collection.

43. Louisa May Alcott to MMD.

44. Louisa May Alcott to MMD.

45. Louisa May Alcott to MMD, 20 Sept. [1878?], Dodge Collection.

46. "Herewith I forward to you the remainder of suggested scenes for illustration. Hope this may save you some trouble in giving directions to your artist. I have indicated a greater number of scenes than are likely to be illustrated; but the best can be selected from them." Mayne Reid, letter to MMD, 26 Sept. 1883, Dodge Collection.

47. Louisa May Alcott, *Jack and Jill*, SN 7 (Dec. 1879–Oct. 1880).

48. In one of her letters, Miss Alcott regrets not having saved Mrs. Dodge's half of their correspondence, and so Mrs. Dodge's responses would seem to be lost.

49. Louisa May Alcott, letter to MMD, undated excerpt in "Swann Gallery Auction Catalog" for Thursday, June 24, 1982, Sale 1263, lot #5.

50. Louisa May Alcott, letter to MMD, 16 Aug. [188?], Wilkinson Collection of Mary Mapes Dodge, PUL.

51. Ten letters from Celia Thaxter to Mrs. Dodge, written between Feb. 1882 and Mar. 1890, PUL.

52. Celia Thaxter, letter to MMD, 9 Mar. 1890, Wilkinson Collection of Mary Mapes Dodge, PUL.

53. MMD, letter to Lucy Larcom, 29 Aug. 1879, in Spencer Mapes unpublished biography of Mary Mapes Dodge, Dodge Collection.

54. Henry W. Longfellow, letter to MMD, 11 July 1877, Mapes 166.

55. Rodman Gilder, letter to Spencer Mapes, 24 Mar. 1936, Dodge Collection.

56. We also have Reginald Birch's drawings for Frances Hodgson Burnett's *Little Lord Fauntleroy*, SN 13 (1885), whose androgynous characteristics are clearly interpreted in Alan Richardson's "Reluctant Lords and Lame Princes: Engendering the Male Child in Nineteenth-Century Juvenile Fiction," *Children's Literature* 21 (1993): 3–18. Anticipating Birch in the magazine's first frontispiece, William Brooke created a decidedly androgynous figure of a boy lying on his belly and elbows, one foot in the air, a round cap set upon long lush feminine curls. He is a feminized boy. In addition to the long hair, his shirt is draped negligently over a soft, round shoulder, while his upraised leg boasts a well-turned calf. With soft, round cheeks and round dark eyes and a full red mouth, he may be taken for a girl dressed as a tomboy. *SN* 1 (Nov. 1873).

57. John Townsend Trowbridge, letter to MMD, 31 Mar. 1874, *St. Nicholas* Correspondence of Mary Mapes Dodge, PUL.

58. MMD, letter to Charles Scribner, Esq., 5 Mar. 1879, Archive of Charles Scribner's Sons, PUL.

59. The remaining vote-getters were Etheldred B. Barry, Ernest Thompson Seton, Frederic Remington, Charles Allen Gilbert, Peter Newell, Alice Barber Stephens, Maxfield Parrish, Henry Hutt, A. B. Frost, Penrhyn Stanlaws, Andre Castaigne, A. I. Keller, A. B. Wenzell and Thomas Mitchell Pierce.

60. Susan Gannon and Ruth Anne Thompson, *Mary Mapes Dodge* (New York: Twayne, 1993): 14.

5

"Here's to *Our* Magazine!" Promoting *St. Nicholas* (1873–1905)

SUSAN R. GANNON

In 1873, a year's subscription to *St. Nicholas* cost three dollars. The monthly issues— small cream-colored booklets with covers intricately patterned in red and black, carried the announcement that *St. Nicholas, Scribner's Magazine for Girls and Boys*, was conducted by Mary Mapes Dodge. Each issue was accompanied by separately paged advertising and promotional material that reveal much about the way the magazine was merchandised. Unfortunately, when the magazine was bound for home or library use, these inserts and surrounds were usually stripped and discarded. So in preparing the following outline of the promotion history of the magazine it has been necessary to consult various library runs of the magazine and to explore the second-hand book market for stray unbound issues. A further survey of reviews and ads appearing in runs of magazines like *Scribner's Monthly*, later the *Century*; the *Atlantic Monthly*; and *Harper's* has indicated the way *St. Nicholas* was assessed in influential venues throughout the Dodge years, and also the way it promoted itself to the readers of other magazines. So what follows is a brief sketch of *St. Nick's* marketing of itself— in promotional material, commercial ads, "Letter-Box" pieces, and retrospective anniversary essays— that should clarify the magazine's agenda and the lines of its development through the years of Dodge's editorship, 1873–1905.[1]

I. Launching the Magazine: The 1870s

In the Christmas season of 1874/75, an elaborate hard-bound volume containing the first year's issues was published, and this four-dollar presentation copy, "elegantly bound in red and gold" was welcomed by many reviewers as the ideal Christmas gift (Announcement, inside front cover, *SN* 2 [August, 1875]). Scribner and Company worked very hard to get that first volume into the hands of well-regarded public figures whose endorsement might impress the kind of upwardly mobile middle-class families who took *Scribner's Monthly*. And soon words of praise poured in from such trusted cultural gatekeepers as poet John Greenleaf Whittier, writers Bayard Taylor and E. C. Stedman, educator T. W. Gunn, Rev. C. S. Robinson, D. D., and essayist and editor Charles Dudley Warner. Since most of those solicited for their opinion of the new journal were friends (and potential contributors), Dodge and her staff can hardly have been surprised by the warm welcome they received, but they had every reason to be gratified.

As a marketing strategy, they printed quotations from some of the "warm and encouraging personal letters" they had received in an ad supplement in the issue for January, 1875 (*SN* 2 [January 1875]: ad. p. 1). The remarks they chose to quote announce major themes of the magazine's future advertising in the Dodge years—and beyond. The first part of the supplement is headed "WHAT SOME EMINENT MEN THINK OF ST. NICHOLAS."[2] In it, one of America's most impressive cultural icons, John Greenleaf Whittier, calls *St. Nicholas* "the best child's periodical in the world"—a precious endorsement that would be repeated so often in the magazine's future advertising as to become a familiar "tag line" inescapably associated with its name. Whittier added that Dodge had "great reason to congratulate herself upon it," thus striking another familiar note: the magazine was, from the first, identified as the creation and personal triumph of its editor (ad. p. 1). Like other, later reviewers, Bayard Taylor was struck by the beauty of the physical object itself: " the typography, illustrations, and general arrangement," he said, "are wholly admirable and delightful" (ad. p. 1). Taylor's comment that his entire family had been charmed with the volume echoed sentiments the publishers of *St. Nicholas* had expressed in their announcement of the new magazine to subscribers of *Scribner's Monthly*: The new magazine would enlighten and delight the *whole* family circle. Dr. Robinson stressed the purity of purpose with which the publishers produced the magazine. "I know the proprietors," he said, "and they are Christian friends." Though *St. Nicholas* made no claim to being a religious periodical, he felt safe in saying, "it is on the side of all that is true and good from beginning to end." T. W. Gunn, the schoolmaster, on the other hand, could claim to "know something of the hearts of boys — what influences and what debases them." To Dodge and her staff he said: "Your magazine is all gold" (ad. p. 1).

Charles Dudley Warner was a good friend of Dodge's, and had been watching the progress of the *St. Nicholas* project from its inception. His kind words must have meant a great deal to her, and were, like Whittier's, widely quoted in later publicity campaigns:

> I have watched the magazine every month of its existence, and have seen its beauties of pen and pencil unfold; but I am surprised, now that it becomes a book — and as handsome a book as St. Nicholas himself can hope to find on Christmas — by the variety and wealth of its contents. Never before, I think, has so much literary and artistic talent co-operated in the service of children, and I will not resist the hearty impulse to say to you that you have made the best magazine for children of all ages I have ever seen; it is even more entertaining for grown people than some of the quarterlies. I know the high ideal Mrs. Dodge had for it, and her desire that it should exert a sweet and ennobling influence in the households of the land. It has been made level with the comprehensions of children, and yet it is a continual corrector of their taste, and of their honor and courage. I do not see how it can be made any better, and if the children don't like it, I think it is time to begin to change the kind of children in this country [ad. p. 1].

The warm praise of the great and the good was immediately followed by a three-page double-columned spread headed "WHAT THE AMERICAN PRESS SAYS OF THE BOUND VOLUME." Selections from reviews in leading papers around the country addressed the purposes to which the reading material in *St. Nicholas* might be put, the place it might hold in publishing history, its editorial policies, and its production values. The *New York Christian Leader* commented on the "wretched quality" of much contemporary literature for the young and the difficulty of finding suitable material for Sunday-school libraries. But it commended *St. Nicholas* for adding "not a few kernels only, but a whole bushel of wheat to every library which includes it" (ad. p.2).

St. Nicholas was highly praised for giving young readers challenging material by the best writers for adults, carefully measured to their needs. "The conductors of this admirable periodical," the *Leader* suggests, "started with the idea, that it was even more necessary for boys and girls than for grown people to have the services of practiced pens — and behind them well-stored minds, vigorous intellects and pure hearts." With the help of the editors, the contributors have been encouraged to contribute skillful but strong and simple writing, and "the result is a delightful playmate, companion and friend, which both instructs and amuses, and *tells the truth.*" As well as being an attractive feature for a well-chosen Sunday-school library, the *Leader* notes that the bound volume would be a perfect Christmas present; while a year's subscription costing just three dollars would see "the linked sweetness long drawn out during a whole twelve-month," and would make a "most excellent school prize" (ad. p. 2).

The *Boston Journal* stressed the "high standard of excellence" with which the magazine was conducted, as well as the care and expense lavished upon it by Scribner and Company (ad. p. 2). The *Evening Chronicle* of Pittsburgh was impressed with the superb education the magazine gave young readers, and called the illustrations, "greatly superior to *Chatterbox*, the bound volumes of which find their way into hundreds and thousands of American homes" (ad. p. 3). New York's *Independent* also attempted to place the new magazine among its peers, terming it "an excellent successor of the children's former favorites—'The Riverside Magazine' and 'Our Young Folks,'" and noting that it had been "about as successful as 'Our Young Folks' and much more successful than 'Riverside' in enlisting the services of well-known writers" (ad. p. 4).

The New York Tribune praised the way *St. Nicholas* exceeded expectation: "It is not often," they said, "that so much ability and literary practice are combined in the conduct of a juvenile magazine. Almost every page bears the mark not only of talent, but tact — a feature in which so many writers for children are woefully deficient." The *Tribune* expressed amazement at the way men of letters who usually wrote for adults had been coached by Mrs. Dodge to write for a new audience. She has, they said, "kept her noble army of subalterns, aide-de-camps, and common soldiers admirably in hand, always making them fire low enough to hit the mark." And there was also a recognition of Dodge's admirable networking skills, which brought to the pages of *St. Nicholas* a particularly outstanding group of women writers, "including besides the editress many of the most brilliant writers of the day" (ad. p. 4).

A common feature of most of the reviews was the judgment that the magazine was the best of its kind yet produced, and that this was largely due to Dodge's editorial management. As the *Liberal Christian* saw it, her "wise editorial hand is felt and recognized all through the pages of ST NICHOLAS, giving a certain uniformity of excellence to the whole" (ad. p. 4). But the *Times* of Hartford noted the importance of the generous support of Scribner and Company, saying that the editorial management of Mrs. Mary Mapes Dodge had here been "strengthened by the various resources of Scribner's great house," so that "in its literary and artistic merits, as well as the happy accuracy with which it hits the taste of its readers, this publication stands alone without a rival (ad. p. 4).

All this commendation amounted to a spectacularly good press. But would it be enough to sell enough copies of a new and rather expensive magazine, especially in 1873, which had, after all, been a "panic year"? The editors were practical enough to realize that *some* potential readers might need a more direct sales approach, one that would provide more urgent motivation to subscribe. So in another advertising section in the front of the same issue that contained the endorsements quoted above, they addressed their first subscribers in bold capitals, offering them premiums for selling subscriptions to their friends and neighbors. By persuading four friends to subscribe, readers might obtain a free copy of Dodge's new book *Rhymes and Jingles*. Six subscribers would mean three free books, including Dodge's *Hans Brinker*, and for fifteen subscribers a hard-working agent might acquire the latest of John Rogers' popular groups of statuettes, this one depicting "THE FAVORED SCHOLAR." Of these premiums the editors add: "No more welcome or tasteful gift could be made than one of these noted and beautiful statuettes, and **even the children can procure them** with the labor of a few hours, while at the same time, supplying their neighbors with **The Brightest and Best Juvenile Magazine ever Published**" (sales ad. p. 4).[3]

Aware that selling a luxury item in hard times might be difficult, the editors even provided a hard-hitting sales pitch, encouraging their amateur sales force to tell parents what the "**The Brightest and Best Juvenile Magazine ever Published**," might do for their children: "The *necessity* of such a magazine to every home-circle can be perceived by noticing the *healthy, earnest, and inspiriting occupation, the practical and hopeful views of life, the lessons in correct taste, the habits of inquiry and investigation, the awakening of new interest*— in short, the varied instruction and pleasure afforded by ST. NICHOLAS, all tending toward a *thorough and general improvement*." And then, of course, "Its articles are from the BEST WRITERS OF THE COUNTRY, and are always *fresh and original*. Its pictures are carefully drawn by the MOST NOTED ARTISTS, and are not only *illustrations*, but are, in themselves, *art-studies*." This hard-sell manages to meet the likely objection — that the magazine is a bit pricey — by arguing that it gives value for money, since each page of *St. Nick* includes more material than three of an ordinary juvenile book, and since "each number has **more,** as well as **better illustrations than half a dozen such books**," so that **St. Nicholas** is not only the "***BEST,*** but the ***CHEAPEST READING FOR CHILDREN***" (sales ad. p. 4).

The seventies, for *St. Nicholas*, brought a good deal of experiment, the cautious development of departments such as Dodge's vivid and original "Jack-in-the Pulpit" feature, and the beginnings of the lively interaction with reader-correspondents through the "Letter-Box." Dodge knew through her experience at *Hearth and Home*, where she had edited a page for young people, what powerful circulation-builders contests and reader-participation schemes could be. An early test of such a device was a campaign to enlist as many children as possible in a Bird Defenders organization whose members pledged not to harm defenseless birds. The success of this venture made it clear that among other things, the readers of *St. Nicholas* loved seeing their names in print. And soon the magazine was full of puzzles, riddles, and contests followed by long lists of those who succeeded in solving them. Appealing series by the likes of J. T. Trowbridge, Louisa May Alcott, and Noah Brooks accustomed families to read-aloud sessions with lively debates over plots and characters, and eager anticipation of new turns of events, discussions that became even more enjoyable as they were shared with the larger community of readers in letters to their favorite magazine. The "Letter-Box" was also used to promote sales. When Dodd and Mead snapped up Frank Stockton's story "What Might Have Been Expected," the editors expressed satisfaction in the "Letter-Box" that the "noble story" "entered the world through the pages of *St. Nicholas*," and hastened to tell readers "it will be good news to you all that Mr. Stockton has promised to write as much as he can for this magazine during the coming year" (*SN* 2 [Jan. 1875]: 196). To reinforce the message for parents, the back matter of the issue included a prominent ad from Dodd and Mead announcing the publication of Stockton's new book and quoting a favorable review of it from the *Nation*. Using the "Letter-Box" to answer "frequently asked questions"—or perhaps questions the editors *wished* might be frequently asked—was another common promotional strategy. The same January 1875 "Letter-Box" begins with an answer to "William B. S." explaining how to send monthly copies to *St. Nicholas* to have them bound. And at the end of the feature there is a letter from a farmer in Missouri one of whose children missed the circus and stayed home to plow the fields in order to earn the $3.00 for the family's subscription. His father wrote that his son's behavior showed how highly the magazine was "appreciated" (198).

　　　Occasionally, *St. Nicholas* published articles directed to parents, suggesting how to assure that young readers get the most out of the magazine. One such piece in the 1870s, Mrs. J. G. Burnett's "Some Young Readers of *St. Nicholas*," was cast as a kind of dream vision—a Christmas reverie in which the speaker, who has fallen into a half-waking dream after reading selections from recent issues to her sons, "sees" how parents and caregivers might have used a Christmas issue to nurture the children in their lives. In one vignette, a large family of children share a moment of happiness as they hear their recently widowed mother read an installment of Alcott's *Eight Cousins* in a determinedly cheerful voice. She encourages them to argue about issues in the story, laugh at the amusing bits, and enjoy the way the baby of the family pushes his way through to peer into the book. In another home, a wealthy but neglected little boy puzzles intently over a picture of chimney-sweeps in his *St. Nicholas*, failing to make sense of it without the needed help from the indifferent adults around him. His futile pleas for just one story to be read to him before bedtime go unanswered, and the bright pages of his *St. Nicholas* lie open on his chair as he is hauled off to bed. In contrast, in a Southern cabin, a loving nurse comforts a very little girl whose mother is ill, showing her how to read the pictures in her old copy of *St. Nicholas*, and relate to the stories. What makes for an effective reading for the children here is the sensitivity and effectiveness with which adults have mediated the text for them (*SN* 2 [Oct. 1875]: 761–763).

Scribner and Company had bought out Horace Scudder's distinguished children's magazine, the *Riverside*, in 1870, on speculation that they would launch their own rival publication in due time. By its third issue, *St. Nicholas* had also absorbed John Townsend Trowbridge's notable journal *Our Young Folks*, gaining not only its substantial subscription list but a number of strong pieces that had been promised readers for the coming year. Within a few years, three more magazines had joined the list: the *Children's Hour* and the *Schoolday Magazine* of Philadelphia and Chicago's *The Little Colonel*, giving *St. Nicholas* a national audience. "Cards" expressing the goodwill of the editors of these magazines toward *St. Nicholas* were printed as they were assimilated, and their subscribers were formally welcomed into the growing *St. Nicholas* family. By the time it was advertising its list of prospective wonders for 1876, *St. Nicholas* could boast of several years of prosperity "unexampled in the annals of juvenile literature" during which it had "not only met with the most hearty reception from the boys and girls of America," but had "fully satisfied the most critical grown-up readers," had "won golden opinions from the press," and "consolidated with itself all its strongest competitors" (*SN* 2 [Oct. 1875]: ad. p. 4).

II. Instruction with Delight: The 1880s

In a review of the 1881 annual volume of *St. Nicholas*, its sister publication, the *Century*, approved both the moral tone the magazine had set and its proven ability to provide lively, appealing reading. Children's literature, it said, had moved beyond "goody-goody books, conducted upon the principles of the most inexorable justice" and "dull disquisitions on the universe in general." But the reaction against past "priggishness" had led to the development of "sensational blood-and-thunder stories of the lower class of weeklies, the dime novels and so forth." However, "a purer literature," was "making its way rapidly with the children, not because it is pure so much as because it is bright, and lively, and true to nature." And, based on what the magazine had done to date, the writer concluded that "the recognition of what will please children, and at the same time, help them in forming high ideals of life, of literature, and art, is probably due as much to the editor of 'St. Nicholas' as to any one person living."[4]

During the eighties there was increasing emphasis on educational features. Historical articles, art history, the "Treasure Box of Literature," the natural science reports and projects of the "Agassiz Association," all provided what the reviewer for the *Century* had praised as "solid information" (953). There was much fun to be had, of course, but also a new interest in exploring the latest developments in technology, transportation, and current events. The magazine became more handsomely produced during this period, and this was above all the period of the great *St. Nicholas* serials—*Little Lord Fauntleroy, Juan and Juanita, Donald and Dorothy, Davy and the Goblin, The Hoosier Schoolboy.* Readers at this period had developed strong likes and dislikes, to which the editors paid close attention. Ads for each coming year were very explicit about the names of favorite writers who would turn up in *St. Nick*. Frances Hodgson Burnett, John Townsend Trowbridge, Louisa May Alcott, Palmer Cox, Rudyard Kipling — writers who might be said to "have a following" among the magazine's readers— were valuable assets who commanded top prices and favored treatment from the editors.

By the eighties, the look of the magazine was becoming more modern. More pictures, different type, a change of paper, and the use of color made for a more sophisticated and elegant product. Ads of the period often boasted that the magazine contained a thousand pages and as many pictures. Artists could count on their work being beautifully reproduced, and the editor was ready to experiment even with a successful editorial formula. Instead of trying for the usual mix of themes throughout a yearly volume, she decided that 1889 would be billed in advertising as "An All Around the World Year" in which young American readers would be introduced to what goes on in the world outside their country. There were to be features about life in Europe, Asia, Africa, Australia, and the Arctic regions, and though three serials were advertised, the content promised to be more challenging than usual. On the eve of the nineties, the decision was made that with the seventeenth volume there was "only one way that Mrs. Mary Mapes Dodge, its editor" could "make it better, and that is by making more of it," so it would be enlarged and printed in new and clear-faced type, and of course, this was to be managed at "NO INCREASE IN PRICE."[5]

III. Writing for Another Generation: The 1890s

In 1890, a promotional article was written by someone at *St. Nicholas*, and made available to a number of magazines.[6] It was the kind of piece that today would be printed with due warning that it is an "advertisement," but was not always so handled by the magazines that picked it up. The piece was headed "CHILDREN'S LITERATURE. WHAT 'ST. NICHOLAS' HAS DONE FOR GIRLS AND BOYS," and it was illustrated with attractive cuts from *St. Nick.* In a passage very much in the Dodge spirit, the writer suggests that "men and women are just as truly the result of the atmosphere in which they have passed their childhood, as the trees and herbage of a country are the result of its soil and climate. It is by the subtle something we call *atmosphere*, rather than by direct teaching, that the home molds a child." *St. Nicholas's* "supreme quality," then, is identified as the "bright, healthful and invigorating atmosphere" which does its good work without "unreadable prosing on moral subjects." Citing Froebel's view that "'the first work of a child is play,'" the piece draws attention to the striking sympathy of the magazine "with the spirits and pursuits of young people," to whom it offers such a wealth of home amusements, plays, riddles, charades, and puzzles—as well as tempting features on outdoor games and athletics—all subjects "of prime importance to boys and girls" (667).

This remarkably shrewd "info-mercial" notes the up-to-date-ness of recent issues of *St. Nicholas* dealing with subjects "fresh in the public mind," ranging from the building of the Brooklyn Bridge and the Statue of Liberty, to innovations in cable-telegraphy and the explorations of Stanley in Africa (668). "Children are interested in children," the piece goes on to say, and the editors use this "principle to amuse them and to attract their attention to many important subjects," including the sufferings of the homeless and the dreadful working conditions in factories that employ child labor.

St. Nicholas is said to have published a wide range of fiction, strong and lively work, but never "of the hot, unhealthful sort—the sort that tends to produce a harvest of renegades, highwaymen and pirates" (668). On this point, Dodge herself is quoted at length, and since she was often criticized for being over-bold in offering her readers the realism of Trowbridge or Twain, here is her forthright defense of her policy:

The mayor of Philadelphia says that he could rid the jails of
two-thirds of the boy criminals in the next year, if he could
banish bad plays from the boards of the variety theaters, and
put bad books out of print.

Now it will not do to take fascinating bad literature out of
boys' hands, and give them in its place Mrs. Barbauld and Peter
Parley; or worse still, the sentimental dribblings of those writers who think that any "good-y" talk will do for children. We
must give them good, strong, interesting reading, with the blood
and sinew of real life in it, — heartsome, pleasant reading, that
will waken them to a closer observation of the best things about
them.

It is right and natural for a boy to want to see the world. It
is right and natural for him to wish to read books that, according to his light, show him what the world is.

The evil is the impression given to young minds that *seeing
the world* means seeing the badness of the world. Let a boy
understand that to *see the world* in a fair, manly way, one must
see also its *good* side, its nobleness and true progress, and you
at once put his soul in the way of wholesome growth [668].

Like the "eminent men" who commended the magazine to readers in
1875, the author of this promotional piece in 1890 praises the magazine
for supplanting "unhealthful literature with stories of a living and healthful interest, uncontaminated and invigorating as the open air of heaven"
(668). The moral influence of the magazine is again seen in religious terms,
but now *St. Nicholas* is seen as "a teacher of religion — not in cold, dog-
matic form like a catechism" and "not in any sectarian sense." Instead it
teaches a kind of "'applied Christianity'"— the principles of religion as
they are applied to ordinary life. "Unselfishness, faithfulness, courage,
truthfulness— these things are taught in a hundred ways by stories, poems,
and precepts" (669).

It wasn't hard, by the time this promotional essay was sent out in
1890, to come up with an impressive list of distinguished American writers who had graced the pages of *St. Nicholas*. And since by this time, an
edition of the magazine had been published in England, there was also an
opportunity to quote what the foreign press had said in praise of the magazine, and especially of its art direction and production: "'The Thunderer,'
the London 'Times' itself, pronounced *St. Nicholas* superior to anything
of its kind in England, and said that its 'pictures are often works of real
art, not only as engravings, but as compositions of original design'" (670).

The 1890 essay ends with a reference to the opinion of the "eminent"
Charles Dudley Warner, expressed "when the magazine began." He had
said, "'if the children don't like it, I think it is time to begin to change the

kind of children in this country.'" The writer of this piece adds, "well, the children do like it, but all the same *St. Nicholas* has changed the kind of children. It cannot be that multitudes of them should see such pictures and read such stories and poems without being better, more thoughtful, more refined, and in many ways another kind of children than those who have gone before them" (670).

During the nineties, the magazine's first generation of readers were beginning to raise children themselves, and their families constituted a tempting new market. In 1893 *St. Nicholas* assimilated Boston's *Wide Awake*, the annual bound volume which had, like *St. Nicholas,* been successfully merchandised as a Christmas gift. In 1898 the annual magazine ad for new subscriptions tried to capitalize on young parents' memories of their own passion for *St. Nick.*[7] The ad was headed by a drawing of a young highwayman, holding up a startled Santa with a bundle of toys on his back and a magazine stuffed into his pocket. The caption reads: "ST. NICHOLAS OR YOUR LIFE!" The ad copy asks parents to "keep in mind the fact that the young people of today are just as anxious to read ST. NICHOLAS as you used to be — and how many of them can you subscribe for and make happy?" The copy stresses that the quality of the magazine had stayed the same, and the same editor was at work to provide "the best things in literature and art that money can buy and young folks will enjoy and thrive under." But in keeping with the stress on current events in the nineties, parents were assured that the magazine was up-to date. The editors knew that young people loved the adventure tales of Henty, so he was persuaded to contribute an exciting serial that year, and other celebrities of special topical interest would also contribute to the fun: Admiral Peary, the wife of the commander of the *Maine,* and Robert Louis Stevenson's stepson and collaborator, Lloyd Osbourne.

Two important new departments appeared in the late nineties: "Nature and Science" and "The St. Nicholas League." Both were described in ads as having aroused immediate enthusiasm among young readers, and as having substantially increased circulation. Potential subscribers were promised that the editor of the science department would give careful attention to every question asked by his readers, and there was frequent mention of the prizes and fame to be won by young contributors to the League. The League would of course become enormously important to the readership and would nurture the talents of many future writers and artists.[8]

During the nineties, Dodge's own "Jack in the Pulpit" department gradually ceased to appear, as did another of her special interests, the little pieces directed to the youngest of readers. As the period drew to a close, she was less involved in day-to-day management activities, which fell to her associate editor, William Fayal Clarke; Albert Bigelow Paine, whose St. Nicholas League had proven an instant success; and the other staffers who carried on the magazine's major departments.

IV. The Turn of the Century: 1900–1905

When Dodge herself looked back at thirty years of editing the magazine, she was struck by how much it had changed over time. Much as the early praise of those "eminent men" must have gratified her, she had always known better. She was self-critical and very much aware of how much her achievement as an editor had fallen short of her aspirations. But as she looked back and saw how far the magazine had come toward deserving the praise so generously lavished upon it, she felt at least that her editorial agenda had been sound, and that the result of all that effort had been worth the struggle.[9] In the last five years of her editorship, as Dodge's energies flagged, she relied increasingly on Clarke, and upon her death in 1905 he became editor-in-chief. Clarke endeavored to carry on in the Dodge tradition, and edited the journal ably for another quarter century.

In 1923, fifty years after *St. Nicholas's* debut, Clarke looked back over *his* years at the magazine in a retrospective piece very much in the tradition of the other promotional literature, called "Fifty Years of ST. NICHOLAS: A Brief Compilation of Chronicle and Comment" (*SN* 51 [Nov. 1923]: 16–23). The essay, as its title indicates, is a curious hodge-podge of history and endorsements. There are the usual "'golden opinions'" from famous people — Whittier's remark in 1875: "ST. NICHOLAS is the best child's periodical in the world," being prominent among them (17). But in 1875, most of the endorsements had been from cultural leaders who spoke to parents in generalities about the good influence the magazine might have. Now, though only one of the endorsements is from a woman, the celebrities cited come from many walks of life –politics, music, athletics, journalism, law, library science — and most of them speak from personal experience, out of appreciation for what the magazine brought to their own childhoods. Walter Damrosch wrote: "I dare not say how many years ago I read my first ST. NICHOLAS, but its pages are inseparable from my memories of boyhood days; and as my children came along they proved themselves equally devoted to it" (17). It is not just the entertainment value of the magazine that is savored by parents: writer George W. Cable confided, "nothing else that has ever come into my household of children has been, in equal degree, the stimulus to their artistic and literary taste" (17). Some familiar refrains from notable newspapers declare the magazine to be in various ways the best of all possible reading for children. And Clarke cannily includes a promotional idea proposed by the "Catalogue of a Children's Library": "If it were possible to bring a new number of the St. Nicholas magazine, with its wealth of entertainment and instruction, into every home and school-room in the land, every month, it would be a desirable thing to do" (18).

Clarke devotes an extended section of his "Compilation" to a selection from an overview of the history of the magazine written a few years before by Leroy Fairman, who produced a summary of the "ideals" that shaped St. Nicholas, based on his study of the magazine. The list resembles aims expressed in a general way in Dodge's essay "Children's Magazines" and in the early editorial copy and promotional material cited above, and since it has the hearty approval of Clarke — one of only two editors-in chief the magazine had had in fifty years, suggests a remarkable continuity in the way the magazine saw and presented itself during that time.[10]

Ads, reviews, and promotions may have drummed up a good bit of enthusiasm and business for *St. Nicholas* over the years, but the proof of the pudding is in the eating, and the last word must go to the young readers of its primary target audience themselves, who could be, as Dodge and Clarke knew, the keenest of critics. Children, she once said, "take up their monthly or weekly because they wish to, and if they don't like it they throw it down again."[11] In 1898 an urgent advertisement for the new year's *St. Nicholas*, written at a time when "new magazines and papers are ever clamoring for recognition," ended with a sober reflection: "An announcement, however attractive, is of little worth unless insuring a performance exceeding the terms of the promise" (*SN* 21 (Dec. 1898): ad. p. 3). *St. Nicholas* always found its most powerful promotional endorsements in the simple words of readers who poured out their heartfelt admiration in smudgy but eloquent letters to the "Letter-Box." Clarke quotes one child who wrote: "My sister has taken you for six months, but — well, I get the mail!" One letter was addressed to "St. Nick" and the young reader said: "I do not think it is disrespectful to call you this, because one always gives 'Nick' names to the people one loves best." Another began with, "Why does a month seem so long? I am so anxious for the next St. Nicholas!" And it ended with the rousing cheer: "Here's to *our* magazine!" Clarke concludes: "When these words represent the prevailing and continuous sentiment of its young readers, what need to say more?"(22).

Notes

1. Sources for the sort of ephemeral advertising material used here are hard to locate. I have been fortunate in the kindness of several antiquarian booksellers, notably the

late Robert M. Dell, and have looked at runs of the magazine in various libraries. Mary June Roggenbuck's invaluable dissertation, *St. Nicholas Magazine: A Study of the Impact and Historical Influence of the Editorship of Mary Mapes Dodge* documents her careful search for such material and cites many contemporary reviews of the magazine (Ph.D. diss., University of Michigan, 1976). It is to be hoped that when a digitized version of *St. Nicholas* is available, it will include inserts and advertising material. The *Making of America* database at the University of Michigan and Cornell University makes available online some important nineteenth-century American magazines, including the *Atlantic Monthly*, the *Century*, and *Harper's Monthly* with their advertising sections. The Bodleian Library at Oxford University has a run of the *St. Nicholas* edition published in London, with its local advertising. The British Library has a short run of a French variation on *St. Nicholas* published in Paris by Delagrave. It was modeled on the American magazine and recycled a good deal of material from it, quite creatively. Like the English edition of *St. Nicholas*, its advertising was local, but unlike the English edition which was identical to the American one in content, the French *St. Nicholas* included a good deal of original French material and its extensive interactive features for readers were geared mainly to the local French audience.

2. As the title indicates, even a brief survey of the promotional material used by *St. Nicholas* makes it clear that most of the authority figures referenced are male, and, though many features in the magazine were designed to appeal to girls, and women writers were always major contributors, the need to provide wholesome reading for boys was stressed in advertising, especially in the nineties, when the magazine was facing competition for boy readers from *Harper's Round Table*. Wherever caps, bold type, or italics are present in the original text of the promotional material, I will reproduce them to give a sense of their rhetorical effect.

3. Roggenbuck reports a fourteen-page supplement to the April, 1874 issue offering premiums for selling 100 to 500 subscriptions of "organs, a piano, full tuition or full tuition and board to schools and academies in the United States, and a trip to Europe" (27). Roggenbuck also notes that though the promotional material at this time stresses that the magazine is a bargain, almost twenty years later, in 1891, *St. Nicholas* advertised itself boldly as "'the most expensive children's magazine in the world,'" and seems to have begun to target more aᵒuent readers, though once more, times were hard (325).

4. "St. Nicholas, Volume VIII," *Century* 23 (Apr. 1882): 953.

5. Century Company Advertisement, *Garden and Forest* (November 6, 1889): ad. p. iii.

6. *Overland Monthly and Out West Magazine* 16 (Dec. 1890): 667–670.

7. *Atlantic Monthly* 82 (Dec. 1898): ad. p. 10.

8. See Suzanne Rahn, "In the Century's First Springtime: Albert Bigelow Paine and the St. Nicholas League" in this volume.

9. See Susan Gannon, "Fair Ideals and Heavy Responsibilities: The Editing of *St. Nicholas Magazine* (1873–1905)" in this volume.

10. Fairman's list resembles very much a briefer list which appeared later in *Mary Mapes Dodge of* St. Nicholas, Alice B. Howard's biography of Dodge for children (Macmillan, 1943: 208). There it was presented as a list of prospective aims Dodge was supposed to have written out for herself when considering how she might edit *St. Nicholas*. Howard's biography was not always reliable on major points, though she did consult members of the Dodge family when preparing it. We have looked diligently for a source for this list among the Dodge papers in various major collections, but my colleague Ruth Anne Thompson and I have not found anything resembling it. We are aware that this does not mean that one does not exist, or never existed. But until such a document turns up, we don't think the Howard list can safely be attributed to Dodge.

The list of aims from Howard is cited as Dodge's in some otherwise reliable sources, including Cornelia Meigs et al., *A Critical History of Children's Literature* (Macmillan, 1953: 208), and Roggenbuck (13). And it has recently turned up on the Internet. But we think it likely that these references all can be traced back to Howard, who in turn may have adapted the material from Fairman's list as it appeared in Clarke's 1923 article.

It might be noted that Catherine Morris Wright, in her 1979 "life and letters" biography of Dodge quotes meticulously from letters and documents possessed by the Dodge family, but avoids reference to the list as Dodge's, as does Fred Erisman in the standard reference article "*St. Nicholas*," in *Children's Periodicals of the United States*, ed. R. Gordon Kelly (Westport, CT: Greenwood Press, 1984). Erisman carefully cites the list only as it appears in Clarke's article, as he also does in his essay "The Present as Prologue" (in this volume).

11. "Children's Magazines," *Scribner's Monthly* (July, 1873): 53.

Part II

"Jacks and Jills": *St. Nicholas* and Its Audience

6

St. Nicholas and Its Friends: The Magazine– Child Relationship

SUZANNE RAHN

As we read a book, we enter into a kind of dialogue with its author — more layered if we are listening to someone read the book aloud, but still essentially an intimate relationship with one person. Reading a magazine, on the other hand, is like entering a community which authors, editors, and subscribers inhabit to create the whole. This effect is intensified if the subscribers are able, usually through a "letters from our readers" department, to be aware of each other and hear each other's voices. In magazines for adults, the community is often a rather quarrelsome one, whose letters constantly correct, criticize, and argue with editors, authors, and each other. The communities of children's magazines, on the other hand, tend to be peaceful and friendly. Their letters mention favorite features of the magazine, state how long they have been subscribers, and introduce themselves to each other as fellow members of the community, after a fashion that has remained remarkably consistent over the last hundred years. The children who wrote to *St. Nicholas* Magazine in the 1870s, 1880s, and 1890s talked about their pets, their hobbies, their brothers and sisters, and where they lived; sometimes they described an interesting journey, a funny happening, or an exciting personal adventure. So do the children who write to *Cricket* Magazine today.

Of course, the letters published in the magazine do not necessarily represent the full range of letters received. For lack of space, only a fraction of these letters can be published, and an editor can choose those which most closely approximate an ideal type. In the beginning, she may even "prime the pump" a little by writing them herself, but this is at most a temporary expedient.[1] Children are eager to have their letters published, and they naturally emulate those they see in the magazine. Unlike adult subscribers, they seldom blame the editor if their own letter is not chosen; they blame, if anyone, themselves. Not infrequently, one finds a letter in *St. Nicholas,* which mentions that its author has made previous unsuccessful attempts at publication; this time, perhaps, the letter will be "good enough to be printed." Thus, the editor of a children's magazine wields both direct and indirect influence over how subscribers present themselves to the magazine community — and even, perhaps, over how these children see themselves.

Much has been written of the outstanding ability of Mary Mapes Dodge, as editor, to get the best work from the best authors and illustrators of her time. But *St. Nicholas* owes its unquestioned preeminence as a children's magazine not only to the high quality of its text and illustrations, but to the intensity and loyalty of feeling it generated in young readers, notable even in an age so dependent on print for pleasure. Devotion to *St. Nicholas* often outlasted childhood and — as we see from the silent testimony of family sets extending over twenty or thirty years— spanned generations.[2] Sheer quality of material and a keen editorial nose for "what's happening" are not enough to explain this deep and lasting appeal. There was also an unusually strong sense of community among the readers of *St. Nicholas*— a sense of belonging to something real and wonderful.

What kind of community was this and what did it mean to the children who belonged? And what did Mary Mapes Dodge do to create and sustain it? Two departments of *St. Nicholas* provide an answer: "The Letter-Box" with its letters from young readers, and the editorial page, "Jack-in-the-Pulpit."

To appreciate what Dodge did, consider the immediate predecessor of *St. Nicholas. Our Young Folks,* published from 1865 to 1873 by Ticknor and Fields, aimed, like *St. Nicholas,* for the best in American writing for children. It numbered among its authors some of the most illustrious names of its times. Shortly after *St. Nicholas* began publication in 1873, Scribner's purchased *Our Young Folks* and merged it with the newer periodical. This close relationship makes the dissimilarities all the more striking. From its earliest issues, *St. Nicholas* was more spacious and inviting in design, more handsomely and abundantly illustrated, and contained a greater variety of material. It reveals as well its generally higher quality and more innovative content — the difference between good and brilliant editing.

Our Young Folks had no separate editorial page; any editorial messages were incorporated in "Our Letter Box." From its beginnings in January 1866, this department consisted not of letters from readers, but of letters to them — and these were mainly letters of rejection. A department called "Round the Evening Lamp: A Treasury of Charades, Puzzles, Problems and Funny Things" published reader contributions and the editorial letters explained to would-be contributors why their efforts were unacceptable. For example:

> W. Arthur D.: Rebus sketches are well enough in pencil. But your subjects do not quite come up to standard. And — let us whisper in your ear — you must look sharply to your spelling, which is faulty, both in your letter and your puzzles.
>
> Tudor: You must learn the rules of composition — how to use capitals and all marks of punctuation, etc. — before what you write can be printed anywhere. Emma M. D.: Your little note is very pleasant to us, and we thank you for it; but we must put the little puzzle aside [2 (Mar. 1866): 12].

It is hard to imagine that W. Arthur, Tudor, or Emma could have enjoyed seeing their names in print in such a context, and one might wonder at the courage of the children who continued to send in puzzles and conundrums under these conditions.

With time "The Letter-Box" changed somewhat till by 1873 the contents were chiefly inquiries and answers. Letters were generally excerpted or summarized, and the editorial tone remained formal, uncompromising, and rather severe. Warmth of feeling entered only when the writer was a young invalid such as Daisy, who wrote to *Our Young Folks:*

> I love you very much, and have loved you ever since you first came to me, six long years ago, to cheer, to help, and give me glimpses of the happy child-life I had lost. How many weary hours of suffering you have helped me through! And when I grew sad and lonely, longing to be one of the happy, healthy little girls I saw running past to school, instead of the little lame girl who had to lie all day on the bed by the window, I would take my last "Young Folks" from under the pillow, sure to find something comforting [8 (June 1872): 382].

The editor responded, "What you say of yourself is very touching; and when you speak of the comfort which 'Our Young Folks' has afforded you in your suffering loneliness, that is a comfort to us, dear Daisy!" (382).

Readers of the magazine were children who had to work hard to win adult approval. Children were not encouraged to see their own lives as interesting, unless they were invalids, who were called "dear" and allowed to feel thoroughly sorry for themselves.

JACK-IN-THE-PULPIT.

The original heading illustration for "Jack-in-the-Pulpit" (top) and the revised version that replaced it a few years later.

When these readers went to *St. Nicholas,* they found a very different world. On the first page of the first issue Mary Mapes Dodge greeted them with a cheery welcome:

> Why, this is delightful. And how fresh, eager, and hearty you look! Glad to see us? Thank you. The same to you, and many happy returns. Well, well, we might have known it; we did know it, but we hardly thought it would be like this. Hurrah for dear St. Nicholas! He has made us friends in a moment [1 (Nov. 1873): 1].

And there was something even more unexpected — a page headed "Jack-in-the-Pulpit," with a funny little drawing of an odd figure emerging from a flower to address a group of children, animals, and fairy folk. "My name is Jack," it announced. "I am a green thing coming up as a flower, yet I know a great deal. For why? The birds come and tell me" (1 [Nov. 1873]: 46). Despite the "pulpit," "Jack-in-the-Pulpit" was not in the least like a sermon. It began each month with a cheerful greeting and was made up chiefly of droll bits of information — some on strange customs of foreign lands, some on coming features of the magazine, some on unusual plants and animals. Sometimes young or adult correspondents contributed an item; sometimes children were challenged with puzzling questions, the answers to which appeared in subsequent issues. Jack's voice is sprightly, vigorous, humorous, and friendly throughout.

The fiction is maintained that Jack is an actual Jack-in-the-Pulpit flower that grows in a meadow near a schoolhouse, where he can overhear conversations among the children or remarks from their teacher, the Little Schoolma'am. Another character who appeared in 1875, Silas Green, or Deacon Green, lived in "the red cottage across the road from the schoolhouse" (3 [Nov 1875]: 54). The department sometimes contained snatches of the conversation between the Deacon and the Schoolma'am on a coming feature in *St. Nicholas,* or an argument over a question of fact — which Jack, of course, being a mere plant, does not presume to answer for them.

Who was Jack-in-the-Pulpit? His own answer is at once evasive and revealing:

> Am I a real Jack-in-the-Pulpit? you have asked — a true plant, growing and preaching out in the sunshine? Well, perhaps no. Perhaps yes. This much is certain: I do live in the sunshine; I do try to grow; and I do love to talk to the boys and girls of St. Nicholas — to open their eyes and their minds by pointing out all sorts of queer truths here, there, and yonder — and to put into their hearts grateful, loving thoughts toward the Giver of all good.
>
> So, my darlings, if you're satisfied with this explanation, I am [3 (Nov. 1875): 54].

William Fayal Clarke's memorial to Mary Mapes Dodge revealed the truth:

> No mention of Mrs. Dodge's editorial life would be complete
> without reference to the department which was her own spe-
> cial joy and pride — though, all too modestly, she never even
> acknowledged its authorship.... It is no betrayal of a confidence,
> now, to reveal that Mrs. Dodge was herself "Jack-in-the-Pul-
> pit," "Deacon Green," and the "Little Schoolma'am" all in one
> [32 (Oct. 1905): 1065].

A novelist as well as an editor, Dodge found it natural to communicate
through a whole cast of characters. The Little Schoolma'am seems to have
represented her intellectual interests and the Deacon her ethical concerns;
when something purely educational or a bit of moralizing was called for,
they lent her the traditional authority of school and church. But Jack-in-
the-Pulpit, her principal persona, despite his name, was not an authority
figure at all. Who could be overawed by a wildflower, something even
smaller and more helpless than a child? Through Jack, Dodge could talk
to children, not as a teacher, mother, minister, or even editor, but as a
friend — a fellow creature still "trying to grow" and as wide-eyed at the
world's wonders as themselves. And through Jack, she could bring her storyteller's humor and imagination to the editorial page. In one column Jack
advises his readers:

> How to Get Cool
> When the thermometer stands at 90 deg., my warm young
> friends, don't fume, nor fuss, nor fan yourselves into a blaze.
> No. Sit down in some quiet place and think only of cool things.
> Think of snow; think of ice; think of cold water trickling down
> your back. Think of holding a live eel in each hand. Imagine
> yourself under an icy shower-bath, or sitting at night-fall on top
> of an iceberg; then try to shiver. Do all this without once stir-
> ring from your position, and you'll get cool, or my name's not
> Jack [3 (Aug. 1876): 670].

He goes on to describe a cold sea full of floating icebergs. In an abrupt
change of pace, he then quotes an English advertisement for "Dr. Ridge's
Patent Food for Infants in Shilling Packets." Jack comments, "Infants must
be pretty cheap on the other side of the ocean. Cheaper than chromos"
(670). Jack could get away with such flights of fancy and impish humor;
an editor could not.[3]

This created a community Dodge envisioned for *St. Nicholas,* one in
which children would be first-class citizens. By minimizing her role, she
allowed children a greater one. This is even clearer in "The Letter-Box"
which appeared in 1894. It consisted at first of answers to readers' questions — generally not quoting the original letters — with some discourag-

ing responses to children's attempts at verse. "Dear little Elaine!" Dodge exclaimed, "don't write verses yet, cleverly as you do them for one of your age" (1 [Mar. 1874]: 308). Dodge had a strong aversion to any kind of precocity or public self-display in children.[4]

Here there was already a change in tone; the editorial voice sounds less severe, more relaxed, more openly sympathetic to its audience than the voice of *Our Young Folks*. One example is the different responses given to the same question asked of both magazines: Will Brotherton and Oscaretta T. had read "The Owl and the Pussycat" and asked what a runcible spoon was. *Our Young Folks* responded:

> "Runcible" is a nonsense word introduced in the nonsense poem for the comical effect of a well-sounding epithet, without any shadow of meaning [8 (Nov. 1872): 703].

This was *St. Nicholas'* answer:

> Runcible spoons are not made now-a-days, so it is not to be wondered at that Oscaretta did not find the word in any modern dictionary. If our little friend only could find an encyclopedia that was published in the time when all these things happened — when Owls and Pussies, on their wedding tours, really sailed in pea-green boats "to the land where the Bong-tree grows," — she would not long be kept in ignorance. But we'll whisper a word or two in Oscaretta's ear. There's a great big, big volume called Imagination; and in this volume, right among the R's she'll find "runcible;" and, perhaps, among the B's a perfect description of a Bong-tree. Why not? [1 (May 1874): 436].

The *St. Nicholas* "Letter-Box" also encouraged greater reader participation. The second issue included an article, "For the Birds," by C. C. Haskins, which urged children to join a new organization called the Bird-defenders, one of the earliest wildlife preservation groups in America; "The Letter-Box" became the department which published the names and sometimes the letters of children pledging their support.[5]

Dodge also actively encouraged readers to answer each other's questions:

> H. W. Carroll wishes to know who invented carpet-making; also, who invented oil-cloth making. Can any of our young readers answer the questions? [1 (June 1874): 499].
> Who can tell a correspondent, J. H., why salt is used in freezing ice-cream? [3 (Aug. 1876): 678].

Gradually letters from children filled a larger proportion of "The Letter-Box," and the editorial response a smaller one. *St. Nicholas* initiated a

"Young Contributors' Department" with articles signed with initials only (3 [Jan. 1876]: 202), and although it did not last many months, the department helped shift the emphasis of "The Letter-Box" by leaving more room for personal letters rather than "contributions." The real turning point came in the spring when "The Letter-Box" included two letters with no questions to be answered, nor any "useful" information whatever (3 [Apr. 1876]: 404); and in May there were eleven such letters. A new pattern was established in which the children themselves, their opinions, personalities, their individual lives and circumstances, were more important than the objective information they had to offer or ask for.

This pattern was to continue for nearly thirty years. Oddly enough, while the abortive "Young Contributors' Department" had helped establish "The Letter-Box" as an independent feature, the St. Nicholas League, established in 1899, had the opposite effect. This featured competitions for monthly awards for the contributors in creative writing, graphic art, and photography. Its founder, Albert Bigelow Paine, was able to overcome Dodge's qualms in regard to child celebrity, and the unprecedented opportunities offered quickly made it one of the most popular departments in the magazine. Children's letters about the League were initially printed in the League's department, in effect siphoning off a great many letters that would normally have found their way into "The Letter-Box." The latter diminished in size and disappeared in November 1904 and reappeared briefly in January and March 1905. Although it was never again omitted from *St. Nicholas*, it never regained its pre-League length or importance.

While the St. Nicholas League was meant for children with talent and even professional ambitions, "The Letter-Box" embraced and reflected the entire *St. Nicholas* community, a wider-reaching and more varied community than is sometimes realized. It is generally assumed that *St. Nicholas* was a "gentry" magazine, designed for and read by upper middle-class children. Lower income families, it is argued, could not afford magazine subscriptions, particularly for magazines aimed at children.[6] "The Letter-Box" suggests that *St. Nicholas* was intended for, and read by, a much larger audience than "gentry" children.

There were, to begin with, more ways than through subscriptions for children to become regular readers of St. *Nicholas*. Children circulated the issues among themselves. A ten-year subscriber, James Mason K., wrote: "I think if you could see the many invalids, country children longing for books, and friends away from home in the summer time, that have pored over our copies, you would realize what good service St. Nicholas has done for us" (14 [Mar. 1887]: 397). Schools, teachers, and public libraries also subscribed to *St. Nicholas*. A teacher submitting a list of Bird-defenders to "The Letter-Box" added, "I have kept St. Nicholas upon my desk in the school-room ever since it came out, and I find it a capital text-book" (1 [Oct. 1874]: 746). Jack London told the story of how, as a working-class high school dropout, he read a story in *St. Nicholas* in the Oakland Public Library that inspired him to become a writer.[7] Sometimes a generous relative supplied a child or family with a subscription: one letter told of a large and financially straitened family in "a lonely country neighborhood in Virginia" who received a Christmas subscription from "an aunt in a distant city" (3 [Apr. 1876]: 404). In the 1880s an entire town subscribed to *St. Nicholas*. According to Charles Barnard in "A Town with a Saint," the will of a local manufacturer had established a fund to be used "for the benefit of all the people in the town" of North Easton, Massachusetts; its trustees spent part of the money on individual subscriptions for "every family where there are children" (10 [Mar. 1883]: 339).

> Think of it! One copy for every family. The joyful news soon spreads, and the moment school is out there is a grand rush for the post-office. Three hundred boys and girls besiege it at once. The postmaster hands the magazines out as fast as possible, and before night every one is gone. Not one is left, you may be sure. That evening, the entire population begins to read St. Nicholas. Nobody knows when they get through, for father and mother and big brother want their turn [338].

Mary Mapes Dodge herself encouraged the circulation of *St. Nicholas* among children too poor to pay for their subscriptions. A "Letter-Box" response to Emma T. suggests that she and other children give their back numbers to "any boys and girls who are too poor to buy St. Nicholas ... and tell them, when they have read them to pass them on to other boys and girls who may not have them." She also suggested sending back numbers to "some institution for poor or suffering children," such as Dr. Knight's Hospital for Crippled Children (3 [Dec. 1875]: 132). She had made it clear in an earlier issue that the *St. Nicholas* community was not restricted to children who could afford their own subscriptions:

> Oriole: You and all the other young folks are welcome to write to the Letter-Box, whether subscribing to St. Nicholas or not. We look upon every boy and girl who can read English, or look at a picture, as belonging in some way to St. Nicholas. Yes, you may join the army of Bird-defenders, too, provided you are resolved to keep the requisite pledge, even though you never expect to buy a copy of the magazine [2 (Nov. 1874): 57].

Although the social class of the young correspondents is often not evident from what they say about themselves or their families, some letters

Thousands of competitors took part in the contests sponsored by *St. Nicholas* in the decades before the St. Nicholas League. Here children respond overwhelmingly to an 1882 contest called "Historical Pi." *SN* 9 (Mar. 1882): 415.

confirm that *St. Nicholas* was not confined to the well-to-do or "genteel." A young girl named Jo writes:

> I have taken the St. Nicholas for three years, and I like it very much. I take it for my little sister now, but always read it first myself, and enjoy it very much, and so does my little sister. I send it to her by mail after I am through with it.
>
> I have been making my own living for five years, and I do not get much time to read. I almost always read St. Nicholas going and coming from work, as I have to take the street-car.
>
> Seven years ago I came from Sweden and could not speak a word of English, but now everybody takes me for an American [13 (July 1886): 714].

In 1895 an orphanage with a joint subscription sent a cheerful letter to *St. Nicholas* from Cooperstown, New York (29 [July 1895]: 790). And in his report from the "Historical Pi" Contest Committee, Deacon Green mentioned among the contestants who worked under special difficulties, "a poor little working-girl with an invalid mother," "a self-taught orphan," and "a Western farm-boy, who is busy in the fields and has only four months schooling in the winter" (9 [Apr. 1882]: 500).

Since *St. Nicholas'* treatment of African-Americans was stereotypical of its time, it might be assumed that African-American children, both because of prejudice and economic status, were not members of this community. A letter from 1916 suggests that such assumptions should not be lightly made. The Fisk Jubilee Singers mentioned below were African-American students at Fisk University, the first group to perform gospel music on the concert stage and highly regarded in both America and Europe.

> Dear St. Nicholas: Last Thursday night after a concert given by the Fisk Jubilee Singers, the younger Mr. Harrison took you up and looked you over.
> "Have you ever read St. Nicholas?" I asked, as he seemed greatly interested.
> I thought the question provoked him, for he rose quickly and said very earnestly:
> "I have read St. Nicholas from the time I was ten. I've read it when it has taken me an hour to read a sentence. I have taken it with me when I've been picking cotton to get the money to pay for it. I've taken it with me when I've gone fishing. One time I took it with me and propped it up against a tree. About five minutes afterward, I got a large trout on my hook. When pulling the trout in, I upset my St. Nicholas, pushing it into the water. I let go my pole and fished out my St. Nicholas. By the time I got back to my rod, the trout was gone. I told my father, when I got back, all about it, and he said he would whip me the next time I lost a trout for a good-for-nothing book of waste paper. That very night he stayed up until three o'clock reading it. And now," said he, "you ask me if I've read St. Nicholas!"
> Your loving friend, Phil. Lord [43 (Feb. 1916): 382].

Certainly, if social and economic factors posed no impossible barrier, neither did age nor geography. Numerous letters testify to the wide age range that enjoyed *St. Nicholas*, from five-year-olds to parents, and to the reluctance of readers in their late teens to leave it behind. Dodge took pride in its far-flung geographic distribution, and she liked to print letters from distant places, which, in the 1870s, included any place west of the Mississippi. She wrote in "The Letter Box" less than a year after the founding of *St. Nicholas*:

> We are delighted to see many evidences that these pages are as
> thoroughly enjoyed by the children of the far West as by those
> nearer New York. Scores of our stoutest and most enthusiastic
> Bird-defenders send their names from beyond the Mississippi,
> and the Letter-Box constantly testifies to the hearty interest of
> our far-away young friends. Therefore we fully appreciate an
> item in the Nebraska City News, which says: "One of the pret-
> tiest sights we have seen this year was that of a little girl, perched
> upon a hitching-post in Laramie Street, eagerly reading St.
> Nicholas by the light from one of the street-lamps" [1 (Oct.
> 1874): 747].

A number of early letters came from army forts and Indian reservations
on the American frontier.

By the 1880s *St. Nicholas* was extending its reach across the continent
and into foreign lands as well. "The Letter-Box" included children's letters from France and England, in addition to Fort Apache in Arizona and
the "piney woods" of Florida. "I write to tell you," said Nettie F. Little, "that
we got a copy of the St. Nicholas in London, and, although it has a different
cover, inside it is the same old friend that we have known so many years
in America and hope soon to see again (9 [Dec. 1882]: 157). The English
edition of St. Nicholas was eagerly greeted not only by young Americans
abroad, but also by many English children who seemed to prefer it to their
own native magazines. Letters also came from subscribers of other nation-
alities like Louisa H., who wrote from Stuttgart:

> My Dear St. Nicholas: When my eldest sister was in America
> in 1887, she sent me St. Nicholas for a present, and since that
> time I enjoy your coming every month. As a little girl I learned
> how to read English in your stories "for very little folks," and
> now, as I am sixteen, I know how to read your beautiful stories
> all by myself. Though I am a German girl, I like the English sto-
> ries much more than the German ones. I think no German story
> is as beautiful as your "Little Lord Fauntleroy," or your "Lady
> Jane" [20 (Mar. 1893): 396].[8]

Another letter in the same issue from Morse D. in Mexico concludes,
"I am a telegraph-operator for the Central and South American Company
on the Isthmus of Tehuantepec, and am twelve years old" (396).

The November 1886 "Letter-Box" included letters from Maroussa,
Russia (another "Little Lord Fauntleroy" fan), Katie in South Africa, Nina
Louise on Maui in the "Sandwich Islands," Flossie and Erica in England,
and Dorothy, an English girl on Poole Island off the coast of northern Australia (14 [Nov. 1886]: 77–78). The following May there were letters from
children in Ontario, Kauai, Montpellier, Dresden, Cheshire, London and
Wales, Louis in Paris, and Alfonso in Mexico City, who wrote: "I am far-

ther south than that girl in Savannah, and I assure you that the Southern friends love dear St. Nicholas" (14 [May 18 87]: 556).

For American children abroad, *St. Nicholas* brought a bit of home, helped sustain their national identity, and kept them in touch with their own culture. For children from other countries it was a fascinating introduction to the American way of life and a means of learning English. From their letters, these children considered themselves members of the *St. Nicholas* community.

The magazine also reached out to children isolated in other ways. Not a few subscribers were invalids, bed-ridden, or physically disabled, who could not attend school and may have had few contacts outside the home. One early letter and the editorial comments reveal the same tendency to single out invalids for special, sentimental consideration that was observed in *Our Young Folks*. "A little lame boy" wrote saying he learned from *St. Nicholas* how to amuse himself by constructing miniature cities. Dodge comments: "Many of you have written welcome letters to St. Nicholas, telling of the pleasant work you have learned to do from directions given in these pages; but this sweet little note from a Boston boy pleases us most of all" (1 [Oct. 1874]: 746). Later letters from invalids, however, were printed without comment. Children with disabilities mentioned them simply and frankly, as part of the picture of their lives, and had a special reason for appreciating *St. Nicholas*:

> Dear St. Nicholas: I am a sick little boy. I have been an invalid for almost a year, and am confined to my bed nearly all the time. My sister had to write this for me, as I am not able to write. The only thing I can do is read. We have taken St. Nicholas a long time. I can scarcely wait for it to come. My little baby brother thinks the "Brownies" is the nicest piece in the book, and we have to read it over and over again to him.
> Your constant reader, Casper N. [14 (May 1887): 554].

"The Letter-Box" reveals in letter after letter how many American children of this period lived in isolated circumstances — isolated, in many cases, not only from schools but from other children, for many reasons. Some lived at army forts: Mae G. wrote from Fort Apache, "We have no schools out here" (9 [Dec. 1881]: 157). Some families were settlers, not only on the Western frontier but in other parts of the country also. C. D. R. wrote from Florida:

> St. Nicholas is sent to me as a Christmas present from a very kind auntie of mine. I don't know what I should do without it.... The nearest little girl that I have to play with lives nearly two miles away, but I don't get very lonesome. I look forward

with a great deal of pleasure to the day that brings St. Nicholas to me [9 (Dec. 1881): 157].

Some families were missionaries. "I am a little girl seven years old, and live alone with my father, who is a Baptist missionary," wrote Edwina S. from Mexico City (13 [July 1886]: 714). Many other families traveled or lived abroad for extended periods. "We have lived very little in America, as mama is obliged to travel for her health," wrote Sussette and Aggie (22 [July 1895]: 788). Some children were educated at home, like Marguerite H. of Greenville, South Carolina:

> It seems to be the custom of your correspondents to give their ages and a minute description of their occupation, so I will follow. I am fourteen years old, and have never been to school a day in my life, my mother having always taught me at home until this year, when I have a tutor for Algebra and Latin. I continue the study of French with my mother, using Fasquelle's Grammar and reading a pretty story called "Le Petit Robinson de Paris," besides having lessons in English composition, geography, history, declamation, music and drawing [13 (July 1886): 715].

St. Nicholas connected these children to others and to a world otherwise beyond their reach. For rural children, especially, it could provide a source of knowledge and culture beyond what the local schools, if any, could provide. Letters like Casper's and C. D. R.'s are testimonials to its power, and the latter's "I don't know what I should do without it" is echoed again and again. Occasionally, as in the case of "the younger Mr. Harrison" of Fisk University, we learn a little more of what St. Nicholas could mean in the life of a disadvantaged child.

Another detailed and moving account comes by way of a former contributor of the 1870s, who wonders:

> ... whether boys and girls of the present time appreciate St. Nicholas as highly as the juveniles did twenty-five years ago. One of the boys of that time told his aunt the other day what this periodical was to him when he was a little country boy living on an isolated farm situated on the highest point of the State, having but little society, few books, and without a library, even of the Sunday-school sort in a primitive community. As a Christmas gift his aunt subscribed to St. Nicholas for him, as for three or four years he looked forward to the monthly feast of good things that never failed to come on time. The nearest post-office was four miles away, and if a neighbor going to the village did not bring him the precious parcel, he traveled eight miles to get it! After he had finished, his brothers enjoyed the undiminished feast, and then passed it along to other hungry boys who had no generous city aunt.

At length a time came when he waited in vain for dear St. Nicholas, and it was Christmas-time, too. Perhaps there was a delay of the mail. The snow was deep and heavy, and everything was snowed except the great high hill he lived upon. Christmas passed without its usual cheer; something very dear to the boy's heart was lacking, and, alas! The lack was never made up to him, though, encouraged by that same aunt, the country boy went to college and got his degree.

"Oh, my dear boy, why did you not write and tell me how much St. Nicholas was to you?" said the aunt after her nephew had told his story, the half of which has not been told here.

"I couldn't, I felt so wretched; I simply couldn't say anything of what I felt," he replied. Now, I hope that if there are any city aunts subscribing to St. Nicholas for their young country nephews they will keep up the subscription indefinitely and thereby escape the regret of

Yours sincerely,
Annie E. De Friese [32 (May 1905): 670].

Through "Jack-in-the-Pulpit" and "The Letter-Box," Mary Mapes Dodge shaped this far-flung community of readers. Just as her taste in writing and illustration and her concept of what childhood should be permeated the contents of St. *Nicholas*, so her editorial comments and selections for "The Letter-Box" gave the community its distinctive character and particularly strong appeal. Readers living in unusual and distant places had something of an "edge" in "The Letter-Box." Although St. *Nicholas* was published in New York City and had its largest circulation on the East Coast, it was the reverse of parochial in terms of readership. As one might expect from the author of *Hans Brinker* — the first American novel to take children inside a foreign culture — Dodge encouraged children from "beyond the Mississippi" and from other countries to feel themselves part of the St. *Nicholas* community. She also encouraged circulation of the magazine across social and economic boundaries. Nicholas, after all, was the patron saint of all children.

The cheerful, kindly, positive approach to life that characterized St. *Nicholas* as a whole was especially apparent in "Jack-in-the-Pulpit," and made itself felt in "The Letter-Box" as well. No negative letters ever appeared in the magazine, although it is unlikely that none were ever submitted. This selectivity may be regarded as a simple matter of self-interest. "The Letter-Box" helped set the characteristic tone of the magazine, and the steady stream of praise for St. *Nicholas* that runs through it was an effective form of advertising. Children must have suspected that saying something nice about St. *Nicholas* might help to get their letters printed. But the policy also helped give the community the pleasant, friendly atmosphere that was one of its attractions.

From the outset (and unlike the editors of *Our Young Folks*) Dodge also encouraged children to answer questions themselves rather than depending on her. Assisting her father with his agricultural experiments had given her a degree of scientific training unusual for a young woman of the 1840s, and she was fully aware of the importance of fresh ideas and first-hand investigation in an increasingly technological society. So she frequently included challenging questions in "Jack-in-the-Pulpit," or invited readers to try their hand at the questions sent to "The Letter-Box." She even suggested that there was not always a "right answer." She would set the Deacon arguing with the Little Schoolma'am, and when two readers sent in differing but equally plausible answers to a question, she would print them both. When Helen D. wrote to correct a statement in "Rhymes of the States" about the derivation of the name "Minnesota," she praised and thanked her "as a vigilant young correspondent, whose letter is certainly very convincing." At the same time, the editorial note points out "authorities differ, so that one may well doubt which is the true meaning, or whether the true meaning is known with certainty" (22 [July 1895]: 790). Children are encouraged to question what they read — even in *St. Nicholas* — and to recognize that the best authorities may not be certain of the truth.

"The Letter-Box" also occasionally contained letters from adults with information on specialized topics. The Agassiz Association, founded in 1880 for the study of natural history and sponsored by *St. Nicholas*, though primarily for children, had members of all ages: teachers, scientists, and other professionals who shared their expertise. Other movements sponsored or supported by the magazine, such as the Bird-defenders, money-raising for the Fresh Air Fund for children, organizing Christmas Clubs to give poor children a happier holiday, contributing to the Longfellow Memorial, encouraged children to assume a responsible and active role in the larger world.

As members of the *St. Nicholas* community, children saw themselves as mentally self-reliant and resourceful, capable of working with adults and each other toward common goals. And they were aware of being connected through *St. Nicholas*, however isolated they might be. Finally, and not least important, the children of the *St. Nicholas* community were encouraged to see themselves as lovable, not for any special talent or achievement, but for who they were. It is remarkable how often terms of endearment appear in "Jack-in-the Pulpit," how frequently readers are addressed as "my friends," "my chicks," and "my darlings." Despite their more formal tone, the editorial notes in "The Letter-Box" echo this affection and approval. When *St. Nicholas* sponsored a contest, extra pains were taken to prevent the losers from feeling too badly. Commenting on the results of a spelling competition, the Little Schoolma'am had praise for everyone:

> Some of you have worked under disadvantages which would have discouraged many older heads, and all of you have shown a zeal and intelligence which make me the proudest and happiest little schoolma'am in the world.... In conclusion, with a full heart I thank you, one and all, parents and children, for your good letters and the hearty love you show for dear *St. Nicholas* [3 (July 1876): 466].

Deacon Green was even more tenderhearted when he announced the results of a competition to make a perfect copy of the Declaration of Independence:

> The rest of the committee was enthusiastic over the correct and finely written copies, but somehow my heart went out to the blotted sheets whereon chubby little fingers toiled and blundered. While the four wiser ones were ecstatic over the neatness, skill and accuracy of hundreds of bright competitors, I sat wistfully holding the very worst Declaration of the lot, and, in imagination, wiping the tearful eyes of youngsters who couldn't possibly win a prize or get on the Roll of Honor [3 (Aug. 1876): 672].

Although this may sound sentimental to contemporary ears, it is unmistakably sincere. In every detail of *St. Nicholas*, we sense how much its founder cared about her "Jack and Jills."

It is no wonder that children loved, not the editor whose name they never saw, but "dear *St. Nicholas*." Children naturally responded to the openly expressed, unconditional love which valued them as individuals and respected their capabilities. Like the best mothers, *St. Nicholas* provided an environment that both nurtured the young and helped them grow. Its stories, articles, and illustrations, fine though they were, may not have meant so much to these nineteenth-century children as the sense that *St. Nicholas* gave them of who they were and the splendid community to which they belonged.

"It often seems to me," wrote one thoughtful "old boy" of eighteen to *St. Nicholas*, "as if you were the medium of feeling between all the boys and girls in the land. I wish you the friendship and love of all children everywhere" (11 [Feb. 1884]: 340).

Notes

1. Six months after the inauguration of *St. Nicholas*, Dodge was apologizing in "The Letter-Box" for her inability to reply to all the letters she received (1 [May 1874]: 437).

A few months later she told "Oriole," "One entire number of the magazine scarcely would hold half the letters that come to us every month..." (2 [Nov. 1874]: 57).

2. One example of a long term relationship appears in this letter: "Dear St. Nicholas: Our family has taken you for a long time. My great-grandmother (first), my grandmother (second), my mother (third), my uncle (fourth) and now myself (fifth) have been your subscribers, We have all certainly enjoyed you.... Your interested reader, Mildred Fuller (age 11)" (43 [Feb. 1916]: 382).

3. As far as I know, Jack-in-the-Pulpit was the first of his kind. But the non-human editorial persona became almost a convention of American children's magazines. *Jack and Jill* had Finny, the office goldfish; *Boys' Life* has its wisecracking burro Pedro; *Cricket* features a full cast of mostly insect characters like Cricket, Old Cricket, and Ladybug.

4. In another instance, although Dodge printed the poem of "A Little Syracuse Girl," she prefaced it with "We are not fond of encouraging such literary ways in our little folk ..." (1 [July 1874]: 560).

5. For more on the Bird-defenders, see my "Green Worlds for Children," *The Lion and the Unicorn*, 19 (Dec. 1995).

6. The subscription cost $3 a year.

7. Jack London's first published story appeared in *St. Nicholas*.

8. It was apparently not unusual for parents and teachers to use *St. Nicholas* as an aid to language learning. The letter from two boys in Montpellier begins: "Nearly two years ago our grandmamma, in America, sent us your magazine for Mamma to teach us English, for our lessons have all been in French and German, although we are little Americans" (14 [May 1887]: 555).

7

Young Eyewitnesses
to History

Suzanne Rahn

Historians have always ignored children, except for the occasional prince or princess. Even today, when the lives of New England midwives and the humble inhabitants of medieval villages are considered worthy of exhaustive study, children remain largely footnotes and statistics. The few "histories of childhood" still tend to focus on how adults conceived of childhood and child-rearing, rather than on the children themselves.

Children have been ignored not only because they are powerless, but because they have no voice for the historian to hear. Their written records consist mainly of letters—usually dictated or overseen by adults—some fragmentary journals that have happened to survive, and an abundance of samplers and school assignments designed by adults for them to do, with every flicker of spontaneity or individuality suppressed.

Thus, the *St. Nicholas* "Letter-Box" represents a rare cache of historical material. Here, spanning sixty years of history, are the voices of innumerable children, sharing with each other their knowledge, their experiences, and the details of their daily lives. Though produced, to some extent, under adult supervision and selected by adult editors, these letters bring us as close to children of the past as we are likely to get. They also give us fascinating glimpses of a kind of "other" history, in which even the best-known events, from the San Francisco earthquake to the sinking of the *Titanic*—seem freshly experienced, seen through the eyes of a child.

Mary A. Manley, for example, gives us an eyewitness account of General Custer's 1876 expedition, setting out to its rendezvous with disaster in "Indian country." By the time her letter was published, in the September issue of *St. Nicholas*, the Battle of the Little Big Horn had already taken place.

> Fort A. Lincoln, May 18th, 1876
> Dear St. Nicholas: I write you from Fort Lincoln, on the west bank of the Missouri River, opposite Bismark, the terminus of the N. P. R. R. An expedition has been fitting out from here to go into the Indian country, and day before yesterday they broke camp and started off at five o'clock in the morning. I will tell you in which order they marched past the officers' quarters:
> First came General Terry, who is in command of the expedition, accompanied by his staff. Next came a bank of forty Arickarree scouts, mounted on Indian ponies, and singing their horrid war song, which sounded to like "yow-yow-yow!" Then came the regimental band, playing the "Girl I left behind me." Following this came the seventh regiment of cavalry, at the head of which rode General Custer, and by his side his beautiful wife, who was to accompany him to the first camp. Next came a battery of Gatling guns, each drawn by eight horses. Last of all came three companies of infantry, which marched with resolute and steady tread. The expedition was accompanied by a train of one hundred and fifty wagons. It is going to drive Sitting Bull, and his band of hostile Siouxs [sic], on to the Reservation. If it accomplishes anything wonderful, you will probably read of it in the newspapers.
> Fort Lincoln is a very large Post, but we cannot go outside of it alone for fear of Indians.
> As I fear I am taking too much space, I must say good-bye.
> Mary A. Manley [3 (Aug. 1876): 678].

Only eleven years later, the battlefield of Custer's Last Stand — like the newly created Yellowstone Park — had become a destination for sightseers, as this 1887 letter shows.

> Fort Custer, M. T.
> Dear "St. Nicholas": I am a little girl who was born and brought up in the U. S. Army. My home is now in Fort Custer, a post built on the Crow Indian reservation. We see lots of Indians here every day. The post is a large one. We have eight companies and a band. The Custer battle-field is only ten miles from the post, and we have visited it. We spent five weeks this summer in the Yellowstone Park, and saw the geysers and all the wonderful things there. We have taken you a number of years, and we think you are just lovely. I am 'most eleven years old. I have one sister eight years old, and no brothers. Good-bye, dear "St. Nicholas."
> Always your loving reader, Pansy E. H. [14 (Feb. 1887): 317].

Along with the many letters from children like Mary and Pansy whose fathers were stationed on the western frontier, a handful of letters from the September 1880 issue speak out from the other side of the barricade. Four Omaha sisters—Susette, Marguerite, Susan, and Rosalie La Flesche—wrote with surprising frankness to "The Letter-Box;" pieced together, the four letters create a troubling and fascinating picture of childhood on the Indian Reserve.

Dear *St. Nicholas*: I do not know whether you allow "savages" in your "Letter-Box," but my two younger sisters seeming to have no doubt whatever on the subject, Rosalie and I have concluded not to let them get ahead of us; besides, nothing is ever complete unless "we four" are all "in it." As my little brother Mitchell (who, by the way, considers himself the most important member of the family) is unable to write for himself, I will attempt to do it for him. He is six years old, — so old that he constitutes himself our protector on all occasions.

He tries to re-assure mother by telling her that he will keep all the Sioux and Winnebagoes away from us. He can speak only a few sentences in English, although he chatters fast enough in Omaha, our own language. He admires the white people immensely. He said to me once:

"Sister, don't you like the white people? I do."

"I don't know," said I; "why should I?"

"Oh, because they know how to do everything."

He is rather afraid of them, though, when he sees a good many of them together. The members of the "Joint Indian Commission" were out here a short time ago visiting the different tribes, and they called on us for a few minutes. While we were all busy entertaining and being entertained by them, we forgot Mitchell entirely. A gentleman — one of the employees of the Indian Reserve —came to the kitchen where Mitchell was and asked him if the Major (the agent of a Reserve is often called "Major" by Reserve people) was in the front room.

"No," said Mitchell.

"Then please go and tell the Major that I want to see him," said the gentleman.

"Oh, no," said Mitchell, "I can't."

"Why not?"

"Oh! I can't; there are too many white men in there for me."

When our visitors had gone away, we found Mitchell standing by the dining-room window, with the tears rolling down his face, while he shook from head to foot with fright. I never knew him to be afraid of anything except white men, when he saw a good many of them together.

When he was three years old, he began riding horseback. When he was four years old, he rode alone to a neighbor's nearly a mile off, although the road led over steep bluffs near the Missouri River. Now, he can get off and on a horse without any help

whatever. We often see little Indian boys younger than he riding out alone on the prairie, hunting horses with perhaps an
older brother. Mitchell can go in among a number of horses
standing close together, and bring out any one of them without making any confusion or getting hurt.
    Susette La Flesche

Dear *St. Nicholas*: I am an Indian girl fifteen years old. I have
three sisters and two brothers. Two of my sisters are older than
I am. We four girls are keeping house by ourselves at the Omaha
Agency. It is three miles from our own home, where our father
and mother live. We are living on a Reserve, where nothing but
Indians, called Omahas, live, except the employees of the
Reserve.
    Sometimes I am sorry that the white people ever came to
America.
    What nice times we used to have before we were old enough
to go to school, for then father used to take us on the buffalo
hunt. How glad we used to be when the men were bringing in
the buffaloes they had killed! I do wish we could go again. Whatever the white men take away from us, they cannot take away
the love of roaming. I cannot write anything exciting, as nothing hardly ever happens, unless a number of Senators and Congressmen happen to come along and stir us up. All of us girls,
and brother Frank, are very fond of reading and like you very
much. —
    Your reader,
    Marguerite La Flesche

Dear *St. Nicholas*: I am a little Indian girl twelve years old. I go
to school at the Omaha Agency. I study geography, history,
grammar, arithmetic and spelling. I read in the Fifth Reader. I
have three older sisters and two brothers. Sometimes father,
mother and grandmother come to see us. My father was a chief
for fifteen years. My brother Frank once killed a deer, right by
our house. Some Senators and Congressmen came to see the
Omahas. They all came to our house and sang "Hold the Fort"
with us. My oldest sister played backgammon with one of the
Congressmen and beat him. — Yours truly,
    Susan La Flesche

Dear *St. Nicholas*: I am one of four Indian girls who read you
and like you very much. We live at the Agency, where we go to
school with about sixty other Indian girls and boys. Perhaps you
would like to know how we go on the hunt. Sometimes the
whole tribe go, leaving at home the folks who are too old to go.
When we were too young to go to school, father used to take
us every time they went; but when we got old enough, we used
to stay at the Omaha Mission, a boarding-school kept for the
Indian children. One year they were going out on the buffalo

hunt, and, as we were not going to school that year, father took us girls. We were so glad to go, as we had not gone for a long time. Sometimes they would travel almost all day, and I used to be so glad when they all stopped to camp, for I would get tired of riding. In a few minutes all the tents would be up, and the women would be getting dinner, while the men were out hunting. As soon as we girls were off our horses, we used to run down to the creek, or out into the woods, and get poles to make ourselves little tents. When the men came home with a lot of meat everybody was glad. As soon as the men got home they used to roast the buffalo ribs, while the women were getting the meat ready to dry. Mother used to let me have all the little pieces of meat to dry for my old grandmother, who had to stay at home. As soon as they had all the meat and skins they wanted, they would start for home.— Yours truly,

Rosalie La Flesche [7 (Sept. 1880): 918].

After the San Francisco earthquake and fire of 1906 that leveled most of the city, "The Letter-Box" printed a number of firsthand accounts of the disaster. Caroline E. Gibson's was one of the most detailed and interesting.

Dear *St. Nicholas*: You have always come to us as far back as I can remember and I enjoy reading you very much.

I was in the great San Francisco Earthquake and I thought I would try to tell you a little of my experience. I was awakened in the morning by an unearthly noise and the house shaking as a cat shakes a mouse. I jumped up as soon as I could, thinking that the end of the world had surely come. I tried to run downstairs but they were shaking so I could not. When the earthquake ceased we all ran out in the street in our nightclothes where our neighbors were, in the same apparel.

All day long false reports kept coming in from downtown and dense clouds of smoke covered up the sun.

That night we went up on Twin Peaks, where we stayed three nights. The first night the ashes fell all over us. The next two nights we were not bothered by them as we had secured an old shed, in which ten of us slept.

We took five of our chickens with us and tied strings around their legs, the ends of which were tied to a stake. We took these for food as we expected a famine. Most of our blankets, food and other things, we tied on to an old bicycle and a coaster. Each one of us girls had one blanket pinned around us and some of us had more. At the last moment my sister rushed into the house and brought out two tin cups tied around her neck.

On the hill we met a Frenchwoman who had walked about three miles wheeling a baby buggy filled with clothes. The only food she had was a few scraps tied up in her dress-skirt. She could not speak any English which made it all the harder for her. She would look at the fire, clasp her hands and say, "Ter-ri-ble! Ter-ri-ble! La! La! La! La! La! Oo! Oo!" As we look back upon it now it seems very funny.

One of my friends put on her three best dresses, one over another, as she expected her house to burn. The wild birds sang all night long on the hills because it was so light. We also took our dog and two canary birds with us. Saturday we went home as our house did not burn, the fire stopping four blocks away.

My mother who was visiting in Connecticut at the time sent for us, but we all hope to be back some day as we think there is no place like San Francisco, even if we do get shaken up some-times.

Your devoted reader,

Caroline E. Gibson (age 13) [34 (Dec. 1906): 184].

Finally, this firsthand account of the sinking of the *Titanic* was writ-ten by Ruth E. Becker. Ruth Becker Blanchard (as she became) died in 1993, one of the oldest remaining survivors of the disaster.

Bryan, Oregon

Dear *St. Nicholas*: I am a girl thirteen years of age, and have lived in India with my mother and father for ten years. My mother, brother, sister, and myself came to America, and we were passengers on the *Titanic*. My father stayed in India for another year. I am going to tell you about our journey home, and about the *Titanic* disaster.

We started from India March 7, on the steamer *City of Benares*. We had a very nice voyage to Port Said. The sea was very calm. While in the Suez Canal we saw camels and many other interesting objects. When we left Port Said, it began get-ting colder, and the sea was getting a little rougher. We went between the two islands Corsica and Sardinia to Marseilles. There, nearly everybody got off to go shopping. When we left Marseilles, we got into the Gulf of Lyons, and it was very rough there. The waves just dashed over the highest deck. When we went through the Strait of Gibraltar, we did not see the rock, because it was night.

It was rough when we were in the Bay of Biscay, too, but those were the only places. We got to London on the fifth of April, Good Friday. We never were so glad to get off anything, I think, as that boat; we had been on it twenty-nine days, almost a month. We stayed in London five days, so as to make connec-tion with the steamship *Titanic*, which was sailing the tenth of April from Southampton. During those five days, we went to the places of interest, like St. Paul's Cathedral, Zoological Gar-dens, and Westminster Abbey. We also saw the largest clock in the world, which is called "Big Ben."

On the tenth, we left London for Southampton on the train. We got on the *Titanic* about ten o'clock, and sailed at twelve.

We were thinking of getting to New York in about six or seven days, but when we got on the *Titanic*, we heard people saying that we were going to get there in about four or five days, that Captain Smith was going to make his maiden voyage a record one. We were just dazzled when we got on this lovely big boat. Our cabin was just like a hotel room, it was so big. The dining-room was beautiful, with the new linen and silver. There was an elevator, so we did not have to walk up or down. We had been on the *Titanic* for three or four days, when we found it was beginning to get bitterly cold. On Sunday, we all crowded to the inner decks especially made for winter.

On Sunday night, my mother had just gone to bed, it seemed, when she was awakened by the engines stopping; then she heard a pounding noise above our cabin. She got up and asked a steward what the matter was, but he said, "Nothing," and that she should go back to bed. She came back into the cabin; but then our own cabin steward came, and she asked him, and he said to tie on her life-belt and come, that the ship was sinking; so she awakened me, and we all put on our shoes and stockings and our coats over our night-clothes, and went to the upper deck. We heard them sending off rockets for help, and the band was playing. Soon an officer came and told us to all come and get into the life-boats. We went. My mother, brother, and sister got into one life-boat, and then they said it was all for this boat, so my mother told me to get into the next one. I got into another boat, and when they were lowering it, another one nearly came on top of us. We finally did get to the surface of the water, with much difficulty. The *Titanic* was sinking lower and lower. We could see the port lights go under one by one until there was an awful explosion of the boilers bursting, and then the ship seemed to break right in the middle, and, after a bit, go down. When it did go down, we heard terrible screams and cries from the people that were going down with the boat. We rowed for quite a while, then the oarsmen on our boat began singing songs to cheer us up. Sometimes we would think we saw a light, but it would only be a star in the horizon. It was bitterly cold, and we did not have anything on except our coats over our night-clothes. None of our family had any life-belts on at all. Suddenly, in the early morning, we saw a faint green light; it came nearer and nearer. It proved to be the light on the rescue ship *Carpathia*, which was sending off rockets to notify us that it had come to save us. We rowed as fast as we could to it, and were one of the first boats to get there. I was the first to be taken off, and a steward came and took me to the first-class dining-saloon, and gave me brandy and hot coffee; but I could not drink anything, I was so worried about my mother. After a while, though, I found her in the second-class dining-saloon, trying to find me, with my sister and brother. My, but I was glad to see her! The women were hunting for their husbands, and when they could not find them, they knew they had gone down with the *Titanic*. It was an awful sight!

Then, before we sailed for New York, they sent four life-boats afloat so that they could get any one that was drowning.

We had fog all the way to New York, and got there in the pouring rain. We went right to a hotel, and the next day we went on to Michigan.

I have taken *St. Nicholas* for a year now, and like it very much. I can hardly wait until the time for the next one to come.

Your most interested reader,

Ruth E. Becker [41 (Apr. 1914): 573–4].

8

In the Century's First Springtime: Albert Bigelow Paine and the St. Nicholas League

SUZANNE RAHN

They were, Mark Twain is said to have remarked, "either all geniuses or the worst damn little liars you ever saw"[1]— the girls and boys of the St. Nicholas League. From 1899 to 1936, the few pages devoted to the League were the most popular in *St. Nicholas*. Here, each month, were printed the best stories, poems, drawings, and photographs submitted in competition for the gold and silver badges awarded in each category. And here, for a generation of young artists and writers, were encouragement, recognition, the stimulus of seeing what their peers could do, and the ultimate thrill of publication before a highly appreciative international audience.

"The St. Nicholas League," began the original announcement, "is an organization of the readers of the *St. Nicholas* magazine.... It is to be a union of cheerful, fun-loving, industrious young people bound together by worthy aims and accomplishments, and stimulated by a wide range of competitions that offer to every member a chance of recognition and success." The League's ambitious program included "intellectual advancement," "higher ideals of life," "intelligent patriotism," and "protection of the oppressed, whether human beings, dumb animals, or birds." "'To learn more and more of the best that has been thought and done in the world'— to get closer to the heart of nature and acquire a deeper sympathy with her various forms— these are its chief aims, and the League is in favor of any worthy pursuit or pastime that is a means to this end." The League's motto was "Live to learn and learn to live," and its membership button bore the Stars and Stripes (*SN* 27 [Nov. 1899]: 80).

Albert Bigelow Paine, who initiated the League, wrote the rules, invented the competitions, and oversaw its first nine years, believed from the outset that its influence would be far-reaching. "There are many thousands of us now," he wrote in October, 1900, less than a year after the first competition, "and our work is growing better and better."

> Some of those who did not even get on the roll of honor at the start are winning prizes to-day; and some of those who are winning prizes, as well as many of those who are not, are going to be heard from by and by in the grown-up magazines and picture-galleries of the world. For the most talented and intelligent children in the world belong to the St. Nicholas League, and they, as well as their parents and teachers, appreciate the fact that, as a great competitive school, the League has no equal, and that from its classes will graduate those whose names shall not be quickly forgotten by men [27 (Oct. 1900): 1131].[2]

In fact, the roll-call of League graduates is by any standard an impressive one. Edna St. Vincent Millay, Rachel Carson, Reginald Marsh, Elinor Wylie, Ring Lardner, Stephen Vincent Benet, Rachel Field, Eudora Welty, William Faulkner, Edmund Wilson, James Daugherty, F. Scott Fitzgerald, Vita Sackville-West, and E. B. White were among those who first saw their names in print in its pages. Himself an established author, Paine was especially generous to would-be writers, sometimes offering individual criticism or even acting as literary mentor over a period of years (Gannon and Thompson 125).

Nonetheless, Paine did not envision the St. Nicholas League as a private club for this talented elite. The League was designed to embrace the entire readership of the magazine and to spread the readership as widely as possible. Members were directed to organize themselves into chapters, and chapters to recruit new members. Nor was this simply a device to increase subscriptions. As we see from the original announcement, League membership was not restricted to subscribers, but available to any reader of *St. Nicholas*. There was no membership fee, no dues of any sort; one need send only a stamped envelope to receive the League button and leaflet of rules.[3] (Even children who lost their leaflets and buttons could have them replaced at no charge.) The stated aims of the League were concerned not primarily with aesthetic goals but with the conduct of life as a whole, and could be pursued by any child. Chapters of the League, it was suggested, might "become the means of mutual advancement by discussing at the meetings the stories, poems, drawings, puzzles, etc., of the previous month's magazine," but might also "have exercises and games, and by meeting at the members' houses spend many delightful evenings" (27 [Nov. 1899]: 81).

While the League placed a high value on competition, nineteenth-century style, its aims also suggest some major cultural changes which Paine might have hoped to see in the coming century, and perhaps to further through his "graduates." In the League model of society, the highest rewards would go not to business tycoons and lumber barons, but to painters, poets, and novelists. The general level of education would be raised, as its citizens learned "more and more of the best that has been thought and done in the world." Even patriotism would be "intelligent." In this vision of an enlightened America, civilization and nature were not set in opposition. Citizens of the League were to learn from nature as well as from books, and to live in harmony with the natural world. Nineteenth-century chivalry was extended to protect animals and birds as well as human beings.

Although a separate monthly nature study feature already existed in *St. Nicholas*, Paine found an ingenious way to incorporate sympathy with nature into League competitions too. A distinct category for nature photography was inaugurated, whose stated object was "to encourage the pursuit of game with a camera instead of a gun" (27 [Jan. 1900]: 277). Gold badges and cash prizes were offered for "the best photograph of a wild animal or bird, taken in its natural home," resulting in a regular gallery of embarrassed raccoons, deer, possums, antelope, hawks, crows, and owls through the years. Later, as Yellowstone Park became popular with tourists, and Yellowstone bears and buffalo began appearing in "The League," the rules for wild animal photography were altered, to exclude animals photographed in any preserve or protected area — not because these animals were not wild, but because they could no longer be "pursued by a gun" in any case.

In the beginning, however, few expected the League to last so long. Most editors and publishers, according to Paine's "The Story of the League," believed

> that a department of this sort would interest only so long as it was a novelty, and that within a few months, or within a year, at most, it would cease to be of value.... Those who read the first poems and looked over the first drawings, said: "Yes, these are very fine, but they cannot keep it up; no set of boys and girls can continue to do such work as that. It is not humanly possible. We know children, and what they can do" [35 (Feb, 1908): 366–7].

Paine himself did not dream how successful, how famous, and how enduring the St. Nicholas League would be. Within a year after its inception, the League had several thousand members; by November, 1902, three years after its inception, there were forty thousand, fully half of whom were active competitors (30 [June 1903]: 70).

It became at once, and remained, the most popular department in the magazine. "I always turn to the League the very first thing," wrote a typical young reader, while a gold badge winner confessed in the same issue, "I always read my magazine backward, beginning invariably with the League" (28 [Dec. 1900]: 188–9). In 1901, Marie H. Whitman, writing on the subject of "My Favorite Books," voiced her enthusiasm for the League in exuberant couplets; for her, and for many children, it was "the finishing touch" of a magazine that had already given her much to enjoy:

When I was quite a little girl I read my "Brownie Book,"
And "Mother Goose" and fairytales, o'er these I'd ever look;
And then when I grew older I thought "Lady Jane" was fine;
"Lord Fauntleroy" and "Little Women" were favorites of mine.
But one merry, merry Christmas, when the snow was on the ground,
In my stocking in the morning *St. Nicholas* I found.
And then, oh, all the dear friends I found in the many pages,
Birds, beasts, and flowers, and children of all ages.
Thrilling jungle stories; "Teddy and Carrots" so jolly;
Saucy "Miss Nina Barrow," and our pretty, merry "Polly";
"Philip," the boy of ancient France; "Master Skylark" of England old;
And the wild-goose chase of the "Biddicut Boys" for the dog that was often
     sold;
"Denise" and her dear little pony; "Tom Sawyer" and merry crew;
Of all my many favorites these were only a few.
But the finishing touch was added when I saw in those columns so dear
"The St. Nicholas League for Young Folks," at the beginning of last year.
So with the very best of wishes for a long life so well begun,
Among your many readers please count me a loving one [28 (Mar. 1901):
     476].

Although its aims remained unchanged throughout its long lifespan, the League itself evolved, as Paine refined its format and responded to unforeseen contingencies. What subjects to stipulate for the various competitions, for example, was a crucial problem for him to solve. They must not seem childish or too much like the usual dull subjects assigned in school. In the initial competition of November, 1899, the subject for poetry was "The Christmas Tree," and for drawing, "The Christmas Fireplace." These may have proven too restrictive, for in succeeding months Paine's subjects became more general, though still emphasizing the coming season and its familiar holidays. Before long, he was growing inventive, in his efforts to avoid repeating the same subjects over and over. In January, 1901, for example, his set subject for verse was not "Spring" but "The Twentieth Century's First Springtime" (28 [Jan. 1901]: 285), combining the coming season with its unique place in history. In February — looking, as usual, three months ahead — the subject for verse was "A Day in the Fields" (28: 382); and in March, "When School Is Done" (28: 477).

That same month, Paine suggested "A Heading for June" as the drawing subject for the June competition. The original pictorial headings for "The St. Nicholas League" department, incorporating the League motto, had been provided by professional illustrators, but it soon became standard practice for League members to compete with each other to supply headings for each month, as an alternative to whatever other drawing subject had been set.

In his later years with the League, Paine liked to create competitions with a unifying theme. "The St. Nicholas League" for January 1907, for example, included poems set "In Days of Old" and stories and essays on "My Favorite Knight," while the May League featured "Humor" in stories, poems, drawings, and photographs. The November League that year centered entirely on horses; young artists drew horses, photographers took pictures of them, poets wrote about "A Ride," and storytellers about "A Horseback Adventure." Revering and cherishing one's heritage — a favorite theme of Paine's (35: 468) — took the form in March, 1908, of drawings and photographs of "An Heirloom," poems on "The Days of Long Ago," and prose accounts of "A Family Tradition."

In the original announcement, the gold and silver badges were simply first and second prizes. Paine had not yet conceived of a series of graduated incentives for his most talented contributors, nor of how to deal with repeated winners in a way that would reward their achievements without allowing them to monopolize the prizes. In the beginning, he had stipulated that a prize-winner could not compete again until six months had passed, but in August, 1900, he modified this rule in accordance with the suggestions of League members; henceforth, a silver badge winner need not wait six months, but could compete for a higher award without delay — either a gold badge or the cash award offered for wild animal photography (27 [Aug. 1900]: 938). Later that year, an additional award was created — "a cash prize of five dollars" — to members who had already won a gold badge and had placed first again within the year (28 [Nov. 1900]:

93). After winning their gold badge, they were designated "Honor Members" and received cash awards for entries of first-prize caliber. "The cash prize," wrote Paine, "is really in the nature of a graduation honor, and means that the one receiving it has done work worthy of regular acceptance and payment..." (28 [Oct. 1901]: 1138). Edna St. Vincent Millay won her gold badge at fourteen, published several poems as an Honor Member, and won a cash prize for "Friends," before leaving the League at eighteen. Rachel Field was one of the few graduates to proceed directly to "acceptance and payment" from *St. Nicholas*. After winning a silver badge at sixteen for her vividly descriptive essay "A Winter Walk," she re-entered the magazine as a professional at eighteen with her morality play "Everygirl" (40 [Oct. 1913]: 1115–7), and continued to publish poetry there through the 1920s before winning the Newbery Award in 1929 for *Hitty: Her First Hundred Years*.

At first, only one gold and one silver badge were awarded in each category, but by April, 1900, the quantity of first-class work was already so great that Paine was forced to allow two of each in poetry, prose, and drawing; in later years, two or three gold and silver badges were normally awarded in each category, and occasionally as many as four or five. Besides printing the prize-winners, the early "St. Nicholas League" also included a selection of what were called "Gems from Young Poets"—individual verses that Paine considered noteworthy or simply amusing. But "Gems" was not a satisfactory solution; besides favoring poetry over the other categories, it had a somewhat condescending flavor that Paine must soon have realized was out of place. Before the first year was over, he had dropped "Gems" and instead was publishing a small selection of good entries in all categories in addition to the prize-winning pieces. Simple publication in the pages of "The League" became in effect another, slightly lower rung on the prize ladder.

Even the Roll of Honor had to be reconceived to accommodate the swift expansion and burgeoning talent of the League. Beginning as a short list "of those whose work, though not used, has been found worthy of honorable notice" (27 [Jan. 1900]: 276), the rapidly lengthening Roll was soon divided into a list "of those whose work would have been used had space permitted" and a considerably longer list "of those whose work entitles them to encouragement." Young competitors were, needless to say, acutely conscious of the difference. As fifteen-year-old Alice M. Macrae graphically expressed it,

There's a Ladder of Ambition in a far-off happy land,
Where merry children gather, climbing upward, hand in hand.

It is not hard to find it if you have the magic key,
A round and shining button with the badge of liberty;
But the only way to climb it is to work with might and main,
And to never be discouraged, but to try and try again;
And you'll very soon discover that the first step toward the goal
Is the very, very bottom of the second Honor Roll! [35 (Oct. 1908):1142].

"The St. Nicholas League" also included a list of new chapters as they were founded, plus a few interesting letters from individual members. Last of all came the announcement of a new competition, with a reiteration of the basic rules. These rules were simple and practical: drawings were to be done in black ink on white, unruled paper; each contribution must bear the name, age, and address of its contributor; each must be endorsed as original work by an adult, and so on.[4] Yet through carelessness or confusion, children not infrequently managed to disqualify themselves. At intervals, Paine was forced to point out once again the importance of following instructions:

"A very good puzzle," the editor said,
Then softly sighed when the page was read.
"Why, it isn't indorsed [sic], and so, alas,
I'm sorry we'll have to let it pass."
"An excellent poem!" the editor cried,
But the "excellent poem" was laid aside;
For the poet in haste had left her age
And even her name from the dainty page.
"This story is fine! but — the same old song —
'Tis at least a hundred words too long!
This capital drawing in dull-brown ink,
We'll have to lay it aside, I think."
And so it went on till the tale was done,
And the editor said: "There are thirty-one
With never a chance to win, indeed,
Because to our rules they gave no heed" [27 (Aug. 1900): 938].

And there was room for misunderstanding even in Paine's simple rules. In June, 1901, he needed to clarify how many entries each competitor could submit — only one per month, and in only one category, "for if we allowed one of each kind the number received would be so many we could not examine them, and the quality would not be so good.... Others ask if they are obliged to contribute every month. No, certainly not.

League members should enter only such competitions as really appeal to them, and should only contribute when they mean to do careful, earnest work… (28 [June 1901]: 754).

In August, that same year, the worrisome question of rats had to be dealt with:

> Rodney C. Jones wants to know if pictures of rats may be entered in the wild- animal photograph competition. On the whole, we think not. The purpose is to encourage the pursuit of game with a camera instead of a gun, and while rats are game, in one sense, their preservation is hardly to be desired…. In this connection we may say that a Cuban reader has written to ask if the photograph of a Spanish flea would be admissible. He assures us that the said flea is sufficiently wild, and that it appears to have found its "natural home" at a certain point on his left shoulder-blade, where it is impossible to reach him in the ordinary manner. The reader is willing to pursue him with a camera instead of a gun, if the League will make the induce-ment sufficient…. We are sorry, but this flea's photograph can-not compete, either. The flea and the fly — the mouse and the mosquito — the rat and the rattlesnake: they were made for something, no doubt, but we do not believe that it was to be photographed — at least, not for the League department [28 (Aug. 1901): 956].

Even carelessness was organized, beginning in August of 1908. A monthly Roll of the Reckless (later Roll of the Careless) was placed after the Roll of Honor, listing in distinct categories the names of those whose contributions were late, not endorsed, failed to include the age of the competitor, failed to include the competitor's address, were written on both sides of the paper, were in pencil, or had addressed the wrong subject altogether. This device not only served to embarrass and educate the careless ones, but to serve as a continuing reminder to all would-be competitors as well.

The potentially most troubling question, of course, was that of "originality." In any competition on such a scale, and with such strong incentives to win, occasional instances of plagiarism are bound to occur; in addition, children are sometimes genuinely uncertain whether their work is "original" or not. Paine was willing to give the benefit of the doubt, but he did not take deliberate plagiarism lightly. In November 1900, he delivered his first editorial pronouncement on the subject:

> It is to be regretted that now and then some one has sent work that was not original. The rules are very clear on this and other points, and if read carefully cannot be misunderstood. It is hardly possible to believe that any child would wish to deceive,

or, if so, would expect to escape the unpleasant results that are sure to follow. It is not difficult to mislead trusting parents and secure their indorsement [sic], nor is it hard to deceive the editors, who could not possibly read and remember all that has been written in the world, and are used to unusual and even startling excellence in the work of children; but it is utterly impossible to deceive the thousands of League members and readers who stand in judgment each month upon the contributions of their fellow-workers. The single instance of this sort (referred to on another page) was immediately brought to our attention by people in all parts of the world. Let us hope that every child, whether talented or not, will at least begin his or her work industriously, perseveringly, and, above all, honestly [28 (Nov. 1900): 82–3].

This guilty competitor not only failed to receive the gold badge originally awarded (for Longfellow's "Twilight"), but was actually expelled from the League (84).

Wisely, Paine did not put the responsibility for detecting plagiarism on the parents and teachers who endorsed the entries, nor on himself and the other judges, but suggested that the St. Nicholas League would effectively police itself. His confidence seems to have been justified. He reported that a plagiarized drawing had once more been detected "by a number of readers" and added, "this is only another example of how utterly impossible it is to escape the detection of a copied work" (28 [Apr. 1901]: 562–3). Periodically, other such cases would surface, and elicit a short, stern lecture in which the plagiarized work was identified by name.

Judging from their letters, young people hated to "graduate" from the League. Seventeen-year-old Elizabeth M. Dukes expresses a common sentiment in "The Salute":

Yes, dear St. Nick, you have been good to me:
The LEAGUE and I have tramped the way six years,
Till now we reach the end, — my journey's end, —
But not the end of my regretful tears.
"Depart, eighteen, depart!" the bugles call;
You've sown the seed — go now and pluck the fruit.
And while your last "taps" echo your farewell,
In loving gratitude stand silent, yes— stand at salute! [47 (July 1920): 854].

More than one eighteen-year-old asked wistfully if *St. Nicholas* could sponsor a competition for them as well, but Paine was adamant. His response was invariably that "graduates" should move on to the careers for which their great competitive school had prepared them.

> Dear young friend! The pages of *St. Nicholas* and those of every
> other publication are always open to competitions for those have
> passed the League age limit. Every editor in the land con-
> ducts at least one competition every working day in the year.
> These are open to all, and from them he fills his pages, reward-
> ing the winners according to their deserts. The world itself is
> one great competition, and when you have passed the League
> age limit, and won all the League prizes, you have far more
> chance of success in this greater field than in any single contest
> which the League editor might devise. Have no fear! The world
> is your inheritance. Do not stand trembling at the door, but
> enter, and with a brave heart and a firm hand resolutely claim
> your own! [30 (Nov. 1902): 80].

Paine's cheery confidence was upheld not only by his own unswerv-
ing faith in "the most talented and intelligent children in the world," but
by an immediate acceptance and validation of the League by the outside
world which surprised even him. As he later wrote:

> We expected the League would be a success, but we hardly
> thought it would at once become a great educational factor with
> a support so wide and so eminent as it immediately received.
> Wherever in any part of the earth there are English readers the
> St. Nicholas League has members; and in every school and col-
> lege where English is read and taught, instructors have watched
> its growth and in many cases made its work a part of their class
> study. Art teachers everywhere have encouraged their pupils to
> compare the League drawings and to enter the competitions.
> One of the foremost illustrators in the world has written to say
> that he wishes he might have had a St. Nicholas League in the
> days of his early beginnings [30 (May 1903): 656].

This illustrator may well have been Howard Pyle, who had already
written to Paine of his interest in the League — a glowing letter that Paine
shared with all the Leaguers in December, 1901. As a teenager, Pyle had
first published his own work in *St. Nicholas*; now, at the height of his fame
as artist, illustrator, author, and founder of the most important school for
illustration in America, he perused the pages of "The St. Nicholas League"
as eagerly as though he were a young competitor himself:

> I never fail, when the *St. Nicholas* enters the house, to turn to
> the leaves of the League and to look at the pictures that embell-
> ish it, wondering as to who are the boys and the girls who draw
> them, what they are like, what their homes are like, what are
> their ambitions, their desires, their aims in life. Who knows
> but that some great future artist, who is destined, after a while,
> to reach high-pinnacled altitudes, is here essaying his first
> unfledged effort at flight? Who knows but that some future man

of might may sometime look back to the very page of the magazine which I hold open in my hand, and may see in it his first young work that won the glory of his first young prize in life! [29 (Dec. 1901): 178].

Such sentiments confirmed Paine's own dearest hopes for the League; it is clear from his editorial remarks that his ultimate aim in devising and judging competitions was not to encourage youthful imagination or self-expression, but to develop the talents of serious would-be professionals. While his initial suggestions in the League "Announcement" are such as any schoolteacher might give — "Write and draw what you see and know. Do it well and simply. If you fail the first time, try again.... Careful work and perseverance mean success" (27 [Nov. 1899]: 81–2) — by March, he was pointing out that professional artists and writers have to write on one side of the paper too (27 [Mar. 1900]: 461). "Following the rules" was not a matter of obedience to one's elders, but of accepting a professional standard. By 1904, he was able to point to a number of successful "graduates": "We know of a dozen or more — some of them illustrating for papers, magazines, advertising firms, etc., some of them writing stories, poems, articles, and what not" (31 [Apr. 1904]: 560), and by 1908 he could claim that "there is hardly a month goes by that our foremost magazines do not contain something from old members of the League" (36 [Nov. 1908: 80). That February, he wrote a retrospective article, "The Story of the League," in which he fondly boasted not only that the names of his "graduates" "may be found to-day in the Table of Contents of many a grown-up magazine," but that many of the poems and sketches published in "The League" itself had been "clipped and reprinted, and gone the newspaper rounds, not always as the work of children, but as work that was worthy of being read and re-read for its own merit" (35 [Feb. 1908]: 36). Paine's most frequent advice to competitors emphasized the value of studying and analyzing published work — as professional artists and writers do:

> The League is a school of comparative study, and the surest advancement is made in comparing one's own efforts with the work of others — learning by thoughtful study of the successful contributions the faults of our own and the reason of another's success. League members who have graduated into the professional fields have been almost unanimous in declaring that their greatest progress has been made in studying and comparing the published contributions [33 (Nov. 1905): 80].

But artistic merit, Paine warned his "students," is not the only basis for selection. Professionals must consider the particular audience and periodical they are aiming for. By 1907, Paine was stressing — which he had not done initially — that whatever was published in the "League" must be suitable for the general readership of *St. Nicholas*.

> A poem or a story may be ever so good from the technical and artistic point of view and yet not be adapted to every publication. In fact it may be adapted to a very few publications. The League department, for instance, being a part of the *St. Nicholas* Magazine, must be made suitable to *St. Nicholas* readers as well as to its contributors, for there are a vast number of readers who enjoy the League who do not even belong to it, but read it and look at the pictures just as they would find pleasure in any other part of the magazine. Very sad, very tragic, very romantic and very abstruse work cannot often be used, no matter how good it may be from the literary point of view, and while the League editor certainly does not advocate the sacrifice of artistic impulse to market suitability, he does advocate as a part of every literary education the study of the market's needs whereby one may learn to offer this or that particular manuscript to just the periodical most likely to give it welcome. And the beginning of this education may be acquired by considering the requirements of the St. Nicholas League [34 (Mar. 1907): 464].

Paine made young artists aware that even the shape and size of drawings and photographs might add to or detract from their professional success, pointing out that "a drawing stands a better chance of acceptance if it is made into a shape that fits into the general plan of a page. For instance, a heading should be at least twice as wide as it is high, and if it is three times as wide as it is high, all the better.... Concerning photographs, all things being equal, an upright photograph has the better chance.... These are just hints, and may explain why some otherwise good photographs have been put reluctantly aside, because we could use only a very few in the more awkward shapes and sizes" (35 [Sept. 1908]: 1040).

Paine's own history helps explain his pragmatic approach. Though a reader in a family of readers, he had little formal education — a one-room prairie schoolhouse and four winters of a local "academy" — and by his own account, "never dreamed of becoming an author as a boy" (Kunitz and Haycraft 1067). In his late teens, he began sending poems to "family papers" with occasional success; later, after some years in the photographic supply business, he turned to prose, placed some pieces in *Harper's Weekly*, and at thirty-three moved to New York, where he embarked upon a career as a freelance writer and editor. Here he showed himself willing to put his hand to anything. With some other writers, he started a new family paper; when the paper expired with its third issue, he used the experience in a book called *The Bread Line* — which led to a commission to write Thomas

"A HEADING FOR AUGUST."   BY SCOFIELD HANDFORTH,
AGE 17.   (GOLD BADGE.   SILVER BADGE
WON JUNE, 1913.)

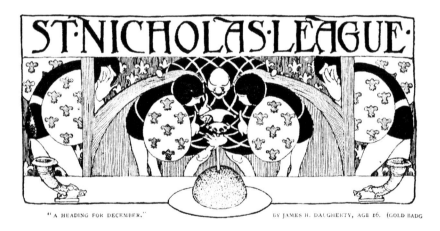

"A HEADING FOR DECEMBER."   BY JAMES H. DAUGHERTY, AGE 16.   (GOLD BADG

The young artists nurtured by the St. Nicholas League included two future winners of the Caldecott and Newbery Awards, Thomas Handforth and James Daugherty — clearly inspired, as teenagers, by the fashionable style of Art Nouveau.

Nast's biography. Of his forty-odd novels, biographies, volumes of short stories, and children's books, none has survived. In *Twentieth-Century Authors*, Stanley J. Kunitz and Howard Haycraft dismiss his magnum opus — the biography of Mark Twain — as "gossipy and uncritical," adding that "there is a touch of condescension in all his work" (1068). A writer without genius and only moderate talent, Paine owed his success to his knowledge of the marketplace, and his ability to seize whatever opportunities it offered. His practical advice to League members was based on realities he had experienced himself.

Even without this advice, of course, most young contributors would have done their best to give Paine what they thought he wanted. Consciously or not, children are aware that they must please adults to prosper, and all have gained some expertise before they reach their teens. E. B. White sardonically recalled how a young friend's suggestion boosted him up the League prize-ladder as a child, advising him to put "plenty" of kindness to animals in his entries. The result? "I won both the silver and the gold badge, and was honorably mentioned several times" (228). While White's fondness for animals was more genuine than he lets on here—some years before he found himself writing a book called *Charlotte's Web*—we can assume that his experience was not uncommon. The rules and subjects of the League competitions set certain parameters of content and form within which young artists and writers were required to work. More subtle guidelines were absorbed through their study and emulation of the prize-winners and other published pieces. Inevitably, Paine's personal preferences in art and literature, as well as his notion of what was suitable for *St. Nicholas*, shaped and limited what was produced by the League.

From the beginning, and explicitly, Paine stressed the value of simplicity and clarity of expression in both writing and drawing. He explained why some talented writers were failing to win prizes:

> [I]nstead of telling their story in short words, simply and directly, as they would talk, they adopt the style of some rather grandiloquent writer, and weaken with long words and flowery sentences the pretty thought that could be expressed so attractively in four hundred short Anglo-Saxon words, divided into brief, crisp sentences. The young poets should think this over, too; and as for the artists, there are a few very talented young people who make such fine marks, and so many of them, and put them so close together, that when the drawing is reduced for publication all the strength and detail and beauty they have labored so hard to obtain are tangled and muddled and lost. Keep your work free and open and strong. [26 (Mar. 1899): 461].

His 1907 editorial on "market suitability" states bluntly that "very sad, very tragic, very romantic and very abstruse work cannot often be used" in *St. Nicholas*. To put it in positive terms, work which was cheerful in tone and outcome, realistic rather than "romantic," and not too hard to understand had a much better chance of publication.

Just what Paine meant by "romantic" and why he discouraged it is the main point of his instructive short story, "Marjorie's School of Fiction," published in *St. Nicholas* in February, 1903, and subtitled "A Story for Young Authors." Its heroine, a talented high-school graduate, is planning her first novel:

> The quaint phraseology of the romantic school attracted her. Already she had done something in that line — a seventeenth-century bit that held class and teachers breathless with the spell of its old-world charm. She had never been abroad, — they had been too poor for that, — but the artist in her had created an atmosphere which had been compared to that of Scott ... [30 (Feb. 1903): 438].

To Marjorie, this kind of novel is "real literature," while "stories of no particular school ... just stories of things that happened, or might have happened, or couldn't have happened, as the case might be" are not (438). As she works away on her Scott-like historical novel, *The Auburn Queen*, she notices with some anxiety that "the book-stalls were simply overflowing with books of every period but our own," but believes that her novel will still stand out above the many others with seventeenth-century settings (438). Of course, *The Auburn Queen* is rejected, and when her father dies, leaving her to support the family, she is forced to get a job, first in a department store, and then, more congenially, as cook for a well-to-do household. ("I have yet to find the woman writer who is not a supremely good cook," Paine comments [440].) In her spare time, Marjorie begins to write — and to publish — little stories based on her real-life experiences as a salesgirl. As the story closes, she is about to see her first book in print, a collection of "quaint people and phases— some humorous, some pathetic, the whole woven into a wonderful march of real life, — with its joys, its sorrows, and its rewards"— a book which belongs to "the school of experience" (444).

"Romantic," then, was the term Paine used to describe stories set in the past rather than the present, written in an elaborate style full of "quaint phraseology," and based on literary models such as Scott and Dumas rather than on personal experience. Such novels were common at the turn of the century, and many were as bad as Paine suggests, with dialogue in a pseudo-Shakespearian style (based on Scott's), cardboard characters, and no sense of historical reality.[5] Paine kept "The League" Scott-free of this kind of writing. Although he encouraged an interest in history, his subjects were such as to elicit essays rather than fiction —"My Favorite Character in History," "A Family Tradition," "My Favorite Episode from French History," and so forth. Indeed, nonfiction was generally more prevalent than fiction in "The League." Even when subjects with strong fictional possibilities like "A Discovery" or "A Horseback Adventure" were assigned, the published pieces would consist mainly of essays, retold episodes from history, and real-life experiences rather than stories, suggesting that young writers who wrote about what they knew rather than what they imagined were likelier to see their work in print. Paine's preference for "short Anglo-Saxon words" and "brief, crisp sentences" rather than "long words and flowery sentences," even in descriptive pieces and poetry, is also reflected in the published selections; in this, he looks forward to twentieth-century tastes.

Other preferences, stated or not, must have grown equally clear to young contributors. While a certain degree of religious feeling was permitted in one's creative work, religiosity was not; *St. Nicholas* was not a religious magazine, and had no place for sermons or retellings of Bible stories. Sympathy with nature, on the other hand, was one of the aims of the League, and was often mingled with a sense of awe or gratitude toward the Creator. Countless subjects for verse, prose, and drawing like "The Song of the Woods," "The Fields of Summer-Time," "The Harvest," "A Winter Walk," and "First Signs of Spring" called for an observant, even rapturous appreciation of natural beauty. Animals were to be enjoyed for their grace or charm, and photographed, not shot; though members recounted some scary experiences with bears, one common type of real-life narrative that never appeared in "The League" was the hunting story. Indeed, any type of graphic violence was taboo. The gore and gruesomeness that boys of a certain age often revel in must have found its way into some submissions, but never into "The League" itself. War as such was not glorified either, though military heroism might be. Paine encouraged "intelligent" patriotism by assigning such subjects as "My Favorite Character in History," "In the Days of George Washington," and "My Country," and awarding prizes to thoughtful, knowledgeable, nonpartisan essays. Cynicism toward one's country — or indeed, toward anything — was nonexistent. An unquestioned idealism pervaded the pages of "The League," as it did *St. Nicholas*.

While Paine favored certain attitudes and approaches, he was receptive to a fairly wide range of creative work. The idealism of the League did not rule out humor; funny stories, poems, drawings, and photographs could be found regularly in its pages. Most set subjects could be treated in a variety of ways, and Paine clearly delighted in an ingenious or unexpected interpretation. Fantasy and historical fiction were uncommon, but not out of bounds. Occasionally, Paine would even indulge his frustrated romantics with a subject such as "The Land of Romance" or "Chivalry," or an entire competition on fairies. He was strict about rhyme and rhythm in poetry (sometimes editorializing on the importance of exact rhymes), but allowed young poets to choose whatever form they liked, including blank verse and the unrhymed hexameters made famous by Longfellow in "Evangeline."

Graphic artists were given the most freedom. Paine accepted drawings in any existing style, as long as it could be effectively reproduced. He encouraged sketching from life, but usually set subjects in very general terms—"A Bit of Nature" or "Drawn from Life"—which allowed competitors to choose what they wished to draw. Imagination, invention, and romance were allowed free play in the "Headings" for various months. Here we can see young artists pursuing their own inclinations with little restriction; "A Heading for December" might embody a detailed sketch of trees in winter, a fashionable young girl in furs, a pattern of fanciful, stylized figures a la Maxfield Parrish, or medieval children bearing a boar's head. Those young artists who only want to draw one kind of thing—fashion plates or horses or cartoons or full-rigged sailing ships—could create headings to fit their specialties, and Paine let them do it. At a time when art classes might consist of drawing only pre-arranged still lifes or plaster casts of Greek sculptures in correct perspective, this creative freedom must have been especially welcome.

Some young competitors may have hoped to win a prize by (perhaps quite sincere) flattery—not of Paine, who kept himself discreetly in the background, but of *St. Nicholas* and the League. If the set subject for drawing was "A Winter Pastime," why not draw a child reading *St. Nicholas*? If the set subject for poetry was "Ambition," why not express one's ambition to win a gold badge? "My Favorite Book"? *St. Nicholas*! "A Book That Has Helped Me"? *St. Nicholas* again! Paine published a certain number of these tributes over the years, but he was canny enough to see the danger. A tribute might be printed in "The League," but the chances of its actually winning an award were vanishingly small.

At the end of 1908, Paine himself was forced to "graduate" from the St. Nicholas League, needing all his energies for the biography of Mark Twain. "And now, at last, the League editor himself is to be among those who go," he wrote in his last editorial. "He began with the League at its beginning, and in sympathy and spirit he will remain with it, come what may. But the active labor will hereafter be performed by another hand, trained and capable, whose owner will be one in full sympathy with the ambitions and the efforts of youth, with time and talent and energy for the place" (35 [Dec. 1908]: 117). And in "A League Good-by," he looked back with nostalgia over the last nine years:

> How long ago, a little group, we gathered
> To weave our stories and to build our rhymes!

How tenderly the vagrant muse we tethered
Through winter eves and drowsy summer-times....
Adieu, adieu, companions of the morning,
My pathway faces to the sloping sun;
The shadows longer grow — I heed the warning,
And trim my fires ere nightfall has begun [176].

His "trained and capable" successor was none other than William
Fayal Clarke, now editor of *St. Nicholas*. In the letter to E. B. White included
later in this section, Clarke describes how he had originally encouraged
Paine to found the League, and how when Paine had to relinquish it, "the
League had grown so dear to me — in fact, my hobby then and ever after,
that I could not consign it to any other hand." Somehow, until he retired
as editor in 1927, Clarke found the time to run the League as well as the
magazine. Sensibly, he introduced no great changes, and most would notice
no difference between Paine's League and his. The format of "The League"
is nearly the same, the quality of contributions is as high, and the set subjects are at least as interesting. Clarke was especially good at inventing
subjects for photography which would stimulate rather than confine the
visual imagination — "Come Along," for example, "Uphill/Downhill,"
"Around the Curve," or "A Flying Start." His major innovation was introduced in 1910. Henceforth, a competitor's first award must be the silver
badge; only after winning the silver, could one progress to the gold (37
[Mar. 1910]: 468). This, he felt, created a more logical system of incentives. He also began cutting down on League letters and news of chapters
in the first months of editorship, and eventually — perhaps simply to save
more space for creative work — did away with them altogether. The last tally
of "New League Chapters" appeared in October that year (37: 1147) — at
which point, 1,159 chapters had been recorded — and the last League letters the following spring (38 [Apr. 1911]: 568).

Clarke's editorials differed, too — not what they said, but what they
tended not to say. Typically, Clarke would comment on the excellence of
the contributions, and on which category had produced the largest number of fine entries. "Last month the young artists of the League seemed to
be slightly in the van of their fellow-workers; but this month the contributions in the Photography competition appear to set the standard for
quality of merit" — and so forth (37 [Mar. 1910]: 468). Paine also used to
make such comparisons, as though the various categories of artists were
competing teams in some perpetual Parnassian tournament. But Clarke
never dwelt, as Paine often did, on the future careers of these young artists,
or on the number of "graduates" who had established themselves as pro-

"A HEADING." BY HESTER MARGETSON, AGE 16. (CASH PRIZE.)

The St. Nicholas League offered talented girls a rare opportunity to compete with boys on equal terms. But what became of Hester Margetson and Lucy Mackenzie when they "graduated" at eighteen? *SN* 3 (Mar. 1907): 464 and *SN* 30.7 (May 1903): 656.

fessionals. Competition had become, in effect, an end in itself — or a means of building character — rather than a means of achieving the goal of professionalism. Yet if Clarke failed to see that goal, or did not care about it as Paine had, by 1909 this probably did not matter much. The success stories of the League had become common knowledge.

If we ask what made the St. Nicholas League so outstanding of its kind — so popular with young people, so successful at nurturing future talent, so durable that it was still going strong decades later, when *St. Nicholas* itself finally went under — we must conclude that Paine's nine years of editorship not only got the League off the ground and flying, but provided its momentum for a generation to come. The intelligence with which he conceived its structure and allowed it to evolve was crucial; equally so was his attitude toward its members.

St. Nicholas had sponsored a series of essay contests in the 1880s, and even experimented with a "Young Contributors' Department" in the 1870s, but neither of these lasted long, or was allowed to develop beyond an occasional page or two. The "Young Contributor's Department" generally consisted of only three or four lengthy pieces; there were no set subjects, no specific criteria, no element of competition — in short, no possibility of using it to train oneself as an artist or writer. Mary Mapes Dodge also had strong feelings on the undesirability of exposing children to fame and publicity, and the Young Contributors were identified only by their initials (see, for example, 3 [Oct. 1876]: 803–4).[6] Paine saw the Leaguers from an entirely different perspective; for him, these were not children to be sheltered, but artists of the dawning century, and ripe for initiation. He vividly remembered his own epiphany at fourteen. As he recounts it in "A Boy of Fifty Years Ago," he had chanced upon an engraving of the Venus de Milo in a volume of *St. Nicholas,* and read the eloquent description which accompanied it.

> When I awoke I was in a different world, in a world that has a light of its own, and different skies; a world where the ideal becomes the real, where dreams come true. I read that article again and again. It became a part of me. I did not know it then, but the marble figure it described had become to me a sort of touchstone of harmony that would influence me through all the years ahead.... In a sense, and in a very real sense, that article and the statue it described have led me whatever distance I may have traveled in the world of creative effort.... There has never been a time since I was grown that I have not had a copy of the Venus in my study; and consciously or otherwise, I have compared with it every other work of art. *St. Nicholas* has done many things for many readers, but for none has it ever done more than for the small-town country boy of fifty years ago who became me [51 (Apr. 1924): 634].[7]

Despite his own mediocrity, Paine believed in great art. He knew that a fourteen-year-old can perceive its power, and that it can change his life. The "touch of condescension" which Kunitz and Haycraft see in his writing is markedly absent from "The St. Nicholas League." Paine did not condescend to the Leaguers, because he respected them for what they were and for what they would become. His faith in "the most talented and intelligent children in the world" was real, and his editorials did not hesitate to tell them so. Other aspects of the League seem to reflect this attitude. If the structure of competitions and awards was meticulously worked out on the national level, the local level of individual chapters was left entirely in the hands of their members. Few suggestions were offered as to how chapters should be organized, or what they might do; more remarkably, no adult supervision or even presence was presumed necessary. (An incidental benefit of this "hands off" policy was that when chapter activity declined in later years—due partly, perhaps, to competition from such fashionable new youth groups as the Boy Scouts and the Camp Fire Girls—the national organization was unaffected.) Paine's reliance on Leaguers rather than adults to report instances of plagiarism is another instance of his encouraging the young to take charge.

As we have seen, Paine himself gave his "students" minimal guidance on how to produce a prize-winning entry, except to stress repeatedly that failing to follow the rules would disqualify it. Instead, he advised contributors to study the prize-winners, to figure out for themselves what made a poem or a sketch outstanding, and then to incorporate these qualities into their own work. This was wise from Paine's point of view—commenting in detail on winning entries would have been a lot of trouble, and would have forced him to assume an expertise in the visual arts which he did not have—but it also implied that young people possessed their own power of analysis and self-criticism, and did not need adults to tell them how to improve their work.

Finally, and most importantly, Paine treated his "students" not as schoolchildren, but as would-be professionals on the edge of the adult world. Again and again, he reiterated his conviction that "some of those who are winning prizes ... are going to be heard from by and by" (27 [Oct. 1900]: 113). He gave competitors professionally oriented advice, and encouraged them to try their wings after "graduation" in the open competition of the marketplace. To children, nothing is more appreciated than being treated with such respect as Paine gave them, and nothing thrills them more than the prospect of taking their place among adults. Every aspect of the St. Nicholas League combined to nurture what we would now call the self-esteem of its members; yet at the same time, its promises rested on a foundation of reality. Working over a period of years through the process Paine had created—meeting deadlines and specifications, experiencing rejection, studying editorial preferences, analyzing published

This illustration of the Venus de Milo, from an early volume of *St. Nicholas*, greatly impressed the young Albert Bigelow Paine. *SN* 8 (March 1881): 399.

work, analyzing and regularly submitting their own — all this actually did prepare young artists for the conditions of the marketplace and increase their chances of success.

And yet Paine's editorship was only half the story; the other half was *St. Nicholas* itself. By 1899, *St. Nicholas* had a prestige equaled by no other children's magazine before or since. To be published in *St. Nicholas* meant far more than to be published in any children's magazine today. The possibility of displaying one's best creative work in an international forum of such stature would have been enough to motivate the most talented young artists and writers in America, without the added incentives of gold and silver badges. Although the League and its competitions were imitated by other magazines and newspapers in the early years of the century, no other magazine for young people could offer them such a degree of fame — while no publication for adults could have accorded them such importance, or presented them to so large and appreciative an audience of their peers.[8]

That *St. Nicholas* provided a safe haven from the prejudice and active discouragement that many of these young artists— particularly the girls— would have met at home, at school, and even professionally may not have been of negligible importance either. When we pay attention to what Paine does *not* say, we find his editorials free from the slightest suggestion that girls are less talented or less career-oriented than boys— or indeed, different from them in any respect. Girls' achievements in the League are certainly as numerous, and in every category. Recent immigrants, who had to contend with so many barriers elsewhere, are also accepted without question here; among the names of members and prize-winners are many of Italian, Eastern European, Armenian, and Jewish origin — even a few from Japan. All citizens were truly equal in the League's version of America.

Today, the young contributors' department has become a standard feature of children's magazines—*Cricket* Magazine's is even called "The Cricket League"—but no one thinks of it as a "great competitive school," nurturing the next generation of artists and furthering the "intellectual advancement" of a nation. No children's magazine today has the influence that *St. Nicholas* could claim in a more literate culture, or the age range of eight to eighteen in which to train a "student" to the level of professionalism. And yet, as an organization designed to encourage young talent in the arts whose long-term success remains unparalleled, the St. Nicholas League surely deserves close study. Here, we can say, is how it worked a hundred years ago. Thus it was designed, and these are the qualities that made Albert Bigelow Paine its first, best editor. Here was the national stature that such an organization would need, then or now. And here are the creative talent, the ambition, the enthusiasm, the idealism of the young — reborn in every generation and awaiting only their chance to flower. For as ten-year-old Gwendolen Gray Perry wrote in "The First Springtime of the Twentieth Century:"

Welcome to the springtime of nineteen hundred one!
In the hundred years before us we expect great things to be.
The years will change, and every year new marvels will be done;
But springtime always is the same, O twentieth century! [28 (Apr. 1901): 563].

Notes

1. Among the working notes for Spencer Mapes's projected biography of Mary Mapes Dodge is the transcript of notes from an interview with William Fayal Clarke and his wife conducted on December 8, 1935, during which Clarke recalled this comment by Mark Twain. The notes can be found in the Donald and Robert M. Dodge Collection of Mary Mapes Dodge, Box I 1, Folder 35, in Firestone Library at Princeton University.

2. All quotations by Paine, unless otherwise noted, are from his editorials in "The St. Nicholas League."

3. Children living in foreign countries did not even need to stamp their self-

addressed envelopes—which, of course, would have made it impossible for them to join. Paine assured them that "the League will gladly pay postage on their badges and leaflets for the honor of having representatives in so many different parts of the world" (28 [Apr. 1901]: 570). Such members were also given a five-day extension on competition deadlines.

4. In 1904, the rules for the drawing competitions were extended to allow black-and-white "wash" (watercolor) as well as ink; from December 1907 onward, entries in colored "wash" were allowed too, even though these did not reproduce as well in the magazine. These changes reflect trends in contemporary illustration at the professional level — the shift from engravings to halftone illustrations at the end of the century, and the increasing use of color reproduction.

5. For the subsequent history of the "quaint phraseology" Paine complains of, see my "'It Would Be Awful Not to Know Greek': Rediscovering Geoffrey Trease" in *The Lion and the Unicorn* (14 1: 23–52).

6. Dodge announced the "Young Contributor's Department" in her "Jack-in-the-Pulpit" for December, 1875: "Jack has news for you! A little bird tells him that Deacon Green thinks there ought to be a "Young Contributor's" department to *St. Nicholas*, and that it will not do the children one bit of harm, provided the vanity of unfledged authors is not fed by printing their names" (3 [Dec. 1875]: 130). "Jack" and "Deacon Green" were both, of course, personae of Dodge herself, and her lingering uneasiness over the prospect is reflected in the tone of the announcement. The first "Young Contributor's Department" appeared the following month.

7. The article was "Venus of Milo" by M. D. Ruff and appeared in 2 (Nov. 1874): 47–9. The engraving which so transfixed young Paine was less than six inches tall.

8. One of the magazines which sponsored competitions for children in the early twentieth century was *The Woman's Home Companion*. E. B. White won a prize from it at the age of nine, for a poem about a mouse; as his essay on "The St. Nicholas League" makes clear, however, it was the League that represented the "Big Time" to him as a child.

9

Onward and Upward with the Arts: The St. Nicholas League

E. B. WHITE

December, 1934

There is no doubt about it, the fierce desire to write and paint that burns in our land today, the incredible amount of writing and painting that still goes on in the face of heavy odds, are directly traceable to the *St. Nicholas Magazine*. In the back pages of that wholesome periodical, in the early days of the century, there flourished a group of minors known as the St. Nicholas League. The members wrote poems and prose, took snapshots with box cameras, drew pictures at random, and solved puzzles. They submitted the results of their fervor to the League, and the lucky ones pocketed the Gold or Silver Badge of extreme merit.

A surprising number of these tiny geniuses are still at it today, banging away with pen or brush for dear life. A hardy and sentimental old League alumnus like myself comes across their names in odd places—in the fall book list, in the classified phone directory, or among a bunch of Pulitzer Prize winners—and thinks back to that "union of cheerful, fun-loving industrious young people, bound together by worthy aims and accomplishments and stimulated by a wide range of competitions that offer to every member a chance of recognition and success." We were an industrious and fiendishly competitive band of tots; and if some of us, in the intervening years of careless loving, have lost or mislaid our silver badge, we still remember the day it came in the mail: the intensity of victory, the sweetness of young fame, a pubescent moment immortalized by one of our League members in October of 1904, a lad named Robert E. Jones, who wrote to the editor, from Milton, N.H.:

> Dear St. Nicholas: My badge came last night and I am more than delighted with it. I shall always keep it, and shall always look back with pleasure to the time "when my first picture was printed." I mean to work hard this summer all by myself, and shall send in more drawings, even better, I hope, than the one which was printed. Thanking you again for the beautiful badge, I remain, Most gratefully yours, Robert E. Jones.

Incidentally, the hope expressed in Robert's letter was fulfilled. He did work hard. Late that same year he was crowned with the badge of pure gold and became an Honor Member. They say he is even now doing the same high grade of work in the field of stage design.

Occasionally a writer or artist, in a fit of biographical confession, jokingly admits to his public that he once won a badge from the St, Nicholas League. His jocosity is to hide his emotion. Nothing has ever taken the place of the League in his life. The Pulitzer Prize was a pleasant reward to Edna St. Vincent Millay, I have no doubt; but it was faint fun compared to her conquest in 1907 when, as E. *Vincent* Millay, 15, of Camden, Me., she opened her August number of *St. Nicholas* and found, "accepted for publication," her poem beginning "Shine on me, oh, you gold, gold sun." This poem was called "Vacation Song." Here are the first and last stanzas:

> Shine on me, oh, you gold, gold sun,
> Smile on me, oh, you blue, blue skies,
> Sing birds! And rouse the lazy breeze
> That in the shadow, sleeping lies,
> Calling, "Awaken! Slothful one
> And chase the yellow butterflies."
>
> Oh, mower! All the world's at play, —
> Leave on the grass your sickle bright;
> Come, and we'll dance a merry step
> With the birds and leaves and gold sunlight,
> We'll dance till the shadows leave the hills
> And bring to the fields the quiet night.

Even in 1907 Edna was already an honor member of the League. She had won honorable mention in June 1904, for a prose piece called "A Family Tradition." She had scored again in November 1905, February and September 1906, and really hit her stride in the spring of 1907. Three years later, her bureau drawer heaped with all the trophies the League could bestow on an illustrious member, Miss Millay, now a ripe girl of eighteen, sat down and penned her valedictory, published in the October issue:

> Dear St. Nicholas: I am writing to thank you for my cash prize and to say good-bye, for "Friends" was my last contribution. I am going to buy with my five dollars a beautiful copy of "Browning," whom I admire so much that my prize will give me more pleasure in that form than in any other.
>
> Although I shall never write for the League again, I shall not allow myself to become a stranger to it. You have been a great help and a great encouragement to me, and I am sorry to grow up and leave you.
>
> Your loving graduate, Edna Vincent Millay

Thus Edna walked statelily [sic] out of the League, a copy of Browning in her hand, leaving a youngster named Scott Fitzgerald holding the fort in the same issue with a prize-winning photograph called "Vacation Scene." The poem "Friends," for which she received five dollars, is reprinted hereunder. The editor seemed to have had some vague notion that he was dealing with an authentic talent, for the verses appeared at the head of the League section and were prefaced with this editorial comment: "This composition is a little gem in smoothness and perfection of its rhythm, in its deft use of contrast, and in its naturalness of expression from first to last."

Friends

I. He

I've sat here all afternoon, watching her busy fingers send
That needle in and out. How soon I wonder, will she reach the end?
Embroidery! I can't see how a girl of Molly's common sense
Can spend her time like that. Why, now — just look at that I may
        Be dense,
But, somehow I don't see the fun in punching lots of holes down through
A piece of cloth; and, one by one, sewing them up. But Molly'll do
A dozen of them, right around
That shapeless bit of stuff she's found.
A dozen of them! Just like that!
And think it's sense she's working at.
But then, she's just a girl (although she's quite the best one of the lot)
And I'll just have to let her sew, whether it's foolishness or not.

II. She

He's sat here all the afternoon, talking about an awful game;
One boy will not be out till June, and then he may be always lame.
Foot-ball! I'm sure I can't see why a boy like Bob — so good and kind —
Wishes to see poor fellows lie hurt on the ground. I may be blind,
But somehow, I don't see the fun. Some one calls, "14–16–9";
You kick the ball, and then you run and try to reach a white chalk line.
     And Bob would sit right there all day
     And talk like that, and never say
     A single word of sense; or so
     It seems to me. I may not know.
But Bob's a faithful friend to me. So let him talk that game detested,
And I will smile and seem to be most wonderfully interested.

I suppose there exist a few adults who never even heard of the St. Nicholas League — people whose childhood was spent on the other side of the railroad tracks reading the *Youth's Companion;* whose fathers didn't give them a subscription to *St. Nick* and who consequently never knew what it was to stand, as we League members stood, "for intelligent patriotism, and for protection of the oppressed, whether human beings, dumb animals or birds." I well remember how vital to one's progress in the League was kindness-to-animals. Without kindness-to-animals, you didn't get far in the St. Nicholas League, unless, like Edna Millay, you were really talented. (A lot of us boys had no perceptible talent, but were just sissies who stayed indoors and read magazines while normal kids were out playing I Spy.) It was a buddy of mine two houses up the block, an observant child named E. Barrett Brady, wise in the ways of the world, who put me on to kindness-to-animals in its relation to winning a silver or a gold badge. Barrett said it was worthwhile to put plenty of it in. As I look back through the numbers and examine my own published works, I detect running through them an amazing note of friendliness toward dumb creatures, an almost virulent sympathy for dogs, cats, horses, bears, toads, and robins. I was kind to animals in all sorts of weather almost every month for three or four years. The results were satisfactory. I won both the silver and the gold badge, and I was honorably mentioned several times. This precocious anticipation of an editor's needs is a sad and revealing chapter in my life; I was after results, apparently, and not writing, or drawing, for Art's own sake. Still, the League motto was "Live to learn and learn to live."

     Membership in the League was anyone's for the asking. The first thing that happened when you joined was that they sent you a copper button, engraved with the League's name and the League emblem (the stars and stripes) in colors (red, white, and blue). This button was, as advertised, "beautiful in design and workmanship." Sweet as it was, it was just a starter, just a taste of what life was to be like. That was the beauty of the League — it came through handsomely every so often with some tangible reward. Each month six silver badges and six gold badges were distributed among the twelve successful adolescents of the month, for the best two drawings, the best two poems, the best two stories or essays, the best two amateur photographs, the best two puzzles, and the best two sets of answers to the puzzles in the previous issue. These puzzles, let me say, were sons of guns. It was a never-failing source of wonder that anybody ever managed to get all the answers. Someone always did, though. A child named Ringgold W. Lardner was on the honor role for puzzles in April 1900; and Stephen Benet, John C. Farrar, Alan Dunn, Wilella Waldorf, and Louis Kronenberger all made the puzzle award in their time. Each month subjects were suggested for drawings and poems (or you could choose your own subject). In the drawing group there was always the chance to try a "Heading for January" or a "Heading for September" or whatever the forthcoming month happened to be. There were no dues of any sort, which perhaps accounts for the League's piling up some two hundred thousand members in thirty-five years of existence.

We Leaguers were busy youngsters. Many of us had two or three strings to our bows and were not content till we had shone in every department, including wild-life photography. Little Robert Benchley was an exception. He was elevated to the roll of honor in September 1903, for a drawing called "The Dollies' Lesson," the same month that Newman Levy won distinction in drawing and Conrad P. Aiken was mentioned for a poem called "A Lullaby." But although Benchley got in near the start of the League (it was organized in 1899), he showed no perseverance. "The Dollies' Lesson" was his only appearance. He dropped out early and was never heard from again, reminding one forcibly of one of the tenets of the League, that "book study alone is not followed by the best results. Direct friendship with the woods and fields and healthful play are necessary to the proper development of both mind and body." Benchley, knowing little of the woods and fields, and nothing about kindness to animals, was an ephemeral member.

Most of us were stayers. Aiken appeared in print four times in 1903 and once in 1904. E. Babette Deutsch rang the bell no fewer than nineteen times during her childhood; John C. Farrar twenty-two; E. Vincent Millay twenty; Susan Warren Wilbur twenty-one. Joseph Auslander made ten successful appearances in two years, and was twice publicly reprimanded by having his name published on the "Careless Roll"— once for no address, once for sending in a contribution without the proper endorsement. (All League contributors had to get a parent or guardian to write on the back "This is Joseph's own work" and sign it. If you forgot to, your name was published among the Careless.) Morris Ryskind was careless twice in the spring of 1913, but later redeemed himself with a poem, "Dawn," and a prose piece, "A Family Tradition," both of which would have been published had space permitted.

It would have been unsafe to predict the professional future of the Leaguers from the type of work they turned in. Viola Beerbohm Tree drew pictures for the League and turned out to be an actress. Benet wrote several prose pieces and turned into a poet. Elinor Wylie (Elinor M. Hoyt) distinguished herself twice, both times for drawing; and that young comer Ringgold W. Lardner gained double honors—in verses and in puzzles. (Note: his poem was not considered good enough to publish, and was merely mentioned.) Cornelia Otis Skinner wrote a poem. J. Deems Taylor and Janel Flanner, in a Mad May of 1901, rose to fame together, each with a drawing called "Household Joys," a suggested subject. Master Taylor scored again later, copping a silver badge in December 1901, for his photograph "Moonrise in December," a snapshot of an extremely peaceful snow scene. Alan Seeger succeeded with a photograph "From My Best Negative." Sigmund G. Spaeth, with his eye on timely topics, wrote a poem about the first springtime of the twentieth century. John C. Mosher took signal honors with his camera in 1906, and, had space permitted, would have enlivened the January 1906 issue with his pleasing photograph "The View from My Home." Norman Geddes was mentioned in 1909 for a drawing, "My Best Friend's Favorite Occupation." And so it went. They were happy days.

Contributions came even from across the sea. A little English girl named Vita V. Sackville-West, bursting with an ancient pride, wrote in 1902 from Knole, Sevenoaks, Kent, England:

> Dear St. Nicholas League: This story about my home is quite true, and it may amuse you. The archbishops of England possessed Knole first. Then it passed into the hands of Queen Elizabeth, who gave it to my ancestor, Richard Sackville, who was Thomas's brother. It then became the seats of the dukes of Dorset, and then it belonged to the earls of that county, and from then the Sackvilles have had it. There are 365 rooms in Knole, 52 staircases, and 7 courts. A priest's cell was found this year. The altar in the chapel was given by Mary of Scotland just before she was executed. Knole began to be built in 1100 or 1200 up to 1400. Most of the kings and queens of England have made Knole a present. We have here the second organ that was made

"A HEADING FOR NOVEMBER." BY ROBERT EDMUND JONES,
AGE 17. (HONOR MEMBER.)

As E. B. White points out, "It would have been unsafe to predict the professional future of the Leaguers from the type of work they turned in." Eudora Welty won her Silver Badge at ten for this quaint beach scene. *SN* 47 (Aug. 1920): 951. Robert Edmund Jones, one of the greatest innovators in twentieth-century stage design, sent in drawings of fashionable ladies — though by his late teens, he was already incorporating them into bold, semi-abstract compositions. *SN* 33 (Nov. 1905): 80.

in England. There are 21 show rooms in the house. Vita V. Sackville-West.

And another little English girl, Stella Benson, was taking cash prizes for her verses, and writing thank-you letters to the editor telling him she didn't really deserve any money.

We Leaguers even grew up and married one another. I married a League girl (silver badge for prose); and I see by the files that William R. Benet did, too. His girl was Elinor M. Hoyt, who received honorable mention for "A Heading for March" in 1901, three months before William received honorable mention for a poem "When School Is Done." My girl's sister was a gold-badge holder: she won it in the wild-life photography by sneaking up with her camera on an affable duck in a public park in Worcester, Mass. And speaking of photography, one of the most unflinching of the League's camera enthusiasts, judging from published results, was a tot named Lois B. Long. Apparently she was banging away with her Brownie from morning till night, and as a result we have, credited to her, a picture of a girl standing in a wheat field, a picture called "Face to Face," another called "At the Corner," and another called "Where I Spent My Vacation."

We were a hard and versatile lot, all right. There were William Faulkner, Alice Hughes, Norman Klein, John Macy, Corey Ford, Frances Frost, Ward Greene, John S. Martin, Margaret E. Sangster, Niven Busch, Jr., Robert Garland, Peggy Bacon, Faith Baldwin, Margaret Kennedy, Clarence C. Little, Reginald Marsh, Bennett Cerf, Kay Boyle, Alice Harvey, Frieda Inescort, Weare Holbrook, Horatio Winslow, Lee Simonson, Marjorie Allen Seiffert, Richard Whorf, Anne Parrish, Leane Zugsmith, Clement Wood, Edmund Wilson, Lyle Saxon, Marion Strobel, Mary F. Watkins, all the Benets, Jeanne de Lamarter, Henry Dreyfuss, Susan Ertz, Elizabeth Hawes, and how many others I'll never know.

For ten years (from 1899 to 1909) the League was edited by Albert Bigelow Paine. I bought a copy of *St. Nicholas* the other day to see what changes time had wrought. The magazine is now grown tall and limp, like *Colliers*— strange to the touch. The format is changed, but the league goes on, in its fashion. The proprietors have, it seems, eased the bitter problem of silver, gold, and cash awards by tying up, in the approved American manner, with manufacturers of the indispensable tools of the arts, fountain pens and drawing materials. I noted, uneasily, that a current minor named Ruth Blaesing, 13, was receiving for her "Ode to the Earth" not the silver badge of courage but the Waterman Pen Company's award of a fountain pen. And that Rose Doyle, 13, was receiving, for her drawing, the "First Higgins' Ink Award."

But the cheering thing was that the contributions in the current issue showed the same tenderness for life, the same reverent preoccupation with Nature, the same earnest morality that we early Leaguers showed in the days of our glory. No graduate can read over the old copies without a lump in the throat; for beneath the callow phrase and the young solemnity, the roots of beauty sometimes throve. Listen to the Miss Millay of November 1908, and you can already hear the singer singing:

> How lovely is the night, how calm and still!
> Cool shadows lie upon each field and hill,
> From which a fairy wind comes tripping light,
> Perching on bush and tree in airy flight.
> Across the brook and up the field it blows,
> And to my ear there comes, where'er it goes,
> A rustling sound as if each blade of grass
> Held back a silken skirt to let it pass.
>
> This is the bedtime of the weary day;
> Cloud wrap him warmly in a blanket gray;
> From out the dusk where creek and meadow lie,
> The frogs chirp out a sleepy lullaby;
> A single star, new-kindled in the west,
> A flickering candle, lights the day to rest.
>
> O lovely night, sink deep into my heart;
> Lend me thy tranquillity a part;
> Of calmness give to me a kindly loan,
> Until I have more calmness of my own.
> And, weary day, O let thy candle-light,
> And let thy lullaby be mine tonight.

And hark to the William R. Benet, of Watervliet Arsenal, West Troy, N. Y., examining the harvest at the age of fifteen:

> Yon lie the fields all golden with grain
>   (Oh, come, ye Harvesters, reap!)
> The dead leaves are falling with autumn's brown stain
>   (Oh, come, ye Harvesters, reap!)
> For soon sinks the sun to his bed in the west,
> And cawing the crows fly each one to his nest;
> The grain will soon wither, so harvest your best.
>   (Oh, come, ye Harvesters, reap!)

Hear young Briton Niven Busch, Jr. before he had discovered the cinema, finding peace in August 1919, in a calm sonnet beginning:

> Beneath the radiance of the quiet stars
> The earth lies beautiful as in a dream.

And search the heart of youth with fourteen-year-old Stella Benson:

> Borne upwards on its gold and silver wings
>   Rises the Heart of Youth,
> With its fond hopes and sweet imaginings
> It wanders through this sordid world, nor brings
> To mind the hard, undecorated truth;
> And future cares and sorrows left behind
> Are spurned, because the Heart of Youth is blind.

The League is still our white plume. We graduates know what it was like to wear it. These later, slight victories, such as they are, fail to make the heart pound; the twilight of an Honor Member is a dim and unsubstantial time. Give me again October 1914 and my drawing (which would have been published had space permitted) called "The Love of a Mother Rabbit."

10

A Debut in the League

SUZANNE RAHN

There is a special fascination in the childhood beginnings of artists and writers. And, as E. B. White points out in his essay written for the *New Yorker*, a considerable number of twentieth-century artists and writers took their first public bows in the St. Nicholas League. White quotes a number of them in his essay, and we have included one of the prize-winning stories, "A Winter Walk," written by White at the age of eleven. It was actually the second publication of "Elwin B. White," who had won a prize from the *Woman's Home Companion* for a poem about a mouse. He did not include his *St. Nicholas* piece in his essay, but we have reproduced it here, along with a submission by Katharine Sergeant, later White's wife.

"A Winter Walk"
by Elwyn B. White (age 11)
(Silver Badge)
I awoke one morning in my little shanty to find the ground covered with snow. It had fallen rapidly during the night and was about six inches deep. I dressed, ate a good breakfast, did some of the camp chores, and set about taking down my snow-shoes and preparing them for wintry weather. Soon I heard a short yelp which reminded me that Don, my pointer, had been left hungry. I gave him some bones and a few biscuits, then, pulling on my heavy overcoat and buckling the snow-shoes on my feet, we started out in the frosty morning air to pay the forest a visit.

Such a morning! There was a frosty nip to the air that gave life to everybody and everything. Don was so overjoyed at the prospect of a walk that he danced and capered about as if he was mad. Jack Frost was busy for fair! My nose and ears were victims of his teeth.

After a small stretch of smooth ground had been covered we entered the forest.

All the trees wore a new fur coat, pure white, and the pines and evergreens were laden with pearl. Every living creature seemed happy. Squirrels frisked among the branches, chattering because we trespassed on their property. Once in a while we caught an occasional glimpse of a little ball of fur among the fern, which meant that bre'r rabbit was out on this cold morning. A few straggling quails were heard piping their shrill little notes as they flew overhead.

All these harmless little wood creatures were noticed by Don and he wanted to be after them, but I objected to harming God's innocent little folk when He had given the world such a bright, cheery morning to enjoy [38 (June 1911): 757].

"A Discovery" (A True Story)
     by Katharine Sergeant (age 9)
     (Silver Badge)
     Once a friend of mine showed me something that interested me very much. It was a spider's nest. The spider had made it out of red clay. It had, at one end, a little door that opened. When the spider was inside, all he had to do was to push the door and it opened out. When he went out, he left the door open. If you looked carefully at the inside of the door, there was a tiny hole, so tiny that you could hardly see it. So when the spider went in he put his leg in the hole and pulled the door shut after him. Anybody who tried to open the door from the outside would have to tip the nest upside down.

For the inside of the nest the spider had spun a web which made it all soft and silky. The nest was small and round and just the color of the ground, so it was very hard to find. I think a spider who had a house like that would be very happy [29 (August 1902): 947–8].

It has been suggested by some critics that Katharine White was her husband's inspiration for Charlotte, the most famous of all fictional spiders. This sympathetic and finely observed essay also suggests the possibility that she first taught him to notice spiders and admire their special skills.

E. B. White sent a copy of his *New Yorker* essay on the St. Nicholas League to William Fayal Clarke, who had been Mary Mapes Dodge's assistant editor and became editor-in-chief of *St. Nicholas* after her death in 1905, until his own retirement in 1927. The League had been Clarke's favorite department of the magazine, and at seventy-nine, he clearly retained all his fondness and enthusiasm for it. He was delighted by White's essay and responded with this account of the League's founding.

Clarke's letter has never before been published. His copy of it can be found in the Donald and Robert M. Dodge Collection of Mary Mapes Dodge at the library of Princeton University.

Scarsdale, N.Y.
  December 21, 1934
  Mr. E.B. White
  Editorial Rooms "The New Yorker"
  25 West 45th Street
  New York, N.Y.
  Dear Mr. White:
  Your letter of last week and the marked copy of "The New Yorker" which you kindly sent me form as fine a Christmas gift as I could possibly have desired.

  Thanks, and again thanks—and then some!

  I always knew, or felt it in my bones, that the St. Nicholas League would come into its own some day. The experienced and gifted pen of Mrs. May Lamberton Becker has recently recalled the glories of the League for the readers of St. Nicholas in the series "Who's Who in the League" and a truly effective series it was.

  But I mean that I knew that the League was bound to get the mention it deserved in public print quite outside the pages of the magazine itself. And if I confess that I never anticipated its first and crowning recognition would appear in "The New Yorker," let me assure you that I am all the more proud and grateful that the honor you have accorded it was published in your brilliant magazine.

  As for the article itself—which you modestly say "might amuse" me — that is putting it with exceeding mildness. For no "movie" thriller ever held such thrills for me as the tribute to our League which you have set forth in words so glowing and sincere. Assuredly, the League editors and its host of readers owe you a debt they cannot repay for reviewing in your masterpiece of appreciation the days that were so happy for all of us and their marvelous fruitage in later years o' grace. And it is a joy to all Leaguers to find your ardor for it still burning as brightly as in the days when your contributions enriched its pages, and when you took all the League badges and honors—in your stride.

  In the final years of the last century, when I was Associate Editor of "St. Nicholas," Mr. Albert Bigelow Paine was editing a Children's Page in the New York *Herald*. As one of its features he had formed a club or organization among its young readers. Both as friend and editor, I was interested in Mr. Paine's work and when we were dining together one evening, he told me that he was expecting to relinquish his position on the *Herald* ere long, and he expressed real regret over leaving the organization he had founded.

  "Why not form another on even better lines," I asked, "and we'll make it a feature of St. Nicholas? We could make room for it, I am sure, and it would be quite as congenial work for you." "Well! Why not?" he answered, evidently liking the idea.

And little else was talked about, that evening, except the pros and cons, and possibilities of the suggested project. Before we parted, it was agreed that he should bring me at an early date a lay-out and prospectus of the proposed "St. Nicholas League." This he duly did, and I submitted it to Mrs. Mary Mapes Dodge, the Editor-in-Chief of St. Nicholas, who gave it her hearty approval. So, in November, 1899 — after a few conferences about final details and adjustments — the League was launched in the pages of the magazine. It was inaugurated and conducted as a regular department under the sole charge of Mr. Paine, who had originated all the conditions of the competitions, the rules and regulations, and the badges and honors to be awarded.

How ably he fulfilled his task, the League reports of that time, the acclaim of its young readers and the roster of "future-greats" in the Honor-Member roll fully attest. All this, as well as the way the members simply astonished us, month after month and year after year, by the remarkable quality of their contributions is a matter of history admirably recorded in your article.

Emerson said, "Nothing great was ever achieved without enthusiasm." Paine and I had plenty of it from the beginning, but the young League members soon showed us that we didn't even know the meaning of the word. Their enthusiasm was simply unquenchable, and promptly assured us that our new project was not to be a mere flash in the pan or a short-lived venture. Even so, we could not foresee what it was to become within the next decade and to continue becoming for another.

Quite as remarkable as the quality of their contributions was the patience and devotion of those eager young workers. "Alps?" exclaimed Napoleon; "there shall *be* no Alps!" — and there *were* none — for him. Nor for our young Leaguers, either! What their patience, ambition and perseverance accomplished, your laudatory article has summarized more completely than anything heretofore printed in the line of major-compliment. I must be content by way of a postscript to your tribute to say that the work of the League members in the aggregate of more than a quarter of a century, set a standard of intellectual and artistic achievement never equaled, or even approached, in the annals of American youth.

After nine years' success with the League, Mr. Paine had to give up the work as its editor — much to his regret, and ours — for he had to undertake the writing of his famous biography of Mark Twain.

The lamented death of Mrs. Mary Mapes Dodge occurred in 1905, and I became Editor of St. Nicholas. And when Mr. Paine left us in December, 1908, the League had grown so dear to me — in fact, my hobby then and ever after, that I could not consign it to any other hand. And for nineteen years, from December, 1908 to the beginning of 1927, I kept the editorial work of the League under my own supervision and control. In

May, of 1927, I retired from the editorship of both St. Nicholas and the League — indeed, from all active work — at the age of 72.

Mr. Paine and I, of course, never dreamed on that evening of long ago, after our little dinner together, of the great success that our new project was to bring — nor that 34 years later we should have the great pleasure of reviewing its history and chortling over it, as pictured so vividly and admirably in your article in last week's "New Yorker." There is glory enough for us all in what you have recounted and for your unique and memorable tribute to the League, Mr. Paine and I, the two co-founders and first two editors of the League, "were but little grateful if we could say how much."

And so you married a Leaguer! Lucky man! Let me offer, along with belated congratulations, my salaams and salutations to both of you and assure you that you two Honor Members will henceforth shine with *especial* honor in our happiest memories of the League.

Very sincerely yours,

(signed) William Fayal Clarke

11

The *St. Nicholas* Advertising Competition: Training the Magazine Reader

ELLEN GRUBER GARVEY

> From the advertisers' point of view, these competitions are most
> valuable. They make our young readers and their elders thor-
> oughly familiar with the business announcements in the mag-
> azines, and cause these to be read and re-read with closest
> attention. The young people, too, learn much ... and are enter-
> tained besides.[1]

Children at the turn of the century were not thought of as consumers.
Nonetheless, *St. Nicholas* carried a moderate quantity of advertising and
conducted a vigorous campaign to persuade advertisers of the value of
advertising in its pages. Advertisers undoubtedly assumed that adults
would see the ads, but they may also have fallen in line with ideas current
in advertising psychology and advice to advertisers that ads directed to
children would influence their later purchases in adulthood. *St. Nicholas's*
advertising department drew on and made such ideas explicit in several
booklets addressed to advertisers. One, *A Good Line of Advertising*, frames
advertising to children as an investment in future rather than present sales,
and as virtually a moral duty:

> There is no period of life at which impressions can be so deeply
> made as in early youth, and as the youth of America are trained,
> so will the next generation of men and women be. Proper train-
> ing ought, all educators agree, to consist in familiarizing young

people with the conditions that will surround them in adult life.[2]

St. Nicholas augmented this "proper training" by publishing a monthly advertising competition beginning in 1900. Since advertisers lacked measures of how readers responded to ads, publishers sought to demonstrate to advertisers that their magazines were a congenial environment for advertising, and that ads in them would be read attentively. A number of magazines sponsored contests that focused on advertising to reassure advertisers that readers noticed their ads.[3] Magazines that separated ads from editorial matter and ran them in the back of the issue, like *St. Nicholas* and its parent *The Century,* had a special need to do so. In effect, *St. Nicholas's* contests trained its audience as consumers and as magazine readers who would be attentive to advertising. Booklets addressed to advertisers like *A Good Line of Advertising, Alice in Blunderland* and *A Visit from the St. Nicholegions* made sure advertisers appreciated this training, telling them "the object is to make certain that the advertising pages of *St. Nicholas* and of other magazines of the better class shall be read and read with discrimination."[4]

The focus on deep "impressions" best made in early youth comes from the psychology of advertising promoted by Walter Dill Scott in the early 1900s. Scott, an empiricist follower of William James, held that purchases were most shaped by habit, and habits impressed in childhood were particularly effective:

> As a boy I associated certain names with certain articles of merchandise. I saw a particular soap advertised in various ways. Perhaps it was used in my home — I am not sure about that. The name and soap were so habitually associated in my mind as a boy that when I think of soap this particular soap is the kind I am most likely to think of even to the present time, although it has not been called to my mind so often in recent years as other kinds of soap.... The associations formed in youth are more effective than those formed in later years. The effectiveness is lasting and will still have influence as long as the person lives. Hence goods of a constant and recurring use might well be advertised in home or even children's papers, and the advertisements might be constructed that they would be appreciated by children.[5]

Advertisers believed that an ad had to be consciously noticed and carefully read for it to be effective, as opposed to the later idea that close analysis might destroy an ad's power. In line with this, the *St. Nicholas* contests sought to develop a critical and attentive eye for advertising by setting readers' tasks "in such a manner as to compel close study of the advertising pages of *St. Nicholas* and the *Century*."[6] *A Good Line of Advertising* goes on to point out the advantage such training gives the advertisers:

> The readers of *St. Nicholas* have become the most intelligent
> constituency an advertiser can address, and a constituency that
> is of growing importance and value. The greatest advertisers in
> the country have recognized this, and have directly and indi-
> rectly lent their aid to this school of advertising, and of adver-
> tisement writers and artists.[7]

The publishers were eager to show advertisers that noncommercial creativity would not be rewarded. Contest judges have:

> no use for the efforts of budding genius simply as such.... It is
> the object of these advertising competitions *to train young girls
> and boys so that they may become practical makers of advertise-
> ments,* if they choose, or at least may be appreciative of the work
> of others—an intelligent public to whom the advertiser may
> appeal with the certainty of a response.[8]

Appreciation was seen as the desirable response to the ads. As the *St. Nicholas* editors tell their readers in their introduction to the January 1905 contest: "It is necessary to educate in the appreciation of good advertising not only those who will make a business of publicity but the whole public to whom their efforts are addressed."[9]

St. Nicholas thus articulates the need to train readers to respond to ads, and proposes the middle-class reader as the proper and desirable object of such training. While *St. Nicholas's* contests prompted readers to try on the advertiser's role, and so see themselves as having interests in common with the advertiser, the magazine elsewhere directed advertisers to see *St. Nicholas* readers as young versions of themselves, and therefore worth reaching. One such message to advertisers assumes that the advertisers' own store of "engravings" and "impressions" was stocked by this genteel magazine:

> Looking Backward
>
> You were brought up on *St. Nicholas* and remember still some
> of the stories, pictures, and possibly the advertisements which
> you saw there when you were young. *St. Nicholas* is the same
> magazine today. Don't you want to engrave upon the impres-
> sionable minds of the best boys and girls in the land your firm
> name, trade-mark, or commodity?[10]

And yet *St. Nicholas* was an elite magazine. E. B. White, asserting the universality of its readership, actually reveals its opposite when he writes in 1934: "I suppose there exist a few adults who never even heard of the St.

Nicholas League — people whose childhoods were spent on the other side of the tracks reading the *Youth's Companion.*"[11] But since *St. Nicholas* claimed a circulation at 50–60,000, and *Youth's Companion's* has been estimated at half a million in this period, the other side of the tracks was clearly better populated."[12] Advertisers or ad managers might not have come from such well-off backgrounds, and other pitches proposed *St. Nicholas* as the advertiser's source of entree into such a household. *St. Nicholas's* readers

> are constantly invited to close critical, intelligent scrutiny of its advertisements, which make them remembered. Examine any copy of *St. Nicholas:* what kind of family is it likely to enter? When you persuade the boys and girls that there is pleasure and profit in studying your advertisements, you surely reach the heart of the whole family.[13]

An article on the competitions in an ad trade journal, after praising the nearly professional quality of the ads the children turned out similarly concluded, "the greatest value, measured by a commercial standard, accrues to those advertisers who are shrewd enough to appreciate having an army of bright young people studying their announcements in the family circle, and so making their wares and trademarks household words in the best families everywhere."[14] Not only is the advertiser thus assured that the merchandise *St. Nicholas* offers it — the reader — is of high quality, "boys and girls of the right sort,"[15] but it is promised a seat at the table, introduction into family conversation. The structure of the advertising competitions furthered this end.

The Two St. Nicholas Competitions

Late twentieth-century ads addressed to children dramatize pleasure in the realm of consumption and enjoyment of ads themselves as an opposition to the dull realm of parental values of discipline, order, and respect for rules. Consumption becomes the field for celebrating freedom and for disruption and antiauthoritarian rule breaking.[16] Already in place in the early twentieth century, this opposition is played out in the differences between *St. Nicholas's* ad competition and its ongoing non-advertising St. Nicholas League Competition, which began in 1899. The non-advertising competition ran in the body of the magazine and set readers under 18 non-advertising-related themes for poetry, essays, drawings, and photographs. The advertising competition ran in the ad section of the magazine, and variously set readers to do such things as create ads on particular subjects or using particular phrases, or in the form or a dialogue between historical or fictional characters, or to hunt through the magazine for ads in which certain pictures or phrases had appeared, or to complete a puzzle using ad phrases.

Rules for the two competitions were initially nearly identical, but gradually diverged in ways that reveal much about the ways readers were encouraged to see and participate in advertising. The non-advertising competition required adult certification that a child had submitted an entry and that the work was original. Despite this, nearly every issue carries news that a child's prize has been revoked because it was found to have been given for copied work. The advertising contest eventually required no such warrant, did not bar copying, and invited entrants to obscure the traces of individual effort as they played with the already-existing texts of advertising. Advertisers, represented by the "advertising editor" of *St. Nicholas*, invited readers to the freest possible play with the advertising, even transgressive play. Rules against plagiarism would be counterproductive since the advertising materials are offered for playful appropriation by all. They thus move into a quasi-folk realm, consistent with the fostering of a new common language built on nationwide familiarity with advertising characters and slogans. In another sense, the companies are extending their corporate largess in the form of the advertising figures and slogans: they allow readers the treat of being praised and rewarded for playing with private intellectual property as though it were public.

Contestants were initially told to "try to remember than an advertisement is primarily intended to sell goods. It is amusing perhaps to receive suggestions that 'Pears' Soap floats,' that it may be 'used as a laundry soap,' but suggestions of that kind are not likely to win prizes."[17] A later contest, however, invited them to the wilder, freer play of making comical collages of different pieces of ads.[18] This contest not only licensed burlesque and parody, but also capitalized on the status of the ad pages as something a parent might allow a child to cut up. And yet the humor here depends on familiarity with the proper form of the ad so that one can see its incongruity with the new form.

"Everybody Try"

"Remember that there is no age limit to these competitions, that you may have help, and that whole families may get together and combine on a clever idea."[19] Working on advertising, playing at creating advertising, and playing with advertising slogans were proposed as worthwhile family pastimes. Inserting ads in *St. Nicholas* "where they will become a part of these competitions" was the right strategy for advertisers if "you would see your products, your name, and trademark made the subject of household discussion."[20] Some *St. Nicholas* competitions extended the invitation to work together to the larger community of the school. Schools could earn reference books in a contest that asked answers to advertising-related questions. The rules recommended even wider participation in the contest:

> There is no restriction as to obtaining aid in answering the questions; on the contrary, each school is urged to secure the help of any one who is interested in their winning one of the prizes offered for the answers. Teachers and parents and grown up friends are asked to help their children to win the principal prize.[21]

Even before adults were invited to enter *St. Nicholas's* ad contests, it was reported that one family, at the father's suggestion, had gone over an issue and voted the ad contest the most interesting subject in the whole number. The family set to work with enthusiasm, first submitting the work to the mother for preliminary judging before the entire family's combined work was sent in.[22]

Opening the contest to readers of all ages could help bring advertisers more immediate results via adult purchases, of goods both for children, such as Educator Animal Crackers, which "delight and nourish youngsters … just the thing for Christmas," and for the household, like Postum, whose full-page ads appeared monthly in *St. Nicholas* for at least a decade.

Allowing collaborative and group work on the competitions not only made the ad contest a freer area than the main competition, but also imbedded products in social situations and got people talking about them, something any individual advertiser would see. The school competition was hailed as having "proved of distinct value to the cause of advertising generally and to hundreds of advertisers specifically."[23] The attraction to advertisers of having their products enter family conversation becomes an attraction to children: Advertising offers pleasures forbidden in the non-advertising St. Nicholas League competition. One ad contest credited the new advertising manager in 1911, Don M. Parker, with giving the competition judges this suggestion:

> You have never given the boys and girls a single advertiser to work upon. Take just one and ask for new ideas. Take the first one in the book [a special position for which the advertiser usually paid a premium] Swift & Company. Ask them to read Swift & Company's advertisements; tell them to talk with the man their mothers buy their meat from; ask their fathers how Swift & Company can do business on a margin of three per cent.... There are at least a "Heinz" number of varieties of reasons why Swift Premium Hams, Swift Premium Bacon, Swift Premium

Lard or any other thing that is Swift & Company's which has been advertised in the *St. Nicholas* should continue to be advertised in the *St. Nicholas* Magazine....[24]

Like an earlier competition that told readers to "be on the watch ... for incidents showing the use or popularity of articles advertised in the magazine," Parker explicitly tells readers to seek out brand-name knowledge, thereby infusing their conversation with neighbors, and local merchants with it.[25] Moreover, his own writing is a model of lively, casual enfolding of brand-name references: "There are at least a Heinz number of varieties." The reader is told by example that this type of slang is acceptable, even within *St. Nicholas's* standards of decorum, although contestants had previously been warned to avoid the vulgar.[26]

White claimed that for Edna St. Vincent Millay, a twenty-time St. Nicholas League competition winner, winning the Pulitzer prize must have been a letdown after getting her gold or silver League medal as a child.[27] But by 1911, entrants in the advertising competition were being told that their work *as consumers* was helping to create the magazine. "We are proud of our advertising department and want every one of you boys and girls to take more interest in what we are doing from month to month. The more interest you show in these pages the more able we are to secure for your reading and study interesting and instructive stories about all sorts of good things."[28]

The advertising work readers produced served as evidence of their attentiveness as consumers, and thus enhanced the magazine. While the work rarely appeared in *St. Nicholas*, some can be found in ads and articles in trade magazines addressed to advertisers, presented as evidence of readers' attentiveness to ads. Competitors were required to consume, to take in the ads carefully. The rhetoric of the ads was evidently regarded as so powerful that study of ads was seen as likely to produce the desired effect: that is, to leave impressions for later use. Moreover, the contests' requirement that readers respond in writing to the ads accords with psychology-of-advertising's promoter Walter Dill Scott's prescriptions on making ads memorable. A reader's "intensity" of response to an ad will cause him or her to remember it.

The intensity of the impression which an advertisement makes is dependent upon the response which it secures from the readers. The pedagogue would call this action the "motor response," even though it were nothing more than the writing of a postal card. Such action is vital in assisting the memory of the readers. An advertisement which secures a response sufficient to lead to the writing of a postal card has a chance of being remem-

bered which is incomparably greater than that of other advertisements.[29]

This principle is at work in instructions for a 1911 letter-writing competition:

> The Judges want you to write a letter to a friend, real or imag-
> inary, in which you describe the virtues of some article adver-
> tised in this number of *St. Nicholas*.... Don't begin the letter
> until you have sat and thought about your subject — go over all
> the advertisements carefully before you make up your mind
> which one to choose, and then write to your friend about it.
> You may tell how you used this article yourself, or any other
> facts that will show that *you understand the claims that the mak-
> ers set forth*.... Your friends the judges get a little boastful some-
> times about your abilities, so take care not to disappoint them.
> Make your manuscript just as real as you can, so that each will
> be a credit to you as a member of the great *St. Nicholas* fam-
> ily.[30] [Emphasis in original.]

Two published winning responses demonstrate the readers' attentiveness to ads and emphasize social involvement with advertising materials and products. The first letter, by John Ketcham, smoothly touted the
superior ability of LePage's liquid glue over flour and water paste for
holding together model airplanes, embedding the mention of the glue
within the writer and correspondent's mutual interest as hobbyists. The
second published winner, Elliot Weld Brown, wrote about a Colgate
product. Brown's letter to his cousin seems less precisely on point than
Ketcham's. The letter's scenario, however, inserts advertising into the
family far more firmly:

> Dear Freddie:
>   Look on the back cover of the March number of *St. Nicholas*
> and see if you think the boy in the "Colgate's Ribbon Dental
> Cream" advertisement looks like any one you know! Mother
> says it's the image of *me* only I haven't got curly hair, thank
> goodness. Mother says she's going to take a picture of me in the
> same position, brushing my teeth, just to compare them, and *I*
> use "Colgate's Dental Cream" too, do you? And don't you love
> it? Mother says I never brushed my teeth so often or so long,
> as since we began using "C.D.C." It is such fun to squeeze the
> tube and let the cream ran out so neatly onto the tooth-brush,
> don't you think so? And it leaves such a good taste in your
> mouth, yum, yum. Just as if you'd been eating candy.... I used
> to mail out the postal cards that came wrapped around the tubes
> with the names of my friends, and they received sample tubes
> of the cream. One day I wrote down, just for fun, "Miss Beauty
> Walter," the name of Uncle Frank's and Aunt Vic's little white

dog, you know, that they always speak of as "your little cousin
Beauty," just as if it were a real child....[31]

Colgate sends the dog a sample with a card addressed to her saying that
Brown had sent her name. But now uncle and aunt use Colgate's, "so Colgate & Co. ought to forgive me for the joke I played on them, don't you
think so?"

Evidently it did. The Colgate Company seems to have seen advantages
for itself in this technique of encouraging play with the product and its
advertising, since it announced its own similar contest in the same issue.
The advertising manager of *St. Nicholas* was to be one of the judges.[32]

Brown's letter features many ways to incorporate the product into
play, social interaction, and even social commentary. He makes it part of
his conversation with his cousin, explaining how he will play at stepping
into the ad by posing for a photographic tableau of it. To do so, he must
take up the proper product as well as the pose, and while holding the toothpaste, he tells his friend about the incidental as well as the utilitarian pleasures of using it. As Brown acts as Walter Dill Scott's ideal ad reader,
bringing his memory-aiding motor response into play by filling out the
cards for samples, and thereby modeling this action for the *St. Nicholas*
readers, he gives gifts with the cards. He sends one of these to a dog whose
owners treat it too much like a person and thus finds in advertising license
to mock adult authority: his knowledge of this realm lets him wield the
power of a large company within his own family. The pleasures of posing
for pictures, of teasing older relatives, are all claimed in the name of advertising.

And yet the contests directed less emphasis on the advertised product and more on the instructions for how to reenter the world of advertising, what next to look for in it. The instructions for this contest
suggested that understanding the advertising was more important than
experience with the product. Entrants were to demonstrate that they
understand the claims of the makers.[33] To write only "from personal
knowledge ... is to be absurdly scrupulous. The makers of advertisements
are but the mouthpieces through which others speak, and their only duty
is to help the advertiser in the method of making the suggestions."[34]

Through its contests and such explanations as these, *St. Nicholas*
instructed readers to understand ads as a set of promises. Readers were
invited to see ads as fictional structures they could participate in both by
creating some themselves and by accepting the premises of advertising in
a register that did not require anyone to compare them with the actual
goods. Readers were inculcated in the pleasures of advertising as a kind

of story making that animates products and creates a mythology of products separate from any experience of the products themselves. A crude version of this story making took visual form in the St. Nicholas Zoo, which sets trademarks and other brand references cavorting.[35]

Children learned both to enjoy ads and play with them, and to look to ads for some of the same pleasures of fiction. Ads supply satisfying framing and explanatory structures, and readers learned to understand that these were not literal descriptions of the products, subject to disappointed expectations, but rather that these were stories about products in which they could participate either by creating more stories about products, or by buying the product. Readers were not being encouraged, consumer-education-style, to evaluate the truthfulness of ads' promises and resist believing them, but neither did *St. Nicholas* tell them to believe the ads. Rather children learned that the issue of believing or not believing the ads was relevant to the pleasures of participating in advertising. Instead, like Elliot Weld Brown, they could imbed the product within a complicated interplay of product use, ad-world play, and fictional construction, where the only product claims advanced — that the toothpaste is fun to squeeze, and that it tastes like candy — are perhaps the least important parts of his letter.

Ads and Fiction

One function of the ad contests, whether planned or inadvertent, was to encourage readers to disregard distinctions between advertising and fiction, by inviting readers to fantasize with the materials of the ads, and to join them to approved worlds of fiction. One competition, for example, invited contestants to use figures from Roman myths to advertise items that had been advertised in *St. Nicholas*; others incorporated figures from children's literature.[36] But ads emerge superior to fiction: they offer options for participation that the noncommercial stories do not. Eating the cereal that turns Jim Dumps into the popular advertising character Sunny Jim opens a door to the world of this attractive character that fiction does not offer. It allows the consumer to be with his or her friend Sunny Jim, whether or not the cereal fulfills its implied promise to make the consumer sunny.

Other editorial matter helped to orient *St. Nicholas* readers toward contests and to identify with advertisers. At about the time the competitions began, contests became a frequent topic in *St. Nicholas* fiction. Similarly, both contests and stories showed making advertisements as an enjoyable social pursuit. In "The Corner Cupboard" by Margaret Johnson (1905), for example, art students Kitty and Grace rent the small seaside cottage of the title to use for a studio and store where they serve tea and sell fudge, decorative objects, and drawings to earn money for art school.[37] But it goes badly; summer boarders are not buying. Their friend Billy has an inspiration:

> Are we too proud to advertise? Something unique and fresh in the way of posters is the very thing the Cupboard needs to make it go; something to catch the public eye, to fix the wandering fancy of the S.B. [summer boarder].

They rewrite Samuel Woodsworth's sentimental favorite "The Old Oaken Bucket" as an ad. Billy begins, Grace joins in, and "They finished all together in a jubilant chorus" (780). The poem they are parodying is so familiar, and what should be done to it to make it an advertisement is so evident, that they perform the impossible task of thinking together, all reciting at once precisely the same words as they compose them. Producing advertising thus makes possible astonishingly social acts of creativity, a kind of closeness that bonds the group together as it taps broader cultural knowledge in service to an entrepreneurial goal. The product of this brainstorming, put on posters, turns the tide and brings them business, and finally the patronage of the governor. Advertising becomes the way for the girls to help themselves, and yet to be rewarded for the character virtues of pluck and independence that inspire the governor's interest and patronage. Advertising is necessary to make the evidence of their industry and pluck visible. As in the advertising contests in the magazine, talent and noncommercial artwork aren't sufficient: advertising has to be added. And yet advertising is presented as the non-drudgery part of running the business. It is, if anything, *more* creative and appealing than *making* the knick-knacks the girls sell.

Conclusion

Advertising's invitation to readers to come play with it, to fantasize using its images and perhaps within its terms, was issued both by the advertisement itself and by magazines such as *St. Nicholas* acting in the interests of advertisers. An individual advertiser could encourage attention to its own products through its ads, even running a contest that rewarded attention to the virtues of its own product. But a magazine, whose loyalties were to advertisers as a whole but not to any one advertiser, could more readily highlight for its readers the pleasures of playing with advertising by directing their play, inventing games that used the ads, and rewarding their attention and participation. Advertisers, then, had the use of the institution of the magazine to represent their interests. *St. Nicholas's* advertising contests encouraged readers to bring advertising materials into their lives, and to incorporate brand names and advertising slogans into their conversation and writing. Here, advertising figures become their companions and advertising can be looked to as a reliable source of cheerful friendly characters. Advertising's bright and lively sayings are evidently not considered slang and therefore not condemned as they might be elsewhere in the magazine, in a period in which language of middle-class children was monitored for such lapses.

In its contests, *St. Nicholas* overtly offered advertising itself rather than the thing advertised as a desirable commodity, something readers would want to invite into the home, would want to learn more about, and would be "properly trained" to look for throughout their magazine reading lives.

Notes

1. The St. Nicholas League, "'Advertising-Patchwork' Competition. Report of Judges." *SN* (Aug. 1902): ad p. II.
2. *A Good Line of Advertising*, St. Nicholas League Advertising Booklet No. 5; bound into the *Profitable Advertising* 13 (Jan. 1904): 817–32 of *Profitable Advertising*, but paginated separately; p. 2.
3. For further discussion of advertising contests, and connections between contests and other ways in which readers were prompted to notice advertising, see Ellen Gruber Garvey, *The Adman in the Parlor: Magazines and the Gendering of Consumer Culture 1880s to 1910s* (New York: Oxford University Press, 1996).
4. *A Good Line*, p. 7–8.
5. Walter Dill Scott, *The Psychology of Advertising in Theory and Practice* (Boston: Small, Maynard, 1902–3, 1908, 1910, 1921): 92–93.
6. *A Good Line*, p. 3.
7. *A Good Line*, p. 4.
8. *A Good Line*, pp. 7–8.
9. *SN 33* (Jan. 1905): ad. p. 16.
10. Advertisement in *Profitable Advertising*, May 1905, insert following p. 1328.
11. E. B. White, "The St. Nicholas League" in the column "Onward and Upward with the Arts," *New Yorker* (8 Dec.1934): 42.
12. *St. Nicholas: Alice in Blunderland: To St. Nicholas Advertisers of the Past, Present, Future*, advertisement bound into *Profitable Advertising*, December 1902, p. 12. *Youth's Companion*: Frank Luther Mott, *A History of American Magazines 2* (Cambridge: Harvard University Press, 1938, 1957): 268.
13. *A Good Line*, p. 12.
14. "The St. Nicholas Competition," *Profitable Advertising*, March 1903, p. 873. The unsigned article's close echoing of *SN's* own publicity suggests that it may have been dictated by the magazine, a frequent advertiser in *Profitable Advertising*.
15. *Alice*, p. 12.
16. For an extended discussion on this point, see Ellen Seiter, *Sold Separately: Chil-*

dren and Parents in Consumer Culture (New Brunswick: Rutgers University Press, 1993).

17. *SN* 28 (Apr. 1901): ad p. 13.

18. Entries in the Advertising-Patchwork Competition (Aug. 1902, pp. 10–11) called for "the most amusing or surprising combination of text and pictures from the advertising pages."

19. Instructions for Competition 108, *SN* (Dec. 1910): ad p. 24.

20. Advertisement in *Profitable Advertising* February 1905, following page 968. This claim appeared even before the rules were changed to allow collaboration and adult entries.

21. "A Century of Questions," *SN* (Dec. 1904): ad p. 26

22. Report on Competition 43, *SN* (Apr. 1905): ad p. 14.

23. "Number Forty-Two: Latest Advertising Competition of the *St. Nicholas Magazine* and How It Caused the Examination of Thousands of Ads," *Profitable Advertising* (Mar. 1905).

24. *SN* (Apr. 1911): ad p. 6. The April 1911 competition page announces that a Mr. Don M. Parker has been installed as advertising manager; the style of writing changes to this punchy, breezy tone from March on; from April on, the signature of Tuttle, the Advertising Editor disappears from the end of the column.

25. "Vacation Advertising Competition of the St. Nicholas League," *SN* 30 (June 1902): ad p. 10.

26. Report on Competition 40, *SN* (Dec. 1904): ad pp. 26–28.

27. E. B. White, "The St. Nicholas League." Among the later famous who won non-advertising St. Nicholas League competitions as children, White found Vita Sackville-West (writing about Knole, of course), Ring Lardner, Conrad Aiken (four times), Robert Benchley (for a drawing), Edna St. Vincent Millay (twenty times), Elinor Wylie, Cornelia Otis Skinner, Janet Flanner, Alan Seeger, William Faulkner, Norman Geddes (for a drawing), Morris Rysking, and many others. The only other later famous writer I recognized is Robert Moses.

28. *SN* (Sept. 1911): ad p. 8.

29. Scott, p. 14.

30. *SN* (Mar. 1911): ad p. 6.

31. *SN* (July 1911): ad p. 12.

32. It is likely that Colgate's proposed contest was the impetus for this rare publication of winning entries for *SN* ad competition, since they appeared several months after the winners' names were announced.

33. *SN* (Mar. 1911): ad p. 6.

34. Report on Competition 47, *SN* 32 (Sept. 1905).

35. The St. Nicholas Zoo variously animates the trademarks of *brands* (the Pettijohn breakfast food bear), puns on brand names (an elephant's tusk marked Ivory Soap), refers to a slogan (a camel marked "see that hump"), or more jarringly refers to the source of products (a calf emblazoned Knox Gelatine and pigs marked Swift's and Armour's Ham and Bacon). Even in this crude form in which not only does the lion lie down with the giraffe but Armour's uses the same symbol as its rival Swift's, and the Pettijohn bear eats Quaker Oats, readers are encouraged to imagine products as characters pleasurably cavorting, and to think of ways to include more characters. The pictures prime readers to notice references to brand names everywhere, so that the sight of a lion should make one think of Lion Collars or Royal Baking Powder (Dec. 1900; May 1901).

36. Competition 44, *SN* 32 (Mar. 1905): ad p. 10.

37. Margaret Johnson, "The Corner Cupboard," *SN* 33 (July 1905): 777–84.

12

"Work Well Done": Louisa May Alcott and Mary Mapes Dodge

Daniel Shealy

In the spring of 1873, Mary Mapes Dodge mailed an announcement of a new, forthcoming children's periodical, *St. Nicholas,* to many of the leading writers of the time. Her prospectus touted the "profusely illustrated" magazine and promised that "'[t]he spirit of mirthfulness shall be invoked from the first, and all good things fresh, true, and child-like, heartily commended, while every way to juvenile priggishness shall be bolted and barred'" (qtd. in Gannon and Thompson 128–29). One of the writers she attempted to lure to the pages of *St. Nicholas* was Louisa May Alcott, arguably already the country's premier children's author. By 1873, Alcott had published numerous works, including *Little Women* (1868–69), *An Old-Fashioned Girl* (1870), *Little Men* (1871), and two volumes of *Aunt Jo's Scrap-Bag* (1872), with a third volume being prepared for press. She was also a regular contributor of short stories to Daniel Ford's *The Youth's Companion,* the periodical that was certain to be Dodge's greatest rival for *St. Nicholas's* intended audience. Thus, Alcott's career as a children's writer was secure; she already possessed fame and fortune. Obtaining her services as a contributor would certainly have been a coup for the fledging magazine. While Alcott was reluctant, at first, to commit to a new periodical, especially one without a proven track record, she eventually became one of *St. Nicholas's* leading authors, one whose name would be closely associated with the publication for almost fifteen years during the 1870s and 1880s. Much of the success of the relationship between Alcott and *St.*

Nicholas can be attributed to its editor, Mary Mapes Dodge, who was only one year older than Alcott herself. Not only did Alcott find a lucrative market for her tales and novels, but she also found a compassionate editor who understood the pressures of juggling a professional career alongside domestic responsibilities. She discovered, true to the journal's prospectus, that its editor was serious about creating a unique magazine for America's youth, one that cherished high standards and quality work. The relationship that existed between these two major nineteenth-century children's writers forms a fascinating tale of a literary partnership between author and editor.

When Dodge sent her initial inquiry to Alcott in the spring of 1873, requesting stories for her new venture, the Concord author had recently completed a long serialization of her adult novel *Work: A Story of Experience* for *The Christian Union* (for which she received $5000) and was busy writing stories and compiling old ones for her third *Scrap-Bag* volume. Since returning from Europe in 1871, she had been furiously capitalizing on her good literary fortune by publishing new works and recycling old. She responded to Dodge's request on 8 May 1873, informing her that "I cannot engage anything at present as I am a housekeeper this summer & shall have no time for new engagements." She would not, she declared, even consider a "serial story" since she "dislike[s] that style of thing more than ever after my winter's experience" with *Work*. In fact, she was not promising anything for the new publication because she already had an ongoing, profitable relationship with Daniel Ford's magazine: "Do not depend upon me however, for I may find that I can only write for The Youth's Companion, an old friend & excellent paymaster." Of course, she was not about to shut off any opportunity for a market for her work and closed her reply with "best wishes for success." Perhaps Alcott remembered the difficulty of editing a periodical and securing authors for each issue. She too had performed just such a task in 1867 when she was asked by Horace B. Fuller to edit *Merry's Museum*, a

This portrait appeared in Louise Chandler Moulton's memorial tribute "Louisa May Alcott," which acknowledged Alcott's long association with *St. Nicholas. SN* (June 1888): 624.

children's magazine created by Samuel Goodrich (the author of the Peter Parley tales) in 1841. Dodge herself was not the type of editor to lose the possibility of attracting one of America's leading juvenile writers, and in March 1874, Alcott's first contribution to *St. Nicholas* graced its pages—the short tale "Roses and Forget-Me-Nots," a story which earned her $100 (*Journals* 193). Her second piece, the story "The Autobiography of an Omnibus" followed in October of that year, again netting her $100. Alcott was obviously aware that a new avenue for placing her work was performing well in the marketplace.

Dodge, pleased with the success of her new publication, seemed intent on having Alcott become a regular contributor, and she requested more tales from her pen. However, by 1874, Louisa's mother, Abigail May Alcott, was declining in health and her final illness was upon her, forcing the daughter to spend more and more time at home in Concord, performing her duties as a nurse rather than creating new stories for the young. On 8 October, she confessed to the persistent Dodge that "I am so busy with home affairs just now that I have no time even to think of stories." But she promised that if she could "get any leisure this winter I will try to send one or two." She was willing, however, to offer her professional opinion on illustrators. Dodge had requested the address of Elizabeth B. Greene, the artist who had illustrated Alcott's *Morning-Glories, and other Stories* in 1867 and provided drawings for *Merry's Museum*. Alcott had another suggestion: "I like Mrs. Innis' drawing better than Miss Greene's. Mrs. I. is illustrating a book for me now…. Her children are altogether charming, thier [sic] little fat legs captivate me entirely. But I love E. B. G. & dont mind her infant's dropsical heads very much" (Stern 368).

Despite her refusal to write more tales, Alcott had already agreed to serialize her new novel *Eight Cousins* in *St. Nicholas*. Even though she had just a year earlier expressed her dislike for serializations, she no doubt was tempted by the handsome fee of $2000 that Dodge offered. To perhaps appease her other lucrative market for short stories, Alcott agreed to serialize another lengthy piece she was writing, "Silver Pitchers: A Temperance Tale," in *The Youth's Companion* during May and June 1875. She also had learned by her experience with *Work* that she could command several fees for the same product, and she was not above getting paid twice for her books—once in the serial form and again when the novel was published in book form. Now she was considering a third possibility—European royalties. This venture would, however, lead to conflict with *St. Nicholas*.

In order for an American author to receive a British copyright during the late nineteenth century, the work had to be published first in

England, even if it were only a day's difference. The confusion this procedure would cause for Alcott and Dodge, as each attempted to protect her rights, would try their patience greatly. In fact, Alcott even resorted in writing directly to Scribner and Company to clear up the dispute. On October 30, 1874, she expressed her dismay over the proceedings to the publisher: "If the copyright matter annoys publishers it certainly bewilders authors & leaves them in very defenceless [sic] positions at times, for there seems to be no law to guide or protect them." She, of course, did not wish to upset Scribner or Roberts Brothers, her own publisher since 1868, as it was in her "own interest to keep faith with American publishers as I find them far more generous, active & obliging than English ones." She even admitted that she "should prefer to lose the little John Bull pays me than to be worried by delay, small returns & the very peculiar way in which business is done there." Alcott planned to have her English publisher, Sampson Low, print the first chapter "in pamphlet form" which would appear two weeks before *St. Nicholas* started the serial. She would also instruct Sampson Low not to publish the piece in any magazine which would appear in the United States. Hoping to satisfy Scribner, she asked: "Does not that protect us all & make things safe on both sides of the water?" (*Letters* 186–87). All of her explanations, however, failed to make Scribner happy since they saw potential competition from British publishers.

On December 2, Alcott wrote Dodge herself, exclaiming that the "whole affair has seemed like a tempest in a teacup to me." Scribner, she protested, "have evidently got a bee in thier [sic] bonnet, on this point, & I cannot find out just what it is in spite of the many explanations so kindly given me." She reiterated the problem to her editor: "To me the matter appears thus. I make an agreement with S. & Co. about Eight Cousins exactly as I have always done with other serials. Reserving all rights to the tale outside of thier [sic] magazine." Without British copyright, Alcott insisted, she would be "at the mercy of any English publisher who chooses to take the story." She felt Scribner now was placing "so many obstacles in the way." They were also asking for "so many stipulations that the English publisher is perplexed." Alcott felt ready to raise up her hands and surrender: "I telegraph, write, explain, & try to be as obliging as I can. Change the name of the tale to suit others, put in babies to suit the artist, & endeavor to go on writing with the whole affair in such a coil that my genius refuses to burn & the story is put away till calmer times." She would, she insisted, "gladly give away the whole Eight or put them in the fire if it were fair for others." Appealing to Dodge's sense of what an independent career woman goes through, she added: "I am not well, & with little relief from pain day & night worry wears upon me more than [I] like to have it.

Eight Cousins (1875) was the first Louisa May Alcott serial to appear in *St. Nicholas.*
*SN*2 (Jan. 1875): 135.

If it were not for the blessed fact that everything has its comic as well as tragic side I should have lost my wits long ago with three publishers thundering at me all at once. As a sister woman you can understand this, & know that neither tears nor laughter can keep one from losing patience & spirits sometimes" (*Letters* 187–88). Although it appears Scribner was never fully satisfied with the bargain Alcott had agreed upon with Sampson Low, they did not hold up publication. *Eight Cousins* was first serialized in England in *Good Things: A Picturesque Magazine for Youth of All Ages* between 5 December 1874 and 27 November 1875, and appeared in *St.*

Nicholas from January through October 1875. It was to be the first of several Alcott serials the magazine would print.

In preparing the manuscript for *Eight Cousins,* Alcott, for the most part, accommodated Dodge's requests. Writing to Frank Stockton, *St. Nicholas's* assistant editor, on 10 January 1875, Alcott announced that her work "was finished with the old year & has been waiting for the last touches which are most effectually given after an author has got out of the composing 'vortex.'" The story, according to Dodge, was a bit longer than she wanted, but Alcott declared she could "easily take out two chapters, which will bring the tale to the right length." Perhaps Alcott even remembered Dodge's prospectus for *St. Nicholas,* which claimed the magazine would "avoid anything like formal teaching or preaching" (qtd. in Gannon and Thompson 129): "Pictures of boy & girl life & character with as much fun & as little preaching as possible; this is all the short space allowed will permit me to do, & if the young people get an idea or a laugh or two out of it I shall be satisfied" (*Letters* 190).

The next few years saw little from Alcott's pen appear in Dodge's magazine. Alcott wrote Dodge in September of 1875, indicating that her time was already occupied: "I cannot undertake any long job of pen work as I have another book on hand. But an occasional story is at your service, & one or two papers to the girls if no better person can be found. I have put so many bits of advice into 8 Cousins that I haven't much left" (*Letters* 195). In early 1876, Dodge published two Alcott works: "Marjorie's Birthday Gifts" in January and "Helping Along" in March. By June, Alcott recorded in her 1876 journal, everyone desired new work from her: "Try to get up steam for a new serial, as Mrs. Dodge wants one, and Scribner offers $3,000 for it. Roberts Brothers want a novel; and the various newspapers and magazines clamor for tales. My brain is squeezed dry, and I can only wait for help" (*Journals* 200–01). The next year, 1877, saw no Alcott fiction appear in *St. Nicholas.* Instead, Alcott decided to concentrate on her novels, publishing *Rose in Bloom: A Sequel to Eight Cousins* in late 1876 and *A Modern Mephistopheles,* her contribution to Roberts Brothers' No-Name Series in 1877. However, she had not severed any ties with Dodge; she was, during 1877, busy writing another novel, entitled *Under the Lilacs,* to be serialized in *St. Nicholas.*

By summer 1877, Alcott was hard at work on *Under the Lilacs.* On June 3, she bemoaned to Dodge the fact that the book "goes slowly owing to interruptions, for summer is a busy time & I get few quiet days." She was pleased to report that twelve chapters were done and would "make about six or seven numbers in St Nicholas." The illustrator Mary Anna Foote had been engaged to do drawings for the work, so Alcott promised

to send Dodge "the first few chapters during the week for Mrs. Foote …
so that my infants may not be drawn with whiskers & my big boys & girls
in pinafores as in Eight Cousins." Concerned about past illustrations of
her work, she confessed to Dodge that "I do feel a natural wish to have
one story prettily adorned with good pictures, as hitherto artists have much
aºicted me" (*Letters* 222–23).

Alcott also revealed her own frustrations with the serial and provided
some valuable insight into her creative process: "I am daily waiting with
anxiety for an illumination of some sort as my plot is very vague so far &
though I don't approve of 'sensations' in childrens books, one must have
a certain thread on which to string the small events which make up the
true sort of child life." In order to generate ideas, Alcott told Dodge she
planned "to go & simmer an afternoon" at A. Van Amburg's Mammoth
Menagerie and New Great Golden Menagerie in Boston so she could "get
hints for the further embellishment of Ben & his dog." She also declared
that she had included a poem by Franklin Benjamin Sanborn's young son
and believed that "bit will give Mrs. Foote a good scene with the six-year-
old poet reciting his verses under the lilacs" (*Letters* 223). On 26 September 1877, she sent Scribner the last six chapters, noting that "I have selected
the parts I should prefer for illustration. Mrs F[oote] does not choose lively
ones, & half the fun is spoiled by a spiritless picture." She was also willing to let Dodge use her own professional opinion in editing the piece:
"When you send me proofs just mark here & there any alterations as to
length &c. which must be made & I will try to adjust matters to suit." She
was also ready to remove the young poet from the manuscript if Dodge
preferred: "Shall I take out all about 'Tennyson Jr?' It was put in to please
F. B. Sanborn's boys. But the poems can be suppressed, also the poet if you
think best, though I may not be able to suffer anything better." The editor, however, decided to keep the episode in the published version, even
noting with an asterisk that the poetry was actually written by a child.

Under the Lilacs started its publication in the December 1877 *St.
Nicholas*, and ran in monthly installments through October 1878. As her
own critic, Alcott knew the serial was not among her best: "Some of these
chapters were written in mother's sick room & are a sight for gods & men."
Her hand, which had been causing her problems since she wrote *Work* on
impression paper so as to make three copies at once, was again experiencing pain, and she vowed that "as soon as I get time I'm going to have
my paralyzed thumb cured or there will be an end to story writing" (ALS:
NjP).

Although the end to "story writing" was still a decade away, Alcott's
literary output was indeed slowing down. By now, she considered Dodge

not only to be a fine editor, but she also was a good friend. A few years earlier she had visited her in New York, and in February 1879, Alcott reciprocated as host by inviting Mary Mapes Dodge to Concord for lunch, along with Frances Hodgson Burnett and her son Vivian, who would later serve as the model for her famous novel *Little Lord Fauntleroy* (1886). Both Alcott and Burnett had been "guests of honor" at the Papyrus Club in Boston earlier. Alcott found Dodge and Burnett to be "[m]ost agreeable women" (*Journals* 214).

By July 1879, Alcott had written "Jimmy's Cruise in the Pinafore" for *St. Nicholas* and was paid her usual fee of one hundred dollars (*Journals* 215); however, Dodge wanted another serial, knowing that the Alcott name would attract readers for issue after issue. Dodge had apparently suggested a tale based around the American Revolution, but Alcott felt reluctant. She wrote to Dodge on 21 August 1879 with plans for a different direction: "The Revolutionary tale does not seem to possess me.... I hope you will not be very much disappointed about the old time tale. It would take study to do it well, & leisure is just what I have not got & never shall have I fear, when writing is to be done." Besides, Alcott explained, she believed her readers preferred the domestic stories on which she had built her career: "I have casually asked many of my young folks, when they demand a new story, which they would like, one of that sort or the old Eight Cousin [sic] style, & they all say the latter." In an effort, perhaps, to ease Dodge's disappointment, Alcott declared that she had a title selected, was ready to begin writing, and felt it would proceed quickly — news that Dodge certainly wanted to hear: "It would be much easier to do as I have a beginning & a plan all ready, a village & the affairs of a party of children." The plot, she divulged, would be based on real-life experiences since there were "so many little romances going on among the Concord boys & girls & all sorts of queer things which will work into 'Jack & Jill' nicely." She promised to send a few chapters for Dodge to review and "decide if they will suit." Knowing that Dodge wanted her to attempt new literary territory with historical fiction, a staple in *St. Nicholas,* Alcott promised to make the new serial "unlike the others" she had written. However, that would be a difficult feat, since "the dears *will* cling to the Little Women style" (*Letters* 235).

Dodge was pleased with the few sample chapters from *Jack and Jill,* and Alcott confessed in September that the editor's "cheery word" had been her "best 'starter.'" Alcott was ready with four more chapters and wished that "the artist will be inspired & have some good pictures for us." She wondered if her manuscript chapters were the correct length: "From 30 to 35 of mine are about what you put in to three or four of yours with pictures." If she knew the needed length then she could "plan to have each month's allowance complete in itself, or end with an interesting episode." Encouraging Dodge in her role as editor, Alcott wrote: "Don't let me *prose*. If I seem to be declining & falling in to it pull me up & I'll try to prance as of old. Years tone down one's spirit & fancy though they only deepen one's love for the little people & strengthen the desire to serve them wisely as well as cheerfully." Alcott not only had the young readers in mind, but she also thought of the adults: "Fathers & mothers tell me they use my books as helps for themselves, so now & then I like to slip in a page for them, fresh from the experience of some other parent, for education seems to me to be the problem in our times." Dodge must have taken great delight in Alcott's preview of her youthful critics: "'Jack & Jill' are right out of our own little circle, & the boys & girls are in a twitter to know what is going in, so it will be a 'truly story' in the main" (*Letters* 237). The following month, Alcott recorded in her journal that the first proofs had begun to arrive from Scribner. Once again she noted the intent interest the serial's progress was creating among the Concord children: "Young folks much interested in the story & all want to 'go in.' I shall have a hornet's nest about me if all are not *angels*" (217). However, for the second time, tragedy would interfere with work.

Louisa's younger sister May Alcott, who had been studying art in Europe, had recently married a Swiss businessman, Ernest Nieriker, and on 8 November 1879, their daughter was born in Paris. May honored her sister by naming the baby Louisa May Nieriker. But the family joy was short-lived. On 29 December, May Alcott Nieriker died in Paris, most likely from complications caused by the birth. Distraught that she had not been able to sail to France to help her sister during the latter stages of pregnancy, Louisa found some solace in the fact that Ernest had agreed to May's last wish to have the little girl raised by her older sister. The child, scheduled to arrive in September, was also certain to change Louisa's literary lifestyle — perhaps for the better — since she would now have her "own" child for whom she could spin stories.

On January 20, 1880, Alcott conveyed her grief to Mary Mapes Dodge, along with a report on the progress of *Jack and Jill,* which had started its serialization in *St. Nicholas* in December 1879. "I never get a good chance to do a story without interruption of some sort," she confessed. Alcott's last serial for *St. Nicholas, Under the Lilacs,* had been completed during her mother's final illness, a fact that, in the author's opinion, hurt the tale. Now *Jack and Jill* was completed "when my heart was full of care & hope & then grief over poor May." The serial was finished, all except copying the last chapters, and Alcott "thought it best to let them lie till I could give my mind to the work." She hoped, however, that despite her sadness "the misery did not get into the story, but I'm afraid it is not as gay as I meant most of it to be." The letter closed with a despondent tone: "A sweeter little romance has just ended in Paris than any I can ever make, & the sad facts of life leave me no heart for cheerful fiction" (*Letters* 244–45).

Despite Alcott's own personal grief, readers enjoyed *Jack and Jill*, and it appeared each month in *St. Nicholas* until October 1880. In March of that year, Alcott again wrote to Dodge about the tale and hoped that her editor was "as much relieved to see the end as I am." She had done her best, given the situation, and she even tried to please her audience as much as possible: "People told me to make the tale 'a little pious,' so I have here & there tried to suit them without being too preachy." The local reception of the new work seemed good: "The Concord children enjoy the numbers as they come out, & my other infants seem satisfied, so I trust the delay & dark days have not done any great harm" (Stern 371).

Before *Jack and Jill* ended its run, Dodge was in the market for another long piece of work from Alcott. However, with the lingering sadness of May's death, the prospect of a new baby, plus the care of her older sister's two sons (Anna Alcott Pratt was a single parent, her husband having died in 1871), Alcott did not feel like undertaking another long commitment: "Mrs Dodge wants a new serial, but I doubt if I can do it. Boys, babies, illness & business of all sorts leave no time for story telling. Reality makes romance seem pale & flat now" (*Journals* 225). On May 29, she told Dodge the disappointing news: "If I write a Serial you shall have it; but I have my doubts as to the leisure & quiet needed for such tasks being possible with a year old baby. Of course little Lu is a *very* remarkable child, but I fancy I shall feel as full of responsibility as a hen with one chick, & cluck & scratch industriously for the sole benefit of my daughter." Of course, there was always the chance that the child would "have a literary turn," becoming Alcott's "assistant by offering hints giving studies of character" for her stories (*Letters* 248).

She did offer *St. Nicholas* hope as she proposed an idea for a possible work. She asked Dodge, "If I do begin a new story how would 'an old fashioned boy' and his life do?" Referring to Martha Farquharson, who published *An Old-Fashioned Boy* (1871) on the wave of Alcott's success with *An Old-Fashioned Girl* (1870), she noted that "I meant that for the title of a book, but another woman stole it." Her plan was to use material based on Bronson Alcott's own life: "You proposed a Revolutionary tale once but I was not up to it; for this [*An Old-Fashioned Boy*] I have quaint material in my father's journals, letters & recollections. He was born with the century & had an uncle in the war of 1812, & his life was very pretty & pastoral in the early days." She added, "I think a new sort of story wouldn't be amiss, with fun in it, & the queer old names & habits. I began it long ago, & if I have a chance will finish off a few chapters & send them to you if you like" (*Letters* 248).

However, over a year later, August 6, 1881, Alcott was no longer satisfied with her idea, and she was certainly aware that it had been eight months since her work last appeared in the pages of *St. Nicholas*. She apologized to Dodge: "I am sorry for the children's disappointment, & dont delay for want of urging as the twenty boys & girls here ... clamor for more stories & suggest many plans." Dodge's old idea of a tale about the American Revolution was once again rejected: "None seem to think that a Revolutionary one would be interesting, & I fear that patriotism is not natural to the youthful soul." Even if she could get up the energy to write, Alcott felt unsure about the results, and she told Dodge that "[a]s I lead the life of an oyster just now I fear it wont be a very thrilling tale, but it may appease the little people till we can promise something better" (*Letters* 254).

However, literary work proceeded slowly. During the summer, Dodge, as was sometimes her practice, sent Alcott some illustrations, hoping they might provide inspiration for new fiction. On August 16, 1881, Alcott responded: "I have been looking at the pictures with all my eyes hoping an idea would start up. As yet ideas are not heard from, but I shall continue to stare *hard* & cudgel my brain till something comes." One illustration in particular "took [Alcott's] fancy"—a cat and a spinning wheel. Looking at the picture, Alcott felt "a little tale of an old fashioned Thanksgiving looms vaguely before me." One possibility was to do research on the Pilgrims at Plymouth in 1621: "If I could get at the books I'd try 'The First Thanksgiving.' But it might be too grim & sad." She confessed that she had "often written up to pictures & find them very suggestive, especially now when invention is at low water mark" (*Letters* 255). Obviously the illustration worked, and *St. Nicholas* published "An Old-Fashioned Thanksgiving" in its November 1881 issue. The tale, set in 1820s New Hampshire, even included a spinning wheel and a cat, complete with the illustration! However, the story would be Alcott's only contribution to the magazine during that year. In fact, it would be December of 1882 before the next Alcott tale, "Grandmamma's Pearls," appeared.

Despite her period of little creative work, Alcott never forgot her craft, always remaining sensitive to possible ideas for tales or novels. Spending part of the summer at the seaside resort of Nonquitt, Massachusetts, Alcott, who could not escape her reputation as the "children's friend," often entertained large groups of boys and girls. In her letter of

August 16, 1881, she related to Dodge how these experiences were useful to a weary writer:

> Twenty eight children last night sat round the big chair I occupied, on the arms & back thereof, & clamored for stories. In the exciting crisis of The Three Pigs in the wall of faces before me I saw one little red ear pushed through a narrow place "listening tight", as a small boy expressed it. On examination a flushed and beaming child appeared, saying contentedly, "I couldn't see but I was 'termined to hear, & I did."
>
> Such an audience must inspire even my used up wits; so, as it is rainy, they all come to my cottage this evening &, sitting round the open fire, have a storytell. I have an eye to business, & out of their hints, chat & pretty ways hope for the germ of the forthcoming work [*Letters* 255].

This forthcoming work, "Mrs. Gay's Summer School," would never be published, although such events as she describes in her letter must have done much to reassure Alcott. Instead, Alcott would focus on short tales, which could then later be collected and printed in book form. With a new idea dancing in her mind, Alcott seemed anxious to begin. In fact, Dodge had even sent her a picture for inspiration, and in her letter of 15 August, she told Dodge that the picture of a mother and child "would come in nicely for the first tale, — 'Grandma and her Mother.'" Ready to abandon the thought of a longer serial, she claimed that "the spinning-tales come tumbling into my mind so fast I'd better pin a few while 'genius burns.'" Would, she wondered, *St. Nicholas* "like to start the set Christmas. The picture being ready and the first story can be done in a week." She added: "If you don't want it yet, I will take my time and do several" (*Letters* 271–72).

A few weeks later, on September 7, 1883, Alcott had not yet heard from Dodge about the plan. She had already made the decision, however, about her progress: "I find that neither head nor hand go very well, so you had better announce 'Spinning Wheel Stories,' simply, & let Mrs Gay come in as a second title if I can do the serial or be dropped if I can only string my stories." Ready to start publication, Alcott asked, "How soon do you want to begin?" With three short stories and the introduction completed, she could "have a wide variety & so suit all tastes." Even though she was departing the coast and leaving behind the quiet life away from the distractions in Concord and Boston, she was delighted to "have got a start, & promising to spin away till you play Fate [and] cut the thread" (ALS: NjP).

Dodge herself was also ready to begin another of Alcott's long-range projects. After all, it would insure that an Alcott story would appear in *St. Nicholas* every month for the next year. Dodge already had a long Alcott tale, "Little Pyramus and Thisbe," scheduled for the September and October 1884 issues, and Alcott had recently completed "Sophie's Secret," another long tale planned for November and December publication. The first "Spinning Wheel Story," entitled "Grandma's Story," ran in the January 1884 *St. Nicholas,* with the illustration of a mother and child by Ellen Oakford, which Dodge had supplied earlier. By June 6, 1884, Alcott could write Dodge that she was "glad to be done spinning. Wish they were better & brighter, but the old cheeriness is gone, & one cant bring it back however hard one tries" (*Letters* 282). As the twelve "Spinning Wheel Stories" appeared in consecutive issues, Alcott once again made her presence felt in the pages of America's most popular children's magazine. However, after January 1885, little of Alcott's work would run in *St. Nicholas.*

Alcott herself knew that the genius was burning out. Ill health was plaguing her more and more, tiring her out mentally and physically. Her aging father, who had suffered a stroke in October of 1882, began to weigh on her nerves, and her growing niece consumed more of her time. Added to the family matters was the fact that she was partially supporting her older sister, Anna Alcott Pratt, and her two sons. Dodge, who was a widowed working mother herself, must have had compassion and understanding for Alcott's condition.

By the mid-1880s, the two had become close friends as well as business acquaintances. They had visited in each other's homes and they had comforted each other in sorrow. In early 1884, Dodge's mother had died, and Alcott, true to their friendship, had written a comforting note: "There is no loss like that of a good mother whom one has had the happiness of keeping till one can enjoy as a woman the love that has been fostering sunshine

Mary Mapes Dodge sent Alcott this picture by Ellen Oakford of a Colonial mother and child to inspire her new series, *Spinning Wheel Stories*; it became an illustration for "Grandma's Story" in January 1884. *SN* 11 (Jan. 1884): 212.

since babyhood." Perhaps thinking of her own mother's death almost seven years earlier, Alcott remarked that the bond between mother and daughter "seems so near that even death cannot break it & 'Mother' never deserts us though her visible presence is gone." She added that Dodge should find solace in her work: "May time be kind to you, & the loving labor which makes you like a carefree mother to many young people comfort you as work seldom fails to do" (ALS: NjP). A few weeks later, she again wrote about Dodge's loss, confessing that she had "felt like an orphan ever since my mother went." However, she claimed, she still felt her presence at times: "Nothing takes its place, & if now & then there did not come a blessed sense of her nearness, & the certainty that such love must be immortal, I think it would be much harder than it is to get on in this weary work a day world. Yet work is good without it life is only a selfish thing" (*Letters* 281).

Work would indeed continue for both Alcott and Dodge. Although Alcott was nearing the end of her illustrious career, *St. Nicholas* magazine was in its prime. When Thomas Niles, her longtime editor at Roberts Brothers, announced in late 1883 that Louisa May Alcott was writing the third book in the March family saga, to be called *Jo's Boys,* Dodge promptly requested that Alcott serialize the novel first in her magazine. The publisher's literary notice was premature however: "About 'Jo's Boys,' I can only say that it is not written, & I see no prospect of its being done for some time…. Niles urged the advertising when I thought I could go at it, but other duties prevented it." Since she always enjoyed being paid twice for the same work, Alcott herself had no qualms about the novel eventually appearing in *St. Nicholas,* but Thomas Niles felt otherwise: "*He* thinks, I believe, that it is better for a tale to come out all together, as many read it in a magazine who would otherwise buy the book to our profit" (ALS: NjP). Niles did feel that Alcott and Roberts Brother lost money on serializations, and he convinced Alcott to turn down Dodge's request. She communicated this decision to Dodge: "T. N. says *No*" (Envelope: NjP). She later replied that "T. N. is so very kind & useful that when he decidedly expresses a wish or opinion I like to comply with it." To soften the disappointment, she admitted, "The prospect of 'Jo's Boys' is a very uncertain one, & I have a serial which I think will be done first, if any quiet time ever comes" (*Letters* 281).

The quiet time never came, and another serial would never follow. In April of 1886, Alcott wrote to Dodge that she could not "promise anything, but hope to be allowed to write a little, as my doctor has decided that it is as well to let me put on paper the tales … as to have them go on worrying me inside." Still she promised to work on material for *St. Nicholas* if she could keep her health: "So I'm scribbling at 'Jo's Boys' long promised to Mr Niles & clamored for by the children. I may write but one hour a day so cannot get on very fast, but if it is ever done I can think of a serial for St N. I began one & can easily start it for 88 if head & hand allow. I will simmer on it this summer see if it can be done" (*Letters* 297). During July, she noted in her journal that she needed the money a serial would bring: "What next? Mrs Dodge wants a serial & T. N[iles] a novel. I have a dozen plots in my head but think a serial better come first. Want a great deal of money, for many things. Every poor soul I ever knew comes for help & expenses increase. I am the only money maker & must turn the mill for others though my grist is ground in the barn" (*Journals* 277). *Jo's Boys, and How They Turned Out: A Sequel to Little Men* would be published only by Roberts Brothers in 1886. Besides two more collections of short stories (one published posthumously), it would be Alcott's last major work.

The year 1886, however, saw only one publication by Alcott in *St. Nicholas*— the tale "The Blind Lark," which appeared in November. The tale, written in the waning months of 1885, was especially tailored for the "Blind Asylum people," who had often requested that Alcott "write a story to interest children in the Kindergarten." Sending it to *St. Nicholas,* the magazine they had asked that it be published in, Alcott apologized to her editor: "It isn't what it might have been if I could have used some of the true stories told me. But the parents are very sensitive, or the blind boys & girls, so I had to invent my heroine &c." The money earned, she informed Dodge, would be given "to the Kindergarten Fund." Ending her letter on a positive note, one that was sure to please Dodge, Alcott included a message from her niece, now six years old: "Lulu crushed me latel[y] by saying decidedly, 'On the whole, Aunt Wee, I like St Nitlus more better than your books. Such lots of pishers in it.'" The prolific author added, "I quite agreed with her" (ALS: NjP).

Instead of the long-promised serial, Alcott focused her attention on a collection of short stories. It would be her last complete work that she would see to print. Writing Dodge about her plans on May 4, 1887, she informed her that she was preparing the collection for book publication by Roberts Brothers: "About the stories for St N. I am not sure, for, though my first plan was to do several to send you for the coming year, I found Mr Niles so disappointed at my failure to give him another book that I offered the 'Garland for Girls' instead." The book, she insisted, must be "ready to issue" by October, and if Dodge wanted any of the tales for *St. Nicholas*, she would have to make certain they would be published "before that time": "One is done & you can have the corrected proofs in a day or two if you want it. Others I shall finish as fast [as] my head will allow; but I cannot do much yet, so go slowly." She elaborated on her concept for the book: "The idea is some eight or ten tales for girls, with flowery names as a sort of emblem of the moral or meaning of the stories. Books, travel, charity, home duties, & girlish trials of various sorts are to be illustrated." She even envisioned the project as "a companion volume for 'Spinning Wheel Stories.'" Even though the book would be published by the new year, she wanted Dodge to know that she was thinking of *St. Nicholas* and was willing to offer her what she could: "I wish there were time to send them all to St N. but you shall have as many as you want, & I will do such as are best for your purpose first? ... Which will you have? Or is it too late for any with your fare-handed people?" (*Letters* 310).

By 23 June 1887, Alcott was hard at work on writing the stories for the collection. Knowing that the tales were being written for a book and not for the magazine itself, she requested that Dodge feel comfortable editing them freely: "Pray cut up the 'Ivy Spray' to suit your space. I'll trust you to arrange it prettily even with some of its leaves gone." More tales, she told her, were being readied. Instead of her usual practice of sending Dodge the manuscript first, she was now mailing her the proofs from Roberts Brothers as fast as the type was being set: "'Pansies' is in the hands of the printer, & you shall have the proof as soon as I get it." In order for Dodge to plan for the length to fit the magazine, Alcott offered some comparative information: "It is, I think, about fifty pages of note paper like that on which Ivy is written. This also can be cut, & I will do what I can when it comes to me. Writing for a book I let my pen go & so it may be too long for you. It takes eight of my pages to make one of *St N.* I think." Alcott hoped for more stories to follow, but reluctantly she added: "An hour a day is my limit now, so I accomplish very little, & long to rebel, but dare not" (*Letters* 315). Dodge eagerly accepted the offerings; "An Ivy Spray" appeared in the October 1887 issue of *St. Nicholas*, and "Pansies" followed in November. These two stories were the only ones published by Dodge when *A Garland for Girls*, a collection of seven tales, was issued by Roberts Brothers in December 1887.

In November 1887, Alcott, writing from a type of rest home in Roxbury, Massachusetts, sent Dodge an advance copy of the book, "not for any merit of its own but as a little thank-offering for the kind contribution to my charity fund which the last two stories in St. N. brought me." Her payment of $250 had "put coal, food & clothes into the home where a good woman, deserted by a drunken husband, was trying to keep her little girls safe under her wing, & nearly starving rather than part from them." But that was not all, she told her: "It has also given comforts to a young girl dying of consumption, & made easy the heart of a woman at the hospital by paying rent during her absence." She noted that these "'little chores done for my neighbor,' as mother used to call them, are my best medicine & amusement during this long year of exile from home at Saint's Rest, where the victims of over work slowly climb back to health" (*Letters* 322–23).

Alcott never completed her slow climb. On 4 March 1888, her father, Bronson, died at Louisa's Louisburg Square house on Beacon Hill in Boston. Visiting her father a day before his death, Louisa, on her return to Roxbury, forgot her winter wrap for the carriage drive home. Her already exhausted body could not resist the cold, and she fell ill. Two days later, on March 6, 1888, she died, never realizing that her father, with whom she shared the same birthday of November 29, had passed away. The thousands of readers of *St. Nicholas* had lost a cherished author, and Mary Mapes Dodge had lost a longtime friend. Almost up until her death, Alcott had contributed steadily to *St. Nicholas*. In November 1887, she had written Dodge, saying, "I see my name in the list of St N. writers" and offered her more tales (*Letters* 323). In fact, one month after her death, "Trudel's Siege," a tale she had written for her last collection of short stories, appeared in *St. Nicholas*. Two other stories, one in 1902 and another in 1903, would also be published; no Alcott manuscript sent to Dodge's magazine would go unused. Her professional collaboration with the periodical and her personal friendship with its editor would leave behind a lasting legacy. In the May 1888 issue of *St. Nicholas,* two tributes to the famous writer would mark the magazine's recognition of its beloved writer. Louise Chandler Moulton, a popular poet, would pen a three-page biography, claiming that "hundreds of letters to the editor, from children all over the English-speaking world attest their dear love for the author" whose stories and novels had entertained them in *St. Nicholas* (626). The other piece, entitled "The Advice of Miss Alcott," was written by John Preston True, a children's author and later editor at Houghton, Mi⁹in. True, who had once asked Alcott for her professional advice, noted that "readers of ST. NICHOLAS have met with a great loss. Before this is read by you, the telegraph will have carried the sad news far and near that our dear 'Aunt Jo' has passed away." The young author went on to praise her value to children's literature: "How many happy hours are due to her! How many young lives are the better, and braver for the words she wrote, and the examples of her little men and women!" (545).

The young readers had indeed lost "the children's friend." Her thirty-two contributions to *St. Nicholas* would be among some of the magazine's best fiction, and her name and work had certainly helped Dodge make the periodical the leader in its field. On December 22, 1887, a few months

before her death, Alcott had mailed one of her last letters to Dodge, saying that "I hope you are well & full of the peace work well done gives the
happy doer. I mend slowly but surely, & my good Dr. says my best work
is yet to come" *(Letters* 327–28). Dodge must have been pleased with
Alcott's positive words of hope, and at the end of their illustrious careers,
both Louisa May Alcott and Mary Mapes Dodge surely were "full of the
peace work well done gives."

Notes

1. Louisa May Alcott, autograph letter signed, to Mary Mapes Dodge, 8 May 1873,
Mary Mapes Dodge Collection, Princeton University Library. Hereafter all manuscript
letters cited as "ALS: NjP." All manuscript letters are used by permission of the Princeton University Library.

References

Alcott, Louisa May. *The Selected Letters of Louisa May Alcott.* Ed. Joel Myerson, Daniel
    Shealy, and Madeleine B. Stern. Boston: Little, Brown, 1987.
_____. *The Journals of Louisa May Alcott.* Ed. Joel Myerson, Daniel Shealy, and
    Madeleine B. Stern. Boston: Little, Brown, 1989.
Moulton, Louise Chandler. "Louisa May Alcott." *SN* 15 (May 1888): 624–26.
"Prospectus." New York: Scribner, 1873, qtd. in Susan R. Gannon and Ruth Anne
Thompson, *Mary Mapes Dodge.* Boston: Twayne, 1992.
Stern, Madeleine B. "Louisa Alcott's Self-Criticism." *Studies in the American Renais-
    sance,* 1985. Ed. Joel Myerson. Charlottesville: U.P. of Virginia, 1985.
True, John Preston. "The Advice of Miss Alcott." *SN* 15 (May 1888): 545.

Part III

St. Nicholas
and Its Worlds:
Cultural Messages

13

The Utopia of *St. Nicholas*: The Present as Prologue

Fred Erisman

When the publishers of *Scribner's Monthly* launched *St. Nicholas Magazine* in November 1873, their aim was clear. The newcomer, edited by Mary Mapes Dodge, was to be the qualitative equivalent of the adult magazine, conveying and reinforcing the values of its upper middle-class readers. The two were to be "harmonious companions in the family, and the helpers of each other in the work of instruction, culture and entertainment."[1] This aim remained remarkably constant throughout the magazine's history. As late as 1923, it was restated thus:

> [*St. Nicholas*] builds character; it fosters true manliness and womanliness through the doctrine of labor, courage, fortitude, self-respect, and the golden rule.
>   It keeps pace with the world and the important things that are going forward in it.
>   It prepares boys and girls for life as it is, and stimulates ambition for a life of usefulness and service to mankind.[2]

These are clearly extensions of the original goal. They are also something more.

In its goals lies much of the importance of *St. Nicholas*. The magazine consistently presents to its readers the basic ideals of middle-class America — a clear-cut sense of right and wrong, a regard for the Puritan work ethic, and a sense of personal responsibility. In doing so, it implies that these values are desirable and published between 1890 and 1910, both sides of this split appear. Throughout the years immediately prior to World War I, the magazine transmits, in its non-fiction, a sense of the technological competence necessary to prosper in an urban, mechanized world, even as it presents, in its fiction, the professed values of the middle-class world of the American dream. Taken together, the two groups of literature make up a singularly utopian body of writing as they equip young readers to survive in — and to improve — the world in which they find themselves.

The non-fiction of *St. Nicholas* poses and answers three didactic questions: "What is the world like?" "How does the world operate?" and "How can I best get along in the world?" The first of these is dealt with by descriptive articles embracing topics from matter-of-fact travel accounts to discussions of significant world events. Typical of these are Theodore Roosevelt's "Hero Tales of American History" (May-October 1895), Annie C. Kuiper's "Queen Wilhelmina's Lessons" (October 1903), and Bertha Runkle's "Child Life in China and Japan" (January 1905).

Two themes emerge from these articles: that the well-rounded person must have a general understanding of the world and its history, and that the individual can benefit from the examples of others. The examples, however, are inevitably couched in ideal terms. William Abbatt, citing Captain James Lawrence's dying injunction, "Don't give up the ship," goes on to suggest that persistence and optimism are qualities applicable to all facets of life: "[These words] are a good motto in every trouble of life. Don't give up the ship — don't despair, lose heart, surrender, but take courage, and, like General Grant, 'Fight it out on this line if it takes all summer.'"[3] What the individual learns from history are the lessons of courage, industry and fortitude. If he patterns himself upon these lessons, he will find himself attuned to the world in which he lives.

The second question, the "how" of the world, is answered by a host of scientific and technological articles. Representative of this are Lieutenant John M. Ellicott's history of explosives (July 1896); Tudor Jenks's "Mirrors of Air" (January 1897), on mirages; and George Ethelbert Walsh's "What a Lump of Coal Could Do" (October 1904). These articles, without exception, stress the importance of general knowledge in its own right, and man's ability to mold nature to his will through technology. Thus, Walsh's essay concludes:

> The harnessing of the waves and wind for generating electric
> power, or the focusing of the sun's rays on a boiler ... are but
> further illustrations of man's efforts to cast his burden of hard
> labor upon forces which are all around us, if we but know how

to release and employ them. When some of the potential power
of a pound of coal was first released and harnessed ... a vital
step in the progress of humanity and civilization was taken.[4]

The message is plain: precise knowledge of the world and the harnessing
of its knowledge are among the keys to success.

The final question, "How can I best get along in the world?" is the
subject of numerous practical articles, presenting to the reader of *St.
Nicholas* his environment, the organization and operation of his culture,
and assorted skills and accomplishments likely to be of use to him. Among
these are Ernest Ingersoll's discussion of city-planning, "Reasoning Out a
Metropolis" (January 1898); Cleveland Moffett's several articles on
"Careers of Danger and Daring" (1901) ; and H. Irving Hancock's two-
part article on jiu-jitsu, "Japanese Athletics for American Boys" (January-
February 1904).

Despite all this practicality, though, professed American ideals appear,
quietly but explicitly. Cleveland Moffett, after describing several technical and dangerous occupations, drives home the lesson: "These every-day
heroes ... may give us a bit of their spirit for our own lives, the brave and
patient spirit that will keep us unflinchingly at the hard thing (whatever
it be) until we have conquered it. And perhaps we too may feel impelled
to cultivate ... the habit of courage."[5] Even if the life is that of the twentieth century, the ideals are those of an earlier, simpler America — courage, patience, and unquenchable fortitude.

Throughout the nonfiction of *St. Nicholas,* one finds a sense of
learning about reality. Facts abound, presented without apology, to be
appreciated for themselves. Beneath these facts, however, lies a humane,
conservative world somewhat at odds with the practical world of reality.
These worlds, the editors seem to say, exist concurrently; the ideals of the
American dream are at least partially compatible with the facts of a technological society. Despite this compatibility, though, a division is clear.
Bound by facts, the authors at times have to struggle to reconcile their
ideal view with the real society of which they write. Significantly, no such
struggle appears in the fiction. Here the authors, unfettered by the need
to assimilate cold facts, are free to portray the ideal world.

In its way, the fiction of *St. Nicholas* is as unabashedly didactic as the
nonfiction. Its primary purpose, to be sure, is entertainment. But even as
it provides quality entertainment, the fiction also supplies cultural ideals,
standards, and models to assist the young reader in directing his life. It
reinforces at every turning the child's sense of his place and role in a middle-class world. Whatever the type of story being presented, the plot line
is paralleled by a strong current of cultural indoctrination.

The first major class of fiction, that of fantasy and science fiction, is a mixed group. Like the nonfictional works, many of these stories glorify technical competence, as in Clement Fezandie's "Through the Earth" (January-April 1898), telling of a tunnel to the Antipodes. Others, however, move into the imaginative realm of fantasy and the supernatural. Regardless of the subject matter, though, the stories stress the familiar values of obedience, industry, and contentment, implying that these are the traits that make their imagined worlds attractive. Thus, for example, a boy who suddenly acquires magical powers finds that they bring him only grief. He surrenders them without regret, remarking afterward that "since then, I have never longed for anything that comes without effort — for whatever is worth having is worth working for."[6]

The second notable class of fiction, historical fiction, although somewhat restricted by its basis of fact, advances the same cultural attitudes. The stories are of a familiar type: a young person, aged between ten and eighteen, comes into contact with notable events or persons, and learns something of himself, his times, and the world. Typical are Roberta Nelson's "The Field of the Cloth of Gold" (January 1899), Annah Robinson Watson's "Eleanor's Colonel" (July 1900), and Gensai Murai's "'Kibun Daizin,' or 'From Shark Boy to Merchant Prince'" (July-November 1904). The lessons taught by the stories, like the stories themselves, are familiar. Adherence to duty, for example, is highly regarded, as is self-reliance, in all its forms. Thus, the editors, introducing the story of a seventeenth century Japanese boy, remark: "The shrewdness and dauntless ambition of the young hero of this story will commend him to the admiration of American boys."[7] Though the stories exist primarily to entertain, they obviously also teach, stressing the attitudes and ways of behavior professed by turn-of-the-century America.

The largest class of fiction in *St. Nicholas* is that dealing with ordinary persons under ordinary conditions, such as Carolyn Wells's "The Story of Betty" (January-October 1899), or Frances Courtenay Baylor's "In the Cavalry" (July 1903). In every case, the stories, through the actions and attitudes of a sympathetic central character, provide an example for the reader to follow. Ralph Cruger, for example, a city-bred sixteen-year-old, grows in wisdom under the guidance of his country cousin, Harry:

> Each day was marked by some new experience, some new thing learned, some step forward toward manliness and self-reliance and self-control, frankness, and truth. Ralph, under the tutelage of Harry's constant example, had learned ... to know that a quick hand and ready brain and fearlessness were things of steady value, and to have driven into him, so deeply that they

were never uprooted, the old, old lessons that success comes
only through repeated failure, and that he is thrice brave and
thrice a conqueror who conquers self. He had good stuff in him,
this boy, and the semi-rough life brought it out.[8]

The lessons of *St. Nicholas* are "the old, old lessons": they stress the
importance of duty, industry, thrift, and self-reliance, arguing in the
process that these are the major virtues. In doing so, the magazine per-
petuates qualities that one of its authors admits are old; it presents them,
however, not as museum pieces, but as viable standards, as valid in an
urban setting as in a rural one, as valid in the twentieth century as in the
eighteenth. In doing so, it creates a tantalizingly utopian situation.

Karl Mannheim, in *Ideology and Utopia* (1929) speaks of two kinds
of "situationally transcendent ideas," which illuminate the utopianism of
St. Nicholas. Ideologies, says Mannheim, are the ideas that, although never
achieving realization, are the ones usually cited as the rules and values by
which the society claims to live.[9] Utopias, on the other hand, are those ideas
that can potentially change the existing order: "When they pass over into
conduct [they] tend to change it." This tension between ideology and
utopia appears quite clearly in *St. Nicholas.*

The years during which the magazine was in its prime were years of
social and technological change in which the American individual was
asked to reconcile an increasingly impersonal, mechanized society with a
system of values based upon individuality and open, decent personal relations. This change however is not apparent in the magazine. If one takes
the contents of *St. Nicholas* at face value, one finds that they present a society in which man and machine live in harmony, a culture in which the
comforts of the industrial era are complemented by the ideals of an earlier America. It is an interesting society, and an appealing one, but it is not
the one in which the young readers of the magazine would find themselves
as adults.

If *St. Nicholas,* despite its own professions, does not truly prepare its
readers for "life as it is," it does equip them to change that life. Although
the ideologies of middle-class America permeate the magazine, they are
presented as workable ideals; the contrast between the real and the ideal
is absent. Lacking a sense of this contrast, but finding in life that the contrast exists (as would be inevitable for these children, who would come to
maturity in the years following World War I), the child, as adult, might
reasonably be expected to set out to change his life. The change, presumably, would be one enabling him to practice those ideals in the context of
modern life. If effected, the change would indeed tend to shatter the prevailing order of things.

In its presentation of the compatibility of the modern world and traditional values, *St. Nicholas* is, in the best sense of the word, utopian. Implicitly and vaguely dissatisfied with the shifting present, it looks to the future, recognizing that change must come about through the individual. Recognizing further that the children of the present are the adults of the future, it presents to its readers the ideals of the past in the context of the present, giving them the means with which to change the future.

Notes

1. "St. Nicholas," *Scribner's Monthly*, 7 (Nov. 1873), 115.

2. "Fifty Years of St. Nicholas," *St. Nicholas*, 51 (Nov. 1923), 20. A thoughtful account of the magazine's history and stature appears in Florence Stanley Sturges, "The *St. Nicholas* Years," in *The Hewins Lectures, 1947–1962*, ed. Siri Andrews, (Boston: Horn Book, 1963), pp. 267–95.

3. William Abbatt, "The Chesapeake Mill," *St. Nicholas*, 24 (July 1897), 730.

4. George Ethelbert Walsh, "What a Lump of Coal Could Do," *St. Nicholas*, 31 (Oct. 1904), 1120.

5. Cleveland Moffett, "The Locomotive Engineer," *St. Nicholas*, 28 (Oct. 1901), 1068.

6. Tudor Jenks, "A Magician for One Day," *St. Nicholas*, 24 (Oct. 1897), 1016.

7. Gensai Murai, "'Kibun Daizin,' or 'From Shark-Boy to Merchant Prince,'" *St. Nicholas*, 31 (July 1904), 777.

8. H. S. Canfield, "The Boys of the Rincon Ranch," *St. Nicholas*, 29 (Apr. 1902), 525.

9. Karl Mannheim, *Ideology and Utopia*, trans. Louis Wirth and Edward Shils. (1929; reprinted New York: Harvest-Harcourt, Brace, n.d.), pp. 194–95.

10. Mannheim, p. 192.

14

Two Narrative Formulas

R. GORDON KELLY

Carelessness is worse than stealing. "Behaving," *Wide Awake* (1876)

A comparatively narrow, often rigid, and marked conventionality has long been regarded as one of the principal qualities differentiating mass or popular literature from serious literature. Detective fiction and westerns are familiar examples of popular forms characterized by patterns that have remained relatively stable over time. We expect that detective stories will be about crimes successfully solved by suitably shrewd or dogged individuals and that westerns will pit the forces of lawlessness and savagery against the forces of civilization. These expectations amount to prescriptive rules governing popular forms, and they have rather high predictive capabilities. To learn that a book is a detective novel is, after all, to know a good deal about what will happen in the story. Similarly the stories published in *St. Nicholas,* the *Youth's Companion,* and *Our Young Folks* in the generation following the Civil War reveal a stable pattern of repeated elements.[1]

It is not uncommon for the rules governing a popular genre to be formulated explicitly either by aficionados seeking to guide public taste or by editors seeking to define the qualities of desirable manuscripts. In his autobiography, Ray Stannard Baker, a contributor to the *Youth's Companion* before he became famous as a muckraker for *McClure's* magazine, recalled the rules Daniel Ford and his staff laid down to contributors.[2] Early in his career, Baker had worked as a reporter on the *Chicago Record.* Learning

From Mother Was a Lady: Self and Society in American Periodicals, 1865–1890, *R. Gordon Kelly; © 1974 by R. Gordon Kelly. Reproduced with permission of Greenwood Publishing Group, Inc., Westport, CT.*

that the *Companion* paid fifty dollars for stories and hoping to supplement his reporter's modest salary, Baker wrote to the *Companion*. In reply, he received a cordial letter and a two-page leaflet entitled "The *Youth's Companion* Story," which outlined and explained the principles authors hoping to contribute to the popular periodical should follow.

These formulas, Baker suggests, were the key to popular acceptance: they constituted "the chart for sure-fire success; which is to be sedulously followed. Don't experiment. Don't originate; repeat!" In economic terms, the rules represented what a particular audience "wanted and would pay for," although few periodicals of the time "ever set down their formula so explicitly in black and white as the *Youth's Companion*."[3] Baker's description of the *Companion's* rules as defining a measure of continuing public acceptance is suggestive. By implication, the rules or formula met (or were thought to meet) certain unspecified needs of a particular audience — needs that the repetition of a rather limited number of elements did not satisfy once and for all. People continued to buy and to read material characterized by simple, familiar patterns. Critics of mass culture have frequently cited this stereotypical quality as presumptive evidence that popular formula literature blunts discrimination and simplifies and falsifies experience. More perceptive students of cultural history have used the conventionality typical of popular forms as an instrument to examine widely held beliefs and values rather than as a club with which to harry cultural sinners to repentance. The works of Horatio Alger have been particularly attractive to students of late nineteenth-century American life because Alger's hundred-odd juvenile novels were enormously popular — and strikingly repetitious in terms of an overall pattern of character, incident, and reward. Those historians who have sought to explain the reasons for and the implications of Alger's appeal have done so by concentrating initially on the structure of Alger's principal motif — a boy who struggles with little success to achieve a measure of respectability and security until a fortunate encounter provides him with a powerful benefactor.[4]

The analyses of Alger's formula by Richard Wohl, John Cawelti, and others hinge on the recognition that Alger's work was ordered by a relatively stable structure of elements, varied slightly from novel to novel and that this structure, which Cawelti terms "formula," constitutes an important kind of cultural data. In a seminal essay he defines formula as a "conventional system for structuring cultural products" and distinguishes it from such familiar critical concepts as myth, theme, medium, and genre, which, he argues, tend to be overly general.[5] More specific and limited than a myth, for example, a formula is a frequently repeated particular sequence of plot and character elements: "Westerns must have a certain

Little Lord Fauntleroy — here in one of Reginald Birch's illustrations from *St. Nicholas* — exemplifies the "gentry ideal" of "a figure who embodies the moral values of gentility and whose moral force brings about a change in the values of others." *SN* 13 (June 1886): 569.

kind of setting, a particular cast of characters, and follow a limited number of lines of action. A Western that does not take place in the West, near the frontiers, at a point in history when social order and anarchy are in tension, and that does not involve some form of pursuit, is simply not a Western."[6] Historically, popular formulas are created, achieve a degree of acceptance, and can persist for long periods of time. The detective story and the western, though products of the nineteenth century, remain popular today, while the seduction novel and, to a large extent, the Biblical epic have disappeared in the twentieth century.

The prevalence in popular literature of the formula, defined as a sequence of conventional elements, lends itself to several kinds of analysis. It is conceivable that some personality types may be attracted by the repetitive, highly structured nature of this kind of literary creativity.[7] Such an approach, emphasizing a personal psychological component of the writer, is complicated historically by the relatively anonymous (and pseudononymous) world of popular literature and the lack of adequate biographical data. It is also possible to approach formula fiction as a logical response to the enormous demand for quantities of material that is a conspicuous characteristic of mass publishing. Where speed and sheer volume of material become essential, as they do in periodical publishing or broadcasting, some degree of standardized form becomes a functional necessity. Such explanations of formula, however, furnish no key for understanding individual formulas nor the differences they exhibit.

A more fruitful kind of analysis assumes that a reciprocity exists in the production and consumption of popular literature. The formula can be regarded as a common ground on which a relatively small group of producers meets with a particular audience. The formula embodies the values, expectations, assumptions, hero types, and needs of a social group and perhaps resolves tensions that originate in conflicting needs.[8] The precise nature of these needs and their relation to a social group in a given historical period is a complex and difficult subject. It seems likely that the social functions of popular formulas, and especially formulas for children's literature, have their origins, in part, in the precariousness of social order and the consequent need in any society or large social group to reaffirm continually the structure of meanings, the cultural knowledge, that orders social behavior.[9]

With its biological basis in prolonged childhood and man's limited instinctual structure, cultural knowledge implies the centrality of socialization in any society. Children must learn the language of their society, its various social modes, its taboos—all that passes for knowledge among members of their particular group. The process of socialization is never complete but continues to be supported by the day-to-day activities of the members of a society. A measure of precariousness is always present because cultural patterns are never completely internalized by any member of a group—and because individuals are always acting, always choosing. Any social act ultimately has implications for the existing social order, which persists only so long as members of a group consent to, and can sustain in daily activity, the world view or conventional structure of meanings they learned as children. To focus on the transference of culture from one generation to another, then, as children's writers must, carries the increased probability of becoming sensitive to the situations that threaten social order and which must be controlled. In the context of the cultural pluralism that has increasingly characterized the American experience from the beginning of the industrial revolution, the young are a perpetual source of challenge to a particular social group's conception of reality. The world into which they are born is initially opaque to them. It must be given meaning, explicit justification, and explanation. The ways of society are not self-evident, as any parent knows. Children constantly ask "Why?" and they must be persuaded that the parental ways, the given ways, are *the* ways and warrant acceptance and allegiance.[10] By definition, children are incompletely socialized. On the one hand, they do things that would bring chaos if projected on the future as the actions of adults. On the other hand, they are weaker and less able to cope with experience than adults. Consequently, they may at any time reveal, or be used to draw attention to, the precariousness of social existence as a whole. Juxtaposed against certain institutions, they may call into question patterns of behavior that adults take for granted. As the embodiment of the future, finally, children are essential to society. They are often consciously invested with the hopes and aspirations that adults have for the maintenance of their own way of life.

A single popular formula will never mirror all the problems of a given period. The basic pattern in the novels of Horatio Alger center almost exclusively in matters of economic mobility, financial success, and the qualities considered efficacious in striving for social respectability. In contrast, the formula stories in popular children's periodicals like *St. Nicholas* and *Youth's Companion* emphasize quite different concerns. They suggest which threats to the social order particularly exercised the social group with whom the principal writers and editors tended to be affiliated. Moreover, they demonstrate the efficacy of a particular constellation of values and assumptions about the nature of social order in a democracy. Thus, the code of the gentleman, the problem of economic security in an age of economic instability, and the destructive impact of urban environments on childhood needs were important elements in the formulas of children's domestic fiction. The child reader was asked to become self-conscious about his own behavior and to see it in relation to a moral position dramatized in the stories. This position was never called into question or shown to be a style of life to which alternatives existed. The stories defined the way things were and ought to be and illustrated the modes of behavior that are consonant and rewarding, given the principles that organize and define "reality."

Finally, these formulas probably allayed, in some degree, parental fears about the split between generations caused by widespread preoccupation with personal and social mobility, rapid social change, and shifts in the social sources of moral authority. The stories frequently dramatized a faith in the reasonableness of the child and his willingness to be guided by parental values and judgment. Children, in turn, were assured that parents know what children need for the future, however different that future may be from the experience of the parents. The apparent changes taking place with such rapidity in American society during the 1870s and 1880s did not imply the obsolescence of the parental definition of things. Their world remained subjectively plausible within the formulas of children's fiction.

In *St. Nicholas* and the four other magazines selected for study, two formulas dominate the fiction that attempted to entertain children with realistic incidents from the everyday lives of ordinary families. This editorial ideal proved elusive in practice; some very extraordinary, though usually plausible, events occur in these stories. A third group of stories suggests the possibility of another formula, but it appears so infrequently that I have discussed it as a distinct variation of one of the others. None of these magazines published westerns, detective stories, or romances— the staple narrative formulas of the story papers and pulps such as *Frank Leslie's Boys' and Girls' Weekly* and *The Boys of New York*.

The writers who worked primarily within the restrictions imposed by the editors of the quality magazines tended to settle with impressive regularity on a single generalized situation. They most frequently dramatized an incident in which a young person (more rarely an adult) acted out an attitude, a stage of self-knowledge, or a virtue — and experienced the appropriate consequences. As I have suggested earlier, the moral framework that gives significance to the pattern of incident, resolution, and reward is the code of the gentleman modified to suit the needs and, to some extent, the interests of children. Not all of the stories that dealt with domestic life can be fitted into this schema, to be sure; formulas do not exhaust the possibilities for popular literature although they account for a large portion of it. The two or three formulas in the children's fiction sampled may be considered ideal types, created abstractions with which few stories coincide perfectly but toward which many tend in the arrangement of plot and character elements.

For want of more incisive labels, I have chosen to call the two major formulas the "ordeal" and the "change of heart." A third formula, a variation of the change of heart, I call the "gentry mission." Aspects of the first two, and occasionally all three, may be found in some serial stories. About

90 percent of the stories I read, however, are quite short (the *Youth's Companion* story, for example, was limited to 3,000 words) and the formulas, while not totally exclusive, are useful in describing the primary impulse of a given story.

In the ordeal, a child or young person is temporarily isolated from the moral influence of adults (generally parents or other family representatives, though occasionally teachers, ministers, or other professionals who might symbolize the demands of society at large). Beyond the aid or influence of adult experience, the child undergoes an experience that requires him to respond decisively. Often, very little time is permitted for reflection; his reaction frequently suggests the force of instinct. Having proved himself in action, the child returns to the safety of the family or the supervision of adults and is rewarded. The circumstances of the trial and the kinds of temptations confronting the isolated child are suggestive of the social stresses to which the adults writing for these children's magazines were sensitive. The narrative rhythm of the ordeal resembles the characteristic movement of ritual rites of passage, the three phases of which, according to Arnold Van Gennup, are separation from society, a period of isolation and transition, and finally incorporation into a new social world or reintegration with the old.[11]

A conventional realization of the ordeal is "Nellie in the Lighthouse" (1877) by Susan Archer Weiss, a story which takes place on the Carolina coast.[12] At first, Nellie, a little girl of seven, is surrounded by the adults — her father and an elderly black couple — who have reared her and her brother since their mother's death several years before. Soon after the story opens, the family begins to disperse, leaving the children isolated: Nellie's father leaves for the mainland to pick up needed supplies, and shortly after his departure, the family's black housekeeper is called away to nurse a distant neighbor. When a sudden squall blows up, their elderly black companion collapses with a stroke, leaving Nellie and her panic-stricken brother to operate the lighthouse alone. A broken window in the tower and Nellie's general unfamiliarity with the equipment make it impossible for her to light the beacon her father will need to guide himself home. Consciously resisting the temptation to panic, Nellie suddenly remembers a hymn her mother used to sing. In the moment of calm that follows, through some process of association the author chose not to delineate, the girl recalls that pine knots will burn even in a high wind. Hastily gathering as many as she can, Nellie again climbs the long stairs to the tower and successfully rekindles the light. Her father, caught in the squall, is guided safely home by his daughter's improvised beacon.

A similar drama of fortitude, tested and sustained in crisis, is evident

in Louisa May Alcott's "Bonfires" (1873). Phebe, the twelve-year-old daughter and only child of a charcoal burner, braves a stormy evening and the
subtle terrors of a treacherous, desolate landscape to warn an approach-
ing train of a washed-out bridge.[13] For her presence of mind and self-
reliance, qualities nurtured by her lonely life in nature where her only
playmates are the woods creatures, Phebe is generously rewarded by the
train's passengers, whose dress, manners, and speech identify them as ladies
and gentlemen. Like Nellie, Phebe is completely isolated from adults who
might have aided her. Her father is away, her mother is ill, and the nearest neighbor lives too far away to be of any help.

Sudden, potentially bewildering isolation overtakes children in story
after story based on the formula of the ordeal. Without warning, the family, a central symbol of stability, may be dissolved, leaving a young person
to manage as best he can amid hardship and the loss of a taken-for-granted
framework of expectations and relationships. A story entitled "Charlie's
First Doughnut" (1882) makes explicit that this pervasive symbolism of
isolation is rooted in the very conditions of American life.[14] The freedom
that Americans enjoy demands of them great individual restraint and
responsibility, the author emphasizes. Charlie has been reared in Italy by
his mother, a sculptress who has often described to him the delights of
American doughnuts. For unexplained reasons, he has never had one.
Clumsily contrived, to be sure, these improbable circumstances are
designed to make clear and certain his temptation when a friend of his
mother's gives him a box of doughnuts and tells the boy to take them
home to his mother.

Going up into a garden overlooking Rome, young Charlie struggles
to resist temptation to eat one of the doughnuts on the spot and say nothing to his mother. She, after all, will never know how many doughnuts
the box originally contained, so it will not be a lie exactly to eat one without admitting it. Uneasy perhaps over the apparent triviality of the situation she has created, the author breaks in to interpret, lest her readers fail
to recognize what is going on: "It was a fateful time for our little American — a time in which his young nature was the battle-ground of good and
evil; the scene of one of those terrible conflicts that we all of us have known,
and perhaps yet know, and the issues of which are mighty, no matter how
trifling their causes."[15] Charlie, poised on the brink of knowing himself
forever hence a liar and a thief, hesitates, as well he should. He goes so far
as to take a bite, but seeing a group of Italian schoolboys go by, he recalls
his mother saying that they never faced temptations like the one facing
Charlie because of the formal restraints placed on their lives. Never trusted
as children, they were never free — nor could they be. Americans, by con-

trast, were free—free to face temptation and, if sufficiently strong, free to conquer it. Temptation, Charlie learns, is the price of freedom. Fortified by his insight, he chooses to go home and to confess the stolen bite to his mother, who thereafter cherishes the box as a symbol of a "great victory." To make the moral uncomfortably explicit, the woman who gave Charlie the doughnuts happens to be present when he gets home, so he would have been caught in the lie he contemplated. We are left with the uncharitable suspicion that our hero has been badly used.

Charlie's honesty, like Phebe's courage, is tested in isolation, in situations that suddenly arise and leave no opportunity for consultation with others. Such unforeseen trials, these stories suggest, are to be expected, but they are not to be taken lightly or assumed to have purely individual relevance. The wrong decision may imperil a trainload of passengers or threaten the affection and trust on which the family—and beyond it, society—depends. Children who read these stories were invited to regard every moment of life as precarious, unpredictable, and invariably serious. Americans, including children, were free, but they were frequently alone, uninsulated from sudden temptations and dangers. In variations of the ordeal formula, courage and self-reliance emerge as the virtues most often tested.

The second formula, the change of heart, often proceeds according to the same rhythm of separation, isolation, and incorporation that characterizes the ordeal. In the ordeal, however, the child is assumed morally capable, and the events of the story satisfy us that he is indeed. On the other hand, the change of heart almost invariably proceeds from a moral stance that varies from the merely inappropriate and embarrassing to one that is personally dangerous and socially vicious. As in instances of the ordeal, a wide variety of possibilities exists. The key element in the formula, with certain exceptions to be noted later, is a species of moral conversion, a dramatic shift in perception, which combines a conscious recognition of the erroneous nature of the individual's former behavior with a conscious resolution to do better. The change of heart is made manifest in useful and appropriate activity following the individual's conversion.

The great majority of stories in the five magazines (excluding Leslie's) follow this pattern, perhaps in conscious recognition that, given the nature of childhood, young readers might better identify with fictional children who still displayed thoughtlessness, pride, or impatience, the three failings which recur most frequently.

"Charlie Balch's Metamorphosis" (1867) is a model of the change of heart except in its setting—a private boarding school.[16] Charlie Balch enters the story a sullen, lazy, and withdrawn boy. His mother is dead, and his father, a politician, has little time for the boy. Without a mother's love or a father's guidance, Charlie is ill equipped for boyhood, which is at best a time of trial. Character, if left to form itself, becomes selfish and idle, the author warns, and we are given abundant evidence that this is true. Charlie quickly falls in with the school's less principled boys, yet an inextinguishable spark of reverence remains, hidden beneath Charlie's "unpromising exterior" and capable of being fanned into flame under appropriate circumstances—in this case a sermon. Charlie suddenly recognizes that "probably there is no such thing as an indifferent moment, — a moment in which our characters are not being secretly shaped by the bias of the will, either for good or evil."[17] In this recognition, the author announces, "the change had commenced." Charlie emerges from the chrysalis of apathy and idleness slowly, however. Success and reward are not immediate, for his resolution must be tested. Gradually his character and manners improve, his disposition grows more cheerful, and even his appearance changes. Charlie was a "hard case," but his successful redemption provided a lesson in the responsibility, which those of "gentle feeling" have, for aiding others.

European visitors to America during the nineteenth century commented frequently on the degree of freedom enjoyed by American children in contrast to their European counterparts.[18] Charlie Norton successfully resisted the temptation that was the price of that greater freedom, we recall, but it is the province of change-of-heart stories to explore the problems raised by children who chose to use their freedom irresponsibly. "When Book Meets Book" (1886) tells of a socially prominent mother who could no longer cope with society life or with her two sons, spoiled by an indulgent father and by inappropriate reading.[19] Off to Europe to rest her shattered nerves, she entrusts her sons to her brother, a Boston gentleman. He refuses to allow their misbehavior to go unpunished as had their father, for whom "boys will be boys" furnished an easy absolution to any mischief.

When the boys' carelessness in his house results in damage to the furnishings, their uncle questions their sense of honor: "I thought that my sister's children, boys twelve and ten years of age were old enough to have the simplest instincts of gentlemen," and, as rarely happens in these stories, invites them upstairs for a whipping.[20] Besides being destructive, their pranks, they are told, would be detrimental to their mother's need for peace and quiet when she returned. The fiction that they have fed on and the storybook boys whom they have emulated do not provide fit models for behavior, not in Boston at least. It requires more to be a gentleman, they discover, than merely to appear well mannered and to speak truthfully. Their every act must speak what they know, but may not like to admit, is right. Absolute congruence between moral knowledge and even the most seemingly insignificant act defines the standard of the gentleman, which they are expected to meet.

Unwarranted pride and a treacherous romanticism frequently combine to bring about the isolation and suffering that characterize the change-of-heart formula. In "Jenny, the 'Flying Fairy'" (1888), a young girl is forced to quit school after her father dies and leaves his widow with Jenny and four other children to support.[21] Jenny has had the education of a lady, but unfortunately it has borne little fruit in her behavior: she remains blindly self-centered and concerned exclusively with "her own success and amusement." She will have nothing to do with her mother's suggestion that she take a position as a governess or a maid for a family in the country. Although her mother had held such a position before her marriage without feeling degraded by it, Jenny is sure no lady could submit to such an arrangement.

Refusing also to go back to school, Jenny fears that she will never be a lady as a consequence of her misfortune. Her self-pity is transformed, however, when she sees a poster advertising a circus wintering nearby. She imagines herself supporting her family while living a glamorous and stylish life as a bareback rider, although she is appalled and frightened by the squalid quarters and the coarse, rough men she encounters at the circus. Nevertheless, she applies for a riding job and, self-conscious in a skimpy costume provided by the circus owner, a predictably lecherous foreigner, is ridden around in a practice harness. Knocked unconscious in a fall, she comes to her senses to find that her mother has rescued her. Humbled by her experience, she agrees to become a governess. Ten years later, the reader learns in the last paragraph of the story, Jenny has successfully finished her education and become a teacher, wife, and mother — and, most importantly, a true lady. The willingness to serve is the beginning of wisdom — and redemption.

Suffering is proportionately greater in change-of-heart stories in which an adult is the central character; those few who, refusing all help, defy the moral assumptions on which the stories are grounded experience disaster. Such is the case in "The Fatal Fire-hunt" (1876).[22] Pierre Estrin, a morose and impatient, if famous, hunter gives in to his only son's pleas to go on a hunt one evening in spite of his wife's intuitive uneasiness about the venture. The boy tires quickly on the trail, and Pierre pushes on into a swamp where he becomes confused in the darkness. Impatient at finding no game, he finally fires unhesitatingly at the first hint of a target, mortally wounding his son. The event shatters his reason, and Estrin, involved later in several murders, is eventually assassinated himself. He "did not profit by the teachings of his misfortunes," the author informs her readers.

The significance of the story would appear to be in three related attitudes that define Estrin's flawed character. He is antisocial and impatient, and the latter finds concrete expression in the fatal shot. Second, he ignores his wife's intuitions, the unreasoned promptings of a more reliable moral nature than his own. Finally, he fails to benefit from his misfortunes with an appropriate change of heart. He remains oblivious to the moral organization underlying reality, and his subsequent murders are evidence of the degree to which his initial antisocial bias becomes overtly destructive in a social context. In this way, his own destruction, which takes place, presumably, at the hands of similar moral outcasts, is justified. Estrin's impatience results in the destruction of the family just as his violence outside the family, if not stopped, would result in the destruction of society.

There is often little drama or suspense connected with the change-of-heart process. The child is always viewed not by another child but by the adult author from the outside. The suspense or dramatic interest that might arise as the child struggles to decide what is right remains hidden. The child's recognition of his responsibilities can be made visible only in activities that embody the new knowledge. Because a happy ending is expected, indeed required, the sense that there was ever a possibility of moral failure is almost always lost. Only in rare situations, and usually when an adult is the central character, can the possibility for moral failure exist. The principal interest is not primarily in how the change of heart occurs but in the fact of its occurrence.

In the third pattern common in the gentry fiction, the civilizing possibilities of the code of the gentleman are acted out, sometimes with explicit reference to its efficacy for the rawest kind of economic competition. The basis of the gentry mission is a figure who embodies the moral values of gentility and whose moral force brings about a change in the values of others. Several stories show how the loneliness and frustrations of elderly persons are dissolved by a younger figure. Others present a young college graduate taking over and bringing order to a rural school. Perhaps the best example of the motif, however, is "Naylor o' the Bowl" (1873), a story by Rebecca Harding Davis.[23] Miss Davis's characters are a motley group of young men, most of them mill hands, who are drawn to western Virginia about 1859 in hopes of making a rich strike on the petroleum lands being developed there. They soon discover, however, that their capacity for cooperation deteriorates steadily amid the frustration borne of their unsuccessful drilling. As mill hands, according to the author, these rough, irreligious young men lack the shared fun, friendships, and courtesies that would have provided a more stable basis for a group of college students in similar circumstances. Moreover, because none of the men are married or even related to each other, the only grounds for their uneasy and brittle alliance are dependence and greed. Given these circumstances, violence is almost inevitable.

Conditions begin to improve, however, when Naylor, the grandfather of one of the men, arrives unexpectedly to live with his grandson. Although the old man has lost both his legs and is confined to a makeshift wheelchair, he has accepted his impairment with grace and dignity. He is carefully identified as a gentleman, and as his quiet strength of character gradually invigorates and purifies the camp's atmosphere, a true community begins to emerge where none had existed previously. We are to understand, it seems clear, that Naylor's moral strength and courage are sufficient to compel, in his rough companions, a particular response — a recognition that character is the only basis for an orderly society of freely competing individuals. It is no accident that soon after Naylor arrives, his grandson begins to think about the existence of God for the first time in years; the basis for character, in turn, is seen to be an understanding of the universal principles of order. When Naylor dies peacefully after a short illness, the men's memories of the old man's moral force cement the group in friendship and cooperation, for their mutual recognition of Naylor's character establishes an essential basis for social order — the shared recognition and acceptance of a compelling ideal.

Thus, the terms of Mrs. Davis's justification of the gentry ideal are readily apparent: because his moral authority derives from universal law, the gentleman is capable of bringing order into the rawest kind of economic competition, that which characterizes the scramble to exploit the nation's natural resources. The code of the gentleman softens the rigors of such competition (but does not destroy it) and fosters a sense of community without impairing either initiative or self-reliance. After Naylor's death, the drilling goes on, but it goes on efficiently and harmoniously, or so Mrs. Davis would have her readers believe.

The three formulas contrast with the fiction that appeared on the cheaply printed, flamboyantly illustrated weeklies—*Frank Leslie's Boys' and Girls' Weekly*, for example — as well as with the work of the period's most popular juvenile author, Horatio Alger. In the *Weekly*, the adventure of the isolated child remains prominent, but the values, settings, experiences, and moral framework assumed in the stories are radically different. The hallmark of the *Weekly* and its numerous competitors was the serialized dime novel, which emphasized continuous and rapid action, violent encounters, and hairbreadth escapes, all of which occurred amid exotic settings, The stories are populated by a cast of conventional stereotypes blended from the nineteenth-century western and sea story, the gothic romance and the sentimental novel.

"The Magician" (1867), for example, delineates a series of incidents that would never have occurred in a gentry magazine like *St. Nicholas*.[24] Carl, a young boy, later revealed to be an Eastern prince, is the sole survivor of a shipwreck. Taken into a family living in an isolated coastal town, he is taught English and matures pondering the classics. No snob, he is friendly with a poor boy, but he can move in other circles as well and he falls in love with a girl who lives in a beautiful castle. There Isabel entertains him in the lush splendor of her "boudoir"—where, we are told, "the days passed, glorious with dawn and dusk. Weeks, held together by God's golden links of the Sabbath, came and went."[25] With the coming of spring, however, a rival intrudes to break this splendid chain. The girl's cousin, Reginald Booth, quickly forces Isabel to forget Carl. Vowing revenge, Carl tears up his apartment in a rage and disappears. A body which seems to be his washes ashore soon after. Twenty years go by. A magician comes to the castle to perform before Isabel and Reginald, long since her husband. During the performance it becomes clear that Reginald tried to kill Carl years before but killed instead a fisherman disguised in the young man's clothes. The day after this revelation, Reginald lies murdered, and Carl, revealed as the magician, is gone again, accompanied and comforted by Isabel's only daughter whom Carl, it is revealed, had stolen from her parents at the age of four.

The theme of unrestrained passion and revenge, combined with the undercurrent of sexual dalliance and indulgence suggested by Isabel's incense-laden bedroom, conveys markedly different attitudes towards experience, character traits, and children's reading needs from the attitudes implicit in the formulas to be found in periodicals like *St. Nicholas*.

The works of Horatio Alger also differ significantly in attitude from the quality children's periodicals. No one knows how many Alger books were produced, but the number has seemed sufficiently large to require explanation of his popularity: "Frozen into a host of clumsily written novels," Alger's formula, R. Richard Wohl writes, "has many times been picked out ... as characterizing a fundamental and crucial aspect of American culture."[26] Alger's "gospel of thrift, hard work, and endurance" and respectability appear to echo the nation's absorbing interest in material achievement, in getting and spending, in self-aggrandizement rather than self-culture. Recent commentary on Alger has questioned whether he should continue to be regarded as an unambiguous spokesman for the self-made man and for the virtues of rugged individualism. Shifting historiographical perspectives on the Gilded Age impose limitations on Alger's usefulness as a cultural symbol also. In an important recent synthesis, Robert Wiebe argues that during the Gilded Age massive changes in population distribution, new patterns of industrial organization, and new ideas worked together to undermine the structure of values and meanings that had ordered the lives of most Americans prior to the Civil War.[27] The period from 1877 until after World War I is conceptualized best, according to Wiebe, as a "search for order." The values that had effectively organized life in small, relatively isolated communities began to seem inadequate for promoting social order in large urban centers characterized by ethnic heterogeneity, corporate organization, and industrial working conditions.

Alger's stories evidence little concern with the problem of sustaining social order in an aggressive, competitive democratic society. Instead, the emphasis is on success, economic opportunity, and the values judged most instrumental and useful in achieving the kinds of secure clerkships to which Alger's heroes aspire. But the fiction characteristic of *St. Nicholas* and similar children's periodicals often speaks directly to the problem of maintaining social order under democratic conditions of competitive individualism and of nurturing those qualities of character which would stimulate a sturdy self-reliance without threatening the stability of the community. The ordeal and the change of heart were designed, as we have seen, to display those qualities of character in bold relief.

These formulas were intended to facilitate socialization — and doubtless they did, but the effect of the stories concerns us less than the striking similarity between the structure of the fictional experience and the process of socialization as explained from the perspective of social role theory.[28] This approach to socialization, or enculturation, owes much to the work of George Herbert Mead and recognizes "that a child is born into an ongoing society with common symbols, established patterns, and recognized positions, and that it is through others that a child learns these elements of the social world."[29]

A key concept in this approach is that of *role*, a pattern of expected behavior associated with a given social status or position in a social structure. Roles are symbolic forms in the sense that they are vehicles of communication and the means by which a person expresses himself in society. To function in society, the child must develop the ability to judge his own behavior against the role expectations he has learned to associate with his several statuses— as child, brother, student, Little League shortstop, or whatever. Acquiring the ability "to designate to himself that he is or is not acting appropriately" is the essence of the socialization process.[30] Only gradually does he relinquish the egocentrism that characterizes the very young child and come to possess a sense of self, to be able to regard himself from the outside, and to shape his behavior on the basis of that recognition.

Both formulas, the ordeal and the change of heart, dramatize the origins of self. The stories provide opportunities for the child as reader in the experiences of the fictional child to see the consequences of values and attitudes which initially are taken for granted in the context of the fiction. In the change of heart, the child character frequently learns that intense self-centeredness, issuing variously in selfish, careless, or thoughtless behavior, leads to isolation and suffering. Psychologically, the heart of the formula is the conscious recognition that the old habits and attitudes are unacceptable combined with an equally conscious resolution to adopt more appropriate patterns of attitude and behavior. To the extent that a child reading such a story is led to participate imaginatively in its resolution, he may gain vicariously the same salutary perspective on self.

Often the new perspective is dramatized in a dream or metamorphosis. A boy who longs to escape the irksome restraints of home by going to sea is dissuaded when he dreams of hard work and harsh discipline. Another lad, prone to being distracted from his duty, falls to dreaming about a land of short memories. He experiences a world whose only order is the logic of forgetfulness. He cannot discover who he is or where he is and awakens with relief to the recognition of his folly.[31]

In the ordeal, however, the morally capable child seldom expresses a dramatically altered perception, although his experience of isolation and even suffering may be similar to that encountered in the change-of-heart formula. He seldom comes to a conscious recognition of the connection between the values he has absorbed and his triumph over temptation. Instead, the child reader seems expected to supply the necessary recognition and to realize that, like the child in the story, the hymns he learns at his mother's knee have implications for his experience beyond the cozy warmth of hearth and home. The family is a magic circle of safety surrounded by subtle and hidden dangers. The proper attitude toward that fact is certainly not morbid fear. A decent respect and a proper prudence, combined with self-control and self-knowledge, are essential if one is to remain free.

The ordeal carries a measure of reassurance to both the children who read the periodicals and to the adults for whom socialization was a constant, and no doubt often problematic, concern amid the turmoil of the Gilded Age. Children are reassured about the social utility of the values that are justified in the home but must find their ultimate legitimation outside the family. Similarly, the stories, written by adults, continue to sustain the plausibility of adult values in the midst of social and intellectual uncertainty.

The change of heart implies reassurance of a different kind, for the formula confronts, though not always directly, the problem of social control. Here, I shall consider briefly what might be called the problem of consent — the assumptions concerning the means by which individuals, in this case children, who are free to pursue "wrong" activities, come to recognize their error and to change their behavior. This is a central and recurrent, but still largely unexamined, problem in democratic thought. The traditional model for the transformation or character frequently affected in the change of heart is religious conversion. Purged of doctrinal and institutional trappings, conversion appears in these stories in situations which dramatically juxtapose deviant values against accepted ways. Forced to perceive and to evaluate his behavior in the new context, the individual chooses, and is able to will, behavior more consonant with his altered perception. Thus, the formula, from the child's point of view, encourages a cluster of values by dramatizing the penalties—fear, pain, isolation — that attend adopting (or maintaining) the deviant ways. On the other hand, the writers may be said to be acting out their faith in the accepted norms and values of their group by demonstrating the inevitable punishment and suffering that attend the transgression of those accepted ways. Further, the formula may be said to act out the writers' faith, or will to believe, in the ability of the young to perceive things as the writers did as well as their belief in the willingness of the young to act on that perception and to persist in the ways of righteousness in spite of temptation. Writers who used the change-of-heart formula tried to avoid overt preaching as a means to stimulate the shift in perception that signals conversion. A speech made by one of Rose Terry's characters puts the matter clearly: "I don't approve of talking to or at children, myself; it always exasperates me and why not them. Help 'em to use their eyes, and see for themselves, if they're not fools; if they are — why let 'em alone."[32]

Both formulas encourage children to use their eyes, to become self-conscious of the impact which even their most trivial behavior could have on the lives of others—first in the family and then, by extension, in society at large. What if everybody behaved that way? is the mirror held up to the child reader. He is asked to recognize and to judge, in the fictional lives of children supposedly just like him, the necessary consequences of the daily deeds that, he was prodded to acknowledge, formed the iron links of character and thus shaped the future.

Notes

1. See, for example, Fr. Ronald Knox, "Introduction," in *The Best Detective Stories of the Year: 1928* (London: Faber & Gwyer, 1929), pp. vii-xxiii, and Marie F. Rodell, *Mystery Fiction: Theory and Practice* (New York: Duell, Sloan and Pearce, 1943).

2. Ray Stannard Baker, *American Chronicle* (New York: Scribner's, 1945), pp. 69–70.

3. Ibid. See also [The editors of *The Youth's Companion*], "Editorial Talks with Contributors," *The Writer* 9 (1896): 143–45.

4. R. Richard Wohl, "The 'Rags to Riches Story': An Episode of Secular Idealism," Seymour M. Lipset and Reinhard Bendix, eds., *Class, Status and Power* (Glencoe, Ill.: Free Press, 1953), pp. 388–95; John Cawelti, "From Rags to Respectability: Horatio Alger," in *Apostle of the Self-Made Man* (Chicago: University of Chicago Press, 1965), pp. 101–24; Michael Zuckerman, "The Nursery Tales of Horatio Alger," *American Quarterly* 24 (1972): 191–209.

5. John Cawelti, "The Concept of Formula in the Study of Popular Culture," *Journal of Popular Culture* 3 (1969): 381–90. A somewhat expanded discussion of the formula concept, together with an analysis of the western formula, is available in Cawelti's *Six-Gun Mystique* (Bowling Green, Ohio: The Popular Press, 1970).

6. Cawelti, "The Concept of Formula," p. 388. The concept of formula serves, first, as a rudimentary theory. It defines the elements appropriate for analysis and in this respect is conventionally literary in emphasis. The elements Cawelti identifies as significant are the familiar ones of setting, character, conflict, and resolution. Meaning is seen to be a function of the relationships, first, among the elements of a given work (thus preserving the structural integrity of that work) and, secondly, a function of a marked similarity between works. The concept of formula is also regarded as having explanatory significance. The popularity of certain formulas may be accounted for in terms of the social functions they perform. Given the scarcity of audience data, these functions remain speculative, especially since the content of the formulas admits of various plausible functional interpretations. Consequently, I have confined my discussion of function to the producers of children's fiction, on the assumption that the stories constitute better evidence for authorial than for audience behavior.

7. Baker remarks in his autobiography that he had little difficulty in adjusting to the limitations of the formula and soon felt quite free in them.

8. The sociological literature on effect is summarized in J. T. Klapper, *The Effects of Mass Communication* (New York: Free Press, 1960) and in Wilbur Schramm and Donald Roberts, eds., *The Process and Effects of Mass Communication*, rev. ed. (Champagne: University of Illinois Press, 1971). See also: Warren Breed, "Mass Communication and Sociocultural Integration," in Lewis Dexter and David Manning White, eds., *People, Society and Mass Communications* (Glencoe, Ill.: Free Press, 1964), pp. 183–200.

9. Peter Berger and Thomas Luckmann, *The Social Construction of Reality* (Garden City, N.Y.: Doubleday, 1966); Hugh D. Duncan, *Symbols in Society* (New York: Oxford University Press, 1968); Erving Goffman, *The Presentation of Self in Everyday Life* (New York: Anchor Books, 1959). The inherent stability of any given society reflects in large measure the principal given qualities of human life. Human behavior, compared with that of other animal species, appears to be relatively unstructured by biologically based imperatives. What serves man in place of instinct is culture.

10. Arnold van Gennep, *Rites of Passage*, trans. Monika B. Vizedon and Gabrielle L. Caffee (Chicago: University of Chicago Press, 1960). Bernard Wishy, in *The Child and the Republic* (Philadelphia: University of Pennsylvania Press: 1968), suggests a different analysis of late nineteenth-century children's fiction, noting the recurrence of three child types: the lovable, erring child; the pure child who is rejected by a corrupt world; and the child redeemer.

11. Susan Archer Weiss, "Nellie in the Lighthouse," *SN* 4 (1877): 577–80.

12. Louisa May Alcott, "Bonfires," *YC* 46 (January 9, 1873): 10.

13. Margaret Bertha Wright, "Charlie's First Doughnut," *WA* 15 (1882): 295–99.

14. Ibid., p. 298.

15. "Vieux Moustache" [pseud. Clarence Gordon], "Charley Balch's Metamorphosis," *RM* 1 (1867): 106–12.

16. Ibid., p. 110.

17. Richard L. Rapson, "The American Child as Seen by British Travelers, 1845–1935," *American Quarterly* 17 (1965): 520–35.

18. G. Hamlen, "When Book Meets Book," *WA* 23 (1886): 206–10.

19. Ibid., p. 209.

20. Mary Barker French, "Jenny, the 'Flying Fairy,'" *YC* 61 (August 30, 1888): 413–14.

21. Marie B. Williams, "The Fatal Fire-hunt," *YC* 48 (February 3, 1876): 35–36.

22. Rebecca Harding Davis, "Naylor o' the Bowl," *SN* 1 (1873): 65–69.

23. "The Magician," *Frank Leslie's Boys' and Girls' Weekly* 3 (November 9, 1867): 21–22.

24. Ibid., p. 21.

25. Wohl, "The 'Rags to Riches Story,'" p. 390.

26. Robert Wiebe, *The Search for Order*, 1877–1920 (New York: Hill and Wang, 1967).

27. Frederick Elkin, *The Child and Society* (New York: Random House, 1960), pp. 3–44. Cf. Berger and Luckmann, *The Social Construct of Reality*, pp. 129–84.

28. Elkin, *The Child and Society*, p. 19.

29. Ibid., p. 33.

30. See, for example: Mrs. A. M. Diaz, "Jimmy's Dream," *YC* 49 (June 1, 1876): 174; S. S. Colt, "The Land of Short Memories," *SN* 7 (1880): 217–18; Walter Babbett, "How Conrad Lost His School-Books," *SN* 13 (1886): 514–17.

31. Rose Terry, "Isabella," *OYF* 7 (1871): 346.

15

Money: The Change of Fortune Story in *St. Nicholas*

ANNE MACLEOD

In America 1873 was a bad year. The post–Civil War boom slid into financial panic and depression. Banks failed, wages fell, unemployment soared. By most measures it was a chancy time for a publisher to launch a new magazine, especially a children's magazine designed to be lavishly illustrated and stocked with material by the best — and the best paid — periodical authors of the day.

But Scribner and Company went ahead anyway. They chose Mary Mapes Dodge as editor on the strength of her past editorial work, and, even more, because of her now-famous essay setting out her idea of a children's magazine, which should be, she said, "a child's pleasure ground." The first issue of what would become the most celebrated American periodical ever published for children appeared in 1873. *St. Nicholas* was not inexpensive — $3.00 a year for a subscription was not trivial when $1200 a year was an adequate income for a family, and when many families lived on far less. Nevertheless, the magazine was successful, financially as well as artistically, from the first.

That success was grounded in Dodge's clear understanding of the broadly held middle-class American attitudes of the time toward children and childhood, attitudes that Dodge herself not only shared, but understood well how to express in editorial direction. The magazine taught facts and imparted values, but its editor also took care to please her child readers. That was the formula Mary Mapes Dodge applied with success for

" SHE SLOWLY ADVANCED INTO THE PARLOR, CLUTCHING HER DOLL."

A suddenly impoverished Sara confronts Miss Minchin in Reginald Birch's illustration for *Sara Crewe* by Frances Hodgson Burnett. *SN* 15 (Dec. 1887): 100.

thirty years. And everything about the magazine, its entertaining fiction and informative non-fiction, its educational purposes tailored to a child's tastes, its inclusive approach to its young audience — all these fit the concept of childhood widely embraced in late nineteenth century America.

A stroll through the first three decades of *St. Nicholas* publication —

that is, through Dodge's tenure as editor—finds much that would be expected of middle class American views tailored to conventional ideas of what was suitable for children. The outlook was optimistic, the tone kind, friendly, interested and occasionally sentimental. A good deal of the fiction was domestic, about children of three or four years old up to fifteen or sixteen, in contemporary American settings, or, sometimes, in other countries or other times. None of this is surprising. What is a considerable surprise is how many of these stories were about money.

The stories were about getting money, losing money, managing and spending money; about poverty, riches, wages and charity. In other words, they were about a society in the process of reorganizing its hierarchies along economic lines and a middle class struggling to maintain both its financial balance and its values. *St. Nicholas* stories dealt with money in a variety of ways, some direct, some allusive. But for the youngest as for the oldest of its readers there was fiction that testified to the uncertainty of the economic climate and to the questions that troubled a society rapidly dividing along class lines in which money played an ever-increasing role. And if money was essential for security and status—as it was—it was also the key to the new-found joys of a consumer society. These, too, found a place in *St. Nicholas's* stories for children.

The change of fortune tale was a staple of nineteenth century literature. As Dickens and Horatio Alger well knew, a sudden, dramatic financial shift was a sure source of drama. *St. Nicholas* authors knew it, too; such tales were reliable favorites in the magazine. "The Wyndham Girls" is an example. It is a long story by Marion Ames Taggart (29 [Jan. 1902]: 208–47) of a wealthy family abruptly brought low, and of how they coped and what they learned. The opening episode introduces the Wyndham girls, two sisters and a cousin Phyllis who lives with the family, and Mrs. Wyndham, widow of a successful businessman who gave his family every luxury. The three girls are choosing silks for new dresses, while Mrs. Wyndham, "a frail creature, sweet and gentle" rocks in her chair: "one felt that she had been properly placed in luxury, fortunately shielded from hardship." But hardship is about to knock at the door in the person of the family lawyer, come to inform them that their fortune is lost, through the "speculative" treachery of the late Mr. Wyndham's trusted partner. Frail indeed, Mrs. Wyndham screams and sobs and is carried to her bed by a servant "as if she had been a child."

Mrs. Wyndham's efforts never rise above this feeble standard, but the three girls set themselves to coping, and the story becomes a rich stew of entertaining narrative, uplifting homilies about the real meaning of happiness, mild romance and, through it all, exact reckonings of income and outgo for the nouveau poor. Inevitably, it is also an insight into the author's philosophy concerning the privileges of refinement and the uses of adversity.

One of the privileges is a "residue" of the family fortune that will provide $2000 a year in income. While this is unquestionably a long way down from wealth, it was not, by the standards of the time, penury. (A 1907 study put the threshold of middle class status at $1200 a year.) On the other hand, a downside of refinement is that it will be hard to add to their income. Mother is obviously no help and none of the girls has been trained to "practical labor." "Jessamy's drawing, Bab's music, Phyllis's clever stories and verses were all too amateurish to find a place in the arts." As their great-aunt unkindly remarks, "I believe there's nothing you can do decently ... you are only fit for nursery governesses" (213–214).

And, at first, the girls do not try to find work. Instead, they find a place to live, a cheap boarding house, for which they pay $28.00 a week for two rooms. A friend more experienced with fallen fortunes does the arithmetic for them: "That's fourteen hundred and fifty-six dollars year. That leaves five hundred for washing, clothing, possible doctor's bills, and so on." She recommends a small flat instead: "Cheap boarding is unwholesome, vulgar, and generally horrid," but the Wyndhams decide they must board because they know nothing of housekeeping. They soon find that "in spite of all ... prudence, money slipped away; laundry bills took on alarming proportions, and they had never dreamed how fast five-cent fares could swell into as many dollars" (222).

So the question of work must be faced. Prodded by their great-aunt, two of the girls decide to try for employment, causing their mother to burst into laments. "Pride," Aunty sniffs, but Mrs. Wyndham denies it. In an outburst that clearly expresses the author's opinion, she declares that "unwomanly women are a misfortune to themselves and all the community, and it is impossible to knock about the world without losing something of that dear and delicate loveliness ... no girl should be placed in the thick of the fight, striding through the world in fierce competition with men" (223).

Nevertheless, Bab does take a job as cashier (in a "protected" situation) only to find that she is incompetent to do the work: "Accomplishments she had, but practical knowledge, especially of arithmetic, she lacked." After a week, she is "kindly dismissed." Meanwhile, Aunty arranges for Phyllis to read her "perfect" French to two girls of the "newly rich" class for two hours a day, at a fee of $25.00 a month. Phyllis's experience quickly confirms the moral dangers of employment to girlish innocence. The "four foolish girls of fifteen" discuss "flirtations, theaters, trashy novels ... betraying the most sordid ambition, till innocent and honest Phyllis was horrified." This time, a young doctor delivers the author's message, assuring Phyllis that her own standards are the right ones: "You've been shown the highest standards in everything, and they can't be common ... keep your own ideas and steer by them.... Girls don't understand that the whole world is in their hands; we're all what women, young and old, make us" (225–6). Phyllis, too, lasts only one week at work, then falls ill of typhoid.

Illness, winter, low funds and no work bring about a new decision, presented, as usual, with exact financial calculations. "We are going to take a flat, the best we can find for the money, at forty dollars a month. We are going to have a woman come in two days each week to wash, iron, and sweep, at a dollar and a quarter a day, making about a hundred and twenty-six dollars a year. We are going to cook on gas ... seventy-two dollars more. And we're going to live plainly ... for six hundred a year.... That makes a total of thirteen hundred dollars ... three hundred dollars less than we spend now. When one of the girls objects that "we can't do anything, any of us. I'm not sure mama understands cooking" (233), another points out that they might learn and, if they can't, they could hire a servant and still spend no more than they now do.

Now that they've made the right decisions at last, hardship fades dramatically. The girls find a seven room flat, with a "rosy-cheeked German janitor's wife," only two blocks from Central Park. And it turns out that a rich friend had bought many of their "dearest things" at the home auction and has had them stored away all this time. Miraculously, they have money for extensive redecoration, replacing "ugly" wallpapers and putting down "tasteful rugs." Arithmetic falls silent as they serve steak for dinner, learn to sweep and agree with Longfellow that "home-keeping hearts are happiest." They even decide that financial collapse is a blessing: "I suspect it isn't misfortune [but] good luck that has come to us, and that if we had stayed rich we should have missed getting into the heart of things, and the real fun of living" (238).

That said, the real story is over. In the last nine pages, the author arranges two romances, the beginnings of a modest writing career for Phyllis, and the restoration of $40,000 of the Wyndham fortune. Except for the $40,000, figures disappear from the story, but if $30,000 produced $2000 annually, the reader can easily calculate that the Wyndham income has more than doubled and that the family is now, if not wealthy, at least very comfortable. Its lessons taught, adversity departs.

Themes like these turn up often in *St. Nicholas*. The idea that hardship built character was popular. For the very well-to-do, a dollop of economic distress was often seen as a tonic, as it was for the Wyndham girls.

If the protagonists' values are askew, the right amount of struggle corrects them; if their values are sound, the struggle proves their worth. At the same time, the strugglers learn about everyday realities and get closer to "the heart of things." It is noticeable, though, that the genteel in fiction were seldom left in permanent poverty with only their improved characters to see them through. Even if real wealth was not restored, enough money for comfort always found its way back somehow.

St. Nicholas authors took a remarkably tolerant view of adults who wilted in hard times. Mrs Wynham's sweet, unworldly nature apparently deserved the comforts of money and, when money was gone, protection from the effects of her own poor judgment. (She had refused advice from the family lawyer that would have prevented the disaster.) Other stories told of fathers just as ineffectual as Mrs. Wyndham, with neither frailty nor sheltered lives for excuse. Susan Coolidge's story "Eyebright" (6 [Feb.-Oct. 1879]) tells at painful length about a little girl growing up in the shadow of her father's depression. He has reason to be down-hearted, to be sure: his wife died after a long illness, and he lost his job as manager of a mill when the company failed. But he makes things worse by moving himself and his daughter to an island off the Maine coast, where it is impossible for him to make a living, and where he grows more and more dispirited. Eyebright (this is her name, I regret to say) knows that it is her duty to make a cheerful home for her father and she does that, against great odds. She can't even go to school, but Coolidge finds a silver lining: "No geography or history can take the place of the lessons which Eyebright was now learning — lessons in patience, unselfishness, good-humor and helpfulness" (675). After several years, unfortunately for papa but fortunately for Eyebright, he is drowned in a storm and she is adopted by an aᵒuent family, far from the lonely island where life is so hard.

Stories that let adults off the hook so easily focused the drama on the young characters, certainly, but they also served up clear messages about the duties of girls and the essential qualities of womanhood. Coolidge's "lessons" for Eyebright covered much of the ground, but there was more. A pleasant, well-ordered home was a sex-linked responsibility. In family crises, it was up to girls to stretch scarce resources, make a "simple" home "cozy and inviting" and, above all, to cultivate a cheerful outlook for the sake of others. In "Nora's Oil Well" by Sophie Swett (6 [Sept. 1879]: 757–61) a poor Irish girl resists selling the poor shack where she makes a home for herself and her brother because it is home. She gets her reward when oil is found on the land, and she and her brother make a "snug little fortune." There was, of course, another possibility: Women could find paid employment. The author of the Wyndham tale admitted the practical uselessness of the girls' expensive education, but she refused to draw the obvious conclusion. The only kind of work she approved for women was home work. If Jessamy could learn to draw well enough to illustrate books, if Phyllis could sell her "little stories," well and good. For girls to go out to work, however, was to risk their femininity. The Wyndham girls' most important lesson was to learn domestic skills, that they might make a happy home on a modest income.

Not every *St. Nicholas* author saw it that way. Elizabeth Stuart Phelps responded vigorously when Dodge asked her to write for girl readers her opinion of women supporting themselves. In "Supporting Herself" (11 [May 1884]: 517–9), she said, "Do it!" and second, "Do it thoroughly!" She countered every conventional objection: "If a lady is less a lady for earning her own living, she never was a lady at all." And she allowed for exceptions: "*Some* girls must stay at home and accept a dependent life." "*As a rule*," however, "it is honester, safer, nobler and more womanly for a woman to be able to care for herself and for the father, or mother, or brother, or husband, or child, whom a hundred changes may ... fling upon her warm heart and brave hand for protection" (517).

The second piece of Phelps's advice — "do it thoroughly" — was a bluntly realistic assessment of the commercial world. Paid work, Phelps says, is not for amateurs; it must be done properly. "To offer incomplete work for complete market price, is to be either a cheat or a beggar. The terrible grinding laws of supply and demand, pay and receive, give and get, give no quarter to shilly-shally labor." Intentions, poverty or need are beside the point. "When you have entered the world of trade, you have entered a world where tenderness and charity and personal interest are foreign relations." Phelps's views of the business world were not so far from Mrs. Wyndham's, but her conclusions were entirely different (518).

Fall-of-fortune stories reflected middle class anxieties about economic security, an uneasiness well warranted by the fluctuating economy of the age. In the midst of expansion there were repeated financial panics, in 1873, 1883 and 1893, each of them followed by prolonged depressions. Since speculation was implicated in every panic, it is not hard to understand the terrified scorn authors packed into the word "speculator." Fiction never spoke of systemic causes of economic problems; business failures were always ascribed to speculation, cheating or mismanagement.

The middle classes, especially city dwellers, also saw the ever-increasing reality of urban, industrial and immigrant poverty. That concern, too, spilled into the pages of *St. Nicholas* in the form of stories flavored by attitudes that ranged from sympathy to fear to condescension to scorn. Whatever the authors felt about the poor, two responses were almost always clear: first, that their strongest sympathies went to the children, and second, that they had little to suggest, in practical terms, about what could be done beyond personal charity. The result was fiction grounded in reality, but also greatly given to a belief in luck, pluck and the benevolence of the rich.

One rather ambiguous tale, "Mary Elizabeth" (7 [Feb. 1880]: 316–9) written by the same Elizabeth Phelps who was so brisk on the subject of work, tells of a little girl who is "poor … sick … ragged … cold … hungry … frightened," a child with "no place to go to and nobody to care" who begs for her supper on Boston's streets—in vain. Finally, she tries her luck in a great hotel. There her innocent questions shame a dissipated young man into repentance and she gets not only her supper, but a spontaneous charitable donation of forty dollars from several "gentlemen," and a referral to someone who will "know what to do" with an orphan. None of the "gentlemen" shows any genuine interest in the child, however, and Phelps implies that the really important beneficiary of the encounter is the young man, who turns to better ways.

Another *St. Nicholas* story for the very young shows condescension ingrained at an early age. "The Poor Dol-ly" (written with its words divided into syllables) tells of two little girls holding a tea party for their dolls (9 [Oct. 1882]: 977–9). They decide to have a poor dolly, "hun-gry and cold and [in] rag-ged clothes" invited by their dolls, "who have ev-ery-thing they want." They use a discarded doll without arms, tear her clothes, "which were pret-ty old any-way" and make her look "ver-y rag-ged and cold." One little girl speaks for the fortunate dollies, the other for the poor one, in a conversation very patronizing on the one side, and grateful on the other. The little girls show a surprising awareness of the plight of the working poor. Asked about her brothers and sisters, the poor dolly says, "They go out to work at five o'clock ev-ery morn-ing. They are ver-y young…. They make but-tons." The poor dolly leaves with some leftover teacake and some second-hand clothes, and the little girls are happy for "e-ven hav-ing played at kind-ness." The benefit of giving to the giver was rarely overlooked.

While middle class adults wanted their children to learn kindness, they didn't want them seriously distressed over social problems. An 1879 article by Oliver Thorne, "The Little Housemaids" (6 [Apr. 1879]: 403–10), reassured the child who might be harrowed by the stories or sights of poverty: "Little Housemaids" begins by telling fortunate children that the unfortunate also have good times. "Small houses, cottages, and even 'rooms' hold many happy little folk." And now, the essay goes on to say, even street children have happy days because "one kind lady has thought of a way to

"Those chil-dren of ours," said Su-sie, in a thought-ful tone, "ought to be much hap-pi-er for hav-ing been kind to that poor dol-ly."

"I think they look hap-pi-er al-read-y," said lit-tle Jen-nie, who looked hap-py her-self for e-ven hav-ing played at kind-ness.

"The Poor Dol-ly" by Anonymous reveals an unconsciously condescending attitude toward the poor. *SN* 9.12 (Oct. 1882): 979.

open to them a better life." The author describes a school for servants, with girls of five or six brought from the streets to learn washing, cleaning, marketing and kitchen work, that they might be placed with respectable families, to earn wages "suitable to [their] years" (twelve or older) and so have "useful" lives, saved from "miseries you cannot imagine" (410).

Lives useful to their employers, however, might still be hard lives for the redeemed children of the street. The little girls of the doll tea party apparently understood one of the grimmest facts of late nineteenth century economic life: that work, even work at fourteen to sixteen hours a day and employing every member of a family, including "ver-y young" children, did not guarantee a decent life for the working poor. The last two decades of the nineteenth century were desperately hard on workers, especially the many who depended on their skills as handworkers for a living. As immigrants poured into the country, the poor were undercut by the poorer yet. The work that offered a living in 1880 could not, a few years later, keep a family, as employers turned from wages to piece payment, as steam replaced human power in some operations, and as less skilled new arrivals stood in line to take work at starvation pay.

Helen Campbell was a journalist with a mission. She wrote vividly about the women who worked in the garment industries of New York, often quoting from her many interviews with them. Most of the women were immigrants who worked at home and were paid by the piece in a system that consistently exploited and cheated them. No family could get by on the wages of one or even two adults, though most of the work was at least semi-skilled. So children, from the age of four, worked beside their parents the same long hours, in the same wretched surroundings.

Campbell's 1887 book, *Prisoners of Poverty*, describes the lot of poor working women with the kind of financial precision *St. Nicholas* authors applied to the lesser problems of the formerly wealthy, and her relentless arithmetic does indeed outline a prison. She tells of a shirtmaker who in 1880 worked ten, twelve and sometimes fourteen hours day to make nearly $9.00 a week. In 1887, the same work brought no more than $4.50 per week and sometimes only $3.50. She paid $1.50 a week for the single room where she lived with her crippled mother and three younger sisters. They bought what food they could, and no clothing at all. Coal and oil, for heat and light, broke the budget because the poor could only afford to buy them in small, expensive quantities. Wages (but not rent) continued to fall until a dozen shirts brought only eighty-five cents. The end of this particular story comes when the shirtmaker brings five dozen shirts to the foreman for her pay. He finds a half-inch flaw in one shirt, and docks her for the whole dozen, leaving her with $3.40 for her week's work. In despair, she turns to prostitution. The children, the author observes, are warm now and no longer cry from hunger.

Campbell told desperate stories, far removed from the mild scrimping of the Wyndham family. She also detailed the cold-hearted ways by which employers cheated women of the scanty earnings of unending labor. Is it fair? Campbell asked one businessman. "Anything's fair in business," he replied. And to any objection from the women themselves, the reply was always the same: "There's plenty waiting" for the jobs.

St. Nicholas was never so stark, of course, yet the same realities haunt its pages. Even a wholly sentimental story might hint at some of the raw truths Campbell wrote about. In an 1881 tale, "Angel in the Ulster" by Washington Gladden (9 [Dec. 1881]: 106–14), rich, benevolent Mr. Todd, on his way to Cincinnati, finds himself stranded in an Eastern city on Christmas Eve. Chance arranges for him to overhear a conversation between a girl of twelve and a boy of ten ("neatly but plainly dressed") as they are leaving a garment factory. They have just delivered four dozen nightgowns made by their mother and themselves as pieceworkers, and they have been cheated by the foreman. "The price was two dollars a dozen, but the man said that some of them were not well made, so he kept back a dollar." When the boy wants to accuse the man of lying, his sister echoes the women Campbell interviewed: "Oh, no, that wouldn't do any good ... and he might not give us any more work.... [But] only seven dollars for two weeks hard work of all three of us!" They can't spend $1.50 for a Christmas turkey, they agree, since rent is $2.00 and they must buy coal (111).

Mr. Todd's sympathies go out to these children and he soon learns the family's story from an old friend who "happens" to know them. "The father was the master of a bark in the African trade, and he was lost on the west coast a year and a half ago.... They had a home of their own, bought in flush times, and mortgaged for half its value, but in the [depression], everything was swept away." In other words, we are not looking at the "real" poor here, but at a respectable middle class family down on its luck, always an easier proposition. Mr. Todd supplies gifts and a glorious Christmas dinner for the children and their mother. Fortunately, he also happens to encounter the seafaring father, whom he happens to know and who is looking for his lost family, it happens, just in the street outside their tenement. All are reunited, joyous and (of course) grateful to Mr. Todd, who takes the train to Cincinnati (114).

Sentiment aside, the pivot on which this story turns is the economic precariousness the middle class rightly feared — the few sentences about the mortgage and the depression say it all. And the children's conversation at the beginning of the narrative is a sobering glimpse into the abyss of poverty: the long work for small return, the pinching calculations for the most basic necessities, and above all, the powerlessness of the poor. The sunny surface doesn't quite hide the darker truth just beneath.

Fortunes could change for the better as well as for the worse, and though it was doubtless less likely, it was surely more fun. In 1899, *St. Nicholas* published "The Story of Betty" by Carolyn Wells (26 [Jan.-Oct. 1899]), a wonderfully class-conscious tale of a young Irish-American girl who comes into a fortune and spends most of the story happily making a home with both love and money — lots of money. It's a long story, full of remarkable coincidences and suffused with conventional contemporary attitudes. Betty Maguire grew up in an orphanage until she was ten, when she was sent out to earn her living as a servant. When she is nearly fourteen, remarkable coincidences bring her to a lawyer who is looking for the heir to a fortune made in Australia by — it turns out — her grandfather. Luckily, Betty, though a servant girl in a nasty boardinghouse when she is found, has qualities that recommend her to the genteel. She is spirited but humble, attractive and amusing, *and* her low-class Irish accent drops away magically when she is with educated people. Therefore, a wealthy, refined and strictly honorable family takes on the task of guiding Betty as she learns to be a millionaire.

Since Betty has always wanted home and family, the next episodes in her story are wholly taken over by shopping, at the level of wildest dreams. The home Betty buys is a mansion in the choicest neighborhood, with park-like grounds and rooms without number to be furnished. A trip to New York provides the furniture, and then Betty turns her attention to the family she also wants to "buy." She finds a grandmother, in the form of a refined housekeeper, brings in a lame friend as her brother and selects a baby from an orphanage to be her little sister.

She has a tutor for her education and lots of coaching on dress and decorum from her genteel friends, but as time goes by, she knows she is missing something. What it is, of course, is something she can't buy — a mother. A whole new series of remarkable coincidences produces her real mother, who was injured but not drowned all those years ago, and who is beautiful, refined and overjoyed to find her daughter again. All are united (no one seems to miss father) and live happily ever after in the mansion.

Class consciousness permeates "The Story of Betty," as it does many *St. Nicholas* tales, but with a particular emphasis. Throughout "Betty," class is closely associated with money, without the usual pious claims that one has nothing to do with the other. Privilege, too, is thoroughly linked with wealth: it is the privilege to have and do pretty much what she wants that comes to Betty with her inheritance — as she understands from the start. She accepts a few restraints, but the only real check to her wishes comes when she yearns for real family — blood relations — and knows of none. Even then, her money serves her well as she follows up slender leads until she does in fact find her grandparents (wealthy, respectable Bostonians) and her mother.

And along with the pleasures of money, status and privilege Betty also embraces what can only be called consumerism. An impressive portion of the story consists of descriptions of luxurious expenditure. The house, with "frescoed garlands on the walls and ceilings, the shining, flickering glass prisms on the chandeliers, and the carved scrolls of the tall mantels," the furnishings "a dear little dressing-table with a wide, low mirror ... a wide, soft couch upholstered in blue ... a dear little rocking-chair, a lovely work-table of inlaid wood ... a carpet of blue and white ... the musical instruments for the music room, the leather chairs for the library" and so on and on and on. Clothing gets the same loving attention and so does a birthday party with "wonderful fruits and confections and cakes, and a great big salmon ... and boned turkeys ... and sandwiches rolled up and tied with ribbons ... ice-cream [and] chocolates [and] cake...." For the reader, whatever else it may be, Betty's story is a vicarious orgy of consumption.

Consumerism marked one major cultural difference between early and late nineteenth century literature for children. Though Louisa May

Alcott wrote after the Civil War, her outlook on children and reading was characteristically pre-war. In an instructive little piece, "Pansies" (15 [Nov. 1897]: 12–19), in *St. Nicholas*, Alcott targeted exactly the literary materialism so popular in late nineteenth century fiction. A young girl in the story excuses her "sentimental and impossible novel" by saying, "Well, I'm poor and can't have as may pretty things as I want, so it *is* delightful to read about women who wear white quilted satin dressing-gowns and olive velvet trains with ... lace sweepers to them. Diamonds as large as nuts, and rivers of opals and sapphires and rubies and pearls, are great fun to read of, if you never even get a look at real ones." But her wiser friend deplores this not very vicious taste. "That's the harm of it all. False and foolish things are made interesting, and we read for that, not for any lesson there may be hidden under the velvet and jewels.... Now *this* book [the one she is reading] has a true and clean moral that we all can see, and one feels wiser and better for reading it" (12).

But Alcott was scolding the rising tide. The Gilded Age was all about money. Great fortunes made in steel, oil and railroads brought gargantuan — and conspicuous — spending on houses, art, clothes, carriages and luxuries unthought of in pre-industrial, pre-war America. Spending money became an occupation for those who could afford it and who had little else to do. Advertising, magazines devoted to furnishings for the home or clothing for the well-dressed, department stores — all the artifacts of a consumer society flourished in the second half of the nineteenth century. Of *course* the girl too poor to hope for velvets and diamonds for herself liked to read about them in books. Authors knew it and publishers knew it and both were happy to supply her yearning. *St. Nicholas*, too, though it believed with Alcott that literature should improve the mind and morals, published many a tale spiced with vicariously enjoyable possessions.

And it was not only the middle classes who dreamed consumer dreams. Like peasant storytellers who filled their fairy tales with gold coins and bountiful food, the poor in American fiction dreamed of the consumer symbols of success. "Mike Deehan's Spree" by Mary Densel (29 [Aug. 1902]: 918–21) tells of Mike Deehan, poor, cheerful and Irish-comic, who does a lot of imaginary shopping on Broadway, which had "block after block of shops [with] windows full of tempting goods." Mike's fantasy purchases are specific, since he can see the goods he can't possibly hope to have. He (mentally) "buys" a cutaway coat, shiny boots, a blue vest and a "bookay" and he charges them all. At home again, he eats mush for supper as he did for breakfast, but he calls it stuffed turkey, "blue monge," herring, "an' iystrs [oysters], an' ice-cream, an' orange-jelly." The ideal poor boy in a consumer society was Mike, aspiring, but not resentful. "And — who knows?" wrote the author in cheery conclusion, "perhaps Mike's dreams of happiness will come true. For Mike was a bright, hard-working lad, with push and energy enough to earn himself a place in the world."

That money, in a variety of ways and forms, was highly visible in *St. Nicholas* does not suggest crassness on Dodge's part; it simply attests that the magazine belonged to its time and place, as, indeed, it had to, to be as successful as it was. Nothing about the selection of material for the magazine was accidental or absent-minded. Dodge knew her clientele, shared its values and reflected those values back to her readers. If the theme of money ran through so much of *St. Nicholas*'s highly varied material, it was because money had become, by the last quarter of the nineteenth century, integral to the value system of the middle classes *St. Nicholas* served.

Not that American attitudes toward money were uncomplicated, as these stories demonstrate very well. Genteel tradition deplored open ambition, vulgar displays of wealth, and social climbing — all the failings of the "new rich" scorned by both the older privileged classes and the genteel middle classes. But the hope of financial success and the fear of financial disaster were also real. The unstable economy made the middle classes uneasy and faced them with anguishing questions about how to reconcile such conflicting values as preserving womanhood from the marketplace, on the one hand, and coping with financial crisis, on the other. On the question of poverty, *St. Nicholas* stories are a fair guide to the sentiments of the time. The social casualties of urban and industrial growth, heavy immigration and unmitigated capitalism troubled many Americans, yet for a long time, society at large dealt with them pretty much as *St. Nicholas* stories did — with an unsystematic mix of personal and organized charity and attitudes that ranged from sympathy to dismissiveness. *St. Nicholas*, which meant so much to so many children and parents in its halcyon days, is a rich sourcebook for understanding how the American middle classes felt and thought about their own time.

Reference

Helen Campbell, *Prisoners of Poverty: Women Wage-Workers, Their Trades and Their Lives,* Boston: Roberts Brothers, 1887.

16

St. Nicholas and the City Beautiful, 1893–1894

GRETA LITTLE

Mary Mapes Dodge's tenure as editor of *St. Nicholas*, from its inception in 1873 until her death in 1905, coincided with a particularly turbulent period of American history. Much of that turbulence was centered in the rapidly growing urban areas of the country. The Industrial Revolution had called workers to the cities from the less productive farms and from foreign shores. Unprepared to accommodate such large numbers of new residents, the city centers became hotbeds of civic unrest and human misery. The resulting strikes, riots and events like the Haymarket bombing prompted national fears about industrialization, immigration, family disruption, religious change and deepening class divisions (Boyer vii). Civic-minded middle class citizens saw themselves facing an "increasing ethnic and cultural heterogeneity and escalating threat of disorder" (Hall 176). Thus in January 1893 when *St. Nicholas* published the first in a series of articles about American cities, the nation was facing grave concerns about its cities and their future.

The essays must be read and interpreted in this historical context. The series included eleven articles featuring nine cities—Boston, Philadelphia, New York, Washington, Chicago, Baltimore, New Orleans, St. Augustine and San Francisco. They were presented as a major attraction of the magazine; three served as the lead article of an issue. Each contained a good deal of factual information and was accompanied by maps, drawings and photographs of the city, showing important buildings, monuments and thoroughfares. For the larger metropolitan areas, growth statistics constituted a major portion of the articles. The cities of the South and West were presented in a more anecdotal way, emphasizing each city's appeal for youngsters.

The Chicago World's Fair, which opened in May 1893, provided the avowed motivation for the series. The fair, held to commemorate the anniversary of Columbus's discovery of America, generated widespread interest throughout the nation. The *Century Magazine*, successor to *Scribner's*, and parent to *St. Nicholas*, had run numerous feature articles calling public attention to the fair, its plan and its exhibits. The size and beauty of the buildings and grounds, said to excel the Paris exhibition in 1889, were cause for national pride. *St. Nicholas* also featured several articles about the fair ("*St. Nicholas* At the Fair," 20 [Aug. 1893]: 790–1), including an essay by Tudor Jenks with illustrations borrowed from the *Century* articles. His article, "The World's Fair Palaces," (20 [May 1893]: 519–28) too expressed pride in the Chicago fair, applauding "American pluck, capacity, and achievement" (520).

However, Dodge also saw in the fair and its foreign visitors an occasion for *St. Nicholas* to teach its readers about American cities. In the initial article, "Boston" (20 [Jan. 1893]: 170–9), Thomas Wentworth Higginson, minister, reformer and author, explained the series' purpose:

> This is simply one of a series of papers, each with a specific subject and each confined to its own theme. In view of the large number of foreign visitors to be expected, during the coming year, on this continent, it is desirable that all curious persons should be informed what kind of a place each city is, and what are its points of interest [178].

The series provided the opportunity for comment on the issues and fears raised by the increasing urbanization of American society.

Prominent representatives of each city wrote the articles, presenting his or her views of the city. Although each was different, the essays included information about the city's history, a catalog of interesting sights to be seen and some distinguishing characteristics to set each apart from the others. As usual, Dodge was able to recruit outstanding writers for her series. Senator Henry Cabot Lodge wrote of the nation's capital in "The City of Washington" (20 [June 1893]: 572–80), as did Frances Hodgson Burnett in "A City of Groves and Bowers" (20 [June 1893]: 563–571). George Washington Cable, author of *Creole Days* and a native of New Orleans, contributed a two-part essay on that city. For other articles Dodge enlisted authors, poets, journalists and university presidents to tell readers of *St. Nicholas* about their cities.

Many of these contributors belonged to Dodge's New York circle of friends and shared an interest in progressive reform. She was tied to a number of those most active in the movement through her publisher, Scribner and Company. Richard Watson Gilder, editor of Scribner's *Century*, headed the 1894 New York State Tenement House Committee. Frank Stockton, Dodge's former assistant editor, had also written for Gilder and *Century*. Burnett, Lodge and Cable as well as Edmund Clarence Stedman and D. C. Gilman were fellow *Century* contributors or members of the same circle. While their views cannot be expected to be identical, their essays reveal a common approach to urban reform, an approach shaped at least in part by Scribner's.

In 1890 the publisher agreed to print Jacob Riis's sketches of tenement life, *How the Other Half Lives*. The book had a major impact in the battle for adequate housing. Social historian Roy Lubove described it as "a plea for understanding and sympathy" (58) and attributed Riis's success to the concerns of contemporary readers:

> Americans in the 1890's were anxious to learn about those things which he described in his books and lectures. Puzzled and fearful, they needed social critics like Riis to interpret the significance of the big city and immigration, poverty and tenement life; to explain how America could safely make the transition from an agrarian-rural society to an urban-industrial one [55].

A Danish immigrant himself, Riis was very articulate in describing the plight of the immigrant child. His goal was to mobilize the public and initiate change. He wanted reform that would transform, "guide the child's impulses into socially constructive channels, plant in his neighborhood attractive and wholesome counter influences to the saloon, street gang, and similar evils, and the tenement would surrender its power to produce moral and social decay" (Lubove 72). Riis placed his faith in schools, parks and playgrounds:

> These were the tools which would civilize the child, Americanize the immigrant, reconstruct the tenement neighborhood, and reduce the importance of the policeman's night stick as an instrument of social control. In Riis's eyes, no greater challenge confronted the housing or social reformer than the creation of new primary group relationships based on the neighborhood in geography and a common Americanism in spirit [Lubove 80].

His view of the city producing moral and social decay and of children as the most effective defense against such decay was consistent with Dodge's philosophy (Sturges 270–71) and the attitudes of late nineteenth-century American writers, who were ambivalent or even antagonistic toward cities and city life (MacLeod 45). Although Dodge's views might have been similar to Riis's, his descriptions of urban poverty were far too negative and graphic for readers of St. *Nicholas*:

> In the midwinter, when the poor shiver in their homes, and the dog-days when the fierce heat and foul air of the tenements smother their babies by thousands, they are found, sometimes three and four in a night, in hallways, in areas and on the doorsteps of the rich…. Few outcast babies survive their desertion long…. The high mortality among the foundlings is not to be marveled at. The wonder is, rather, that any survive. (Riis 141–42)

The themes, however, that Riis had identified are prominent in the articles of the city series. For example, in the first essay on Boston, Higginson stresses the importance of schools, parks and playgrounds. He lauds the colleges and universities of Boston and its environs, as well as the public-school system, and the partly established park system. His attention to physical education is particularly interesting. He praises athletic clubs and a public open-air gymnasium with classes for women and children, saying that it "is accomplishing great good" (20 [Jan. 1893]: 177). In speaking of school playgrounds that remain open for public use during summer vacations, Higginson is careful to mention proper, efficient supervision, noting that nearly a thousand people used the Charlesbank facility "without casualty or insubordination" (178). Without ever acknowledging concerns about disruptive city crowds, he reassures readers that no such problems exist where supervised playgrounds are available for children.

The availability of parks constituted a major attraction in the essays on Chicago. John F. Ballantyne, managing editor of the Chicago *Morning News*, later the *Record*, called Chicago's parks its "crowning glory" (20 [July 1893]: 658–72). The system included some 2000 acres and had three large parks north, west and south of the city with several smaller "breathing spaces for the masses" spread throughout the city (669). These parks featured green fields, shade trees, artificial lakes, rare flowers, serpentine walks and drives that "lure people from the noise, and dust, and worry of a crowded city" (670). The sporting life too was convenient for Chicagoans. According to Ballantyne, both game fish and birds were available within the city's limits: "In this advantage Chicago is probably unique; it is not likely that there is another large city that can furnish duck- and snipe-shooting, and occasionally goose-shooting, within its corporate boundaries" (671–72). Yet even in 1893, Ballantyne made it clear that the city would soon outgrow its parks and that the fish and game were being rapidly depleted.

Charles H. Shinn, a journalist who wrote for several magazines, praises San Francisco's open spaces and magnificent views, mentioning especially the gardens that "are a surprise to every visitor" (21 [Apr. 1894]: 519–30). He describes the people of San Francisco as "an outdoor race" (522), with a passion for "an abundance of light and air" (524). In his view the people are "overflowing with health and vitality … [and] ride, walk, and live outdoors" (524–5). The city's several large public parks as well as scenic surroundings provide useful distractions for all citizens. Even the poor people take their children to the Golden Gate Park several times a week (526).

For her essay on Washington, Burnett chose the title, "A City of Groves and Bowers," allowing her to describe in great detail the natural beauty of the nation's capital. Trees were so numerous—"rows and rows of them as far as one can see up the avenues and down them …" (564)— that she found it "almost impossible to believe that one is in a town. The plan of the city gives so many vistas of green" (567). Indeed, Burnett's Washington had quiet streets, "well-dressed, well-bred and respectable" citizens, and no ugly smoke from tall factory chimneys (564–65). For his part, Lodge too commented on open spaces planted with trees and shrubs that helped make Washington a pleasant place in which to live. He was especially impressed with a new public park planned for the land surrounding Rock Creek: "It is not too much to say that it will make a park of greater natural beauty than is to be found in the neighborhood of any great city in the world" (580).

Parks or open spaces were deemed crucial to the success of any city and consequently were mentioned in virtually every essay of the series. If a park system was not yet established, then private gardens and the proximity of nearby forests were part of the discussion. Cable, in his article "New Orleans" (20 [Dec. 1893]: 150–4), could think of no other city "so green with trees or so full of song-birds and flowers" as New Orleans (150). Stockton spoke repeatedly of St. Augustine's orange groves and rose gardens, and then guided visitors to the rivers and forests in the heart of Florida (21 [Jan. 1894]: 207–14).

Adequate housing is another of Riis's concerns that the *St. Nicholas* writers addressed in their essays. Several essays mention crowding, but they give few details, avoiding graphic descriptions that were not appropriate for young readers. Writers for adults in *Century*, such as M. G. van Rensselaer, are more forthright in addressing the problems. In "The People of New York," van Rensselaer takes readers to the city's East Side:

> You might see dreadful things in the streets of this region, more
> dreadful things in its flaming bar-rooms and dance-halls, things
> most dreadful and pitiful beyond words in its damp and filthy

cellars, in its naked attics, which are cold past sufferance in winter, and in summer pestilential with a tropic heat ... through these black hives where vice and crime are once fostered and excused by ignorance, poverty, and pain [49: 546–47].

Descriptions such as this along with mention of the want of morals found in boarding houses would not have made fit reading for *St. Nicholas* readers. Stedman's article "New York" (20 [Apr. 1893]: 403–19) addresses the problems directly, but it lacks the descriptive detail of the *Century* treatment. He admits the city's defects, "the contrasts of splendor and squalor; the want of evenly distributed beauty and comfort; the want of civic spirit; the need, shared in common with various American cities, of 'municipal reform'" (413). Although he does not ignore the area from Broadway to the East River, acknowledging the misery in the thickly crowded foreign neighborhoods, he paints an optimistic future. Readers "will ... gaze upon the residential city to the east, with its series of magnificent parks, its beautiful mansions set in garden-closes, its speedways, plazas, and broad shaded streets" (419). The article apparently presented a challenge to both writer and editor. In spite of their shared progressive orientation, Dodge urged Stedman to revise his initial article in order to insure that she and *St. Nicholas* were not drawn into New York City politics by becoming identified with local factions.[1]

In his essay, "Philadelphia — A City of Homes" (20 [Mar. 1893]: 324–36), Talcott Williams, a writer and editor for the *Philadelphia Press*, approached municipal reform by looking at what he called the first business of cities, namely the comfort of children. He saw individual home ownership as the key:

The only way to make families comfortable and the best way to make families comfortable is to put each in a separate house which it owns.... If the families of a city are cramped and crowded, if each lives in a house it does not own, and dreads rent day; if it sees the sky only through a window-pane, and has neither roof nor yard it calls its own; if it has to share its staircase and its doorway with other families...; if the street is not a family street, and the seething and turbid tide of city life wells and swells past its door, then neither the family nor the children will be comfortable. The city has failed [325].

Williams' answer to middle class fears of social unrest was to invest everyone with a stake in the future, in essence to make everyone part of the middle class gentry. He saw a home owner as "a 'capitalist' ... [who] will never be a turbulent striker" (331–32).

Related to adequate urban housing was the problem of rapidly growing immigration. For New York City, the influx of foreign immigrants pre-

TENEMENT HOUSES, THE CHEAP HOMES OF NEW YORK.

CHEAP HOMES IN PHILADELPHIA.

In "Philadelphia — A City of Homes," Talcott Williams contrasts inexpensive housing in New York City with that of Philadelphia. *SN* 20 (March 1893): 336.

sented a special challenge. Stedman called the city a "national reception-room — the place of rest for hungry, travel-worn pilgrims" (414). In his view, the government had certain responsibilities: "to take these foreign hordes in hand, to welcome the better class and make Americans of them, and to gain from them labor, taste, color, in return; to receive also the far greater mass of the coarse and wretched, and to make Americans of them, if possible, but certainly of their children" (414). Here again, the *St. Nicholas* approach to immigration was much more upbeat than that undertaken for adult audiences. In an article for *Century* published in 1893, Lodge adopted a position absent in his *St. Nicholas* contribution, demonstrating that Americans of foreign birth constituted an inordinately large proportion of criminals and paupers (John 211). The tendency to blame urban problems on immigrants was widespread: *Atlantic Monthly* printed the following in an editorial on city growth in 1895:

> It is to be remembered that, in America, the problem of municipal government is infinitely complicated by the ethnic charac-

ter of the population in our large cities. In the average American big city at least three fourths of the people are of foreign birth or of foreign parentage and until these have become thoroughly Americanized the difficulty of securing good government is enormously increased [Cook et al. 18].

Stedman, on the other hand, voiced pride in New York's "special, vast, and patriotic task — to receive the living overflow of Europe, to cleanse and distribute it, to retain the most unsightly portion of it and make this ... a portion of its own substance" (414), suggesting tolerance in his comment that the ways of a "foreign" district "are not our ways— its standard of life is not, for the most part, the American standard, and we cannot judge it by the latter" (410). The *St. Nicholas* articles on Boston and Philadelphia were also positive, paying brief compliments to the special skills immigrants contributed and praising the diversity they brought. In the essay on San Francisco by Charles H. Shinn (21 [Apr. 1894]: 519–30), Chinatown was introduced as a tourist attraction with "sensational stories about its wonders and mysteries" (527). Shinn told readers of Chinese gods, food, holidays and customs. Even so, the view was patronizing and offered little concrete information about everyday life within the walls of Chinatown.

The position of ex-slaves in American cities can be glimpsed especially through comments on southern cities— New Orleans, Washington and Baltimore. Cable writes that "black roustabouts laugh and sing while performing prodigious labors" (21 [Nov. 1893]: 40) and tells of "ragged black Samsons" who unload boats in New Orleans (46–47). Later he points out "the dividing line between the New Orleans of the Anglo-Saxon American and that of the Creole" (45), but readers never cross that line to see what lies on the other side. In Burnett's piece on Washington "the only people one sees in rags or asking alms are occasional negroes; and they are very rare, and usually look rather as if their profession were a matter of preference" (565). Unlike more recent immigrants, former slaves are not seen as a threat to peace and prosperity. In his presentation of Baltimore (20 [Aug. 1893]: 723–33), D. C. Gilman, the first president of Johns Hopkins University, includes an observation from Cable about "the contentment of the colored people" there and mentions "the ready and almost friendly service of the blacks" as an advantage of the city (729).

In spite of the problems, turn-of-the-century views of the city also acknowledged the importance of cities' having attractive buildings and statues. *Century* published an article by van Rensselaer extolling the "utility and beauty" of Madison Garden (47:732–47). The *St. Nicholas* series featured outstanding architecture as well as inviting parks. It tied dignified monuments and noble citizens to distinguished cities, making both essen-

MADISON SQUARE GARDEN AND TOWER.

New York's Madison Square Garden illustrates the concept of the City Beautiful in "New York" by Edmund Clarence Stedman. *SN* 20 (Apr. 1893): 409.

tial. In "Philadelphia" Williams identifies Benjamin Franklin as what makes Philadelphia great because "in him a great man had walked her streets" (328). For Ballantyne, the buildings of the Chicago World's Fair are "miles and miles of stately monuments to human industry and enterprise" (667). Higginson sees in Boston's past achievements the promise it "will do its fair share in the development of that ampler American civilization" of the future (179).

Baltimore's major attraction, according to Gilman, lies in its monuments. The city boasts several statues, memorials, art galleries and public buildings honoring important people and institutions. Yet Gilman does not allow these institutions to overshadow the people of the city: "After all, people are more interesting than places" (728). A large portion of the essay is thus devoted to outstanding citizens and their important contributions to the city's welfare. In fact, each essay includes attention to the important people of the city as well as to its architectural and natural attractions. The pictures and the text join to give readers a sense of the grand old buildings, commercial centers and some of the major parks or residential areas. Pictures of specific individuals are rare; they are included only in Williams' essay on Philadelphia.

While the series on cities was presented as an inspiration of the World's Fair, there was little to tie the essays to the fair directly. Scribner's exhibit for the fair featured Williams' essay, "Philadelphia — A City of Homes," in all its stages of production. In addition to Jenks' feature, "The World's Fair Palaces," the magazine printed several short articles on the fair, including an account of Helen Keller's visit by Anna Sullivan (21 [Dec. 1893]: 174–7). Yet in Ballantyne's essay on Chicago, the fair was mentioned only briefly, saying it was "utterly impossible ... to do more than refer to [it] in a general way (668). Nonetheless, the lessons in the essays reflected certain tenets about what makes an attractive city, tenets which corresponded to the principles of the fair's designers. Those principles came to be known as the City Beautiful Movement, an approach to city planning that gained prominence as a result of the fair's White City.

Daniel Hudson Burnham, Frederick Law Olmsted and their colleagues, who were in charge of the architecture and landscaping for the fair, argued that improving the urban environment through beautiful structures and parks would influence the people to improve themselves. "From this grew the notion that the city itself could engender civic loyalty, thus guaranteeing a harmonious moral order; the city's physical appearance would symbolize its moral purity" (Hall 44). Proponents of the City Beautiful found its appeal in the antidote it offered to urban moral decay and social disorder (Boyer 266). According to Lubove, this was the true meaning of the Chicago Fair: "Planned beauty, order and picturesque design were an irresistible alternative to the dirt, monotony, and pervading dinginess of existing cities" (219). The *St. Nicholas* series to hail American cities in preparation for the fair appeared just as the movement was evolving. The idealistic aspirations of the City Beautiful were consistent with the magazine's policy and the utopian notions Dodge and her fellow reformers espoused.

The City Beautiful approach to urban renewal was popular throughout the 1890s and into the beginning of the twentieth century. Burnham's plan to translate his World's Fair triumph into a renewed Chicago culminated in his 1909 *Plan of Chicago*, "in many respects the quintessential expression of the social vision underlying the Progressive city-planning movement" (Boyer 271). The plan was to overcome the urban evils of "poverty, congestion, immorality, ugliness" and crime (Boyer 271). The approach to social control advocated by Burnham is reminiscent of the praises given to *St. Nicholas* cities: broad streets, enlarged park systems and attractive public buildings. Urban historian Paul Boyer suggests that Burnham's goal was "to restore to the city a lost visual and aesthetic harmony, thereby creating the physical prerequisite for the emergence of a harmonious social order" (272). Stedman had also cited this influence of the external on urban populations in his discussion of New York:

> There is a realization of the educational value of the beautiful — testified by such creations as the Madison Square Garden, by financial and other structures equaling in design the best in the world, by the museums, and the new Arts building, and the Washington Arch, each and all of which have aroused local pride, and the desire to advance upon these hopeful beginnings [417].

Charles Mulford Robinson writing for *Atlantic Monthly* in 1899 demonstrated the appeal for Dodge and *St. Nicholas*:

> There is other value in municipal beauty than that indicated by money value. There is a sociological value in the larger happiness of great masses of people, whose only fields are park meadows, whose only walls are city streets, whose statues stand in public places, whose paintings hang where all may see, whose books and curios, whose drives and music, are first the cities where they live. The happier people of the rising City Beautiful will grow in love for it, in pride for it. They will be better citizens, because better instructed, more artistic, and filled with civic pride [reprinted in Cook et al. 106].

This upbeat, positive approach to urban problems was especially suited to the "pleasure-ground" that Dodge required in a children's magazine: "...

pleasant, breezy things may linger and turn themselves this way and that. Harsh, cruel facts—if they must come, and sometimes it is important that they should — must march forward boldly, say what they have to say and go" (Dodge 354). Dodge may have thought children needed to know the harsh realities of turn-of-the-century urban life, but she did not wish to frighten them.

The *St. Nicholas* articles emphasize positive aspects of city life and strongly advocate the gentle kind of social control found in the City Beautiful concept. The darker sides—the ugliness, crime and disorder — are like toads in her pleasure-ground: they "hop quickly out of sight" (Dodge 354). Furthermore, they stay a long way from home where the negative impact is diminished. In these articles the unhappy consequences of urban failure are virtually ignored. A significant exception is a brief reference in Williams' essay on Philadelphia where he explains the possible result of a failed city:

> Children are not at sweet ease in its ways. It has failed. Its day will come, as it came to Paris in 1871. The grim and iron girdle of war will surely bind its beauty, and for soft splendors there shall be desolation. All its garish glory shall be smoke, and garments rolled in blood shall be spread in all its streets. Famine shall devour its people, and fire its beautiful places [325].

Paris is far enough away that children can look upon "harsh, cruel facts." In an earlier *St. Nicholas* series on European cities, Frank Stockton's "Personally Conducted: Queen Paris" (13 [June 1886]: 572–82) had written warning of the necessity to consider the needs of the poor:

> In very many ways the French government offers opportunities to the poor people to enjoy themselves, and it is pleasant to see how neat, orderly, and quiet these people are. It is very necessary that they should be kept in good humor, for when the lower classes of Paris become thoroughly dissatisfied, they are apt to rise in fierce rebellion, and then down go kings, governments, and palaces [13 (June 1886): 579].

In the lesson of far-away Paris young readers can consider the perils of any city. But here at home, the natural parks and handsome buildings inspire all who live there to share the emergent pride of a prosperous and growing nation. The picture of American city life provided in the pages of *St. Nicholas* is that of the idealistic City Beautiful.

Note

1. Personal correspondence from Susan Gannon and Ruth Anne Thompson who have seen the correspondence between Dodge and Stedman about the essay.

References

Boyer, Paul. *Urban Masses and Moral Order in America, 1820–1920.* Cambridge: Harvard University Press, 1978.

Cook, Ann, Marilyn Gittell, and Herb Mack, eds. *City Life, 1865–1900.* New York: Praeger Publishers, 1973.

Dodge, Mary Mapes. "Children's Magazines." *Scribner's Monthly* 6 (1873): 352–354.

Hall, Peter. *Cities of Tomorrow.* Oxford: Basil Blackwell, 1988.

John, Arthur. *The Best Years of the* Century. Urbana: University of Illinois Press, 1981.

Kelly, R. Gordon. *Children's Periodicals of the United States.* Westport, CT: Greenwood Press, 1984.

Kelly, R. Gordon. "Literature and the Historian." *American Quarterly* 26.2 (1974): 141–159.

Kelly, R. Gordon. *Mother Was a Lady: Self and Society in Selected American Children's Periodicals 1865–1890.* Westport, CT: Greenwood Press, 1974.

Lubove, Roy. *The Progressive and the Slums.* Pittsburgh: University of Pittsburgh Press, 1962.

MacLeod, Anne Scott. *A Moral Tale.* Hamden, CT: Archon Books, 1975.

Riis, Jacob. *How the Other Half Lives.* New York: Hill and Wang, 1957.

Robinson, C[harles] M[ulford]. "Improvement in City Life." *Atlantic Monthly* 83 (May 1899), reprinted in Cook et al., 103–6.

Schuyler, David. *The New Urban Landscape.* Baltimore: The Johns Hopkins University Press, 1986.

Sturges, Florence Stanley. "The *St. Nicholas* Years." *The Hewins Lectures: 1947–1962.* Ed. Siri Andrews. Boston: Horn Book, 1963.

van Rensselaer, M. G. "The Madison Square Garden." *Century Magazine* 47 (March 1894): 732–747.

van Rensselaer, M. G. "The People of New York." *Century Magazine* 49 (February 1895): 534–548.

17

"When Did Youth Ever Neglect to Bow Before Glory?" *St. Nicholas* and War

MARILYNN STRASSER OLSON

In the October 1877 issue of *St. Nicholas* magazine, Noah Brooks, Civil War correspondent and friend of Abraham Lincoln,[1] published a story called "A Century Ago" (4: 802–5). Quite unlike any other story published in the magazine during the years of Mary Mapes Dodge's editorship, it nonetheless introduces some of the motifs that recur in war stories in that juvenile publication during its golden age.

The story starts with a chapter set in 1777. Peletiah Wardwell bursts into the home of Dame Perkins and her sixteen-year-old son, Nolly, shouting that the British are coming. In her determination to resist the British by sending her husband's flintlock, bullying the messenger to alert the town, and preparing bullets for the fight, Dame Perkins inspires her son to rush out as a volunteer. As he leaves, Brooks notes:

> The lad lingered an instant in the open doorway, and the sun streaming brightly on him gilded his yellow hair and shed a sort of glory over his fair young face. So full of life, so alert and ardent, he seemed for the moment transfigured in the eyes of his mother. She went swiftly toward him; kissed him, and without a quiver in her voice said:
> "I cannot give you to your country, Nolly. God gave you when he gave you a country. You will do your duty" [803].

The fortunes of war lead to Oliver becoming part of a forlorn hope halfway between the British landing and the understaffed fort, and he falls immediately as the British overrun the thinly held position. Brooks says, "How gallantly the patriots defended this last line behind the town, how well they fought, I cannot stay to tell. It was all in vain. When night fell, the red cross of St. George was flying on the flag-staff on the green, and the British colonel was quartered in Dame Perkins' house." When Oliver's father comes home he says, "It was a foolish thing to do"; Brooks adds, "whether he referred to Oliver's going to the defense, or to Captain Blodgett's attempt to hold the battery, nobody dared to ask. For it was plain that his grief was great" (804).

Chapter two, the other half of the story, is set in the same place in 1877. Two boys going fishing encounter a farmer plowing who turns up a boy's skull in the field. They admire the hole in the skull that proves that the soldier who shot him was a fine marksman. The two boys try to determine what engagement might have taken place there. Abe thinks that it was "wicked that ... this remnant of a cruel war should now be turned up in the midst of the life and beauty of spring." No one knows what the fight was about or what happened, but Jotham declares that the fight was "for independence." The farmer agrees, "They fit for their country. Many a poor feller bit the dust in that war. But they did their dooty, and it's all the same in a hundred years" (805). Fishing tackle found next to the skull affirms to the reader that this is Nolly Perkins's skull. The boys go fishing.

This story embodies three of the ways of presenting war generally displayed in the pages of *St. Nicholas* during the thirty years following Brooks's tale. First, the story of American historical warfare is an important feature of the magazine.[2] *St. Nicholas* sought to promote "intelligent patriotism" and growth in readership, and stories about historical American engagements served both interests. It is clear, too, that the authors of such stories feel that they are writing for readers with a detailed knowledge of historical events and personages connected with the American Revolution and War of 1812, as well as the more recent War Between the States. Letters from the children reflect this knowledge, as they describe the battlefields, relics, historic forts, graveyards, and so on found near their own homes or encountered on visits. It should be remembered, of course, that the letters included in the magazine were a select lot, chosen as particularly interesting and informative (indeed, the children often cite them as a favorite feature), so the editors' inclusion of many military households in the Letter Box can also be seen as promoting historic knowledge or catering to a well-known taste for patriotic pieces.

Second, the practical details of how to use a flintlock, how bullets are made, and the military strategy included in the Brooks story are common motifs in *St. Nicholas*, which devoted many nonfiction articles to such topics as the content of gunpowder, the uses of different kinds of swords, the generals' intentions in various engagements, the variety of ancient armaments, and the pieces of equipment being built for the navy. This feature of *St. Nicholas* can be attributed to many causes: the incorporation of the *Little Corporal* into *St. Nicholas*, a desire to court boy readers, the military as an upper-class interest well represented in the subscribers' families, or the intense public interest in armaments at the time. One immediate reason for this practical emphasis is that some of the men who wrote the military pieces for *St. Nicholas* were themselves veterans of the Civil War, war historians, or active-duty officers with special expertise in the practical arts of war.[3]

Third, *St. Nicholas* was interested in the virtue of self-sacrifice. A young person's ability to give up a pleasure or favorite ambition to relieve an invalid friend or widowed or otherwise needy family member is a familiar test of character in *St. Nicholas* as well as in other fiction of the period. In war stories in *St. Nicholas*, similarly, the emphasis is not usually on the soldier's ability to overpower the enemy. What matters is his courage in facing death and his self-sacrifice in giving his life (or the mother's in giving her son) for the cause.[4] The merits of the cause, indeed, are rarely the issue. Because of the magazine's postwar desire to reconcile the North and South, for example, the value and heroism of soldiers on both sides of the conflict become the emphasis in Civil War stories. While the untidy or scandalous details of battle are generally left out, no one can accuse these stories of encouraging young people to believe that good people survived warfare. Instead, the stories encourage them to feel that death in battle is the appropriate end. William F. Carne, who wrote "A New Leaf from Washington's Boy Life" (14 [Mar. 1887]: 373–5), explains the influence upon Washington of the death of his young cousin Thomas Fairfax in this way:

> A manly boy is quick to listen and ready to respond to the story of manliness in others. To young George Washington the dirges for the dead midshipman at Belvoir came rather as a note of triumph than a song of sorrow, for they told of a heroic death — the epic of a boy, scarce older than himself, who had fallen under the enemies' guns on far-off eastern seas, where the flag of his ship, unstruck, waved at the peak above his ocean funeral [375].

As Chuggins, another manly boy, remarks when viewing the body of a young soldier, "It's nothing to cry about" (H. I. Hancock, "Chuggins: The Youngest Hero with the Army," 26 [Nov. 1898]: 39–52).

Brooks, then, was unusual in his story in two points. He left out

Oliver's moment of sacrifice, focusing the reader's attention instead on his skull and the apparent lack of significance to the war effort of his death: at nightfall his mother was having to quarter the troops who killed him. The second feature is the ambiguity of the farmer's "it's all the same in a hundred years" and in the tension between the mother's vision of glory and the father's "it was a foolish thing to do."

In acknowledging that Oliver was a willing sacrifice to his mother's vision and would have been, no doubt, also influenced by his father had he been at home with different advice, Brooks is apparently making a point that the young are easily influenced to deeds of glory and one can rarely make such a decision with knowledge of the real situation; this was as true of the *St. Nicholas* readers as any other children. Further, in this story, whether Oliver and the other volunteers did the right thing is not apparent to and cannot be determined by the onlookers. The meaning of Oliver's death is not explicitly stated here, as it was in most other stories. It lies both in Oliver's heart and in the bigger picture of the event that the parents and the uninformed descendents cannot rightly decipher. In allowing the readers to ponder inexplicable elements of human warfare, Brooks gives his readers credit for the thoughtfulness and intelligence that often is credited only to a story's hero.

I. War As Text

In 1900 Robert Park, a pioneer American sociologist, described the philosophy of Germany's much-studied army by quoting from a speech given in the Reichstag by General von Moltke:

> War is an institution of God, a principle of order in the world. In it the most noble virtues of men find their expression —courage as well as abnegation, fidelity to duty, and even love and self sacrifice. The soldier offers his life. Without war the world would fall into decay, and lose itself in materialism.[6]

The Elizabethan playwrights would have said that von Moltke was a good servant, but a bad master. They would not, I think, have ignored the very material reasons for raising such an army nor acquiesced in the idea that courage and fidelity were the best requisites for interpreting divine will or national policy. But there is reason to believe that nineteenth-century American people who admired these sentiments did not always bring the same earthy pragmatism to the discussion.[7]

St. Nicholas, with its educational goals, took on a common complaint both then and now: children often do not like studying history and lack information about the past. They addressed this, as did many nineteenth-century textbooks, with rousing stories of heroism on the battlefield: a choice that interprets the subject of war in much the same way von Moltke did, and, indeed, as the popular songs, entertainments, and popular fiction within their society did.[8]

We do not, presently, encourage children's love of history with such stories. We do not regard war with the same optimism — as a forward movement, however high the initial cost, for example. When Mary Stuart McKinney remarked in her essay on "The Goodly Sword" (23 [Mar. 1896]: 392–7) that "though it soaked earth with the blood of her sons, the sword has ever been true to its mission — the progress of society" (397), there are now as then some plausible arguments to support her, but our own age would find more rebuttals.

Nor is the belief that war invariably produces the highest standard of human virtue likely to go unchallenged in our own day, though this was even more generally espoused in *St. Nicholas* stories. We are also simply less given to emphasizing self-sacrifice rather than self-fulfillment. For these reasons, among others, the study of battles and wartime maneuvers has ceased to be our children's text.

We also differ in our definition of "intelligent patriotism." Our experience of wars in which our nation's own defense was not directly at stake has also eroded the concept that love of country means eagerness to serve in the military forces. Ever since war has been critically discussed, there has always been the most solid endorsement for the war that defends native ground. America's Revolution, War of 1812, and Civil War were so construed in America in the nineteenth-century history books. They were also so construed in most *St. Nicholas* features. But whether warfare was presented as self-defense, or simply bloodshed that paid off handsomely to establish the country, American history before the turn of the century provided unusually striking examples of the necessity of war — or of the romantic principle that war carried out divine plans in shaping better nations.

Of course *St. Nicholas* cannot be held responsible for not conforming to our era's ideas about war, nor are our own unassailable. But every age has had its discussions of warfare, and Homer and Shakespeare, for example, brought a more balanced view of war and peace to many generations before *St. Nicholas* and its generation was born. To nearly always confront warfare with what our generation must regard as an innocent, inexperienced eye is, therefore, a matter that will surface for the modern reader. The question of how often war was discussed and the way it was discussed seems important, since it raises questions about censorship in children's literature, as well as the degree to which the military material reinforced or undercut the other messages of the magazine.

Jacqueline of Holland, from E. S. Brooks's series *Historic Girls*. *SN* 14 (March 1884): 326.

In defining the material to be examined, I am arguing that though stories in which battles, armaments, life in the armed services, and war are unmistakably present and were very frequent in the 1880s and 1890s, that peacetime references to soldiers also should be noted in the discussion because the characterization of soldiers influences the way readers will think about their profession; *St. Nicholas* respected the tradition that the exercise of arms produced noble character. The use of kind, upright military characters in stories, even when they are not actively engaged in warfare, is carrying on this tradition and having an influence on the way warfare is to be regarded by the children who read the stories.

Similarly, there are arguably many ways in which "Historic Girls" could be chosen as examples to present to young people (12–15 [Jan., Apr., July, Oct. 1885; Apr., Nov. 1886; Mar., May, Sept., Nov. 1887]). Beauty or chastity or association with well-known male figures, for example, were long popular reasons for remembering the few women who appeared in histories. If, as in E. S. Brooks's series, the girls seem to be noted for moments in which they exhibit physical courage or are associated with feats of arms, it appears that they are instead being legitimized as worthy of remembrance by reference to the military tradition that would similarly legitimize their brothers. Children's biographies of women in the last decade also frequently have discussed women who dressed as men to serve in war, who fired cannons, who were military spies, or who otherwise risked their lives, as worthy role-models for young girls. In order to show equal potential between the genders, the women are shown succeeding at the traditionally male, traditionally military, activities. Thus, though there are obviously fewer women than men who can be shown in actual battle, some young women's activities also deserve note.

Although always perceived positively, the incidence and emphasis of the lessons about war purveyed by *St. Nicholas* responded to external forces as well as internal philosophies during the years of Dodge's editorship.

II. The 1870s

The stories that fall under the military category are considerably varied in kind in the 1870s. They are much more scattered and incidental than the works in the established long-running serials that came later, although Mark West's discussion of the *Little Corporal* magazine in *Children's Periodicals of the United States* points to the great enthusiasm for quasi-military organizations for children in the previous decade and encourages us to see interest in military topics as already well-established in the juvenile market.[9] Ruth Miller Elson's *Guardians of Tradition*, while noting an anti-war movement, also points to the great number of military terms in alphabets, heroic scenes in readers, and pictures of children enjoying war play in the American textbooks of the earlier century (322–334). Children receiving an education in Latin also would be devoting much study to war and military campaigns. *St. Nicholas*, then, was not a notably active espouser of this material in its early years, at a time when many other children's materials were.

In 1879, a year typical in this more incidental material, the January number had Hezekiah Butterworth's story "The Funniest General in All the World" (6 [Jan. 1879]: 191–2) about the conflict between the Hussites and the Procopices in 1424, illustrating warm-hearted behavior on the part of the title character. In "Teddy's Heroes" by Amalie La Forge (6 [Feb. 1879]: 261–4), a little boy who speaks in baby talk discusses various heroic soldiers and explorers and, as the result of this early teaching, is able to rescue a man in the snow. John Lewees's story "Spoiling a Bombshell" (6 [Apr. 1879]: 375–7) tells the story of a boy who runs away to sea and makes good in a battle against Spain; "Rattle-Te-Bang" (a poem) and "Hay-Foot! Straw-Foot!" (6 [July 1879]: 603–4; 614–5) are both about military drilling, the second referring to historical origins in the War of 1812 (and therefore part of the patriotic group for July 4th). Jack in the Pulpit, an editorial column, discusses the need to honor the foe you have beaten. "The Story of a Prince" (6 [Sept. 1879]) describes a young man whose "baptism of fire" includes being killed by receiving nineteen spears through the throat in the Zulu wars. Military figures make brief appearances (telling stories and so on) in Treadwell Walden's "The Boy-Heroes of Crecy and Poitiers" (7 [Nov. 1879]: 64–9) which follows an English lad at Crécy and a French lad at Poitiers. The year ends with Martha C. Howe's "The Knight and the Page" (7 [Dec. 1879]: 99–102) about a page who saves a medieval lady from the fortunes of war on Christmas morning because the besieging knight is touched by the page's innocent piety. J. T. Trowbridge's "An American King David" (7 [Dec. 1879]: 109–10), about a Tezcucan Indian whose life seemed comparable to that of the Biblical David, includes some mention of pre-gunpowder warfare and army campaigns. The genre we shall see developed — varied historical locales, kindly soldier figures, heroic episode, young people who make a difference, and interest in military routines — is already established here, but without the emphasis and volume that is found in the next two decades.

III. The 1880s

Harry Kiefer's "Recollections of a Drummer-Boy" (9–10 [Nov. 1881– Apr. 1882; June-Oct. 1883]) is both the first of the truly engrossing military series and a work that stands apart as an experiment that was never repeated in *St. Nicholas*. Kiefer was unusual in this periodical in being an actual Civil War veteran telling his own war experiences, as well as an unusually thoughtful boy as a volunteer; moreover, Kiefer, himself, showed the signs of having been embued with heroic stories in his boyhood and was speaking to another generation of children who were looking to him for more of the same.

Kiefer's war series was used to advertise the new *St. Nicholas* subscription year, and its reception showed the editors that there was an eager audience for similar stories. It was immediately notable, however, that Kiefer himself was unlikely to read the rest of the magazine's heroic stories uncritically. He clearly notes in his first installment that the "war fever" that resulted in his father giving grudging approval of his sixteen-year-old schoolboy son's enlistment was a species of madness hard to fathom in a later age; the cause that set him to thinking of leaving school was the sight of one of his own (older) school-fellows brought home, wounded by a ball through his shoulder. Of this event, Kiefer says "our excitement knew no bounds!" (16).

Kiefer's story was not a story of unexamined glorious action because he has already passed the point where innocence gives way to experience, a point at which he, as a child in the war, had come to see discrepancies between his dreams of glory and the reality of the battlefield. Until the Battle of Gettysburg, his experiences were a matter of camp incident (Tad Lincoln and his family visited the camp) or learning duties. He and his friend Andy did Latin declensions on picket duty and, at a moment of relief after nearly being shot, recite "All Quiet Along the Potomac To-Night" from memory in their tent: "while soft falls the dew on the face of the dead — /The picket's off duty forever!" (142).

Their duty as drummer boys was primarily to pick up dead and wounded soldiers from the battlefields because drumming on the field had already become a confusing anachronism. Possibly for this reason, the series emphasizes the number of casualties, especially among friends ("an excellent soldier, who afterward fell at his post at Spottsylvania … both McFadden and the orderly went where there is neither marching nor standing guard any more …" (236). Kiefer's turning point came at Gettysburg. He was part of the 150th Pennsylvania Volunteers, who were entrusted with holding a crucial position in front of the Seminary, facing west and north by turns, on the first day of the battle. Although Kiefer's friends and the nearby regiments had all the glory of hand-to-hand combat, bayonet charges, and other gallant maneuvers noted with approval in other *St. Nicholas* stories, Kiefer did not emerge untouched by his experience. His regiment went from 500 to 100 men, 54 to 13 in his own company.

> As we pass along, we stop to observe how thickly they lie, here and there, like grain before the scythe in summer-time, — how firmly some have grasped their guns, with high, defiant looks, — and how calm are the countenances of others in their last solemn sleep; while more than one has clutched in his stiffened fingers a piece of white paper, which he waved, poor soul, in his death-agony, as a plea for quarter, when the great wave of battle had receded and left him there, mortally wounded, on the field.
>
> I sicken of the dreadful scene, — can endure it no longer, — and beg Andy to "come away! Come away! It's too awful to look at any more!"

IN FOR IT!

An actual Civil War veteran, Harry Kiefer, recounted his experiences in the *St. Nicholas* series *Recollections of a Drummer Boy. SN 9.* (Nov. 1881): 64.

> And so we get back to our place in the breast-works with sad, heavy hearts, and wonder how we ever could have imagined war so grand and gallant a thing when, after all, it is so horribly wicked and cruel [9 (Feb. 1882): 308].

Kiefer's article is illustrated with a picture of the boys going to and from Gettysburg, being cheered by young ladies and men in a neighboring town and serenaded with "Rally Round the Flag, Boys!"—a form of encouragement that they could not bring themselves to acknowledge on their return. Although he was not mustered out until the end of the war, Kiefer chooses to ignore most of the other engagements, concentrating on tending the deathbeds of the dying men that he knew (many of whom died of exposure and neglect of wounds); the plight of the black people following their army, whom he and Andy succored as they could; and Andy's disappearance at Petersburg and eventual rediscovery. By the standards of our late twentieth century, Kiefer's seems a credible depiction of warfare and Kiefer's view the inevitable view of maturity. The Northern soldiers who responded to his series apparently agreed.

The "Drummer-Boy" series brought touching letters attesting to his popularity not only as a writer but as a soldier. The April 1882 number printed several expressing gratitude for telling "their" story and testifying to the truthfulness of his descriptions:

> I was so struck with the graphic and vivid descriptions that I was at once convinced it was no fancy sketch, but the actual experience of one who had been there ... again I thank you for placing before the youth of our country so truthful a statement of what their fathers did to preserve the nation.
>
> I take the *St. Nicholas* for my daughter, and casually took it up while smoking my "night-cap" pipe last evening, and I assure you I read it twice over, and it brought back the old times so vividly that the chimes rang out midnight before my reverie was ended.... You remember well how well the One Hundred and Fifty-first Regiment (my old regiment) and the One Twentieth New York held the left that first day, and I trust you will kindly accept the thanks of an unknown comrade for the story you have told so well.
>
> Harry M. Kiefer ... was personally as popular with the boys in the company and regiment as are his contributions to the *St. Nicholas*. A brave soldier, an exemplary, noble youth, a worthy son of pious parents. And he is to-day an influential, zealous, able worker as a minister in one of the leading churches of Eastern Pennsylvania [9 (Apr. 1882): 502].

Such letters provided ample reason to suggest to the editors that the series that they had used to advertise the year was both popular and indicative of a desire on the part of at least Northern subscribing families to hear more true accounts of the late war. The magazine, however, did not print other first-person accounts of the battles.[10] Their military material concentrated, instead, on the purely heroic fictional or biographical stories, essays on historic military figures (the Historic Boys series by E. S. Brooks), two stories about fictional girls making a difference in wartime by defiance and quick thinking: E. S. Brooks's "Little Lord of the Manor," about "Evacuation Day" for the Tories in 1783 (11 [Nov. 1883]: 3–8), and A. J. C.'s "Cornwallis's Buckles" (9 [Feb. 1882]: 296–9), and an introduction, followed by an obituary, of the dashing Captain Mayne Reid, whose heroic Mexican War record is cited by Trowbridge as support for his new (and final) serial story.[11] None of these kinds of literature told, or were likely to tell, the story of war in a way that struck the veterans who wrote the commendatory letters as accurate. All of them were essentially entirely positive, heroic stories.

One can see by looking at 1887 that this pattern continued throughout Dodge's career. The nonfiction material, like the fiction, never again revisited the boredom, horror, or ambiguity in Kiefer's camp and battle scenes, nor was anyone ever again doubtful about the final moments or eternal destination of the dead. Instead, gallantry and purpose characterize these frequent features.

The year begins with a Letter Box commendation of the December "battle panorama" article, mentioning a manufacturer of such panoramas, and another child writes from Fort Custer, near the battlefield. In March, E. S. Brooks's "Historic Girls" series (14 [Mar. 1887]: 326–31) discusses Jacqueline of Holland (1414), a "fearless descendent of those woman warriors of her race."

> Jacqueline the Countess, seeing her cause in danger, — like another Joan of Arc, though she was indeed a younger and much more beautiful girl general, — seized the lion-banner of her house, and, at the head of her reserve troops, charged through the open gate straight into the ranks of her victorious foes. There was neither mercy nor gentleness in her heart then [330].

Noah Brooks's article that month (14 [Mar. 1887]: 340–341) is about the Fairport Nine boys' military company of his youth, who, after hearing a splendidly stirring speech, went on to serve in the Civil War — several of his friends dying. "The lesson in patriotism was not in vain," he concludes. "Paul and Nicolai in Alaska" (14 [Mar. 1887]: 367–72) is a story involving boys caught in a battle between two Indian tribes, and the "New Leaf from Washington's Boy Life" article (14 [Mar. 1887]: 373–5) is about his young cousin who "builded [sic] his life into the foundations of the Empire of

India." General Adam Badeau, one of Grant's friends and staff officers, recounted the strategy of the battle of the *Merrimac* and the *Monitor* (14 [Apr. 1887]: 435–44). In May the Brooks "Historic Girls" series features Catarina of Venice who saves her future husband, Prince Giacomo, by defying a mob of Venetian hoodlums (14 (May 1887]: 483–6). George Putnam begins his serial story "Winning a Commission" about a West Point cadetship (14 May-Aug. 1887), General Badeau recounts Sherman's March to the Sea (14 [May 1887]:5), and The Letter Box includes a letter about the capture of Chiricahua Apaches. In June, Putnam continues the cadet story, Badeau recounts "Sheridan in the Valley," and The Letter Box praises the E. S. Brooks stories and describes *Merrimac* and *Monitor* relics. Indeed, the whole year continues these military serials, with an interesting story by Nora Perry appearing in August (14 [Aug. 1887]: 777–782). A story showing Ruskin's influence, "Marigold" tells of a young girl who is mistakenly denounced by her principal for lack of interest in arithmetic (the school's most fashionable study), and who is praised by a distinguished visiting inspector for her remarkable memorization of and interest in heroic exploits of history — a study considered much better worth knowing.[12] Her principal is suitably chagrined (778).

The following year substitutes the fiction serial "Drill" by John Preston True (15 [Feb.-July 1888) about a military academy for the West Point story; "Drill," as its name suggests, concerns the positive results of a precision drill method applied to athletic endeavors at a boys' military school. Bringing out the best in good boys, saving many through disciplined obedience from a chemistry lab fire, and rescuing the character of a formerly over-indulged and therefore vicious boy, the drill increased every young man's physical strength and also, according to the last sentence, made them better Christians. "A perfectly sound man is not a good subject for temptation" (685).

The late 1880s, in particular, were a popular time for military academy stories discussing the education of young men by army or navy discipline.[13] The Putnam serial "Winning a Commission" (14 [May-Aug. 1887]), "How Bright Benson Got His Appointment to the Naval Academy" by Charles R. Talbot (11 [April 1884]: 432–40), "Louis the Resolute" by Harriet Taylor Upton (16 [July 1889]: 653–61), "Recollections of the Naval Academy" by H. Albert Johnson (15 [July 1888]: 690–9), "The Bilged Midshipman" by Thomas Allibone Janvier (15 [October 1888]: 922–8), and "A Modern Middy" by J. H. Gibbons (16 [Oct. 1889]: 287–95) were accompanied by a number of Letter Box mentions of readers (some of them girls) drilling in quasi-military organizations or attending military school.[14] In this case, muscular Christianity, the era's awakening to the need for physical exercise on the part of increasingly urban youth, the need for expert engineers in the new navy, the varying fortunes of the newly founded Naval War College (1884), and enthusiasm for the military tradition appear to serve each other's interests.

Theoretically the participation in military organizations might be supposed to encourage loss of individuality and individual thinking, which the rest of the magazine supports, but few non-fiction or fiction features indicate this. In most cases, cadet stories are unusually tension-free for school stories, and discuss overcoming great obstacles to going to the school, rather than difficulty in adjusting to it.

To finish the year 1888, *St. Nicholas* also serialized *Two Little Confederates* by Thomas Nelson Page (15 [May-Oct. 1888]), and included more E. S. Brooks military pieces, and many more references to tribal warfare, gladiators, dogs in warfare, German militarism, French militarism, a black child killed in a carriage accident while on the way to put flowers on Yankee graves ("but Joe sleeps peacefully, like the brave men he would have honored" [603]), and the poem "To My Boy — on Decoration Day," by Alice Wellington Rollins (15 [May 1888]):

> If ever the dread day should come again
> When the whole country needs her boys in blue,
> How could I bear, dear lad, among the men
> Marching to war and danger, to see you?
>
> My heart sinks as I watch them through the glass; —
> And yet I know one thing were worse to bear:
> That underneath my window they should pass
> And I should look — and find you were not there [520].

There is every reason to believe, in fact, that the child reading *St. Nicholas* in the 1880s was taught to regard warfare in a sternly positive light.

IV. The Civil War and *St. Nicholas*

Fred Erisman has authoritatively stated that *St. Nicholas* was a true child of *Scribner's* and *Century*, the adult periodical and publishing company that produced the juvenile and hired Mary Mapes Dodge (Kelly 387). The end of the 1880s was not only a time of assessment of the Civil War in *St. Nicholas*, but *Century*'s celebrated Civil War series began in November 1884 and ran until 1887; the Lincoln series continued until 1890.[15]

The *Century*'s Civil War series was a balanced and dignified series of articles, made uniquely objective by the expedient of having commanders from each side write up engagements from their own point of view, a point of view that threatened to be lost as death was claiming the surviving officers, if not the soldiers, of the conflicts of twenty years before. The picture of the aging commanders ending their war in forays in and out of the *Century* editorial offices is a striking one. *Century* also included commentary by privates in the engagements, and had a letter box feature in which correspondents added details and argued points after every article. *Century* often concluded during the series that the conflict had occurred because of *faulty educational views* that had deceived the South. War, to the *Century*, was not inevitable but something a high-minded journal could interpret rationally and perhaps prevent on other occasions. The series was reprinted in handsome illustrated volumes.

Both *Century* and *St. Nicholas* were evidently speaking to a real need in the population by trying to make sense of the great cataclysm of their time. Their policies also suggest, in spite of other forces in society that would keep the wounds of war open, that there was an effort to explain, deal with, and otherwise ameliorate the pain that especially attends a war in which the combatants are united by ties of blood and common background. This was done in large part by insisting on the heroic nature of having participated in the war on either side: the presence of such unusual phenomena as Blue and Grey reenactments and reunions points to the celebrity that was officially given to any veteran. In spite of some similarities, however, the Civil War material in *St. Nicholas* is quite different from the other war features.

The *St. Nicholas* advertisements for the year 1887 held out the series on the Civil War as an attraction, promising that the series would be "neither partisan nor sectional."

> The main purpose of the articles is to present in each case faithful, adequate and spirited pictures of the battle or naval conflict under consideration, thus making of the series a sort of literary picture-gallery of the heroic contests in which the parents of many a boy and girl of today took part [13 (Oct. 1886): 1–2].

The purpose here stated is clearly different from the purpose that Kiefer had in his 1881 drummer boy serial, and, for that matter, different from Page's on his confederate boyhood. Both these stories apparently wished to initiate children into their authors' views of what war was really about, and that it was different in reality from the way it had sounded in stories: they were consciously intending to write from the point of view of age about their own fall from innocence during the war. The series promised in 1886, then, was quite different from these accounts; it not only would be a nonpartisan or neutral account, it also would be an account that emphasized heroic deeds.

The series that *St. Nicholas* advertised, however, is not what they ultimately offered the readers. General Badeau's series on the Civil War, was, in fact, a fine, interesting series, but it could not be called nonpartisan, nor was it an heroic picture-gallery. General Badeau was a staff-officer and good friend of Grant, so he was partisan. However, Badeau recounted the war entirely as the practice of military strategy and instruction in the kind of planning that a general has to do, so the series did not enter into combatants' experiences of the campaigns or battles that it discussed. It was neither concentrating on heroic individuals nor their causes, but on strategies and their success and failure. While bringing the children considerable instruction on this subject, the Badeau series, of course, substantially limited the view of the war that the young people would receive.

For example, a Southern veteran indignantly wrote in to complain about the "Sherman's March to the Sea" article, which contained Badeau's view that "the romantic character of the march is unsurpassed" and "so long as American boys and girls read the account of the nation's achievements, they will find no chapter more fascinating than that which tells of Sherman's March to the Sea" (543). Badeau's enthusiasm for the march was based on his admiration for the Union decision to send a body of its army into enemy territory (where its fate could not be known at home for days) in an unprecedented strategic move. The "cold" recounting of strategic points that the Southern veteran objects to as not doing justice to the starvation of women and children that Sherman's march represented to him, is an issue of both partisanship and philosophy.

The editor responded to the Southern letter this way:

> No, this sad story [related in letter] is not fascinating reading, nor is it the sort of reading that was furnished by the *St. Nicholas* article. Every human being with the least sense of compassion must deplore the sufferings caused by war — and especially that which befalls non-combatants. For war is in itself terrible; and calamities are to be found in its track as inevitably as in the trail of a tornado. The fact that every war involves woe for the innocent does not make its cruelties or wrongs any more excusable or less lamentable. But the task of recording these cruelties and wrongs belongs to the patient chronicler and historian, who will investigate special instances of hardship and abuse on both sides, and sift the mass of testimony concerning them. Any attempt to present in a single magazine article, moreover, an account of a whole campaign must, of necessity, be very general, and the *St. Nicholas* article dealt with its subject simply as a military movement [14 (Aug. 1887): 795–96].

St. Nicholas wished to avoid inflaming sectional rivalries by recounting alleged atrocities on one side or the other. But naturally a war recounted only in terms of whether an objective was skillfully accomplished and not in terms of human suffering is leaving out a great deal: material that adults may know (as the editor suggests) but that children who did not experience the Civil War probably do not. Indeed, Badeau's articles assumed as a starting point that the Southern civilian population had to be considered a military objective because of the loyalty and involvement of the Southern non-combatant in the war effort.

Treating warfare as military strategy, while leaving out all the human consequences of the strategy, cannot help but make war sound like an attractively dangerous game — much like the games of Kriegspiel described in Robert Louis Stevenson's "Letters to a Boy" (23 [Dec. 1885–Feb. 1896]), and in the many children's soldier games described in other features.[16]

Taken as a whole, the *St. Nicholas* reporting of the war would have reinforced the pride that children could feel in their families' participation on either side of the conflict, and would have taught them substantial educational lessons about why the North won. Domestic stories about the Civil War would have shown them good-hearted characters who had sacrificed a great deal on either side; reiterated accounts of historic battles would have emphasized the importance of war to the nation and the importance of soldiering to the nation's strength. The reasons for continuing enmity or bitterness, despair or cynicism, however, were not in evidence.

V. The 1890s

Dodge's father advised her, when she was writing her own story for boys before she took on the *St. Nicholas* editorship, "Enlist a youngster and carry him through this war, make him smart, of course."[17] The idea of encouraging children to identify with quick-thinking and independent children in dangerous wartime situations was, in fact, a common plot device in the *St. Nicholas* repertoire. These stories were particularly prevalent after 1885, in the late 1880s and 1890s. To some extent, this kind of story appears to be on a kind of border between those features intended to instill knowledge of and pride in the nation's past, and those features suggesting that America's destiny was to be involved in war again. Being prepared, after all, implies something to be prepared for, and whether it is prudence or some other emotion that inspires this, the 1890s did, after all, culminate in an American war that was widely held to be popularly inspired.

In some *St. Nicholas* stories such as Ethel Parton's "Betty the Bound Girl" (23 [May 1896]: 530–5), young girls and boys are unusually composed and mature in the face of invasion: "Her little brown feet disdained to run/For fire or sword or Regular's Gun" (531). Some children fool the enemy or warn the town or hide provisions against plundering armies or aid wounded soldiers or support the innocent against tyranny, carrying out defiant acts that save their families from enemy soldiers or otherwise showing American spirit. Such stories demonstrate patriotism in the civilian population in historic wars, and teach details of historic conflicts, while also conveying the impression that children who are clever and do not lose their nerve are able to deal handily with invading soldiers.

More children in the *St. Nicholas* stories are actually in the battles, as drummer boys or volunteers or lads fighting in their first battles. Richard, who rides "With the Black Prince" in William Stoddard's 1897–98 serial (25 [Nov. 1897–Feb. 1898]), successfully wins his spurs. Another tells the story of William B. Cushing, the torpedo boy who volunteered at the age of ten and sank the *Albemarle* in "The Youngest Soldier of the Revolution" by W. W. Crannell (11 [July 1884]: 697–700). Real drummer boys were eliminated from all but the Marine Corps in the 1890s. Con Marrast Perkins, Marine Corps first lieutenant, is looking back nostalgically, then, when he pauses to regret "the daring bravery of more than one beardless boy who has sounded at the critical moment the pas de charge or 'rally' just in time to turn the tide of battle" and "Johnny Clem ... who beat the rally without orders when his regiment had broken ... "(27 [July1897]: 710–5) in "The Last of the Drums." He "sadly and sorrowfully" mourns the martial music in which "there is something that sweeps away the sluggishness of every-day life, and gives a feeling that is akin to inspiration" (714).

St. Nicholas, however, showed many other youths in battle. In the "Historic Dwarf" serial by M. S. Roberts, the young hero, Casan, volunteers to join Genghis Khan's invasion of China and leads his youthful friends in military drills, helping finally to destroy part of the Great Wall (24 [May 1897]: 578–83). The boy "monkey" on the *Richmond* in "The Story of Admiral Farragut" by Charles H. Bodder (23 [July 1896]: 762–6) witnesses the shot that nearly hits the Admiral on March 14, 1863, while gaining instruction from the admiral about why never to bow his head to a shot (766); "The Boy in Gray" by M. Bradley (22 [June 1895]: 672–3) takes water to wounded Union soldiers under Union fire at Marye's Heights; and boys and girls of Greece march with agricultural implements against the Turk El-Abarris in "Leonidas: A Tale of the Turkish War with Greece" by Anna Robeson Brown (19 [Oct. 1892]: 944–6):

> "Sir," he said, "we've come to fight you. Father
> said, the other night,
> Greece had lost her glorious soldiers, not a
> Spartan shield was bright" [944].

The child concludes that "the noblest death that any Greek can die/is defending home." The Turk, gracefully, surrenders.

Louis Grandprée, like Nolly Perkins in the Noah Brooks' story, is an example of a soldier youth who dies nobly. In E. S. Brooks's "The Last Conquistador" (19 [Sept. 1892]: 866–71) the sixteen-year-old, who embodies the "old-time heroism which had marked the days of Paladin and Cid," holds the Spanish fort at Baton Rouge for Spain and the king against the Americans until he dies in battle. His cause might not appear especially attractive to Americans, and he was unsuccessful, but E. S. Brooks, unlike Noah Brooks, identifies within the story the right way to think about this activity: "Not alone to the soldier of freedom does death in the hour of victory or defeat bring glory everlasting. Even to he who, in the face of certain disaster, upholds the honor of his flag, is praise abounding due." In his serial story "Boy of the First Empire" (22 [Nov. 1894–Oct. 1895]), schoolboys, encouraged by the adolescent hero, who is a Napoleon loyalist, also fall defending Paris in the hope that Napoleon will return to save it. The older citizens capitulate, and the story clearly identifies the beauty of the idealism and hope of the children against the wiser but less attractive pragmatism of their elders. All the stories bring children into the narratives by assuring them that youth is no bar to affecting history, and that young people with determination and quick thinking can participate as fully, and perhaps more honorably, than older people.

Different from the war stories in which the focus is upon the individual making a difference are the features and stories attempting to inculcate respect for national symbols, knowledge of national military institutions, and interest in military preparedness. In these stories, routines, drills, and the rituals of military camps, ships, and naval yards are made familiar and attractive to the readership, as they were in the military school stories.

Besides emphasis on the useful and pleasurable aspects of military routine, there are also a good many stories on routines specifically meant to instill love of country. As Lieut. B. W. Atkinson of West Point, explains in his story "Escort to the Color," "There is nothing that more conduces to make a good, true, and loyal soldier than to inculcate in him love and respect for the flag ..." (24 [Oct. 1897]: 1005–7). This educative process is described in such articles as Gustav Kobbe's "From Reveille to Taps" (20 [Nov. 1892]: 68–72) which takes the child-reader through the day at an artillery camp.[18]

Charles Sydney Clark of the State Camp of Instruction of the New York National Guard stated (24 [July 1897]: 760–2), that

> a few years ago, when *St Nicholas* told of "Honors to the Flag" [December 1891], a man or woman in New York who rose in an armory at "retreat" or who saluted a regimental flag, would have been remarked. Now any one who does not do these things will soon be considered as unmannerly as a man who should wear his hat in the house or in church [762].

The *St. Nicholas* articles of this period showed that young people could gain thanks or glory for their wartime service; they were further familiarized with the ways in which their own flag was served militarily in their own time, an interest evidently reflecting interests outside the editorial office.

VI. The Spanish-American War

In the years following the Civil War, the United States became acutely aware that its navy was obsolete.[19] In the early 1880s, under the leadership of William E. Chandler, Secretary of the Navy under President Arthur, the first domestically-produced steel warships were built, the Naval War College was founded, and the first high-velocity, breech-loading rifles made by the Washington Gun Factory were installed on the new ships. The size and technical superiority of the navy increased during the 1880s under Chandler's successor, William Whitney, while the officials overseeing the future of the fleet gradually came to view the Navy as an aggressive rather than defensive unit. These changes were well publicized and debated. For example, during the period of time in the late 1880s that Century was reflecting on the meaning of the Civil War, *Scribner's*, a comparable publication, was urging immediate funding of weapons and defenses for naval warfare.

Scribner's printed a number of articles on the need to defend the coast, such as F. V. Green's "Our Defenseless Coasts" (January 1887); James Russell Soley's "Our Naval Policy: A Lesson from 1861" (February 1887) that concludes that because of a decrepit navy we are living in a "fool's paradise, from which the angel with flaming sword will some day cast us out"; "Modern Aggressive Torpedoes" by Lieutenant W. S. Hughes, USN, in which "the writer desires to correct, so far as he may in a closing sentence, the popular fallacy that our great seaport cities and the coastline of our country can be protected by torpedoes alone ..." (April 1887); and "The Development of the Steamship and the Liverpool Exhibition of 1886" by Commander F. E. Chadwick, USN, in which the author notes "how small our own expansion in the iron and steel ship-building industry has been, in comparison with that elsewhere ..." and decries the "grip of legislation which has throttled our shipping industry" (May 1887).

In 1890 Captain Alfred T. Mahan's *The Influence of Sea Power upon History*, as well as the advice of its author, encouraged Benjamin Tracy, Secretary of War under Harrison, to build battleships and to keep them battle-ready at all times. Efforts were made to admit the cadets at the War College for academic success rather than by political favor, and extra-territorial naval bases to fuel the fleet were established, even when such attempts were risks of American diplomatic policy. The Congressional arguments over a defensive or offensive Navy and whether a battle-ready Navy was necessary to insure international trade also were widely disseminated to the populace by a great many articles in the popular press on both sides.

In keeping with the adult periodicals and interests of its day, *St. Nicholas* ran a number of articles about the Navy and United States defenses in the 1890s, just as it had reflected the popular interest in military school training. "Battling Under Water," by Frederick Hobart Spencer (20 [Feb.1893]: 249–54) discusses the problem of trying to design a boat "that will safely dive below the keel of a hostile vessel and blow her to destruction" since "destruction of a single large warship by a submarine boat would spread demoralization through the navies of the world"—something the Europeans are working on. An editorial in the same month recommends purchasing submarines. Ernest Ingersoll's "The Tricks of Torpedo-Boats" (23 [Aug. 1896]: 864–8) mentions that the US Navy, unlike the European navies, has no torpedo-catchers yet, and urges purchasing them: "officers who know them [torpedoes] best fear them most" (868). "Harbor Defenses" by C. R. Thurston (24 [Mar. 1897]: 397–400) argues the thesis that "a hostile fleet might too easily enter them" (397). J. O. Davidson, who wrote the lengthy "Battle-Ships and Sea-Fights of the Ancients" (20 [Jan. 1893]: 221) combined the naval war scholarship then fashionable with the increasingly familiar regret that modern warfare could not be as interesting and exciting as the fights of Greek and Roman war-galleys he extensively evokes. "The naval battles of those days were battles of Titans afloat. The struggles were of necessity hand to hand, in comparison with which modern naval engagements, where a few shots from long-range guns decide the issue in as many minutes, sink into insignificance" (221).

By 1897 Theodore Roosevelt was assistant to John Davis Long, the new Secretary of the Navy, and many improvements to the Navy, to the Naval Academy, to enlistment procedures, docks, militia training and other indications of support for a more efficient Navy and aggressive foreign policy were put into effect. When it came in May of 1898, the Spanish-American War showed the superiority of the US Navy to the unprepared Army and, in the process, added to the territory of the United States.[20] Theodore Roosevelt's personal involvement in the Army, after extreme impatience with Long's disinclination to use his new navy, put him in line for the presidency.

St. Nicholas reflected the naval successes of the war in many articles. Benjamin Webster details the types and names, with many photos, and weapons of "Some Ships of Our Navy" (25 [July 1898]: 744–52); E. B. Rogers, USN, follows with "Big Guns and Armor of Our Navy" (25 [Aug. 1898]: 818–23) and Tudor Jenks with "The Voyage of the *Oregon*" (25 [Sept. 1898]: 882–7) describing the cross-ocean voyage of the battleship sent to replace the *Maine*. He concludes, "it is no wonder that our ships, our guns, and our men are as good as the best, because, from the men in the foundries to the admirals on their bridges, all work is done by honest, competent, patriotic Americans" (887). In September *St. Nicholas* also printed an article entitled "The Gun-Foundry at Washington" (25 [Sept. 1898]: 920–3) asserting that "our guns are not surpassed by those of any European country" and Gustav Kobbé, still known for his work on opera, wrote the first of two articles on "Battling with Wrecks and Derelicts" (25 [Oct. 1898]: 1004–5) about navy vessels using torpedoes to destroy sunken ships that were menacing the shipping lanes; a fictional story by K. U. Clark, "The Triton's Chase After a Derelict" (25 [Oct. 1898]:1006–10) describes a brave boy who destroys such a vessel when his father is unable to undertake this duty. In November "Margaret Clyde's Extra" by I. G. Curtis (26 [Nov. 1898]: 13–19) is about a girl who scoops Dewey's victory at Manila for her newspaper, and children are introduced to "Pets in the Navy" by C. D. Sigsbee (26 [Nov. 1898]: 61–4) including "Peggie, the Pug of the *Maine*."

"Mark V" by Clarence Maiko is about the humorous exploits of a real torpedo of that name (26 [Dec. 1898]: 119–25). Joseph Groff discussed "Apprentices of the United States Navy" (26 [Mar. 1899]: 364–8):"The grand success of our fleets at Manila and Santiago was due, to a great degree, to the excellent ability and marksmanship of the gun-captains on board, nearly all of whom were ex-apprentices" (364). In the same issue, Henry La Motte, USN, explains in "How We Helped Uncle Sam Prepare for War" (413–21) how he had furthered the United States cause by buying three torpedo boats from Elbing of Germany, after overcoming initial rebuffs from the American embassy in Berlin:

> We had no quarrel with Spain; we had no right to suppose she
> was in any way responsible for the destruction of the *Maine*; and
> in his opinion, the Jingoes were a very poor lot of people, and
> much more likely to have destroyed our ship, in order to pre-
> cipitate war, than the Spaniards.
>   I must explain that this young man had lived so long abroad
> that he seemed hardly to be in sympathy with America at all.
> I'm afraid that before I left him I said something rude [414].

Commander J. Giles Eaton, USN, told about "'Prince' in the Battle Off Santiago," (26 [Apr. 1899]: 452), a non-fiction essay about the fox-terrier mas-
cot of the *Resolute*. Mrs. S. S. Robison published a companion piece about
kittens taken prisoner of war on the *Cristobal Colon*, later given by the crew
of the Oregon to Captain Charles E. Clark who was credited with taking
the *Colon* (26 [Apr. 1899]: 461–2). During the summer, there were also
articles on Dewey, such as "Admiral Dewey's Sword" (26 [May 1899]: 591).
"Our Miniature Navy" by W. Osgood and G. P. Conn (27 [Nov. 1899]: 24–
8) records the visit of the scale model US Navy to an exhibition in France:

> the sight of these grim toys, and the realization that they are
> exact duplicates in minute form of war-ships of our navy, will
> excite the admiration and respect, surely, of any who believe that
> bison yet roam the streets of Buffalo" [24].

Looking back, Jessie Peabody Frothingham's "Some Great Sea Fights" for
a patriotic issue (27 [July 1900]: 762–78) compared the sea-fights of Manila
Bay and Santiago with the tactics used throughout naval warfare, starting
with Salamis. She also praises "constant target-practice in time of peace"
(764) as being the key to America's success.

    Children reading *St. Nicholas* had every opportunity to memorize the
United States vessels and to explore their functions. However, they had
been alerted to Navy lifestyles, rather than simply the weapons, before the
war started. Discussions of military routine in the Navy were regularly
contributed in the 1890s by the popular writer Lieutenant John M. Ellicott, USN, who served in Naval Intelligence during the Spanish-American
War.[21] "What Is Told by the Bell" (24 [June 1897]: 679–81) describes watches
on a man-of-war at sea; "The Lights that Guide in the Night" (24 [Apr.
1897]: 481–7) describes the role of lighthouses; "What the Bugle Tells on
a War-Ship" (23 [June 1896]: 624–9); "Gunpowder" (23 [July 1896]:
758–61); and "What the Lights Tell" (22 [May 1895]: 570–6) rounded out
the readers' knowledge of life aboard a navy ship. "Some War Courtesies"
(23 [May 1896]: 604–7) by H. A. Ogden; "Launching a Great Vessel" (23
[Nov. 1895]: 35–40) by Franklin Matthews; "Ceremonies and Etiquette of
a Man-of-War" by Lieut. Philip Andrews USN (25 [July 1898]: 759–60);

and other stories describing young children visiting their fathers on war-ships such as "'Captain Crackers' and the *Monitor*" by E. McConnell (25 [July 1898]: 780–2); "Margery and the Captain" by A. A. Rogers (25 [Aug. 1898]: 794–803; "The 'Old Blue Vase': A Navy Boy in Japan," also by the same author (20 [Jan. 1893]: 182–91); "Christmas on the Home Station" also by Rogers (27 [Dec. 1899]: 140–9) gave every child an intimate view of an attractive active-duty officer, attractive fatherly military figures, attractive wounded sailors, and the daily life of boys in the military ser-vices and their personal sense of loyalty to the country they served and the flag that was its symbol.

The Navy and interest in Naval armament that concerned the adult members of society was also represented in other children's periodicals. *Youth's Companion* carried non-fiction articles by Hilary A. Herbert, the Secretary of the Navy: "How Boys are Trained for the Navy," (Feb. 21, 1895); "How War-Ships are Built," (Jan. 21, 1897); and "Torpedoes & Torpedo-Boats," (June 23, 1898), but did not really embrace the topic. *Harper's Young People*, however, before either other publication had joined in naval fervor to any great extent (1893), included the "boys of the year" from the Naval Academy and West Point; a fiction serial on a boy entering the Naval Acad-emy, "His Father's Son," by Edith Elmer; "Our New Navy" by J. D. Jerrold Kelley, Lieutenant USN (434); "The Columbian Naval Exercises," by Flavel Scott Mines (472); "A Boy's Prospects in the United States Navy" (596); and "Signalling at Sea" by W. J. Henderson (678) in just one year. The promi-nence of military, especially naval, routine in children's reading material makes it clear that the metaphor in verse such as "My Sailor of Seven" by G. Brennan (25 [Oct. 1898]: 1051) would have been a commonplace to the child of the day. In it, the parent advises the little child about his future life:

> If just be your cause, and the foe's in the offing,
> Ne'er haul down your flag for his threats or his scoffing.
> But stand to your wheel; do not show the white feather,
> Through seas rough or smooth, be it war or bad weather.
> From haven of Home unto harbor of Heaven,
> Your voyage be happy, my sailor of seven! [1051].

It would be wrong to say that all American periodicals were pleased at an opportunity to try out the new weaponry. *Century*, *St. Nicholas's* par-ent magazine, was no supporter of the Spanish-American War. The edi-tors and contributors were neither enthusiastic about martial glory nor worried about the military defenses of the United States. If anything, they were concerned that warfare that did not seem to them particularly well justified would sap the national morals and ideals. *Century* ran foreign views of the Spanish-American conflict (to discourage imperialism on the part of America), and articles on why "Remember the *Maine*" was an uncivilized sentiment. The July 1898 number began its editorial:

> The temptation of the Fourth-of-July orator will be to lose sight, in the brilliance of martial events, of the steady white light of national aspiration so clearly reflected in one of the noblest of our patriotic hymns, "America." The publication of this lofty hymn, in the author's autograph ... may help to remind us that not in victory alone, —certainly not in extension of territory, — but in a steadfast dedication to the principles of liberty and justice, lies the true greatness of a nation. The hymn contains no line of boasting or self-glorification, and the contemplation of its pure sentiment will be useful at this time, "lest we forget" in the allurements of martial success that war is only a means to an honorable peace [474].

St. Nicholas, as its enthusiasm for building the Navy would indicate, was, in contrast, more excited than worried about warfare. One of their authors in the 1890s was Theodore Roosevelt, and his personal enthusiasms helped set the periodical's tone. Roosevelt contributed the "Hero Tales from American History" (22 [May–Oct. 1895]).

Roosevelt was, of course, an ardent supporter of the naval strategies outlined by Mahan. He also was two years away from being an aggressive Assistant Secretary of the Navy and three from being a Rough-Rider at the time he wrote for *St. Nicholas*. Of the five essays that he contributed, three involved battles that, against terribly difficult conditions with insufficient support, added territory to America:

> The Northwest was acquired at the time of the Revolution only by armed conquest, and if it had not been so acquired, it would have remained a part of the British Dominion of Canada. The man to whom this conquest was due was a famous backwoods leader, a mighty hunter, a noted Indian fighter — George Rogers Clark [22 (June 1895): 639–42].

The other two stories in the series are naval battles demonstrating innovative American tactics that had won European attention in the contemporary studies of historic sea power of which Mahan's work was a part.

Although it is evident in the stories that Roosevelt was not averse to using military power to enlarge the United States, the stronger thrust of his articles is his romantic enthusiasm for the lone hero who battled against tremendous odds and made a difference all by himself. Clark, Boone, Crockett, and Cushing all had unusual personalities and skills, but identical disregard for hazards and present death. Further, he defines warfare in ways quite like those of von Moltke in Park's article. In his introduction to Cushing's sinking of the Confederate ram *Albemarle*, for example, he says:

> In no European conflict since the close of the Napoleonic wars
> has the fighting been anything like so obstinate and so bloody
> as was the fighting in our own Civil War. Hundreds of regiments, both Northern and Southern, suffered each in some one
> engagement far more heavily than either the Light Brigade at
> Balaclava, or the Guards at Inkerman, or than any German regiment in the Franco-Prussian War; and yet they have gone
> entirely unnoticed by the poet, and dismissed with but a scant
> line or two by the historian. In addition to this fierce and dogged
> courage, this splendid fighting capacity, the contest also brought
> out the skilled inventive power of engineer and mechanician in
> a way that few other contests have ever done [22 (Oct. 1895):
> 1013–15].

Roosevelt passes back and forth between acknowledgment of the practical achievements of war — political territory and practical innovation — and his admiration for military glory over and over in his series. For example, in essay number four, on the *Wasp* in the War of 1812 (22 [Aug. 1895]: 847–50), he tells three adventures of the ship that went over to the English Channel to harry British ships attempting to convey supplies to the Peninsular Campaign; ostensibly, therefore, this is a story of innovation in naval warfare. However, only one adventure is really about innovation.

The first episode is the story of the *Wasp*'s attack on the English *Reindeer*. This engagement is mentioned, not because it was especially creditable to the *Wasp*, since she was bigger and carried more men and guns than the British *Reindeer*, but because the *Reindeer* refused to surrender and Captain Manners attempted to board the larger enemy in the teeth of defeat:

> Manners sprang to their head to lead them again himself, when
> a ball fired by one of the sailors in the American tops crashed
> through his skull, and he fell, sword in hand, with his face to
> the foe, dying as honorable a death as ever a brave man died in
> fighting against odds for the flag of his country [848].

The Americans fire and sink the *Reindeer* after his death. They then win a battle against the *Avon*, in which they are outnumbered; finally, in adventure three, they sail out into the ocean — never to be seen again, all hands lost!

No one who had read Roosevelt's series could have been surprised by the nature of his contribution at San Juan Hill. His view of heroic death, however, was not unusual in the *St. Nicholas* of this era. We are told in 1893, for example, in M. H. Foote's "The Garret at Grandfather's" (20

[Mar. 1893]: 338–44) about generations of children creeping up to the attic to read old magazines about Lieutenant Strain: "the toils, the resolves, the suffering — character and conduct under trial ... his all but dying words" (342).

The "Boy of the First Empire" by E. S. Brooks (22 [Nov. 1894–Oct. 1895]), a serial that coincided with the Roosevelt essays, echoes Roosevelt's approval of dying under fire as it chronicles the failure of Napoleon at Waterloo, dramatizing

> the last charge of the Guard; the heroic advance of that immortal company who died but never surrendered, who, facing certain death, never faltered, but "went forward into the furnace flame" [911].

Brooks mentions in the following number that although Napoleon's reputation was enviable, "had he died fighting for his lost crown, history would have given him even greater glory" (982). *St. Nicholas's* Spanish-American War story, "Chuggins, the Youngest Hero with the Army: A Tale of the Capture of Santiago" by H. I. Hancock (26 [Nov. 1898]: 39–52) then, while it takes confrontation with heroic death about as far as it will go, was not alone in its point of view.

Chuggins, a "little roly-poly youngster" of thirteen who uses great ingenuity and intelligence to get from New England to Cuba to be in the army, finds out where the front is, and dashes in the appropriate direction. As he nears it, he finds a dead soldier, his first, lying at the side of the road:

> He did not stir, this young soldier, nor even breathe. In the center of his forehead there was a tiny hole.
> Killed in battle — a soldier's death! Frank and manly he looked, even now, when the last stillness was upon him. A smile of exultation hovered on the face. The mouth seemed trying to frame a triumphant "Hurrah!" [48].

The *St. Nicholas* discussion of the building of the American fleet and the undertaking of the war with Spain was a matter of pride and abiding interest: in America's growing technical ingenuity, in her strengthened world role, and in the heroic virtue of her brave and loyal sailors and soldiers.

VII. Dodge's Drummer-Boy

In 1898, the same year as "Chuggins," Mary Mapes Dodge reprinted in a story collection her earlier story "Captain George, the Drummer-Boy," a story that had been among the first of her pre–*St. Nicholas* successes as a children's writer. (*The Irvington Stories* first appeared in 1865, the same year as *Hans Brinker*.)[22] This story differs from the Civil War stories Dodge included in her magazine in that it is frankly partisan, a story about Union soldiers with unattractive Secessionists and Rebels. She made no effort to remove any incitements to sectional rivalry when she republished it, because she felt that by 1898 the Civil War was ancient history to children and factionalism no longer a serious problem. Otherwise, this story appears to confirm that Dodge did indeed endorse and enjoy the kind of military stories that entered her magazine during her more than 30 years as editor.

"Captain George" involves a fourteen-year-old who is invited to join a company by a Union recruiting officer because he is an enthusiastic drummer and has been drilling a company of village boys as a pastime. He is a noble youth who reproves the recruiter's insinuation that he has a father to avenge (his father fell at Bull Run) by quietly stating, instead, that he has "a father's intention to carry out." His widowed mother and older sister are like-minded. After a tearful interview with his mother ("Bigger men than Captain George have shed tears as scalding since the war commenced, in the arms of women, smaller, milder-looking than this heroic little mother" [76]), George enlists. As his sister declares, "You are young, dear ... and will have many hardships to endure, but you are the only one we have to send" (79). A secondary theme in the story is her romantic attachment to Captain Warner, an officer who has promised to look after George, and a man of sterling principle.

Although as Sue Gannon and Ruth Anne Thompson have stated, "Captain George" contains some situations that suggest the coarsening effect that war has, particularly on enlisted men (48), the story relishes heroic conflict and contributes to the military knowledge of its readers. It contains several pages on the strategy of the double line and its historical invention in Napoleon's engagements, it contains an account of the different drum-rolls and their usefulness in the rituals of the military day, and it explains that hand-to-hand combat is not usually a feature of Civil War fighting, though "in the battle of Williamsburg, both sides have had the satisfaction of a hand-to-hand encounter" (93).

George successfully avoids the twin evils of becoming hardened or failing to live up to his mother's standards. When a rebel band tries to make him pledge Jefferson Davis on a Bible, he manages after hesitation to break away and fulfill his duties properly. None of the story's characters is killed or maimed, though George and Captain Warner have potentially fatal wounds, and his company raises $1000, which will pay his mother's mortgage, when he is invalided home.

Unlike Kiefer's drummer-boys who were judged useful in battle only if they picked up the dead and wounded, George is one of the legendary boys who turns a retreat into a charge by encouraging the men by heroic example. He did not care for the shot, as the soldiers did, he "only heard those mocking yells — saw only that the men with Right on their side were yielding to temporary Might" (136).

Jamie and Harrie, Dodge's boys to whom the *Irvington Stories* were dedicated, were evidently in Dodge's thoughts as she tried to write for boys of their age.[23] She gave them the kind of story that they apparently wanted, and she encouraged their desire for glory and heroic action just as she encouraged the other readers of her magazine. As "The Boys' Battle-Song" that concludes *The Irvington Stories* states,

> We are marching on to battle, boys,
> With banners floating high,
> In the field of Life before us, boys,
> To conquer ere we die!
> With brave old Truth for general,
> And Honor as his aide,
> We'll face the thickest of the fight,
> And never be afraid.
> For we are "Young America,"
> And if our hearts are true,
> There's nothing right or possible
> Our army cannot do [254].[24]

In an optimistic and military-minded age, the editor of *St. Nicholas* apparently was as optimistic about justice prevailing in warfare as she was about every other heroic ideal.

VIII. Conclusion

In 1895 Gwendolyn Fairfax first announced, "We live, as I hope you know, Mr. Worthing, in an age of ideals. This fact is constantly mentioned in the more expensive monthly magazines and has reached the provincial pulpits, I am told."[25] The *St. Nicholas* ideals — positive attitudes, lack of depravity and coarseness, cheerfulness and sunshine — are incompatible with warfare as the 20th century perceives it. We cannot hope to become outraged, as Richard Harding Davis, the famous Spanish-American War reporter, was, because an old officer told vulgar stories to his junior officers; faced with bungling, vice, and horror, we would not accuse particular officers for betraying the ideals of war, but innocence for having misled the idealistic victims.[26]

St. Nicholas's position, analogously, is difficult to evaluate. It is hard to decipher which qualities of war in the magazine were the result of adults consciously constructing a view of reality they knew to be untrue and which were simply a matter of passing on the construction they themselves accepted. The undeniable salability of violent, exciting stories or war-related nonfiction makes the choice more difficult yet. We see catering to this taste as catering to human nature; *St. Nicholas* professed to see it as raising the level of human aspiration.

One can argue, however, that in the magazine censoring factionalism in Civil War stories shifted the emphasis from glorifying cause to glorifying the act of war itself. Sacrificial dead soldiers may have been a more convenient commodity than live ones, because they could retain their clear consciences, their positive convictions, and their ability to combine the Christian and pagan virtues. Leaving out the stories that would modify ideals was a case of preserving ideals with more zeal than preserving lives or developing intellects.

In *Century*, in generations of more balanced views by writers well-known to the genteel and educated, in the voices of living veterans, *St. Nicholas* could find abundant evidence that a boy's dream of glory is not the only accurate depiction of a battlefield. Whether the desire to please, to encourage, to shield, or to admire a particular construction of youthful innocence was uppermost, the war material in *St. Nicholas* suggests to the reader with the advantage of hindsight that a day of reckoning for those decisions and that philosophy would come.

Notes

1. Noah Brooks edited Lincoln's papers. "He saw the President alone several times a week from December, 1862, to April 14, 1865, when 'late in the afternoon I filled an appointment by calling on the President at the White House, and was told by him that he "had had a notion" of sending for me to go to the theater that evening with him and Mrs. Lincoln; but he added that Mrs. Lincoln had already made up the party ...'" (3) explains the editor's note by Herbert Mitgang to a new reprinting of Brooks's *Washington* [D.C.] *in Lincoln's Time*. Chicago: Quadrangle Books, 1971 (originally printed NY: Century, 1895).

2. Discussed in Mary June Roggenbuck, "*St. Nicholas*: A Study of the Impact and Historical Influence of the Editorship of Mary Mapes Dodge." Ann Arbor: University Microfilm, 1977.

3. Of the older writers, Noah Brooks (1830–1903) went on official trips to the front with Lincoln; E. S. Brooks (1846–1902) did not see service. He was assistant editor to *St. Nicholas* during 1884–87. George Haven Putnam (1844–1930) served in Company E, 176th New York Volunteers. (*Abraham Lincoln the Great Captain: Personal Remi-*

niscences by a Veteran of the Civil War [Oxford: Clarendon, 1928]). William Stoddard (1835–1925) was one of Lincoln's secretaries, but he volunteered for three months in the middle of his service; he wrote 76 boys' books in his lifetime. An editorial note in the Letter-Box (*SN* 4 [July 1877]: 637) seems to be appealing to the veteran writer as a strength: "The long article on 'Gunpowder' in this number, written by an ex-officer of the U.S. Army, cannot, we think, fail to interest our boy-readers, and give them a useful hint or two."

4. The mother's role is sometimes discussed as part of the literature on "Republican womanhood." See, for example, *The Vacant Chair: The Northern Soldier Leaves Home* (Reid Mitchell. Oxford: 1993); *Women of the Republic: Intellect and Ideology in Revolutionary America* (Linda K. Kerber. University of North Carolina Press: 1980) and "The Republican Wife: Virtue and Seduction in the Early Republic" (Jan Lewis. *The William and Mary Quarterly* (October 1987): 689–721) discuss the creation and attributes of this role in its more narrowly defined capacity.

5. "The German Army: The Most Perfect Military Organization in the World," *Munsey's Magazine* (Dec. 1900): 376–95, reprinted in Stanford Lyman's *Militarism, Imperialism, and Racial Accommodation: An Analysis and Interpretation of the Early Writings of Robert E. Park* (University of Arkansas Press, 1992: 189). See also "Germany" (143–46) in Ruth Miller Elson's *Guardians of Tradition* (University of Nebraska Press, 1964).

6. Marcus Cunliffe's *Soldiers and Civilians: The Martial Spirit in America 1775–1865* discusses the unusual mixture of war and peace sentiments in American popular culture, including those arguments for and against a regular army and military college; the usefulness of the discussion does not end with 1865. An unusual example of the anti-war sentiment, as also discussed by Ruth Miller Elson, is exhibited in "A Hero of Lexington" (W. W. Fink, *SN* 11 [Apr. 1884]: 427). A grandfather is explaining to a disapproving grandchild that he failed to shoot a redcoat at his first engagement. Suddenly pointing at a passing man and sending for his rifle, he reveals that that figure and his first redcoat are the same: the child's father.

7. George H. Callcott's "History Enters the Schools" (*American Quarterly* 11.4: 470–483) and Elson's *Guardians of Tradition* both discuss methods of conveying historic war in schoolbooks of the nineteenth century. The degree to which Manifest Destiny was taught in elementary school is, for example, a point of academic debate.

8. R. Gordon Kelley, *Children's Periodicals of the United States* (Westport, CT: Greenwood, 1984) 278–82.

9. They were available; *Youth's Companion*, for example, preferred this mode.

10. The war serials and stories were published in volumes by *Century* after their success in *St. Nicholas*. Many works of a similar nature by J. T. Trowbridge and other authors were offered as popular premiums by *Youth's Companion* as part of its subscription promotion. See, for example, premiums of 25 October 1888.

11. John Ruskin in *Fors Clavigera* claimed that arithmetic encouraged vulgarity and that learning about St. George of England and other heroic national symbols was much more important to a child's education.

12. Robert E. May discusses the changing public perception of West Point and the connection of military schools to popular military movements in the pre-Civil War era in the extensively-documented "Young American Males and Filibustering in the Age of Manifest Destiny: The United States Army as a Cultural Mirror," *The Journal of American History* (Dec. 1991): 857–886. He closes his article with a reference to a novel by Richard Harding Davis, linking Davis's views in the Dodge era of *St. Nicholas* with those of the mid-century.

13. For example, see *SN* 16 (Sept. 1889):870 and *SN* 15 (Oct. 1888): 956. "Édouard

Frère and His Child Pictures," *SN* 11 (Dec. 1883), explains a picture of a little boy in a military cap teaching a toddler how to drum as follows:

> France is preëminently a military nation. The artists, Berne Bellecour, Detaille, De Neuville, and others, have given us thrilling episodes in the last war with the Prussians. The same military enthusiasm glows in the breasts of the boys, and we can see the *esprit de corps* shining in each of the young faces. Some of the men who served as soldiers in the French army during the campaign of 1870, Monsieur Frère painted long ago as children learning to drum and playing at drill. His own little grandson, Gabriel Frère, figures in the awkward squad of "The Young Guard" [133].

"La Tour d'Auvergne" by M. C. Harrison (*SN* 16 [May 1889]: 533) is a heroic story about a Napoleonic soldier that begins with children besieging their uncle with pleas for information about European military drilling. Of related interest is Cecil Eby's *Road to Armageddon* (Duke, 1987), which discusses Boy Scouting in England during the period from the Fall of Paris to World War I.

14. Robert Underwood Johnson, *Remembered Yesterdays* (Boston: 1923), notes that the Civil War series "created in this country the greatest interest ever felt in any series of articles published in a magazine" (469). It also greatly increased the number of subscribers to the magazine.

15. E. S. Brooks (*SN* 11 [Apr. 1884]: 475) ended his "Historic Boys" article on Prince Harry with the sentence "For war, despite its horrors and terrors, has ever been a great and absorbing game, in which he who is most skillful, most cautious, and most fearless, makes the winning moves." See also Lois Kuznets's *When Toys Come Alive* (Yale, 1994) on toy soldiers.

16. Quoted in a letter (14 May 1864) n.7, p. 161, *Mary Mapes Dodge* (Twayne, 1992), by Sue Gannon and Ruth Anne Thompson.

17. *Youth's Companion* flag campaign was contemporaneous, here quoted from June 16, 1898:

> There are over fourteen million pupils in the free public schools of the United States. Free education may not mean as much to the rich, but to the poorer man it means everything. How many parents of these fourteen million pupils could afford to pay a costly yearly tuition fee for each child? Comparatively few.
>
> The state, therefore, recognizing this and knowing that the stability of our republic depends upon an enlightened citizenship, gladly assumes the enormous expense of educating her future citizens.
>
> In return, then, for a free education, every pupil owes to the state a debt of honor and gratitude. An intelligent, loyal and upright citizenship alone will repay this debt to the state. Indeed, to create such a citizenship is the sole purpose of the state in maintaining our public school system at an annual expense of more than One Hundred and Eighty Million Dollars.
>
> It was with these thoughts in mind that the *Youth's Companion*, some ten years ago, organized the Schoolhouse Flag Movement, which has now become almost universal throughout the land. The flag over the schoolhouse should ever be a reminder to the pupil of his allegiance and duty to the state.
>
> No Public Schoolhouse should be conspicuous because of the absence of a Flag. If any of the readers of the *Companion* know of a school without a Flag, and will send us the name and address of its teacher, we will make it possible and easy for that school to raise a Flag of its own within thirty days.

18. *American Secretaries of the Navy* (Vol. I, 1775–1913), ed. Paolo E. Coletta (Naval Institute Press, 1980); *American Naval History*, Jack Sweetman. 2nd ed. (Naval Institute Press, 1991).

19. The popularly held reasons for America's involvement in the war are reviewed by Louis Pérez in "The Meaning of the Maine: Causation and the Historiography of the Spanish-American War," *Pacific Historical Review* (Aug. 1989): 293–322. Mark Twain, in his unpublished book review "Thirty Thousand Killed a Million" (see *The Atlantic Monthly* [Apr. 1992]: 49–65 for the reprint) made a common distinction between support for the Cuban campaign, which was described in *St. Nicholas* as analogous to our Revolutionary War, and the taking of the Philippines, which he described as indefensible, dishonorable imperialism. For views of militarism as imperialism in other children's literature, see "Signs from the Imperial Quarter: Illustration in *Chums*, 1892–1914" by Robert H. Mac-Donald, *Children's Literature* 16: 31–55, and many other articles cited in that work.

20. "Effect of the Gun Fire of the United States Vessels in the Battle of Manila Bay (May 1, 1898)." *Office of Naval Intelligence War Notes No. V.* Washington: Government Printing Office, 1899.

21. Susan R. Gannon and Ruth Anne Thompson, Chapter 3, *Mary Mapes Dodge* (NY: Twayne, 1992).

22. Gannon and Thompson, 42; Alice B. Howard's *Mary Mapes Dodge of* St. Nicholas (Junior Literary Guild, 1943): 88–89.

23. In April 1891, an ironic correspondent named Gertrude De B — sent a copy of what she calls a "beautiful patriotic poem written by my little nine-year-old brother" to the Letter Box (484): "He composed it one night after being put to bed, as he could not get to sleep. He entitled it 'War,' but now wishes he had named it 'They are Coming,' which seems more appropriate, there not being much war about it."

War

They are coming, they are coming,
To destroy our native land:
They are coming, they are coming,
From every shore and strand.
They are coming in the morning, they are coming in the night,
And now, my fellow-countrymen, we must all take flight.
They are coming, they are coming,
With all their swords erect,
They are coming, they are coming,
Ourselves we must protect.
They are coming in the morning, they are coming in the night,
And now, my fellow-countrymen, we must all prepare to fight.
They're upon us, they're upon us,
Oh, help us every one!
We'll be murdered! We'll be murdered!
The father and the son.
And now we must prepare to flee
Across the meadow and the lea.
Hudson, NY

24. Oscar Wilde, *The Importance of Being Earnest*, Act I.

25. See R. H. D. dispatches for *Scribner's*, September and October 1898.

18

Young England
Looks at America

GILLIAN AVERY

Young Britons of the late nineteenth and early twentieth century felt that American families lived lives enviably different from their own. For one thing there was the ice cream. "I would like to go to America awfully,'" cries Milly in Katherine Mansfield's short story "The Doves' Nest," published posthumously in 1923. When her mother's genial American visitor asks why, she gazes at him with flower-blue eyes and says "'The ice-cream. I adore ice-cream.'" Mr. Prodger tells her benevolently that he's sad he can't ship it across. "'I like to see young people have just what they want. It seems right somehow'" [107]. And in American family stories Milly and her English ancestors discovered not only exotic food — ice cream, doughnuts, wa°es — but indulgent adults, and children who were allowed a freer rein. There was also a far stronger sense of home than they could find in their own books.

They had first encountered their American contemporaries in Jacob Abbott's Rollo books in the 1830s and his Franconia stories of the 1850s, and admired the children for their robust, assured ways. A later generation had seen the girls in *Little Women* (1868) as equally independent. Meg was only sixteen, and Jo a year younger, but they were already out in the world, free of the constricting chaperonage imposed on English girls of their time. And in *St. Nicholas* English readers were to find the same tradition — boys and girls who stood on their own feet and might even support their families, and who did such delightful things as candy-pulling, sledding and maple-sugaring. There was also Thanksgiving, celebrated with the food that children most enjoyed.

They loved *St. Nicholas*. Kipling, later a contributor, had "scrambled" for it as a child, and on many Letter-Box pages we find English enthusiasts. "We have taken *St. Nicholas* for seven years and have them all bound, and we read them more than any other of our books," writes Antoinette from Bristol (13 [1885]: 236). "My brother Gussie and I dearly love your jolly little magazine. We have read it for three years" (25 [1898]: 613). In England there was nothing with such universal appeal. Victorian juvenile publishing was targeted at carefully selected corners of the market. As in the United States, there was an abundance of Sunday school papers whose repellent ugliness was denounced by John Ruskin, catering for the lower social orders. At the other extreme there were blood-and-thunder boys' papers, denounced by the moralists for their sensationalism. In between were journals with a limited circulation like Charlotte Yonge's *Monthly Packet* (1851–98) aimed at upper-class young ladies of the Church of England, and *Aunt Judy's Magazine* (1866–85), a more genial publication but essentially designed for the same readership. Two magazines succeeded in attracting a large and loyal following: the *Boy's Own Paper* (1879–1967) and the *Girl's Own Paper,* founded in 1880 and continuing under changed titles until 1956. These did provide for the wage earner as well as the more privileged, but the tone was distinctly earnest (the publishers were the Religious Tract Society). Though the didactic note was to lessen, they never achieved the light-hearted high spirits which marked *St. Nicholas* from its opening number. "A Merry Christmas to you, my darlings!" calls Jack-in-the-Pulpit one December (5 [Dec. 1877]: 156). No English editor would attempt such affectionate informality.

An additional attraction was its international approach. From the start *St. Nicholas* was outward looking; it imparted information about foreign places, and did it with a light touch. The very first issue had an article on the Blue Coat boys of the ancient London foundation of Christ's Hospital. Later numbers carried articles on other English schools, on such matters as tea-growing in Ceylon, mistletoe gathering in Normandy, the Lord Mayor's Show in London, Easter in Germany. Much fiction had a foreign background. As far as England was concerned there was *Little Lord Fauntleroy* and *Sara Crewe,* by an author who, though American by adoption and marriage, had spent her early childhood in England. Frequently it was foreign *and* historical; John Bennett's *Master Skylark,* a poignant story of an Elizabethan singing boy, was a notable example. And at home the American continent could provide a huge variety of backgrounds and experiences—from well-to-do girl undergraduates at Smith, to boy pioneers pushing west; from Elizabeth Stuart Phelps's cherished little Trotty who loses himself for a few hours in Boston ("How Trotty Went to the

Great Funeral," 2 [Nov. 1874]: 11) to the true story "Lost in the Woods" of a nine year old and his seven-year-old sister wandering for eight days in vast woods on the shores of Lake Superior (J. M. Safford and H.D. Brown, 10 [Sept. 1883]: 856).

English readers also noted how different from themselves American children were — independent, resourceful, spirited, informal with their parents, unabashed by adults and easy with strangers. Frances Hodgson Burnett used Cedric Errol in *Little Lord Fauntleroy* (13 [Nov. 1885–Oct. 1886]) as an ambassador of his kind, a sturdy little republican confronting the Old World. The dry old English lawyer who is sent out to New York to collect this young heir to an ancient earldom is fascinated by his trusting friendliness and grave dignity. Mr. Havisham had known plenty of English children, "fine, handsome, rosy girls and boys, strictly taken care of by their tutors and governesses, and who were sometimes shy, and sometimes a trifle boisterous, but never very interesting" (86). *Sara Crewe* (15 [Dec. 1887–Feb. 1888]) was in the same mold. Though the setting is an English boarding school, Sara is essentially a child of the New World, an independent spirit, standing up to the cruel and vindictive headmistress with head held high, and shaming Miss Minchin by her dignity and resolution.

This was the fair side of the medal. But some *St. Nicholas* writers endorsed the unfavorable impressions of European adult visitors (who had a strong tendency to dislike American children), and showed how parental indulgence could produce little monsters. Frances Courtenay Baylor's *Miss Nina Barrow* (24 [Feb.-Oct. 1897]) is one such. She is twelve, hopelessly spoilt by her doting grandmother, who dresses her in the latest fashions and allows her to gorge herself with ice cream and bonbons and to tyrannize her maid. "Foreigners," says the author, "taking her behavior and manners for a text, wrote home the most unflattering accounts of 'these American children'" (331). When we first see her, she is screaming with rage, belaboring her maid and throwing her expensive clothes round the hotel bedroom. Then she goes downstairs and orders her breakfast.

> "Charles, we want three kinds of fish, remember, and lots of fried onion on my steak. And take away those heavy old rolls you are always bringing, and give us tea and chocolate, both strong. And, Charles, no Saratoga chips, 'cause I'm sick of the sight of 'em. And be quick, for I sha'n't wait a minute" [329].

The novelist Anthony Trollope had observed in *North America* (1862) "adult infants" in hotels lisping their orders for similarly rich and indigestible food (1:37). With deep distaste he had also seen precocious beauties of four years old flouncing and strutting in the same way as Nina who

In such stories as Louisa May Alcott's *Eight Cousins,* even wealthy city girls enjoyed learning traditional domestic skills. *SN* 21 (Aug. 1875): 613.

"swishes her short skirts from side to side with an absurd air of importance" (329).

Nina eventually reaches England and goes to stay with wealthy upper class relations in their splendid country house. Here she is outraged when she is expected to go to the nursery to take her meals with the ten children of the house. The size of English families was always a source of amazement to foreigners. Her cousin Mabel is one of the company, for though she is seventeen, in the English style she is not yet "out" and is still segregated from the adult world. Nina sees the girls in plain dresses, brown holland pinafores and sensible shoes, "adapted to any amount of running, playing, climbing" (671). She herself is wearing a silk and cashmere dress, silk stockings, high-heeled shoes and jewelry and doesn't know what play

is. Meals are traditional English nursery fare, plain roast meat and pota-
toes once a day, otherwise bread and milk, or bread very thinly spread
with butter. The nurse impounds the bonbons she has brought for the
children; these will be distributed but strictly rationed. Nina notices the
decorum of even the youngest, their obedience and orderly behavior, their
attentiveness to their parents, and marvels at the unassuming style in which
these very grand people live. On their part they acknowledge her to be
generous and kind, though hopelessly undisciplined. "'I like Americans,'"
says the father, "'but I like them grown'" (860). However, it is not the
experience of English nursery life that tames Nina, but the eventual loss
of her fortune. The author is concerned to show that adversity, and growing up, will turn even a seemingly monstrous child into the best sort of
American.

In *Betty Leicester's English Christmas* (23 [Dec. 1895–Feb. 1896]) Sarah
Orne Jewett, too, contrasted American and English styles. Betty is a fifteen-
year-old American who has been brought up in England. She is invited to
a very grand country house to help entertain a young American girl. Betty,
in the English manner, dresses in simple, inconspicuous, comfortable
clothes, and does not take it amiss when she is treated as a child. Edith on
the other hand is markedly over-dressed, is loud and brash and woefully
ignorant. However she quickly picks up the right manner, and her easy
confidence makes her popular with the house party; Jewett wished to show
the plus as well as the minus side of American girlhood.

The English travelers frequently remarked on the precocity of the
American young. It has to be remembered that their experience would
inevitably be largely derived from what they saw on rail journeys and in
hotels, and few of them would have encountered country children. Little
boys, they said, were businessmen almost as they could talk, and little girls
lolled on sofas eating candy and chattering about the latest novels and
their sweethearts. "I have never discovered that there were any American
children," Therese Yelverton wrote in 1875:

> Diminutive men and women in process of growing up into big
> ones, I have met with; but the child in the full sense attached
> to that word in England — a child with its rosy cheeks and bright
> joyous laugh, its docile obedience and simplicity, its healthful
> play and its disciplined work, is a being almost unknown in
> America" [263].

But this last was the *St. Nicholas* ideal. The Letter Box of March 1874
tells a little girl who has written a poem, "Don't write verses yet … there
is time enough for that. Put your 'heart and mind in tune', dear, by frol-
icking in the open air; by enjoying your dolls and playmates, and by being

a sweet, merry, good little girl—and not by leaning over your desk writing verses" (308). And there is outrage at "two Country Girls" who had wanted *St. Nicholas* to offer "elegant dolls with full outfits." These are horrible puppets, says Mrs. Dodge, not doll-babies to love and fondle, and she would deplore the publishers doing such a shocking thing (308).

This emphasis on youth and play was relatively new in juvenile periodicals, though one has to remember the honorable exception of Lydia Child's *Juvenile Miscellany* fifty years before. Nor had there been very much of it in fiction either. American life in the earlier part of the century was purposeful and often arduous, and childhood soon over. Isabella Bishop, traveling in the Midwest in 1873, commented on how this still held good among pioneer families.

> One of the most painful things in the Western States and Territories is the extinction of childhood. I have never seen any children, only debased imitations of men and women, cankered by greed and selfishness, and asserting and gaining complete independence of their parents at ten years old [77].

The *St. Nicholas* story "May's Christmas-Tree" by Olive Thorne (2 [Jan. 1875]: 179–82) also shows the bleakness of lives in the mid-West. But here the celebration of Christmas devised by an orphaned little girl for her Missouri cousins melts the heart of the grim aunt who has adopted her.

> "John, that tree has set me a-thinking. We ain't doing just right by our children. It's all work and no play, and they're growing old and sober before their time." That was the beginning of a new life in the plain farmhouse. Little by little, books found their way to the table, an easy-chair or two stole into the rooms, pictures made their appearance on the walls ... [181].

St. Nicholas wanted its readers to be young, fresh and joyful, and its girls to be robust, unaffected and free from that precocious sophistication remarked upon by visitors. Louisa May Alcott, like Mrs. Dodge herself, was always strong on this theme. In *Eight Cousins*, the journal's first major serial (2 [Jan.-Oct. 1875]), Uncle Alec finds the orphaned Rose almost smothered by her aunts' tender solicitude and rapidly becoming a hothouse hypochondriac. He wants to turn her into a tomboy:

> "Let the girl run and shout as much as she will—it is a sure sign of health, and as natural to a happy child as frisking is to any young animal full of life. Tomboys make strong women usually, and I had far rather find Rose playing football with Mac rather than puttering over head-work like that affected midget, Adriane Blish" [530].

Uncle Alec also has strong views about sensible, English-style dress for young girls, and plain simple food such as milk and oatmeal.

Many other *St. Nicholas* writers agreed with Alcott, and the tomboy is frequently commended. In "Why Walter Changed His Mind" by Henrietta H. Holdich (2 [Mar. 1875]: 299–301) "Kitty's just a bully girl ... a regular brick," says a boy who discovers that the unwanted guest is brave and can swim. "She never once thought about her dress" (301). In "Wild Becky" by Emma Plimpton (6 [Dec. 1878]: 74–8) Becky is shown to be the type of the "true lady." Ostracized at first by her rich city schoolfellows for her wild ways, she invites them to her grandfather's farm, "initiating them at once into the most approved way of sliding down the hay-mows, and riding on the great swinging doors" (77). She shows them how to fish for trout, and they chase the colts and hunt squirrels. Becky does however learn to modify her wildness a little, for girls should not outrage all conventions, and in any case tomboyhood must come to an end at adolescence. In Alcott's *Jack and Jill* (7 [Dec.1879–Oct.1880]). Jill's reckless impetuosity leads to a nearly fatal sleighing accident for herself and her boy companion. Her character is formed in the long months she spends on a sofa, learning obedience and self-control. This curiously old-fashioned story of salvation through spinal injury is presumably an example of "the moral pap for the young" that Alcott lamented having to churn out in obedience to the voracious demands of her public.

Ideally, perhaps, a girl should be cautious in trying to emulate the boys, and content herself with being robust and sensible. "'She's first-rate,'" says Donald confidentially of his sister in Mrs. Dodge's *Donald and Dorothy* (9 [Dec. 1881–Oct. 1882]), "'not a bit like a girl, you know — more like — well, no, there's nothing tomboyish about her, but she's spirited and never gets tired or sickish like other girls'" (97). We get some idea of what "other girls" were like from the frequent stories that contrasted the affected nonsense of the city-dwelling slaves to fashion with the plain good sense of country life. One article, "A Talk with Girls and their Mothers" (7 [May 1880]: 521–6) by the Reverend Washington Gladden, a regular contributor, addressed itself to the former type with more directness than was usual in *St. Nicholas*. Corroborating what so many foreigners had observed, he told readers with some severity that American girls were obsessed with fashionable dress, spent too much time reading novels, and were initiated by their mothers into smart society at a ridiculously early age:

> They are not older than [three] when they begin to go to children's parties, for which they are dressed as elaborately as they would be for a fancy ball. From this age onward they are never out of society; by the time they are six or eight years old they

are members of clubs, and spend frequent evenings out, and the demands of social diversion and display multiply with their years. (523)

In "Sophie's Secret" (11 [Nov.-Dec. 1883]) Alcott echoed his sentiments. Swiss Sophie, aged sixteen, encounters wealthy young Americans of her own age:

> Their free and easy ways astonished her, their curious language bewildered her, and their ignorance of many things she had been taught made her wonder at the American education she had heard so much praised…. Yet all were fifteen or sixteen, and would soon leave school 'finished', as they expressed it…. Dress was an all-absorbing topic, sweetmeats their delight, and in confidential moments sweethearts were discussed with great freedom. Fathers were conveniences, mothers comforters, brothers plagues, and sisters ornaments or playthings according to their ages [525].

Gladden had also made the point that too many girls paid little attention to their parents and were only interested in frivolous pastimes. From the age of thirteen a girl regarded herself as her own mistress, left school when she chose, went into society as she pleased and was "constantly seeking the street for amusement" (524). The qualities he wished to see were industry, thoroughness, independence of mind, respect for character rather than money or rank. He knew of no more illustrious type of woman than that of the wife or mother, "though marriage is not for all of you, and should not be for any of you the chief end" (526).

Though they perhaps would not have gone so far as to suggest a tomboy ideal, the English founders of girls' schools in the 1870s and 1880s, the dawn of a new age in female education, also wanted their pupils to lead more active and healthy lives. The account of sensible English clothes given by Baylor and Jewett was in some respects an ideal, as least as far adolescent girls were concerned, and pioneers like Penelope Lawrence at Roedean School and Frances Dove at Wycombe Abbey felt they had a mission to free femininity from delicate health and corsets. They had strong views about fresh air, cold baths and bracing outdoor exercise which inculcated *esprit de corps*. Miss Lawrence, who by all accounts wore no corsets herself and forbade her girls to do so, devised a uniform which concealed the fact. It was waistless and knee-length, made of thick blue serge, and the style was later extended to evening and weekend wear. Some of the early pupils at schools such as these enjoyed playing boys' team games. Others, who might have been tomboys at home, detested compulsory team spirit and being made to hit balls up and down muddy fields every afternoon.

But what was never demanded of this new generation, in spite of all the reforms, was that they should do any household chores; early pupils at Wycombe Abbey remembered with distaste that they were obliged to make their own beds on Sundays. Housekeeping of the sort that was expected of all American heroines was something unknown to middle class English girls, who were excluded from the kitchen, and, when married, were only called upon to give orders to the cook and manage the household accounts sensibly. The frequent descriptions of their American counterparts wrestling with the intricacies of baking and roasting seemed fascinating. Alcott often referred to efforts in the kitchen, unsuccessful more often than not. There had been a memorable occasion in *Little Women* where everything turned out disastrously, and the party had been reduced to picnicking off bread and butter and olives. On farms, of course, such competence was taken for granted. In Alcott's "An Old-Fashioned Thanksgiving" (9 [Nov. 1881]: 8–16) Farmer Bassett's children cope admirably by themselves when their mother is called away on the eve of Thanksgiving.

> There were no servants, for the little daughters were Mrs. Bassett's only maids, and the stout boys helped their father, all working happily together with no wages but love; learning in the best manner the use of the heads and hands with which they were to make their own way in the world [244].

This vanished Arcadia (Alcott had set her story sixty years before) was often wistfully evoked by juvenile writers. Susan Coolidge in "Uncle and Aunt" (13 [Nov. 1885]: 30–6) set her story on Long Island Sound, where a niece brings her city friends back to her uncle and aunt's home four miles from any railroad, telling them there won't be a single party or young man to amuse them. But they love the old house with "its shut-up odor of bygone days" (35), and they admire the old people who preside over it, Uncle, "tall and gaunt and gray of the traditional New England type" (30); Aunt, the equally traditional New England housewife — whose cranberry always jellies and whose sponge-cake never flops. For country ways were indubitably the best.

St. Nicholas heroines, if they were wealthy city girls, often taught themselves domestic skills as a hobby, as in another Alcott story, "The Cooking Class" (12 [Nov. 1884]: 11–7) where friends form a club to cook for each other — having apparently unlimited resources to buy the ingredients, and free access to their mothers' kitchens. In Katherine D. Smith's "Half a Dozen Housekeepers" (6 [Nov. 1878–Jan. 1879]), six girls set up house for a fortnight alone in the cottage belonging to the father of one of them. They soon find the cares a burden and are glad to be invited elsewhere. The father's response to his daughter's request for the cottage is interesting:

> "We don't like to refuse you anything while we are away enjoying ourselves, so, as the house is insured, you may go over and try the scheme.... I have scarcely any hopes but that you will burn the house down; however, I should like you to avoid it, if possible" [48].

This is an indulgent parent of a type unknown then in England. We find an even more extreme example of detachment in Kate Tannatt Woods's "Zintha's Fortune" (10 [Aug. 1883]: 769–72) in which Zintha has been abandoned in Nebraska to support herself as best she may while her father is seeking his fortune she doesn't know where. Year in and year out she hovers near the railroad, for he has told her that one day when he has made plenty of money, he will come back and collect her.

Fathers ever since Catharine Sedgwick's domestic novels of the 1820s and 30s had made a poor showing in American juvenile fiction. It was the mother who was the "arch on which the law reposes" as a Polish visitor, Adam de Gurowski, had said in 1857.

> The husband, the father, acts under her advice; he is the deacon where she is the high-priest. The woman, wife, mother, or even daughter, exercise in all these worldly relations an omnipotence and latitude nowhere conceded to them in Europe [392].

English stories in contrast most often portrayed mothers as frail and invalidish (or dead). There seems to have been some foundation in actual fact; Carola Oman, writing of her Oxford childhood in the early years of this century described the mothers of most of her contemporaries as "sofa mothers." In the books their gentle example may act as a restraint on childish wrongdoing, but they are rarely dominant. It is significant that the most energetic and lively mother in Charlotte Yonge's many sagas of family life — Carey Brownlow in *Magnum Bonum* (1879) — is disapproved of by the author; she romps with her children rather than setting them a serious example, and has to be purged in the fire of suffering.

The English tradition made the father a dignified, often awe-inspiring character. The children might see little of him, but knew that all authority rested with him, and that their mother would invariably defer to his wishes. But American fathers tended to be weak-kneed or ineffectual, absent or dead; frequently they were shown as vicious or depraved. Huckleberry Finn's father is the ultimate example. Even *St. Nicholas* sometimes took this line. L. Duykwood's "Chicken Lizzie" (6 [Dec. 1878]: 94–8) for instance, begins, "Lizzie's father was dead. He had been a troublesome man; so now Lizzie's mother said: 'We've no one to hinder us; let's pack our bundles and travel'" (94). Or perhaps they were so busy with their own affairs that they were an irrelevance. In *Eight Cousins,* for instance, the boy cousins, three families of them, would all seem to be fatherless. However, tucked in as an aside is the information that Uncle Jem and Uncle Steve are at sea, and "Uncle Mac was in such a minority … he dared not open his lips and let his wife rule undisturbed" (207). In any case, like Uncle Mac, American fathers tended to be subservient to the women of the family. Though she is only fifteen, Betty Leicester in Sarah Orne Jewett's *A Bit of Color* (16 [Apr.-June 1889]) is used to taking care of her father who is "very apt to forget important minor details" (456), and who has a habit of pretending to ask "his girl's leave to do anything that was particularly important" (459). This particular girl, during her father's absence in Alaska, takes herself off to elderly relations in New England. She makes her own travel arrangements, and copes with a difficult journey alone at a time when no English young lady would have been allowed to undertake any journey unescorted. In Betty's case money is no problem, but had it been, we know she would have been resourceful and inventive. An English contemporary could only earn a precarious living by becoming a governess, but *St. Nicholas* had many suggestions to offer. Zintha Dierke, mentioned above, has had virtually no schooling when her father deposits her in Nebraska. She supports herself by minding a baby, and teaches herself to write and work with figures to such effect that the foreman of the local lumberyard calls her in to deputize for his clerk in an emergency. James Otis's fourteen-year-old Jenny in "Jenny's Boarding House" (14 [Feb.-Aug. 1887]) starts a boarding house for newsboys when her mother can no longer work. Margaret, the sole prop of her family, in "Margaret Clyde's Extra" by Isabel Gordon Curtis (26 [Nov. 1898]: 13–9), works in a newspaper office. Alone there one night, she on her own initiative sets up stop-press news that can't wait and makes a scoop. "'You have the makings of a great editor in you, and that is what you will be some day, or I am mistaken,'" the editor tells her (18). Even wealthy girls are resourceful fund-raisers. By the turn of the century the fashionable set castigated by earlier writers had, in the pages of *St. Nicholas,* become purposeful college students. In "The S.P.O.U." by Agnes Louise Provost (29 [May 1902]: 583–91), a group of friends start a Society for the Prevention of Uselessness. "'Suppose, for a moment, that your father should fail in business, or die and leave you without a penny. What would you do to support yourselves?'" (589) Each girl decides on a career for which she feels she has a talent: librarianship, physical culture, a dancing school, millinery. What is more they decide to put their skills on the market straightway, and to allocate the money they

BETTY AND HER FATHER IN THE GARDEN.

Betty Leicester looks after her father in Sara Orne Jewett's *A Bit of Color. SN* 16 (June 1889): 579.

earn to a central fund that will pay for a student unable to afford college education.

St. Nicholas however did not go in for militant feminism, and this was a great point in its favor so far as the English were concerned. There was a type of American female enthusiast that they particularly dreaded. Novelists represented her as having a rasping voice, an assertive manner and a way of forcing her feminist views on reluctant auditors. In *Is He Popenjoy?* Anthony Trollope described the type in Miss Doctor Olivia Q. Fleabody, who wears tunic and trousers, and in Wallachia Petrie, the strong-minded opposer of men and Englishmen in particular, in *He Knew He Was Right.* Mrs. Dodge would have liked them no better. In "Mollie's Boyhood" by Sarah E. Chester (5 [Nov. 1877]: 7–12) little Mollie, fired by a lecture on women's rights, decides to "throw off the yoke of her girl-hood." She has no idea what this means, but feels that if she were a boy she could better support her mother. There is no father, as is almost tra-ditional. She cuts off her hair, dresses her doll in boy's clothing and finally gives it up altogether, goaded by a teasing neighbor. Trying to emulate boys' feats, she overestimates her powers, jumps, falls and decides to give up the nonsense. "And pleasant visions of a gothic school-house, where she should some day be mistress of sweet rosy-cheeked children rose grace-fully on the ruins of her manly aspirations" (7). No English girl then could have regarded the prospect of teaching with such rapture.

Twenty years or so later Jessie M. Anderson's serial *Three Freshmen: Ruth, Fran and Nathalie* (22 [Jan.-May 1895]), about three sixteen-year-olds at Smith, also distanced itself from feminist issues. The author indeed seemed wary of taking any line of her own. In the second installment Fran debates the sense of sending a girl away for four years "from her life as daughter and sister at home, with all the training there is in that life for the future home-making that comes to most women in some shape" (329). Ruth says that Fran is disloyal to the whole question of "the Higher Edu-cation of Women." "'Does knowing Greek unfit a girl for making biscuit?'" The question is never resolved. Fran is taken out of college when her father loses all his money. Ruth decides to be "a child's doctor," but tells her mother that she does not wish to do anything "in the women's rights line" (595).

In *St. Nicholas* there was the occasional bundle of femininity, like Editha in Mrs. Burnett's "Editha's Burglar" (7 [Feb. 1880]: 326–32), who watches a burglar stealing the family silver, merely begging him to be as quiet as he can so as not to disturb Mamma. But Polly in Kate Douglas Wiggin's *Polly Oliver's Problem* (20 [Nov. 1892–May 1893]) is a truer type, the mainstay of the household, both father and mother, wage-earner and home-maker, tenderly caring for her widowed mother.

> Every word she utters shows you that, young as she looks, she
> is the real head of the family, and that her vigorous indepen-
> dence of thought and speech must be the result of more care
> and responsibility than ordinarily fall to the lot of a girl of six-
> teen [8].

Though she longs for a father to say "Steak, Polly dear" instead of her having to ask the lodgers "Steak or chops" (10), she has resigned herself to carrying the responsibility for her delicate mother on "her strong young
shoulders." She is "cook, housekeeper, nurse, banker, all in one," her
mother says tenderly. Polly has to be tamed a little: this might be predicted
from the auburn hair, the saucy nose and the willful eyes. She is tried in
the conventional fires of woe — her mother dies, and the uninsured house
burns down. But undaunted, she becomes Pauline, a much-loved professional storyteller to children. The conventional English happy ending
would have provided her with a husband, or perhaps an adoptive father.
Miss Secretary Ethel: A Story for Girls of Today by Ellinor Davenport Adams
(1898) shows a resourceful, well-educated girl who knows Greek and short-
hand. Left alone in the world, she goes off to be secretary to a slow-wit-
ted politician. He resents her, but she makes herself indispensable, taking
his place at an important political meeting, keeping him from ignomin-
ious errors. But it is only when she rescues him from a nasty accident that
he is reconciled to her and adopts her as a daughter. After that her secre-
tarial days are over, and she devotes herself to filial duties. "No pains could
be too great which could win her the reward of Sir Edgar's proud glance
and word of approval" (255).

The *Girl's Own Paper* (price one penny) certainly included many
working girls among its readers— shop assistants, milliners, dressmakers
and, by the 1890s, the new species of "type-writer." For them there were
articles on sensible diet, living in lodgings, "Factory girls at work and play."
But there were many other readers at home with time on their hands, waiting to be married, and they could read about how to visit the poor, how
they could help workhouse inmates, "How I painted a tambourine." It is
interesting to see how this paper treated ambition. *Her Own Way* by Eglanton Thorne was serialized in 1894–95; the title alone conveys the moral.
Juliet learns through bitter experience the result of willfulness. She longs
to be a professional singer. Her uncle and her mother tell her that a
woman's place is in the home, and the clergyman who secretly loves her
warns her about the evils of desiring one's own way. Headstrong and
gullible, she elopes to Paris with a man who promises to marry her and
then to allow her to continue with her music. He is arrested for forgery
as they reach France, and when she does in the end sing for the maestro

whom she hopes will teach her, it is only to hear that her musical talent is meager indeed. She returns to England. Miraculously, the clergyman who has tried to save her from herself wants to make her his wife.

> And the mother's heart was no longer afraid. She believed that as spring was renewing the face of the dark earth ... so the life of Juliet, chilled and darkened by errors of her youth, was to break forth into a spring of love and hope. [*Girl's Own Paper* 16 (1895): 451].

Still hammering at the theme, the *Girl's Own Paper* followed this serial with another called *A Willful Ward*. However, Juliet has a far more fortunate escape than Charlotte Yonge would have allowed. Miss Yonge, born in 1823, retained an early Victorian outlook throughout her long literary career. Her last two novels were published in 1900. She believed passionately that a girl's home duties, however trivial, must come before any private concerns, and she took terrible vengeance on Janet Brownlow in *Magnum Bonum*. Janet, strong-willed and clever, wants to be a doctor like her father, in order to use the medical secret (the Magnum Bonum) that he has locked away before his death. In an American book the description of her massive forehead and resolute square-cut chin would have been a signal that she was destined for high achievement, but Yongeians know these are the features of a doomed woman. She studies in Zurich, then falls into the hands of a charlatan Greek professor and is eventually found in New York, abandoned by her husband and earning a precarious living as a cheapjack photographer. She is given the opportunity to redeem herself in a yellow fever epidemic, dies and — a great concession — is allowed the name of Brownlow on her tomb. The Yonge ideal of girlhood is Janet's cousin Esther, all fluttering timidity like a newly-caught bird.

Charlotte Yonge had devoted readers, and was for nearly half a century the doyenne of domestic fiction for girls. She created a landscape in which one can walk, and characters whom even now we recognize as living beings. But the atmosphere is rarified, the warmth of home is lacking. It is the same with other Victorian stories; prosperous families are rigidly stratified, parents, children, servants all living separate lives, the kitchen forbidden territory. Stories about the poor were didactic or tear-jerking, not cozy, and young readers had to turn to American writers for that gratifying sense of united families gathered in harmonious security round a warm hearth. Early settlers had felt that family life could only be experienced in its perfection in the New World, and Alcott in "An Old-Fashioned Thanksgiving," already mentioned, had tried to convey this idyllic state of affairs where the whole family worked as one for the common good.

> Sixty years ago, up among the New Hampshire hills, lived
> Farmer Bassett, with a house full of sturdy sons and daughters
> growing up about him. They were poor in money, but rich in
> land and love, for the wide acres of wood, corn, and pasture land
> fed, warmed, and clothed the flock, while mutual patience,
> affection and courage made the old farm-house a very happy
> one [8].

Edward Payson Roe in his serial *Driven Back to Eden* (12 [Feb.-Oct. 1885]) took up the same theme. Here a father leads his family out of the corrupting influence of New York "to get our living out of the soil" (244). Arriving at the farm after a fearful journey through a snowstorm, the wife exclaims: "Oh Erobert, I have such a sense of rest, quiet, comfort and hominess.... The howling of the storm only makes this place more like a refuge" (423). And the reader rejoices with her. These are real people; the nearest equivalent in an English story would be the arrival of Ratty and Mole at Badger's house after the perils of the Wild Wood (*The Wind in the Willows,* chapter 3).

Home could also be a memory, an ideal even, acting as a powerful magnet to the wanderer. In *Master Skylark: A Story of Shakespeare's Time* (24 [Nov. 1896–Oct.1897) home means the boy's mother. Master Skylark is a Stratford boy who is carried off to London by an ambitious actor who wants to exploit him for his beautiful singing voice. At first he is bemused by the glamour of the actor and his associates, but long before they reach London he is begging to go home and to his mother. Even when he is taken to sing before the Queen he can only repeat this. At last he does come back to Stratford. "And when [his mother] came ... the whole of that long, bitter year was nothing any more to Nick. For then — ah, then — a lad and his mother; a son come home, the wandering ended, and the sorrow done!" [996].

In John Bennett's second serial, *Barnaby Lee* (28–29 [Nov. 1900–Apr. 1902), the hero longs for a home but has none. It is a story of New Amsterdam in 1664, told with great technical skill. Barnaby is an English boy who has been cheated out of the Maryland estate he should have inherited from his father. He escapes from the ship where he is a reluctant apprentice, and after fleeing through the swamps and woods by the Hudson, he is taken in by the sheriff's family, the Van Swerigens. There are two threads to the plot. On the one hand is Barnaby's struggle to get out of the clutches of the villainous ship's captain and then to assert his right to the Maryland estate. On the other is the demise of the Dutch colony, which has to be handed over to the British.

The book ends with defeat for the Dutch, but victory for Barnaby.

The Maryland estate becomes his, but it is a bittersweet experience, because he is alone there. "Master Drew," he said earnestly, "do ye think that by calling a place home ye can make it homelike?" Drew looked down. "Nay, lad," he said gently. "No calling makes a place home. 'Tis the love that is in it which fastens on our hearts like a hook of steel" (537).

Like *Master Skylark, Barnaby Lee* is in essence a celebration of home, and although Barnaby is without a family of his own, the ending leaves him with the promise of one.

> Dorothy Van Sweringen and Barnaby Lee were afterwards married, met happiness and cheerful strength born of mutual trust, were the parents of four children, were loyal, brave, and true, loving each other and their friends with a regard that was never altered by the adversity of circumstances, nor diminished by the flight of time. They saw that the world is full of beauty and good to those who meet it aright; they played their small parts bravely in it, and taught their children to do so; and the world was the better for it [537].

These were the values of *St. Nicholas,* and the last sentence might be used as an epitaph for Mrs. Dodge herself.

References

Adams, Ellinor Davenport. *Miss Secretary Ethel.* London: 1898.

Bishop, Isabella. *A Lady's Life in the Rocky Mountains.* London: 1879.

de Gurowski, Adam. *America and Europe.* New York: 1857.

Mansfield, Katherine. *The Doves' Nest and Other Stories.* London: 1923.

Oman, Carola. *An Oxford Childhood.* London: 1976.

Thorne, Eglanton. "Her Own Way." *Girl's Own Paper* 16 (1894–5).

Trollope, Anthony. *He Knew He Was Right.* London: 1869.

_____. *Is He Popenjoy?* London: 1878.

_____. *North America.* London: 1862.

Yelverton, Therese. *Teresina on America.* London: 1875.

Yonge, Charlotte M. *Magnum Bonum.* London: 1879.

Bibliography

Unpublished Library Holdings

Century Company Archives, New York Public Library
Donald and Robert M. Dodge Collection, Princeton University Library
Horace Scudder Papers, the Huntington Library
Mary Mapes Dodge Letters, Houghton Library, Harvard University
Mary Mapes Dodge Collection, Princeton University Library
Mary Mapes Dodge Letters, University of Virginia Library
Scribner Archives, Princeton University Library
Wilkinson Collection, Princeton University Library
William Fayal Clarke letter, Beinecke Library, Yale University

Suggestions for Further Reading

Alcott, Louisa May. *Selected Letters*. Eds. Joel Meyerson and Daniel Shealy. Boston: Little, Brown, 1987.

Avery, Gillian. *Behold the Child: American Children and Their Books, 1621–1922*. Baltimore: Johns Hopkins University Press, 1994.

Brack, O.M., Jr. "Mark Twain in Knee Pants. The Expurgation of *Tom Sawyer Abroad.*" In *The Yearbook of American Bibliographical and Textual Studies*, vol. 2, ed. Joseph Katz. Columbia: University of South Carolina Press, 1972.

Brake, Laurel, and Anne Humphreys. "Critical Theory and Periodicals Research." *Victorian Periodicals Review* 23 (Fall 1989): 94–5.

Brake, Laurel, Aled Jones, and Lionel Maden, eds. *Investigating Victorian Journalism*. New York: St. Martin's Press, 1990.

Burlingame, Roger. *Of Making Many Books: A Hundred Years of Reading, Writing, and Publishing*. New York: Charles Scribner's Sons, 1946.

Chew, Samuel B., ed. *Fruit Among the Leaves: An Anniversary Anthology*. New York: Appleton, Century, Crofts, 1950.

Clarke, William Fayal. "In Memory of Mary Mapes Dodge." *St. Nicholas Magazine* (October 1905): 1059–1071.

Commager, Henry Steele, ed. *A St. Nicholas Anthology*. New York: Random House, 1948.

"Culture and Progress." *Scribner's Monthly* (November 1876): 36.

Erisman, Fred. "There Was a Child Went Forth: A Study of *St. Nicholas Magazine* and Selected Children's Authors, 1890–1915." Ph.D. diss., University of Minnesota, 1966.

Estes, Glenn E. *Dictionary of Literary Biography*, vol. 42. Detroit: Gale Research Co., 1985.

Firkins, Terry. "Textual Introduction." In *Tom Sawyer: Tom Sawyer Abroad: Tom Sawyer, Detective*, vol. 4 of *The Works of Mark Twain*, Ed. John C. Gerber, Paul Baender and Terry Firkins. Berkeley and Los Angeles: University of California Press, 1980.

Fuller, Lawrence B. "Mary Mapes Dodge and *St. Nicholas*: The Development of a Philosophy and Practice of Publishing for Young People." Paper presented at the annual meeting of the National Council of Teachers of English, Detroit MI, Nov. 1984: ERIC Educational Document, ED 251 847.

Gannon, Susan. "'The Best Magazine for Children of All Ages': Cross-Editing *St. Nicholas Magazine*." *Children's Literature* 25 (1997): 153–80.

_____. "'But I Wanted It to Be the Other Way': Fictions of Rescue and their Function in *St. Nicholas Magazine*." *Nineteenth-Century Contexts: An Interdisciplinary Journal* 21 (1999): 259–88.

_____, and Ruth Anne Thompson. "Mary Mapes Dodge and the Recasting of St. Nicholas." In *Sitting at the Feet of the Past: Retelling the North American Folktale for Children*. Ed. Gary D. Schmidt and Donald R. Hettinga. New York: Greenwood Press, 1992.

_____, and _____. "Mr. Scudder and Mrs. Dodge: A Literary Correspondence and What It Tells Us." *American Periodicals* (Fall 1992): 89–99.

Garvey, Ellen Gruber. *The Adman in the Parlor: Magazines and the Gendering of Consumer Culture, 1880s to 1910s*. New York: Oxford University Press, 1996.

Gilder, Jeanette. "The Newark Life of Mary Mapes Dodge." *Critic 47*, no. 4 (October 1905): 292.

Griffin, Martin. *Frank R. Stockton*. Philadelphia: University of Pennsylvania Press, 1939.

Guthrie, Anna Lorraine, comp. *Index to St. Nicholas: Volumes 1–45, 1873–1918*. New York: H. W. Wilson, 1920.

John, Arthur. *The Best Years of the "Century": Richard Watson Gilder, "Scribner's Monthly," and the "Century Magazine," 1870–1901*. Urbana: University of Illinois Press, 1981.

Kelly, R. Gordon. *Children's Periodicals of the United States*. Westport CT: Greenwood Press, 1984.

_____. *Mother Was a Lady: Self and Society in Selected American Children's Periodicals, 1865–1890*. Westport CT: Greenwood Press, 1974.

Koppes, Phyllis Bixler. "Tradition and the Individual Talent of Frances Hodgson Burnett: A Generic Analysis of *Little Lord Fauntleroy*, *A Little Princess*, and *The Secret Garden*." *Children's Literature* 7 (1978): 191–207.

Lanes, Selma. *Down the Rabbit Hole: Adventures and Misadventures in the Realm of Children's Literature*. New York: Atheneum, 1971.

McEnery, Sarah S. "Mary Mapes Dodge: An Intimate Tribute." *Critic 47*, no. 4 (October 1905): 310–12.

McLeod, Anne Scott. *American Childhood: Essays on Children's Literature of the Nineteenth and Twentieth Centuries*. Athens and London: University of Georgia Press, 1994.

Mott, Frank Luther. *A History of American Magazines*, vol. 3. Cambridge MA: Harvard University Press, 1938.

Murray, Gail Schmunk. *American Children's Literature and the Construction of Childhood*. New York: Twayne Publishers, 1998.

Myers, Mitzi. "Sociologizing Juvenile Ephemera: Periodical Contradictions, Popular Literacy, Transhistorical Readers." *Children's Literature Association Quarterly* 17.1 (Spring 1992): 41–5.

Nelson, Claudia, and Lynn Vallone. *The Girls' Own: Cultural Histories of the Anglo-American Girl, 1830–1915.* Athens: University of Georgia Press, 1994.

Price, Kenneth M., and Susan Belasco Smith, eds. *Periodical Literature in Nineteenth-Century America.* Charlottesville: University Press of Virginia, 1995.

Roggenbuck, Mary Jane. "*St. Nicholas Magazine*: A Study of the Impact and Historical Influence of the Editorship of Mary Mapes Dodge." Ph.D. diss., University of Michigan, 1976.

Runkle, Lucia Gilbert. "Mary Mapes Dodge." In *Our Famous Women, Comprising the Lives and Deeds of American Women Who Have Distinguished Themselves in Literature, Science, Art, Music, and the Drama, or Are Famous as Heroines, Patriots, Orators, Educators, Physicians, Philanthropists, etc. with Numerous Anecdotes, Incidents and Personal Experiences.* Hartford CT: A.D. Worthington, 1884.

Saler, Elizabeth C., and Edwin H. Cady. "The *St. Nicholas* and the Serious Artist." In *Essays Mostly on Periodical Publishing in America: A Collection in Honor of Clarence Gohdes.* Ed. James Woodress with the assistance of Townsend Ludington and Joseph Arpad. Durham NC: Duke University Press, 1973.

Satelmajer, Ingrid. "Dickinson As Child's Fare: The Author Served Up in *St. Nicholas*." In *Book History*, vol. 5. Ed. Ezra Greenspan and Jonathan Rose. University Park: Pennsylvania State University Press.

Sircar, Sanjay. "The Victorian Auntly Voice and Mrs. Molesworth's *Cuckoo Clock*." *Children's Literature* 17 (1989): 1–24.

Smith, Herbert. *Richard Watson Gilder.* New York: Twayne Publishers, 1975.

Sorby, Angela. "A Visit from *St. Nicholas*: The Poetics of Peer Culture." *American Studies* 39.1 (1998): 59–74.

Stern, Madeleine. "Louisa Alcott's Self-Criticism." In *Studies in the American Renaissance.* Ed. Joel Myerson. Charlottesville: University Press of Virginia, 1988.

Tutwiler, Julia. "Mary Mapes Dodge in New York." In *Women Authors of Our Day in Their Homes: Personal Descriptions and Interviews.* Ed. Francis Whiting Halsey. New York: James Pott, 1903.

Twain, Mark. *Letters to His Publishers, 1867–1894.* Ed. Hamlin Hill. Berkeley and Los Angeles: University of California Press, 1967.

Wheeler, Candace. *Yesterdays in a Busy Life.* New York: Harper & Brothers, 1918.

Wright, Catharine Morris. "How *St. Nicholas* Got Rudyard Kipling And What Happened Then." *Princeton University Library Chronicle* 35 (Spring 1974): 259–89.

_____. *Lady of the Silver Skates: The Life and Correspondence of Mary Mapes Dodge.* Jamestown RI: Clingstone Press, 1979.

Index